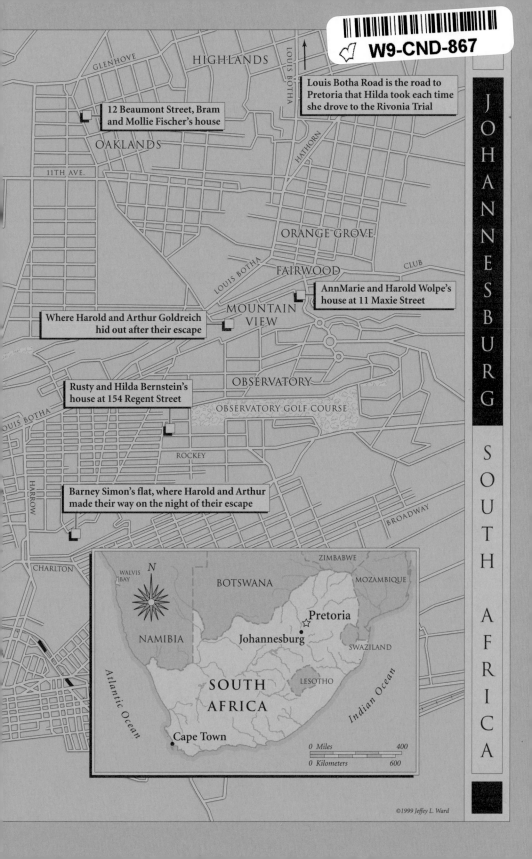

GLENHOVE

HIGHLANDS

LOUIS BOTHA

Louis Botha Road is the road to
Pretoria that Hilda took each time
she drove to the Rivonia Trial

12 Beaumont Street, Bram
and Mollie Fischer's house

OAKLANDS

HATHORN

11TH AVE.

ORANGE GROVE

FAIRWOOD

CLUB

LOUIS BOTHA

AnnMarie and Harold Wolpe's
house at 11 Maxie Street

MOUNTAIN
VIEW

Where Harold and Arthur Goldreich
hid out after their escape

OBSERVATORY

Rusty and Hilda Bernstein's
house at 154 Regent Street

OBSERVATORY GOLF COURSE

LOUIS BOTHA

ROCKEY

HARROW

Barney Simon's flat, where Harold and Arthur
made their way on the night of their escape

BROADWAY

CHARLTON

ZIMBABWE

N

WALVIS
BAY

BOTSWANA

MOZAMBIQUE

NAMIBIA

Pretoria

Johannesburg

SWAZILAND

Atlantic Ocean

SOUTH
AFRICA

LESOTHO

Indian Ocean

Cape Town

0 Miles   400

0 Kilometers   600

J
O
H
A
N
N
E
S
B
U
R
G

S
O
U
T
H

A
F
R
I
C
A

©1999 Jeffey L. Ward

ALSO BY GLENN FRANKEL

Beyond the Promised Land

RIVONIA'S CHILDREN

RIVONIA'S CHILDREN

THREE FAMILIES

AND THE COST OF

CONSCIENCE

IN

WHITE

SOUTH AFRICA

GLENN FRANKEL

FARRAR, STRAUS AND GIROUX / NEW YORK

Farrar, Straus and Giroux
19 Union Square West, New York 10003

Selections from the following books have been used with the kind permission of the authors or trustees: From 117 Days by Ruth First with the permission of the family of Ruth First. From The World That Was Ours by Hilda Bernstein with permission of Hilda Bernstein. From A Healthy Grave by James Kantor and The Long Way Home by AnnMarie Wolpe with permission of AnnMarie Wolpe.

Grateful acknowledgment is made for permission to reprint photographs from the following sources: Photographs of James Kantor and Harold Wolpe, AnnMarie Wolpe and children, James and Barbara Kantor, Ruth First and children, Rusty and Hilda Bernstein, Bram Fischer (photo by Eli Weinberg), Percy Yutar, and Nelson Mandela and Percy Yutar, courtesy of Times Media Limited. Photographs of Communist Party meeting and Joe Slovo, courtesy of the Mayibuye Centre. Photographs of the Rivonia Trialists, Lilliesleaf farm, Rusty Bernstein, Dennis Goldberg, and Lt. Willem Petrus Johannes van Wyk and Arthur Goldreich, courtesy of the Rivonia Trial Archive/SAHA. Photograph of Ruth Slovo, by Eli Weinberg, courtesy of the Slovo family.

Library of Congress Cataloging-in-Publication Data
Frankel, Glenn.
    Rivonia's children : three families and the cost of conscience in
    white South Africa / Glenn Frankel. —1st ed.
        p.   cm.
    ISBN 0-374-25099-5
    1. South Africa—Race relations. 2. Anti-apartheid movements—
    South Africa—History. 3. South Africa—Politics and
    government—1948–1994. I. Title.
    DT1798.F73 1999
    305.8'00968—dc21   99-10757

TO SUE SPARKS

CONTENTS

RIVONIA'S CHILDREN

AUTHOR'S NOTE

The future was already there; it was a matter of having the courage to announce it.
How much courage?—I don't think we had any idea.
Nadine Gordimer
The Late Bourgeois World

We had just finished our first cup of tea when Hilda Bernstein rose and said she would be right back. Several minutes passed. Hilda was eighty-one years old that summer and had acquired an artificial hip not too long ago. She negotiated the staircase with wisdom rather than haste. She came back with a thick manila envelope, whose contents she dumped onto the kitchen table. Out came strips of white fabric, cut in the shape of shirt collars, each one covered in a man's minute handwriting. They contained letters—messages from underground, really—written in 1963 by her husband Rusty, smuggled out to Hilda in dirty laundry from an isolation cell deep in the bowels of Pretoria Local prison in South Africa. Rusty had spent eighty-eight days in solitary confinement there before being charged with sabotage and put on trial for his life alongside Nelson Mandela and nine other antiapartheid activists.

Rusty sat silently in a nearby chair. He was a quiet man, not unfriendly, not unhumorous, but not inclined to speak until spoken to or answer until questioned. His blue eyes twinkled, but his emotions seemed as lukewarm as the tea he was gently nursing. The letters on the shirt collars seemed to come from a different person altogether—a man in the grip of raw despair and on the edge of sanity, agonizingly concerned about his wife and children and his own precarious fate. Hilda read a few aloud. Then I read some. In those moments we were transported back thirty-three years to a prison cell and a country in the process of becoming a police state, and to a family caught in a web in which their political and personal lives were irrevocably entangled.

Hilda and Rusty were white left-wing activists who had worked closely with Nelson Mandela and his comrades at the heart of the anti-apartheid movement for more than two decades. They led double lives, working as middle-class professionals, living in the comfortable white suburbs of northern Johannesburg and raising a family of four children, while at the same time doing illegal underground political work under increasing restrictions and police surveillance. They were integral members of the group that in 1961 set up a secret headquarters in nearby Rivonia at a time when the movement, frustrated by the inability of its nonviolent protest campaigns to compel the country's white rulers to the negotiating table, turned to armed resistance. When the South African regime raided Rivonia in 1963 and crushed the movement, it destroyed the world that they knew. Hilda and Rusty escaped with their lives; others were killed or jailed for life. The cause they believed in and struggled for was set back a generation. It took nearly three decades of defiance, unrest and violence for Mandela to emerge from prison and four more years for a new South Africa based on majority rule to be born. It was a long wait for redemption. Many of their comrades did not live to see it.

In the mid-1960s, shortly after they set up house in exile in London, Hilda wrote a book called *The World That Was Ours* about their ordeal and the trial. It was published in London and republished in 1989 in a small edition distributed only in the United Kingdom. I came across a copy at Foyles, the London bookstore. I had been a foreign correspondent in southern Africa for *The Washington Post* for three years in the mid-1980s and I knew a bit more than most about the 1960s and the Rivonia Trial. Still, the book was a revelation. It was full of passion and anxiety and wonderful scenes and anecdotes, the personal and political powerfully blended. It deserved a larger audience than it was destined to find on a remote shelf in a small back room at Foyles.

Over the years I came across other first-person accounts from the same period. There was *117 Days*, Ruth First's story of her confinement and interrogation, first published in London and New York in 1965 and republished in London after her murder in 1982; *A Healthy Grave*, James Kantor's memoir, published in London in 1967; *The Long Way Home*, by Kantor's sister, AnnMarie Wolpe, which detailed her role in the prison escape of her husband Harold and three other activists and her subsequent interrogation, published in London in 1994; and *The Rivonia Story*, Joel Joffe's record of the trial, which he first wrote in 1965 with the help of Rusty Bernstein but which did not appear in print until it was published by Mayibuye Books in South Africa in 1995. Each of these books weaves together in moving ways the history of the era and the personal ordeals and dilemmas of the participants. Together, they constitute a historical record of great power and importance, and I urge anyone interested in South Africa's past or in the struggle of individuals against state tyranny to read them. A full reference for each book, and for the many others I have relied upon, appears in the Bibliography at the back of this work.

With permission from each author or their heirs, I have used scenes and dialogue from all five books in writing my own. Whenever possible, I have sought to reconfirm and flesh out these stories by using other contemporary accounts, newspaper clippings, trial records and other documents, and by extensively interviewing the surviving authors and others. I have tried to fashion all of these materials into a seamless narrative, though I have stopped periodically along the way to discuss my sources and evaluate both their meaning and their accuracy. The chapter notes in the back describe the sources and research in greater detail. The structure of this book, the choice of characters and situations and, most of all, the conclusions are very much my own, and my collaborators are in no way responsible for them or for any errors that may exist.

While I used the books as both a road map and an inspiration, I have relied more on my conversations with the principals, their friends, colleagues and family members. I have been a newspaper reporter for twenty-five years, have interviewed thousands of people, both in quiet moments and in times of extreme desperation. But nothing has ever been quite as moving as the experience of talking to and getting to know the subjects of this book. I was speaking to people who, for the most part, were in their sixties and seventies about what was for many of them the most crucial moment of their lives. We talked about the details of what happened in that fateful year of 1963 and in the years surrounding it. We also spoke about the decision to turn to armed struggle and the dire consequences that resulted. But what we were really talking about was courage and fear and the fateful choices people make. And of course, lurking in the background of each conversation was the crucial but ultimately unanswerable question: In the same circumstances, what would I have done? What would any of us have done?

I call them Rivonia's Children because Rivonia is the place where their dream of revolution was forever shattered. The 1963 raid was their moment of truth. It destroyed their old order of comfortable, rather benign radicalism and thrust them into a new, dangerous and chaotic world. The regime turned a corner as well, plunging into an era of repression and brutality that is only now coming fully to light. Hilda, Rusty and their comrades came to Rivonia with an innocence and idealism that was both heroic and self-destructive. And the book's title refers not only to the activists themselves but also to their children, who in some ways paid the biggest price for their parents' deeds.

Most of these people were communists, members of a party that was outlawed and driven underground yet continued to function, and we spoke about their ideological commitment and its influence on their thoughts and deeds. The South African Communist Party was one of the most innovative and progressive when it came to the struggle for racial justice inside South Africa, yet one of the most orthodox and hidebound when it came to international affairs and its allegiance to Moscow. Even after Stalin's crimes were confirmed and Stalin's heirs invaded Hungary in 1956, most of South Africa's comrades remained loyal to a morally bankrupt empire. This was partly from belief and partly from pragmatism. As defendant Ahmed Kathrada put it on the witness stand at the Rivonia Trial, "I'd get assistance from the devil, provided it was for . . . the freedom of my people."

Some of Rivonia's Children were dedicated ideologues who would remain Leninists to the end; others suffered from a case of arrested political development caused by the environment in which they labored. Had they lived in the United States or Western Europe, the gates they were pressing at would have gradually opened and, like so many others of their generation, they no doubt would have migrated gradually from communism to social democracy or liberalism. But in South Africa they were up against a rigid enemy with ironclad beliefs and police-state methods who was not susceptible to moral or political suasion. As

Joseph Lelyveld would write of their successor generation, they were "the sort of people who would have been civil rights activists in that period in America," but in South Africa "they faced dilemmas out of nineteenth-century Russian literature in an environment where most whites were deliberately numb to obvious moral issues."

In the end, I concluded that such people must ultimately be judged by their deeds rather than their ideology. While I rejected his ideology, I could draw no moral distinction between a dedicated communist like Rusty Bernstein and a pragmatic liberal like Helen Suzman. Both opposed the regime out of genuine moral repugnance, and both, it seems to me, are deserving of admiration and respect. The tenets of communism have been justly and thoroughly discredited. But it is worth noting in the historical ledger that while communism attracted the murderous and the ruthless, it also inspired a generation of South African idealists who needed its strength to forge their own. Without their ideology, many of Rivonia's Children could not have found the courage to act. "We loved the certainty that Marxism gave us," Norman Levy, one of the comrades, told me, "and we needed it."

As this narrative makes clear, many people—blacks, Asians, whites and those of mixed race—fought in the liberation movement. I decided to focus on a handful of white activists, not because their sacrifices were greater, but because they chose to make those sacrifices. It is surely not hard to understand why Nelson Mandela, Walter Sisulu and other black activists risked their lives for the liberation of their people. But for whites, however small their number, to join with them was a different matter. The comforts and privileges of middle-class life in South Africa were far above its economic equivalent in the West. Housing was cheap and labor was cheaper still, thanks to apartheid. Whites lived well for very little money. To put all of that aside, to resist the temptation to join the mainstream, was a remarkably selfless act. I wanted to understand why. Hannah Arendt contended that true revolutionaries were driven by "the passion of compassion." But were Rivonia's Children driven mainly by altruism? What about the fact that so many of them came from Jewish immigrant origins? And what role did their ideology play? I am not certain my narrative completely answers any of these questions. But it wrestles with all of them.

Finally, I chose to focus on Rivonia's Children because of their distinct contribution to the making of the new South Africa. Nelson Mandela has frequently cited their participation in the antiapartheid movement as justification for the spirit of reconciliation he has preached. The fact that even a small group of whites was willing to put aside their privileged status and fight alongside blacks for racial justice meant to Mandela that people could not be judged solely by their skin color; all whites should be given the chance to participate in the new society. In a real sense, Hilda, Rusty and their comrades bear responsibility for the surprising degree of racial reconciliation in the new South Africa.

Their story is particularly instructive to Americans, who were going through the civil rights struggle at roughly the same time. The role of whites in a black-led movement for racial justice—and specifically the relationship between Jews and blacks—was at issue in South Africa as well as in the United States. Much of my narrative focuses on three women who played dual roles as activists and mothers, compelled not only to participate in a male-dominated movement but to balance the demands of politics with the needs of their families. Hilda Bernstein, Ruth First and AnnMarie Wolpe all emerged from the crucible of the Rivonia years more independent and less deferential, more inclined to trust their own instincts and less willing to accept what they were told by their husbands and their leaders.

I feel a sense of privilege and responsibility to all of those who welcomed me in their homes. This includes at least one person who will be deeply disappointed by my depiction of him. When Percy Yutar agreed to see me, it was the first time in more than thirty years that the man who had appeared for the State as prosecutor at the Rivonia Trial had spoken at length about his role. Percy, who was eighty-six when we talked in July 1997, was an ardent interview subject with one driving message to get across: that while he had carried out his professional duty by prosecuting the defendants, he was also responsible for saving their lives by insisting they be charged with sabotage rather than treason. Both charges carried the possibility of the death penalty, but Percy insisted he knew by instinct and long practice that the presiding judge would not condemn the accused to hang for the former charge, only for the latter. And indeed, in sentencing Mandela, Sisulu and the others to life imprisonment, Justice Quartus de Wet mentioned the charge and stated he was "bearing this in mind."

After explaining all of this in great detail and with great passion,

Percy turned to me at the end of our interview and asked, "You do believe me, don't you, Glenn, that I saved their lives?"

My answer is that although I believe that Percy himself has come to believe this version, I could find no other substantiation for it, and much evidence suggesting it is not so. Percy avers that nothing was written down, and the presiding judge is long dead. There were other compelling legal reasons for charging sabotage rather than treason. And as my narrative recounts, Percy repeatedly argued during the trial that the accused had committed murder and treason as well as sabotage, and he conducted a vitriolic cross-examination of novelist Alan Paton, the one defense witness who testified against imposing the death penalty.

Percy and I were both disappointed that Sunday afternoon. I was looking for an honest account of the pressures and emotions Percy must have felt in handling a highly publicized political trial, but Percy refused even to admit that he had wanted the case, or that it had furthered his personal ambition to become the first Jewish Attorney General. Percy wanted me to accept that he had behaved honorably and with compassion. Neither of us got what we wanted. Percy has said he plans to write his own memoir of the case, refuting the various calumnies he believes have been perpetrated against him over the years. Perhaps he will yet have the last word.

In the end, I see two purposes for *Rivonia's Children*: to tell an important but little-known story about moral choice; and to try to rescue from obscurity a group of people and a body of work that deserves our critical attention, admiration and respect. At the end of this harrowing century we need to collect and retell such stories, if only to remind ourselves from time to time of the need to be vigilant in protecting civil society from police states, large and small.

In *Eichmann in Jerusalem*, Hannah Arendt writes that one of the goals of the police state is to establish "holes of oblivion into which all deeds, good and evil, would disappear." It is our duty, according to Arendt, to preserve history by descending into those holes, rescuing those individual deeds and recounting them to ourselves and our children. The political lesson of individual heroism, she writes, is simple: "It is that under conditions of terror most people will comply but some people will not, just as the lesson of the countries to which the Final Solution was proposed is that 'it could happen' in most places but it did not happen everywhere. Humanly speaking, no more is required, and no more can be reasonably asked, for this planet to remain a place fit for human habitation."

By staying true to their cause and themselves, Rivonia's Children, despite their mistakes, helped keep hope alive in South Africa and pave the hard road to freedom. In the end they redeemed themselves and, perhaps, us as well.

ONE

THE RAID

Communists are the last optimists.
Nadine Gordimer
Burger's Daughter

He was late.
Under normal circumstances, she would have considered it a minor annoyance, a matter of a dinner grown cold, or a delay in helping the children with their homework, or an errand that might not get run for another day. Nothing to worry about. Under normal circumstances.

He had left the house just before noon in the black Chevrolet sedan. "I'm going in to report," he told her. "Then I have to deliver some drawings. And this afternoon I'll be busy."

She knew the routine. For nine months, ever since the Justice Ministry's written order restricting his movements, it had been a daily part of their lives. First he would drive downtown past the gleaming office towers and unruly markets of bustling Johannesburg, past Greaterman's department store, the Sanlam insurance building and the Chamber of Mines, to the red-brick police station at Marshall Square, a squat, brooding fortress that dated back to the turn of the century when Johannesburg was little more than an overgrown mining camp. He would park on the street and march briskly to the tall, studded doors that served like a gate to a forbidden castle. Inside, he would enter the charge office, where the desk sergeant would open the oversized ledger book to the current page, rotate its spine so that it faced him, and produce a pen. Other than a terse "Good afternoon," no words would be spoken; both the sergeant and he knew why he was there. He would sign his name on the first blank line, then return the book to the desk man, who would record the date and time next to the signature. Within minutes he would be back inside the safety of the Chevy and drive off, having once again fulfilled the condition of his daily house arrest.

It was a bloodless, seemingly painless ritual, yet he dreaded each trip to Marshall Square. Every time he walked into the station, he feared he would not walk out again. Sooner or later, he believed, the state would stop toying with him and relegate him to the ranks of the disappeared. The thought of it made his knees buckle and left him in a cold sweat even on the coolest winter day. Marshall Square would swallow him up and bury him in a prison cell tomb deep within its bowels, a place from which he might never return.

But not today. After the mandatory visit he attended to the work he was responsible for as an architect, visiting an engineer, helping him with a project. There had been a time when such tasks would have taken most of the day. But in recent years, as the authorities graced him with their very special attention and he spent more and more time in court fending off their accusations, commissions had dried up, leaving him with little professional work and a shrinking income to support a family of six. Now, on most days, it only took him a few minutes to deal with the work.

After that he headed somewhere else, somewhere secret, to engage in the illegal political work that had led to his house arrest and that, if he were caught, could land him in prison for a very long time.

Under the terms of his restriction, he was required to be home by six-thirty each night and remain there until six-thirty the next morning. If he missed the deadline, even by a minute, he risked a fine and imprisonment. A few times he had cut it close, most recently a few days earlier when a long and cantankerous political dispute had spilled over into the early evening. But he was a cautious man by nature—serious, quiet and responsible, and not inclined to give his wife and children more to worry about than they already had. Usually it was safely before six when she would hear the familiar rumble of the Chevy as he eased into the driveway, and she would start to breathe again. But not tonight.

"I'll be busy," he had said that morning, and she had not asked to be told more. She knew by his very terseness that he would be doing something for the movement. He never told her exactly what or where. This deliberate vagueness was designed to protect them both—she could not divulge what she did not know. Still, she suspected that he was going to Lilliesleaf, a farm north of the city in the suburb of Rivonia. The movement had purchased the twenty-eight-acre estate clandestinely two years earlier, set up one of its members as owner and used it as a secret headquarters for men who were plotting sabotage attacks against the state. All of this she knew and much, much more, all of it guilty and very dangerous knowledge, and it made her uneasy. They both knew Rivonia was not a secure location, that too many people who were under suspicion came and went from there, traveling mostly in their own cars with license plate numbers that the Special Branch men seemed to know by heart. He had complained often about the lack of security, and he had promised her that he would stop going there, but there always seemed to be one last matter that had to be discussed, one last meeting that had to be attended. So far they had been lucky. But they both knew it would not last forever.

They had been married for nearly twenty-two years and they had worked together as comrades in the Communist Party for even longer. Still, there were things they never said to each other, feelings they did not share. That morning she had wanted to plead with him not to go, to tell him it was too dangerous to keep taking such risks at a time when the police were looking for any excuse to strike. But she did not do so, partly because her own years of political discipline had conditioned her to endure stoically, and partly because she knew he would not heed her plea. He understood the dangers as keenly as she did, felt the same turbulent anxiety in the pit of his stomach. Yet he had decided to take the risk. It was a decision she knew she must honor even as she dreaded its potential consequences. "Take care of yourself. . . . Be careful." That was all she said.

She knew the risks so intimately because she was taking many of them herself. Despite the security crackdown, she still attended secret meetings, working to keep alive banned organizations and helping arrange illegal activities such as protest demonstrations and boycotts. Increasingly she could see something many of her comrades refused to admit: that what they were doing was futile. The government was slowly transforming itself into a police state. There were new laws restricting their movements and further contracting their already limited freedoms, and the police were coming down on them with a weight they had never felt before. The few whites like themselves who stood with Nelson Mandela and the black liberation movement were reeling from the pressure and the blows. They had long grown used to the sense that someone was always watching or listening. But now it had gone far beyond that. People were disappearing, swept away in mass raids or sucked into the bottomless pit of recurring ninety-day detentions. Like Germany before World War II, South Africa seemed gripped by a mass fever of desperation and fatalism. Each night they listened for the sound of cars pulling up the drive, footsteps on the pavement and a knock on the door. Their personal lives were not immune to these fears; their own children had become hostages to their cause. Even the house that they had cherished and raised their family in for fifteen years seemed to turn against them.

It was a modest four-bedroom cottage in a leafy, backwoods neighborhood just a ten-minute drive from downtown—154 Regent Street in the eastern suburb of Observatory. There was no thatched roof or split-level flourishes, just a rust-colored, triangular roof of corrugated tin atop a plain, whitewashed, one-story building whose walls always seemed in need of paint. There was a small swimming pool out back where the children seemed to live day and night in summer. But the trees were the real prize. They graced both the front and back, ranging from the six great jacarandas that lined the driveway to the clusters of lemon, fig, apricot, quince, wattle, apple, peach and plum trees scattered throughout the grounds, to the vine that yielded black grapes in summer. Their daughter Frances, who had just turned twelve, thought of it as her own little Garden of Eden, a perfect African paradise. The back yard was not large, but it sloped downward to merge with several others in a long, continuous field with only a low wire fence separating them. The ground was hard and dry and brittle as bone in winter, but the powerful summer rains softened and massaged it and coaxed dark sweet smells from the rich red earth.

When they first lived there, doors and windows had seldom been closed even in winter. Children paraded through both day and night on their way to someone or somewhere. Visitors, whether white, black or Indian—an unusually free mix in a society where race was the ironclad organizing principle of human existence—came and went without ringing the bell. They swam, sat, talked, stayed for tea. And like most white South Africans, they had African servants, Bessie and Claude, to help with domestic chores and child care.

Later she would write that she felt as if the house was itself a living organism; it breathed and murmured and rattled and groaned, and it embraced them in its gentle warmth. But the very openness of the house became a weapon in the hands of the police. Inside, no one could hide from view; onlookers from without could see easily through the glazed windows. Secrets could not be told, nor kept. The phone, too, became an enemy. They assumed it was wired to record not only their phone calls but other conversations as well. Over and over they drilled the rules into their children like a catechism of fear: Never tell callers that we're out, never ever say where we've gone or when we'll be back. It got so bad that the children dreaded hearing the phone ring.

Her husband was an amateur carpenter—he designed a false bottom for her desk, a secret panel for the drying rack in the kitchen and special slots at the top of the kitchen door and the linen cupboard. In these ordinary icons of domestic life, the two of them concealed notes of meetings, forbidden magazines and other documents whose possession could land them a year or more behind bars. They stashed a list of names and numbers as well, far from the prying eyes of police who longed to discover it and whose invasions of their house and their privacy had become more and more frequent. Nothing was off-limits to these officers of the law—the master bedroom, the children's rooms, even the bathroom were all considered open territory to be scrutinized, pawed through and ransacked with contemptuous familiarity.

There were times when she longed for a normal middle-class life, times when she wanted to chuck it all and flee for the nearest border, as many of their closest friends were doing. The Hodgsons had fled, the Bermans too. Joe Slovo, Yusuf Dadoo, J. B. Marks, Moses Kotane and countless others had left on secret missions and never come back. She could feel their pull. But she was too committed, not just to the movement but to her comrades, the handful of people who were as deeply involved as she and her husband. They were like a second family to her; she could no more abandon them than she could her own children. To cut off contact now, to give up in the face of the state's terrible power, would be an act of betrayal not only of her closest friends but of herself.

Besides, as strong as she was, he was even stronger and more determined not to cut and run.

July was the first full month of winter south of the equator, and the African sun set abruptly each night with a brilliant display of crimson defiance. Most nights this glorious ritual gave her strength, but tonight, she would recall later, it only compounded her sense of dread as the time passed and still he did not return. There was nowhere to call, no one to ask, no way to reach him. She could only sit and wonder and wait. As she started preparing dinner, she tried not to look at the kitchen wall clock, but she knew that the sun went down just before six. By six-fifteen the darkness was complete, the night like a lid sealing in her fear. There was no way to see from the window if a police car was hovering up the block. She could send one of the children to sneak a look, but that might alert the security men that something was wrong. It might also alarm the children, whose keen antennae were already sensing her anxiety. Toni, at nineteen the eldest, sat quietly with a friend in the living room before a roaring fire. "Daddy's late," she said matter-of-factly. Patrick, fifteen, sullen and withdrawn, was away at a holiday camp where he tried to escape from the relentless claustrophobia of his parents and their politics. Frances, who was scholarly, dutiful and sincere, was spending the night at a friend's house, while Keith, six, coughed and sniffled, the first signs of a new bout of the septic throat that often kept him awake through the night.

She looked up again. It was six twenty-nine, and she watched the second hand sink to the bottom of the clock and then begin to climb. If something had happened at Rivonia, she knew that their world would come crashing down. All the troubles they had faced in the past would be nothing compared to what was to come. Then six-thirty came and went, and Hilda Bernstein knew. Her husband Rusty would not be coming home. Not that night. Not for many nights to come.

After reporting to Marshall Square early that afternoon, Rusty Bernstein stopped by a local engineering firm's office to drop off a building plan he had designed. Then he went to a nearby Central News Agency shop to pick up some foreign magazines he had ordered. Then he got back in the Chevy and headed north. Soon he was driving on the Oxford Road, a tarred two-lane affair that knifed its way in businesslike fashion through a parade of glossy suburbs. Their names—Killarney, Saxonwold, Riviera, Houghton, Rosebank, Melrose, Dunkeld—evoked Old World tastes and sensibilities that had been grafted with comic imprecision onto the wild, stubborn South African veld. After Illovo, the road visibly relaxed, slipping gracefully into a softer, slower country blacktop. The vegetation changed from the carefully sculpted bougainvilleas and firs of the suburbs to the rural abandon of willows, gums, acacias, jacarandas, cypresses and poplars, stripped of their passionate greens by winter. The road itself changed identities. Now as the Rivonia Road it wound its way past the small, dry suburban crossroads known as Sandown and the turnoff for Alexandra, the vast black township that lay wreathed in an eerie cloud of coal smoke in the valley that for white eyes always seemed just beyond view.

Rusty navigated the old Chevy with deliberate speed; there was no point in risking being pulled over and having to explain to some overeager junior police officer why he, a listed communist who was not supposed to leave the city proper without written permission, was driving around ten miles north of town on a Thursday afternoon. Soon he was passing the dignified, six-foot-high stone wall outside the Carmelite Convent, and then, a block further, the Rivonia police station, a swollen and dusty colonial-style compound set off to the right of the road under a grove of eucalyptus trees. Out of the corner of one eye he could see a white van and a clump of men, but he paid no heed. He concentrated on the road and on checking in the rearview mirror every now and then to make sure no one was following. He knew he was taking a risk by returning for a meeting at a secret headquarters that the police were eager to find and smash, and he was doing so as carefully as possible.

Caution had been forged into Lionel Bernstein's soul at an early age. Born in 1920 in Johannesburg, he had been orphaned at age twelve. His mother developed cancer and his father, a well-to-do accountant, rushed her to England for a futile round of treatment. During the course of his furious attempt to save her, Rusty's father developed pneumonia and died suddenly, leaving his dying widow to bring his body back to South Africa. She herself died a few months later, and Rusty—nicknamed for the shock of tightly curled red hair that made him look like a fugitive from a Dublin betting parlor—was farmed out along with his three siblings to various aunts and uncles. Two years later he was entrusted to the tender mercies of Hilton College, a prestigious all-male boarding school some five hundred miles to the southeast in Natal province where, as he put it, "a gallant but often fruitless attempt is made to turn upper-class South African youths into the sons of gentlemen."

In Rusty's case the results were even more fruitless than usual. All that the experience left him, he later claimed, was a thin veneer of superficially good manners, an enduring hatred for physical exercise and a tolerance for truly bad institutional food. Still, when it came to studies, he was surprisingly adept, finishing at the top of the Class of 1936. Back in Johannesburg, it took him five years to complete a part-time course in architecture at the University of Witwatersrand, South Africa's most distinguished institute of higher learning—known to one and all as "Wits." He worked days as a draftsman at a local firm while attending classes at night. After graduation he joined the army as an artillery gunner. He returned from Italy in 1946 to a job as chief draftsman, his specialty, he wrote, "undistinguished architecture on a large scale." There he designed the city's first drive-in cinema, and worked on numerous houses and small office buildings. "All I can say is that few of them actually offend the eye or have fatal planning defects," he would joke. Humorous self-deprecation was the orphan's chosen weapon.

Rusty wore his conservatism like armor plating. He disliked modern poetry, was mystified by modern art and thought Caruso a far greater singer than Sinatra or Presley. Losing his parents at an early age had made him terminally wary—he had no sense of adventure and no taste for personal risk. His friend Joe Slovo said, not altogether approvingly, that Rusty could easily have been content "sitting hunched in his family drawing room indiscriminately reading thrillers against the background of classical music." He was, by his own reckoning, a laconic soul, almost pathologically unambitious. He dreamt of singing with the purity and control of Maria Callas, of writing with the passion of Jean-Paul Sartre and of becoming a full-time beachcomber. "These I know I will never be able to achieve," he once wrote, "and consequently I never really try." He hated crowds, parties and small talk. He loved books, opera, carpentry and his own children. All of his passions were solitary and private. Except for one.

Influenced by his Latin teacher at Hilton, his fellow architecture students at Wits and the Spanish Civil War, Rusty Bernstein had become a communist in the late 1930s. For a quiet young man haunted by self-doubt, Marxism offered firm, confident answers; it had an explanation for the state of crisis that gripped the modern world—from the Great Depression to the rise of Hitler to the juxtaposition of forces and motives in the new world war that was about to begin. Rusty soon became an ardent campaigner for the republican cause in Spain. He even contemplated joining the International Brigade—but the conflict ended before he reached enlistment age.

Rusty started out in the Youth League of the Labor Party, which modeled itself after its British namesake. It was working class in orientation but exclusively white in membership, and Rusty soon found himself drifting further leftward. The Communist Party of South Africa had been founded largely by foreigners—trade unionists from Britain and radical immigrants from Eastern Europe—and it had started out in the early 1920s with a passionate embrace of socialist idealism and a slavish obedience to the new Soviet Union. Blind faith in Moscow had remained a prerequisite throughout a dizzying series of ideological false starts, sudden reversals and periodic purges. By the time Rusty joined, the party was a semi-clandestine sect with a membership of no more than 500 people and a penchant for internecine warfare and obscure jargon. Its meetings were fiercely argumentative; members seemed to love nothing better than to cast aspersions on each other's intellect and class loyalty. Still, when it came to racial matters the party was a model of tolerance. It was the country's only multiracial political party and its leaders included respected African intellectuals and trade unionists like Moses Kotane and J. B. Marks.

André Gide, explaining why he had become a communist in the 1930s, said that holding a privileged place in a society where most people were mired in poverty was like having a seat in a lifeboat after a shipwreck. "The knowledge of being one of those in the lifeboat, of being safe, while others around me are drowning, that feeling became intolerable to me," Gide wrote.

In South Africa the lifeboat was strictly reserved for those with white skin. Before he joined the party, Rusty gave little thought to racial issues; like most white South Africans, he took for granted his privileged status in a country where two million whites ruled over eight million blacks. But he was astonished to attend party meetings where black members participated freely and viewed themselves and their white comrades as equals. As in a newborn, his eyes were opening.

When they thought about them at all, most white South Africans viewed blacks as slightly less than human. The areas where most whites lived were strictly segregated; schools, shops, restaurants, buses, even public parks were by custom for whites only. Yet blacks were every-where—they did the menial labor in virtually every white-owned store or business, and they worked as servants, maids, gardeners and cooks in almost every white household. At the end of twelve-hour workdays, black employees would retreat to unheated, one-room shacks in the back of their masters' property or else trek to distant shanty towns known as townships, where the air was choked with coal smoke when it was cold and the stench of open sewers when it was not. Servants were poorly paid and poorly fed, and their spouses and children were forced to remain behind in distant rural tribal lands. Africans were even re-stricted to separate plates, cups and utensils, so that a white person would not feel contaminated or at risk from the dangerous act of touch-ing his lips to the same surface a black person had used.

The Communist Party had been slow to identify itself with the strug-gle for racial equality. Early on, many of its members had banked all of their ideological capital on the notion of class struggle and tended to dismiss black nationalism as hopelessly bourgeois. In its futile effort to pander to the white proletariat, the party had even marched during the 1922 miners' strike under the shameful banner "Workers of the World, Unite and Fight for a White South Africa."

But in the early 1940s fresh thinkers like Rusty helped launch a process of revitalization. Riding a wave of popularity during the war, the party enlisted many new black members and organized evening adult education classes and other social welfare projects. Its ranks swelled to perhaps 2,500 members. Rusty became a full-time func-tionary, writing much of the party's political propaganda, and he won recognition as one of the organization's most respected teachers. When it came to foreign affairs, he adhered strictly to the Moscow line, even when it led to the moral contortions of the Nazi-Soviet Pact of 1939, which compelled loyal South African communists like Rusty to turn on a dime—only to shift again after Germany invaded the Soviet Union two years later. But on internal South African issues he was far more creative, steering his students away from the rigid stance of waiting for a white-led proletarian revolution that might never come and moving instead toward embracing the mainstream struggle for national liberation of the oppressed black majority. He was a strong proponent of the budding alliance between the party and the African National Congress, the predominant black political movement. In evening classes and small discussion groups and in the interminable meetings that were the principal fact of communist life, he quickly acquired a reputation as thoughtful, modest and well informed. He acquired something else as well—a full-time girlfriend five years his senior.

Hilda Watts had arrived in South Africa from England just before the outbreak of World War II with impeccable communist credentials. She was the youngest of three daughters born to Simeon and Dora Schwartz of Finchley Park in London. Simeon was a Bolshevik and a Jew who had fled Odessa in 1905 to avoid czarist conscription. In London he met and married Dora, another recent Russian Jewish immigrant. He changed his name to Samuel Watts, dropped all Jewish customs and raised his daughters as proper English ladies. But ideologically Simeon Schwartz never left Odessa, and the 1917 October Revolution rekindled his faith. He became the first Soviet consul to Britain and eventually, under orders from the party, returned to Russia, where he lived out the remainder of his life. He sent money home and invited everyone for visits, but Dora, who stayed behind in London, never understood how her husband could allow his commitment to the Soviet Union to override their marriage.

Hilda believed that all human frailty was susceptible to correction. She had enormous talent; she wrote, she painted, she sang, she orated, all with great skill and fervor. She had all the optimism and arrogance of the young and the deeply sincere. Looking back on herself many years later, she would say, "The meaning of life is not a fact to be discovered, but a choice that you make about the way you live." Hilda made her choices early and stuck passionately to them.

In South Africa, Hilda thrived. The racial situation was stark: there was right and there was wrong and not much gray in between. She may have doubted herself at times, but never her cause. She recalled how an elderly black man once came to the house pleading for work, and a child had said, "There's a boy outside." *A boy.* It was a daily insult to the rest of humanity to live as a white South African in such circumstances. She had no difficulty choosing sides.

She was small, fine-boned and handsome, with gentle brown eyes and a warm, firm smile. Her idealism made her face come alive; it was more than admirable, it was seductive. She was coming off a bad relationship and was attracted to Rusty's powerful intellect and to his rugged good looks. About sex she was liberated and direct; within a few months she and Rusty were living together.

They waited until he was twenty-one to get married. They went with their witnesses to the registry office at lunchtime; afterward Rusty returned to work at party headquarters while his older brother Harold, best man and witness, a man more inclined to respect the niceties of tradition, took the bride to an afternoon movie. She lost her new wedding ring at the theater; she dropped it in the darkness and it rolled somewhere forever, another bourgeois tradition seemingly lost in history's dust.

Having never attended university, Hilda was less of a theoretical thinker than her husband and many of the other men who dominated the Communist Party, but she was broader in her interests. She was deeply committed to nuclear disarmament and became involved in women's issues at a time when many people on the left considered feminism just another bourgeois distraction. She was also interested in children. When the Bernsteins invited comrades and their families over for dinner, most of the adults talked politics and ideology. But Hilda would sidle over to the teenagers to talk about high school, pop music and the opposite sex. For nearly a decade—until her politics made her an untouchable—she was editor of *Childhood*, the monthly magazine of the South African National Council for Child Welfare, where she preached and celebrated the rare art of common sense in child raising. She put a photo of her daughter Toni and two teenaged friends, Ilse Fischer and Barbara Harmel, on the cover of an issue above a lead article entitled "There's Nothing Wrong with Rock 'n' Roll." Yet the same person could write approvingly about China's policy toward ethnic minorities in *New Age*, a leftist monthly edited by her friend and comrade Ruth First. The subject matter demonstrated Hilda's range of interests—and the point of view showed her occasional naiveté.

All in all, the Bernsteins were an unusual pair of communists. He believed in class struggle, dialectical materialism and the infallibility of the Soviet Union and its glorious leader, Joseph Stalin. At the same time, he was also a good father, a caring comrade and a faithful friend. From where he stood at Africa's southernmost tip, he saw in communism the hope of a better world and a better life for the masses; he failed to see the gulags, the firing squads and the lies. The racist regime he fought against reviled everything about the Soviet Union; surely that was another compelling reason for him to stay loyal. Hilda had her doubts about such matters. But this was an era when men still enjoyed a presumption of authority and intelligence that women were expected to honor, and she tended to defer to her husband and his comrades. Only later would she come to recognize how foolish that presumption had been, and regret it.

The personal security of an ideology and of a close-knit band of fellow believers both compelled and enabled Rusty and Hilda to take risks and engage in activities they might never have undertaken otherwise. When the Communist Party was banned in 1950, they helped reconstitute it as an illegal, underground organization. They engaged in many political activities that could have landed them long jail sentences. And when the party turned to sabotage—joining with the outlawed African National Congress in 1961 to form a separate military wing known as Umkhonto We Sizwe, Zulu for "Spear of the Nation"—they followed suit. Other than a brief run by Rusty on the first night of the campaign at a manhole that housed telephone cables connecting Johannesburg and Pretoria, neither of them participated in acts of violence. But Rusty was part of the committee that oversaw Umkhonto, while Hilda knew most of what was going on. If the police came across Rivonia with its storehouse of names and networks, both of them would be in immediate jeopardy.

The idea behind the sabotage campaign was to frighten and shake the white-minority government—"to bring it to its senses" and force it to negotiate before time ran out and the country was plunged into anarchy. But the government was far from cowed. Its leaders orchestrated a furious crackdown, enacting new and more draconian laws further restricting the civil liberties of anyone suspected of opposition. Mandela himself was arrested in August 1962 and sentenced to five years for illegal political activity, although investigators had not uncovered his role in the sabotage campaign.

Frustrated by the lack of progress, the activists of Umkhonto prepared to escalate from sabotage to guerrilla warfare under a rough plan code-named Operation Mayibuye—"The Return." Rusty was one of

those who opposed such a move and he wrote a brief but scathing critique that he had planned to read to the assembled leadership that afternoon. He slipped it under the floor mat of the car, but after leaving
the house that morning, he had become anxious about carrying the
document around with him. He drove back to Regent Street and
stashed the paper at the bottom of a tray of grimy washers and bolts in
the shed at the end of the driveway. He was already carrying too many
incriminating documents as part of his regular duties. In the new South
Africa carrying the wrong papers was in itself a subversive act. Rusty
was not James Bond, or even George Smiley. He could not rely on a few
well-placed karate chops or a Walther PPK with a silencer to deliver
him from danger. He had only his wits, his luck and his innate sense of
caution.

Another kilometer and Rusty turned to the left, heading down a
steep incline toward Lilliesleaf's open gate. It took him several minutes
to wind his way through the narrow wooded drive and pass the stately
main house and the black caretaker in overalls who kept watch. Rusty
pulled around the side and parked near the thatched-roof cottage in the
rear. He was met there by Ahmed Kathrada, a veteran Indian activist
who had spent the night on the grounds. Ahmed was wearing a jaunty
handlebar mustache, long trench coat and theatrical makeup that made
him look like a small-time Portuguese mafioso but allowed him to roam
the streets of Johannesburg undetected. His code name was "Pedro."
Two other vehicles had already arrived. The old Taunus station wagon
belonged to Bob Hepple, a twenty-seven-year-old lawyer who had defended many radical clients and was himself a member of the Communist Party. Nearby was a Volkswagen microbus from Travellyn, another
recently rented hideout. It had been driven by Denis Goldberg, a young
civil engineer and activist from Cape Town, who was due to leave the
country in a few days. Among the passengers were Govan Mbeki, fifty-
three, a veteran journalist and activist from the city of Port Elizabeth,
code-named "Dhlamini," and Raymond Mhlaba, one of Mbeki's closest
comrades. But the most important passenger was a small soft-spoken
man named Walter Sisulu.

He was an elementary school dropout who had been employed as a
clerical worker in the gold mines and factories of Johannesburg. He had
risen quickly within the ANC and had been secretary general of the
African National Congress until the organization was banned in 1960.

With his gentle manner, ready smile, practical mind and abiding optimism he became the perfect complement to the tall, regal and imperious Mandela. He seldom spoke harshly or criticized others. Yet Rusty was among many people who viewed Walter Sisulu as the true center of gravity of the movement. Sisulu was more ideologically grounded than Mandela; he had long believed in Marxist principles and had secretly joined the Communist Party in the 1950s, although he kept his membership hidden from most of his ANC colleagues. At the same time, he insisted that the antiapartheid movement be as broad-based as possible, welcoming Black Sash supporters and members of Alan Paton's small but vocal Liberal Party. As for Nelson, he made no move without first clearing it with Walter, his close friend and mentor. After Mandela's arrest, Sisulu became the ANC's main link to Umkhonto.

Like Mandela, Sisulu had been arrested a half dozen times in 1962 and was finally convicted of political offenses. But thanks to the skillful pleading in court of Harold Wolpe, a radical lawyer secretly involved with Umkhonto, Sisulu had been allowed out on bail while appealing his sentence. He soon fled—Wolpe, who helped engineer Sisulu's flight, feigned indignation—and vanished underground, spending most of his time in hiding at Rivonia and Travellyn. A few weeks later, in June 1963, Sisulu surfaced to make an illegal radio broadcast from a secret location in the northern suburbs, inaugurating something they called "Radio Liberation," the voice of the African National Congress.

"Sons and daughters of Africa!" Sisulu proclaimed. "I speak to you from somewhere in South Africa. I have not left this country. I do not plan to leave."

He told listeners that he and many ANC leaders had gone underground to keep the movement alive. Unity was vital, he said, and black people must develop new ways of struggling against government oppression. "In the face of violence, many strugglers for freedom have had to meet violence with violence. How can it be otherwise in South Africa?"

The broadcast had been a great coup and morale booster for the movement, and it had infuriated the government. Now the police were desperate to find Walter Sisulu. They staked out his house in Soweto and arrested his wife, Albertina, under the new Ninety-Day Act. But even she did not know where he was hiding. Sisulu had straightened his unruly Afro and dyed it a deep black. He had grown a mustache that made him look like Charlie Chaplin impersonating Hitler. His code name was "Allah." Still, he was unmistakably Walter Sisulu—affable, unimposing, unpretentious and South Africa's Most Wanted criminal.

The men who came to Lilliesleaf that afternoon gathered in the thatched cottage, a small outbuilding that Rusty had redesigned and renovated. He had added a bathroom and toilet, hot and cold running water, three beds and an extra mattress and several easy chairs, so that the building could serve as both conference room and hideout. The participants took their place around a coffee table. Govan Mbeki passed around a copy of Operation Mayibuye. They were disputing over not only its contents but its operational status. Mbeki, who was among those pressing for an intensification of armed struggle, argued that the campaign needed no further endorsement because the Umkhonto High Command had already approved it. But Walter Sisulu and Rusty Bernstein insisted that no decision was final until it was approved by Umkhonto's two parent organizations—the ANC and the Communist Party. Neither had done so, and Sisulu and Bernstein were strongly opposed to the idea. It looked like another long, contentious meeting. Rusty knew he would have to start for home by five o'clock in order to safely beat his curfew. He glanced at his watch. It was already three.

Rusty Bernstein was not the only one watching the clock that afternoon. A mile or so away in the dust-caked open yard compound outside the Rivonia police station, Lieutenant Willem Petrus Johannes van Wyk of the South African security police glanced impatiently at his watch. Van Wyk (pronounced *Fon Vake*) was trying to keep fourteen anxious policemen and a spirited Alsatian dog named Cheetah in a state of high readiness while waiting for another of his subordinates to return from central Johannesburg with a search warrant. Already the man was late, and van Wyk was falling far behind schedule. He feared that the trap he was setting would be sprung too late.

For months Willie van Wyk and his fellow officers had been attempting with limited success to track down those responsible for the wave of political sabotage that had struck South Africa. Faced with more than 200 attacks ranging from cherry bombs in post office boxes to the fire-bombing of the National Party regional headquarters in Durban, the police had succeeded only in disrupting a handful of operations in mid-flight and capturing a few low-level operatives. But they had gotten to none of the higher-ups, and did not have a solid piece of evidence that would reveal where the campaign was headquartered or who was in charge.

Not that they had much doubt about who ultimately was responsible. Van Wyk and his superiors believed that agitators such as Nelson Mandela and Walter Sisulu had to be behind the violence. They suspected that these men in turn were being manipulated by white communists such as Joe Slovo, Rusty Bernstein, Jack Hodgson and Michael Harmel in a godless alliance in which Africans served as cannon fodder while their white bosses remained comfortably out of harm's way. The notion that most Africans were fundamentally content under white rule but that some had become mindless tools in the hands of diabolically clever communists was a basic precept for the security police. Another tenet of faith was that most of the communists were Jews—*uitlanders*, or foreigners, whose true allegiance was to Moscow, not Johannesburg. Real South Africans understood the natural justice of white rule. Such beliefs enabled the police to go about their business without the inconvenience of moral pangs. The problem was that Mandela was in jail while Slovo, Hodgson and Harmel had all left the country, yet the bombs kept going off.

Faced with an enemy they could not seem to defeat with standard investigatory techniques, the security police fell back on blunter instruments. They jailed and abused hundreds of activists and harassed thousands more in a heavy-handed attempt to crack the networks. They wiretapped more phones, tailed more cars, raided more houses. And the government bestowed upon them more and more legal weapons. The latest and most draconian was the Ninety-Day Act, which allowed the authorities to detain anyone for up to three months in an isolation cell without charge until he or she answered questions to their satisfaction. Once the ninety days were up, they could arrest the detainee again. And again. And again. "Until eternity," as the government's tough new Justice Minister, Balthazar John Vorster, was reputed to have said.

The makeup of Special Branch, as the security police was called, was beginning to change. It was becoming both more sophisticated and more brutal. A new commander had taken over in January. Hendrik van den Bergh was a lanky six-footer who spoke smooth, elegant English, preferred business suits to uniforms and looked like a high-ranking bank executive. He fancied himself an intellectual. Long Hendrik, as he was known by his men, was appointed to his post by Vorster, with whom he had shared a prison cell during World War II, when both men were interned as Nazi sympathizers. Long Hendrik's methods were unconventional, sadistic and fastidious all at once. When his interrogators began to beat suspects in his presence, he would quietly leave the room. Like his communist opponents, he was more interested in ends than in means. Chris Vermaak, one of the journalists he assiduously cultivated, described him as "a master of the unorthodox . . . with a flair for diplomacy and a lively and inquiring mind." On the other hand, Helen Suzman, who was the sole Progressive in Parliament, called him "South Africa's own Heinrich Himmler."

Van den Bergh's moral calculus was simple. As he later recalled: "For me the choice was between revolution, violence and a bloodbath and the so-called rule of law, about which there was all the noise. I looked at my children and those of others and said, 'To the devil with the rule of law.' "

For years Special Branch had been a haven for mediocrity. Its corridors were inhabited by lifetime bureaucrats, malcontents, mavericks and out-of-shape former athletes—men of unsound mind and body. Its members had spent the last decade trailing after the leaders of the liberation movement, always seemingly a step or two behind. Van den Bergh set about changing all that. He brought in a handful of college graduates to add a touch of class to the operation. At the same time he traveled to France with some of his top men to learn the darker arts of interrogation from the French Deuxième Bureau—the intelligence section of the general staff.

Willie van Wyk was already a veteran criminal investigator when he was reassigned to the Special Branch in 1960 at age thirty-one. He was reluctant to make the switch—he knew the security police's reputation for ineptitude and brutality—but he was given no choice. He had known some of the radicals like Mandela and Slovo as defense lawyers and had been friendly with them; he was uncomfortable treating them as targets. But he quickly acquired a reputation even among activists as a courteous but dogged and dangerous gumshoe whose network of informers was extensive.

Not that he was having much luck tracking down Walter Sisulu. No one was talking. But two weeks after the Radio Liberation broadcast, van Wyk received a call from a fellow officer who had come across an informant with important goods to sell. The man had been detained when a group of Africans were picked up near the Botswana border. They had been on their way overseas for military training, after which they were to be smuggled back into South Africa to take part in Umkhonto's sabotage operations. But this particular prisoner said he had been to the organization's secret headquarters. He said he knew where to find Sisulu and half a dozen other important leaders of the Umkhonto High Command. For a large payment—the man said he wanted the six thousand rand that Sisulu had forfeited when he jumped bail, the equivalent of about twelve thousand dollars—he would take the lieutenant there.

Van Wyk got clearance all the way up to Long Hendrik to offer payment, provided the information proved good. But van Wyk's superiors were skeptical. The informant could be lying, either to try to make money or to throw police off the scent. And indeed, for a week after van Wyk agreed to the man's terms, nothing developed. Each night van Wyk drove the man around the northern suburbs. Van Wyk wore civilian clothes, while the informant wore dark glasses, a cap pulled low over his forehead and a scarf pulled up above his chin. On the first night he directed van Wyk down the Oxford Road but seemed to lose his way once they got past Sandown. "We must watch out for a place called Ivon," he told van Wyk. "I saw the name written on a sign just a couple of hundred yards from the house." There was a church quite near the road, the man said, and a bit farther on, a gate with white posts that opened onto the place where Sisulu was staying.

Night after night they cruised the area without success. Nothing seemed familiar to the informant, and van Wyk was beginning to wonder whether the whole idea was just a ruse. Then one night they headed up Rietfontein Road, a winding road from the valley to the top of the ridge. They had been on this road at least twice before, but both times heading in the opposite direction. This time, the informant rose in his seat. "That's it, Lieutenant! There's the church!"

The "church" turned out to be a gabled private house that looked only vaguely churchlike. The gate with white posts was just around the next bend. From the road, van Wyk could see no house behind it, only trees and bushes, and he did not slow down for fear of alerting someone on the property.

A little further along they came upon a weathered sign bearing the name RIVONIA, but with the letters R and IA faded and almost illegible. Without them, only the middle part stood out: IVON. The informant had not lied; his eyes had simply deceived him.

That night when he reached home van Wyk planned the raid. He figured that the occupants probably moved around after dark and stayed put during the day; it would therefore be best to raid during broad daylight. He made sure that detectives Carel Dirker and James Kennedy came along; they were experienced in handling political documents and would know what to look for. A straightforward police operation using squad cars and uniformed men would almost certainly alert the guards whom the informant said patrolled the grounds. Instead, van Wyk wanted a vehicle that could carry him and his men onto the site without raising suspicion. He thought about using an ambulance, but that might draw too much attention. Then he decided on a dry cleaning van. What could be more innocuous?

In the morning he and a fellow detective drove past the site once more. It was densely wooded and he could still see no buildings from the road, but he could make out a small section of tiled roof behind the trees. They stopped at a neighbor's house. The woman living there was happy to tell them that Lilliesleaf belonged to a Mr. Arthur Goldreich, a local architect and interior designer for Greaterman's. It was a big estate with many outbuildings. He was a nice man, Mr. Goldreich, but she was surprised that he seemed to have a great many African friends who came and went at all hours. "His Bantu visitors are very well dressed," she told van Wyk. "They often have mixed parties in the lounge—Europeans and Bantu hobnobbing and drinking together."

Van Wyk commandeered a dry cleaning van. He dressed two of his best men, Kleingeld and van den Berg, in white lab coats and put them in the front seat. Then he, Dirker, Kennedy and eleven others crammed into the back along with the dog. They stopped off at the Rivonia police compound to borrow a blanket to hang behind the front seat of the van, so that no one looking in would see the men concealed in the back. If challenged, Kleingeld was to claim they were looking for the nearby Sleepy Hollow Hotel.

They were just about to pull out from the station compound at 1 p.m. when Colonel "Tiny" Ventner, van Wyk's newly appointed superior officer, asked to examine the search warrant. Van Wyk did not have one; he told Ventner he had not wanted to risk any leak of his plans by applying for one from the magistrate's office, and in any case the law did not require one in such urgent circumstances. But Ventner, a tall, cadaverous man who had just come to Special Branch, did not want to risk looking bad if some judge of liberal bent decided later to throw out the search. He ordered van Wyk to obtain a warrant. The lieutenant was furious, but there was no appeal. He dispatched one of his men back downtown to the magistrate's court, which would not reopen until 2 p.m. The man did not return with a signed warrant until nearly three.

The timing proved critical. At 1 p.m., the only activist at Lilliesleaf was Ahmed Kathrada in his jaunty disguise. By 3 p.m., when van den Berg turned the key in the ignition and started off for the farm, Walter Sisulu, Rusty and four other important radicals were also on the scene.

The van passed a locked gate, then turned left and entered the grounds through another gate. It meandered for several minutes before pulling up to a large stately house. A black servant blocked the path. Everything seemed quiet, as if deserted.

"Where's the master?" asked Kleingeld.

"There's nobody at home," the servant replied.

Kleingeld asked directions to the Sleepy Hollow Hotel, while van Wyk raced through his options. They could turn around and leave and try again later in the day, but surely the servant would be suspicious next time. Or they could make their move now and trust to luck. Van den Berg had slipped the gearshift into reverse and started to turn around when van Wyk ordered him to stop, *"Ons slaan toe!"* he told his men. "Let's close in!"

From the window of the thatched cottage, Rusty saw the white dry cleaning van pull up. Delivery vehicles appeared in the front yard regularly, and it took him a few seconds to recall why this one seemed especially familiar. "I saw that van in the police station," he told Bob Hepple sitting next to him. Already more than a dozen men and a dog were pouring out the rear of the vehicle and sprinting toward the main house and the cottage.

Rusty watched as Sisulu, Mbeki and Kathrada bolted for an open picture window, climbed through and ran off. He knew he himself had no chance. He pulled the papers from his pocket and dropped them on the coffee table in front of him. Hepple grabbed as many papers as he could, including the six-page outline of Operation Mayibuye, stuffed them into the small coal-burning stove and tried to light them. He fumbled with his matches and nothing burned.

Detective Kennedy shoved open the door. He saw two white men and an African in the room—Bernstein, Hepple and Raymond Mhlaba— and a pile of papers on the table, which he immediately swept up. An officer named van Heerden, with Cheetah in tow, came around the side of the cottage, where he saw the other three men dashing for the bushes. "I order you to stop!" he called out. To his enduring surprise, they froze in their tracks. Denis Goldberg was found in the main house, where he had been about to sit down to a bowl of ice cream. Yet another Umkhonto operative, Wilton Mkwayi, who was dressed in farm laborer's overalls, managed to slip away in the confusion.

Willie van Wyk was astonished to see the considerable haul of men and matériel. He immediately recognized Rusty and Hepple. He also spotted Govan Mbeki, even though the distinguished fifty-three-year-old politician and writer was dressed in a workman's cap and grimy blue overalls. Next to Mbeki was a tall, swarthy man with a mop of red hair and a long coat flopping around his knees. "Who is that red-haired fellow?" asked van Wyk of his fellow officers.

The man burst out in a grin that van Wyk immediately recognized. "Good heavens! Kathrada!"

But the biggest catch was the light-skinned man with the pitch-black hair and silly mustache. Van Wyk had no trouble spotting Walter Sisulu. Neither did Detective Sergeant Dirker, a career bully who had been harassing Walter's family for months. "I've got you now," he snarled at Walter.

He patted down Sisulu and pulled some papers from a coat pocket. "That's all there is, Mr. Dirker," Sisulu told him. "You now have everything you were hoping to find."

Besides the men and the incriminating documents from the coal-burning stove, the raid yielded stack after stack of pamphlets, letters, circulars and communist literature. Among the documents in Nelson Mandela's handwriting were a sixty-two-page notebook entitled "Part One. How to Be a Good Communist," a diary of his trip abroad in 1962 seeking support for Umkhonto from African states and a note describing in convincing detail plans for a jail escape. Police also found his false passport in the name of David Matsamayi. His comrades' decision to save these papers for posterity in a metal trunk buried in a coal pit now meant that Mandela could be linked to Umkhonto with his own words and charged with a capital offense. The police also discovered a handwritten version of an Umkhonto disciplinary code and fingerprints that they quickly matched to those of Harold Wolpe, as well as a notebook in Arthur Goldreich's handwriting entitled "Theory of Demolition." They found in Raymond Mhlaba's shirt pocket a typed copy of the Umkhonto oath of allegiance. Elsewhere they came upon lists of names and addresses that presumably formed networks of Umkhonto members and supporters throughout the country. There were one hundred and six maps pinpointing police stations, army bases, railway lines and other potential sabotage targets. There were fifty-five copies of the pamphlet "Fundamental Principles of Marxism," thirteen copies of the South African Communist Party's "New Draft Program," seven copies of *World Marxist Review* and three copies of *Marxism Today*. One seized leaflet bore the optimistic title "Vorster's Nazi Law Can Never Destroy Communism."

In a separate toolshed, police found a manual entitled "British Coal Mine Explosives," along with nitric acid, ammonium nitrate crystals, benzene, aluminum pipes, time fuses and six pairs of rubber gloves. There was also a duplicating machine, six typewriters and reams of blank paper, as well as a radio transmitter and poles that could serve as masts. They also found documents that led them to the farmhouse at Travellyn in nearby Krugersdorp, where they seized yet more incriminating evidence.

What police did not find anywhere were handguns, rifles or other arms. Revolutionaries they may have been, but the men of Rivonia clearly had no plan or intention of defending themselves against the police or anyone else. They offered no resistance. In the end, they delivered not only themselves but enough documentation to destroy their own networks and convict themselves of high treason, sabotage or any of a dozen other offenses in the state's long and growing list of political crimes.

Long Hendrik arrived just before sunset to survey the find with an entourage of senior police officials and Afrikaner newsmen. He was amazed by the amateurishness of the conspirators in collecting and pre-serving such a trove of incriminating evidence. This was, he quickly real-ized, nothing less than the nerve center of the country's largest sabotage campaign. And now, to his utter pleasure and amazement, it was his. His men had succeeded not only in arresting Umkhonto's leadership but in capturing enough material to permanently paralyze the government's strongest opposition. This could be a turning point in the struggle to en-trench apartheid—and an important feather in his own cap.

Van Wyk set up a pair of men near the gate. When a bearded man in a Citroën drove in at five o'clock and spotted police cars outside the house, he slipped his car into reverse and tried to back out. The two po-licemen stepped out of the bushes and cut off his retreat, and he was taken into custody. It was Arthur Goldreich, the supposed owner of Lil-liesleaf. The car contained a cache of other documents including one entitled "Speaker's Notes—A Brief Course of Training for Organizers" of guerrilla units, "The Revolutionary Way Out," and "Production Re-quirements," which laid out in embarrassingly rich detail the various munitions and explosives that guerrilla warfare would require. In a hubcap of the car they found another copy of Operation Mayibuye. "You see, Goldreich," Long Hendrik told him, "you are all just amateurs and we are professionals. You have always underestimated your ene-mies." Years later, Long Hendrik would still recall triumphantly how nervous both Goldreich and Goldberg had been that day. "You know," he would declare, "when a Jew gets scared, he gets very scared!"

An hour later Goldreich's wife Hazel arrived with their two young sons and a friend. She too was arrested. So was Hilliard Festenstein, a physician who was a close friend of Arthur and medical advisor to Umkhonto, when he stopped at the house later that evening purport-edly to return a book he had borrowed. Eight black servants and farmhands were also placed under arrest. All told, eighteen people were taken into custody.

Rusty, Hepple and Goldberg were handcuffed, then taken to the dry cleaning van. The black prisoners were put in a separate vehicle—apartheid principles remained inviolate. Darkness was falling. As the air grew chilly, the birds began their evening laments—the orange-crested hoopoe cooed rhythmically while crows cackled in mocking retort. The hadedah ibis, a large, restless bird that roosts in the tall trees along the river, cried raucously. Inside the dry, stuffy van, Rusty and his comrades sat in silence, too stunned to speak and not wanting their captors to overhear. Rusty felt like a punctured balloon, drained of all life. His throat was dry, his skin clammy with perspiration. He stared listlessly at his handcuffs and thought about the disaster that had just befallen him and the movement he believed in, what might happen next and how he had gotten to this sad point.

TWO

THE ROAD TO RIVONIA

This is not yet a police state.
Mister Justice Blackwell, 1956
from *Slovo—The Unfinished Autobiography*

The city of Johannesburg is both a fact of geography and an act of imagination. It sits in the heart of the South African interior atop a reef of land called the Witwatersrand—"the ridge of white waters." Yet by the 1940s there was little water and the reef itself was largely buried under man-made development. Its strange hills— "some like volcanoes, some like sand, some with rippling corrugations, like the tombs of ancient kings," writes Nadine Gordimer—were the product of endless pilings of rock and gravel disgorged from mines deep beneath the earth's surface. Down below, beginning a mile under the ground, the Witwatersrand contains the world's richest veins of gold. Its discovery in 1886 set off a frenzied gold rush, and within three years Johannesburg was the largest, brashest and most vulgar settlement in sub-Saharan Africa.

Africans called it Egoli—"the City of Gold." The hotels, canteens, brothels and dance halls that first sprang up were gradually displaced by shops, banks, office buildings and other trappings of modern urban life. Trolley cars replaced ox-drawn wagons, but the frontier swagger remained. When author Lewis Nkosi first came to Johannesburg after World War II, he saw a desert city filled with loneliness and desolation, "which made it so desperately important and frightfully necessary for its citizens to move fast, to live very intensely, to live harshly and vividly, for this was the sole reason for their being there: to make money, to spend it and make more."

In the first half of the twentieth century hundreds of thousands of people, white and black alike, flocked to Johannesburg. White Afrikaners abandoned their shriveling dust-bowl farms in search of work and opportunities. They were joined in the increasingly affluent suburbs by immigrants from Britain and Eastern Europe. But most of those who came were Africans from the vast tribal homelands who were seeking to trade the growing poverty of the rural interior for a piece of urban prosperity. They came to work in the gold mines and in the shops and in the homes of those of privileged skin. Their ranks swelled the squalid, overcrowded slums that lined the edges of a city whose population doubled nearly every generation.

World War II was an enormous engine of growth, as South Africa's mineral wealth fed the Allied war machine. Black South Africans were not allowed to take up arms during the war, and were treated like a lower species of humanity. When a group of African stretcher bearers was buried in a mass grave along with whites after severe fighting at Sidi Rezegh in Egypt, South African Army Headquarters issued an order demanding that the corpses be dug up and reburied in separate graves according to race.

Still, thousands of Africans served in the military in support capacities, coming to the aid of the government in the war against fascism. And the struggle for freedom abroad inevitably heightened expectations at home, feeding a growing sense of impatience and militancy. A new generation of black nationalists such as Anton Lembede, Oliver Tambo, Nelson Mandela and Walter Sisulu pressed their elders in the venerable African National Congress, the black rights movement, to move more aggressively. Black trade unions were emerging with long agendas and deep grievances. The leaders of the ANC, which had been founded in 1912 and conveyed the image and manners of a black gentlemen's club for middle-class professionals and traditional chieftains, at first resisted this challenge to the status quo and to their own authority. Lembede died at an early age, but the other Young Turks, led by the affable but determined Sisulu, pressed ahead. Before the war was over they had convinced the movement's elders to make a straightforward demand for basic human rights known as "African Claims." Still, as the war ended and troops began to return to civilian life, the ANC's leadership was slow to challenge white rule on the only ground where blacks might have an advantage—the streets of Johannesburg and its burgeoning black townships.

Small though it was, the Communist Party showed no such hesitation. The party was a legal institution operating somewhere within the outer borders of the law. In 1944 Hilda Bernstein won a seat on the Johannesburg City Council, one of the party's few electoral successes. Despite the fact she had won on a whites-only ballot, Hilda saw herself as the council's sole voice of the oppressed, and she pushed for lower rents and better services in the hardscrabble townships. She made enough of a nuisance of herself that the city fathers redistricted her into a more conservative and hostile constituency in time for the next election, which she lost.

At the same time, party members launched a campaign of food raids against illegal hoarding and profiteering in the townships by Indian shop owners who were taking advantage of postwar shortages of essentials like rice, bread and soap. Everyone participated. Bram Fischer, a distinguished lawyer who at thirty-seven seemed the epitome of dignified restraint, marched into a shop in his three-piece charcoal gray suit with a crowbar in his hands. He hauled out a crate of Sunlight laundry soap that had been hidden in the back of the store, pried it open and sold it at the controlled price to a line of eager customers. Typical of Bram, he kept precise track of the money he collected and delivered the exact amount to the incredulous shop owner.

The following year the party crossed the thin line into extralegal territory. Spurred on by their communist trade union leaders, some seventy-five thousand African workers struck the minefields just outside of Johannesburg for higher wages and better living conditions in August 1946. The miners lived in appalling company-owned hostels where hunger, disease and crime were rampant. Downing tools, they held out for a week in defiance of their bosses. Rusty Bernstein was one of many party workers who put in long, feverish hours producing leaflets and dispatching them along with food and supplies to the besieged compounds. Each evening he put together a strike bulletin that was printed and delivered to workers at the midnight change of shift. When police raided union offices, he helped move the strike headquarters to the party's own office in central Johannesburg.

The government struck back hard. At the behest of management it dispatched soldiers and police to the mining camps with shotguns, clubs and tear gas to force open mines, beat and arrest strikers and evict from the premises those who resisted the demand to return to work. Miners were forced at gunpoint down the shafts, where some staged underground sit-ins until the police drove them to the surface again. Police savagely broke up an attempt by four thousand workers to march to Johannesburg's city center. At least twelve strikers were killed, hundreds injured, and thousands were fired from their jobs and dispatched back to the rural homelands from whence they came. The strike was crushed.

The government blamed communists for fomenting the unrest, as if the radicals were responsible for the low pay and fetid conditions that had triggered the work stoppage. After the police and the army finished off the strike, fifty-two activists, including Rusty, Hilda and Bram, were arrested and charged with sedition. Bram insisted upon standing in the dock with his fellow accused even though he had been out of town for the entire strike and could easily have had the charge against him dismissed. Eventually, the accused pleaded guilty to a reduced charge of aiding and abetting an illegal strike. Rusty believed the plea bargain was wrong; the charges were political, he argued, and the defendants should resist and force the state to prove its case. But he was outvoted by others, including Bram, who focused upon the impracticality of facing a long trial with an uncertain conclusion. Nonetheless, the mass arrests and the prospect of a political show trial were a foretaste of things to come.

A few weeks after the strike, Rusty played a modest role in the squatters movement that had sprung up among thousands of homeless blacks camping on vacant land outside Johannesburg. The city council had established an official housing area in outlying Moroka Township for blacks whose papers were in order. But many of the squatters were "illegals" with no papers and no hope of obtaining them under the country's increasingly restrictive pass laws. Police had begun raiding the squatter camps for undocumented people, many of whom were arrested, convicted the same day in kangaroo court sessions and dispatched to white-owned farms where they were required to work off their sentences in slave-labor conditions. In desperation, an emissary from the squatter camp showed up at the party's newspaper office late one September afternoon with word that residents were planning to move en masse to occupy plots in Moroka without permission. Hearing that the police had been tipped off about the move, Rusty, Ruth First and Joe Slovo, then a twenty-year-old law student fresh from the army, were dispatched to the camp to plead with the squatters to desist. On the drive over, they came upon a large formation of armed police deployed along the paths that led from the township to the nearby squatters refuge.

The camp was a haphazard collection of makeshift shelters composed of soggy cardboard boxes, burlap bags and reclaimed garbage. Although it was past midnight, barefoot children with dirty faces and runny noses played in the mud alleyways. Rusty and his comrades made their way through the labyrinth guided by a young man who whispered to residents that they were "Ikomunisi" who had come to help. They finally reached a small square where the camp committee had assembled. They described the police contingent they had seen outside Moroka and pleaded with the squatters to suspend their move for at least another night. But the majority were not willing to wait any longer. "Let's try, one day we'll get through," said one young man with resignation.

The result was exactly what Rusty, Ruth and Joe had feared. The thick gray-uniformed line of policemen charged into the marchers wielding batons and *sjambok* whips. Stunned squatters collapsed into the low grass, blood pouring from head wounds and broken limbs. Those who could still run scattered through the veld. No one made it to Moroka that night.

Having failed to prevent the confrontation, Rusty and his two comrades started for their car along the tarred road where the police command group had stationed itself. The officer in charge ordered them to halt. He asked what they were doing out on the veld so late at night. When they did not offer an immediate reply, he took a long, lascivious look at Ruth, then winked at Rusty and Joe. "Jesus, and with all those natives too," he said. "Next time you'd better find a safer spot. *Weg is julle* [On your way]."

That was how it went in those early days. The police, working on a presumption of racial solidarity, had not yet become wary of white radicals. And when it came to women, they sometimes made other, more lurid assumptions. As for the radicals themselves, they could aid and partake in the black struggle but only so far. At the danger point, their privileged status as whites would kick in. There seemed an unbridgeable gap between themselves and the blacks they sought to help. The squatters retreated to their squalid encampment bruised and bloodied that night; Rusty and his comrades drove home to the suburbs unscathed.

There is a photograph of the leadership of the Johannesburg District of the Communist Party of South Africa taken at a conference at around this time. A banner above the speaker's table proudly displays a hammer and sickle inside a red star. Posters of Lenin and party leader Moses Kotane scowl from the walls. Standing at the podium is Bram, wearing a gray three-piece suit and a solemn expression, launched no doubt on one of the meticulous and dispassionate addresses that made him one of the country's most sought-after barristers. Seated to either side of Bram are Ruth First, her dark, curly hair offset by a crisp white blouse, and Joe Slovo, the man she is soon to marry. Next to Joe sits Rusty Bernstein, staring into space, his shyness like an invisible cloak concealing his thoughts. In front of them is a row of Africans who are equally well dressed in coats and ties.

Everyone looks young, earnest and slightly noble. But what is most striking is their innocence. They look like people who think they know where they are going. Time is on their side, their message is taking hold, the revolution is coming, and when it arrives they will be somewhere in its vanguard, guiding and presiding over it just as they are presiding over this meeting. This was their most poignant illusion, one that they cherished for two decades as it led them down the road to Rivonia.

The young lions of the ANC Youth League were wary of these white outsiders, and none more so than Nelson Mandela. He was the son of a village headman in Thembuland, which was part of the rural Transkei. After his father's death, he was groomed for service in the Thembu royal household, but opted instead for a missionary boarding school and, eventually, for the University College of Fort Hare, South Africa's most prominent institution of higher learning for blacks. Like so many men of his generation, he came to Johannesburg in his early twenties to work in the mines, but unlike most, his keen mind and charismatic personality propelled him to law school at Wits and to black nationalist politics and the ANC. He got a break early on when, shortly after his arrival in town in 1941, his new friend Walter Sisulu sent him to a Jewish lawyer named Lazar Sidelsky, who agreed to hire Mandela as an articled clerk. For a white law firm to take on a black law clerk was almost unprecedented in those days.

Youth League members like Mandela called themselves "Africanists" and believed that blacks had to take the lead in their own liberation. At first, he had little use for communists, white or black. Marxism seemed yet another alien, European-based ideology thrust upon blacks by all-knowing white people. Its ideas were a hard sell to blacks like Mandela, who believed that society was fundamentally divided more by race than class. Mandela also feared that the Communist Party had its own secret agenda and was working to take control of the movement under the guise of joint action. The ANC was an organization for blacks only—no whites, Asians or mixed-race members were allowed—but it saw itself in ideological terms as a big tent and there was no prohibition on members belonging to other political movements. Black communists such as Moses Kotane, J. B. Marks and Dan Tloome played an increasingly important role in its leadership. Twice, Mandela and the Africanists sought to have communists removed from the rolls of ANC members. Frustrated both times, they turned to other means. Mandela helped lead several assaults on communist meetings, tearing down posters and capturing the microphone.

But some in the new generation were more open-minded. Sisulu was quick to see the advantages in allying with the communists. They were smart, dedicated and hardworking. They had grown up in a world that Africans like himself and Mandela were only vaguely aware of, yet wanted to be part of. What's more, the communists had access to cars, telephones, newspapers, printing presses and money, all of which were essential tools for building an effective and broadly based political movement. And they were social activists; Sisulu admired the night schools and feeding schemes that the communists ran for Africans, and the assistance they gave to fledgling black trade unions.

The young lions gradually came to power within the ANC. Sisulu became ANC secretary general and he arranged for Mandela's appointment to the National Executive Committee. The movement adopted a Program of Action that called for civil disobedience, boycotts, strikes and stay-at-homes, committing themselves for the first time to mass protest and extralegal tactics. As they did, they had more and more need of outside help—and the communists were more than willing to provide it.

At first no one listened to Sisulu's advocacy of joint action—after one bitter meeting on the issue Mandela and Tambo were so angry that they refused to accompany Sisulu on the train back home. But as on so many other matters, his views gradually carried the day. Perhaps the communists think they are manipulating us, Sisulu told his young friend Mandela, for whom he was quickly becoming a mentor. But who is to say it is not we who are manipulating them?

In the end, each side had much to offer the other. Beyond the obvious material advantages, Mandela and Sisulu found themselves attracted to Marxism for its logical analysis and prescriptions for mass action. No other organized political party with a substantial white membership was prepared to admit black members and work for an unqualified, universal franchise. As for the communists, they desperately wanted a role in a mass movement they both admired and sought to harness. Both sides had the same short-term goal: the end of white domination. After that, they diverged. Blacks like Mandela and Sisulu were great admirers of Western democracy and saw nonracial democratic rule as an end in itself, whereas South African communists tended to see democracy as a means to a socialist state. Even here, however, their views were not so different. Most blacks had no great love for capitalism, having seen it work arm in arm with white domination. Those who gave much thought to the matter believed that some kind of redistribution of wealth was necessary to redress the inequities of the past three hundred years and level the economic playing field.

For Mandela and Sisulu it was no great leap from there to the principles of socialism. Both of them became more and more Marxist in their orientation as the years passed. Sisulu eventually accepted a communist-sponsored trip to Romania, China and the Soviet Union. While in Beijing, he spoke to Chinese officials at Mandela's behest about whether they would provide weapons for armed struggle. The Chinese were supportive but warned that such a move was premature.

Mandela himself was evolving. In his early years, he would later admit, he was far more certain of what he was against than what he was for. But as he grew closer personally to communists like Moses Kotane, an Indian friend named Ismail Meer and Meer's girlfriend, Ruth First, Mandela found it harder to justify his mistrust of the party. He could not quarrel with their dedication to the liberation cause, and he felt he was too ignorant to challenge them on ideological terms. In his autobiography, he recalls acquiring the collected works of Marx, Engels, Lenin, Stalin, Mao Zedong and others and embarking on a personal reading course. While much of it was slow going, he found himself drawn to the idea of a classless society, a concept he found not dissimilar to traditional African culture. He embraced the classic Marxist dictum "From each according to his ability; to each according to his needs."

There were social as well as political reasons for Mandela's increasingly close ties with the communists. Mandela and other leaders of the ANC and the Communist Party inevitably forged friendships, crossing the color line often for the first time. Bram and Molly Fischer's large, comfortable house on Beaumont Street in the northern suburb of Oaklands became a gathering place on Sundays, especially in summer. Their outdoor swimming pool, a common feature in the white suburbs, was an irresistible draw for Africans and Indians for whom even community pools were an unattainable dream. Mandela became particularly close to Bram, a fellow lawyer and an Afrikaner. Blacks were coming to see Afrikaners as the enemy, and Mandela's friendship with Fischer was living proof that men of goodwill could overcome racial enmities. Hilda Bernstein and Walter Sisulu's wife, Albertina, grew to be close friends. The Bernsteins and the Slovos drew similar crowds to their more modest homes.

The postwar era itself was a study in contradictions—a time of growing racial repression yet also of tentative crossing of racial boundaries. Jazz was one of the vehicles that united the races. Todd Matshikiza's jazz opera, *King Kong*, staged at the Great Hall at Wits, and a Township Jazz series at the Johannesburg City Hall brought blacks and whites together. The mere act of socializing was a political statement. On the opening night of the jazz series, Lewis Nkosi, then writing for *Drum* magazine, attended a mixed-race party on the western fringes of town. "Present were Africans, whites, mixed-bloods and Indians, and because of the free admixture of the races the party assumed the proportions of a vast conspiracy against the state," Nkosi later wrote.

For the Bernsteins, Slovos, Fischers and a handful of other white activists who could overcome their own upbringing and prejudices, a rich network of friendship and trust arose that not only helped make worthwhile the personal risks of working against the government but made such work logical and inescapable. When friends like Nelson Mandela, Walter Sisulu and Oliver Tambo were risking so much, how could you stand aside and refuse to share the load?

One activist who never stood aside was Ruth First. Few people better epitomized the optimism, energy and tensions of the postwar era. As a journalist and intellectual she exposed some of the worst abuses of apartheid, while her husband Joe was a popular and skilled lawyer who devoted countless hours to defending victims of apartheid for little or no pay. Friends thought of her as the Rosa Luxemburg of the movement: committed conscientious and contentious, intolerant of those who invoked ideology to justify their mistakes and no sufferer of fools. She was a social figure whose house in the northern suburb of Roosevelt Park became a meeting place for activists and a special target for the police. She was also a mother who attempted to juggle the demands of underground political work with those of raising three daughters, in a climate that became more and more repressive as the decade progressed. And she was the wife in a marriage where both partners were enormously dependent upon each other yet in perpetual conflict.

Born in Johannesburg in 1925, Heloise Ruth First was the first child of Julius and Matilda. Both parents were radical socialists—Julius, who had arrived in South Africa from Latvia in 1910, was elected chairman of the Communist Party of South Africa at its second congress in 1923, and Tilly, who was born in Lithuania and was brought to South Africa in 1901 at age four, shared his beliefs. The Firsts were never poor. Julius started off as an accountant, then began a small business repairing appliances and furniture, and soon owned his own furniture factory. He was a gentle and benign soul, much beloved among the small community of left-wing radicals, of whom he was a major benefactor. Tilly was tough, caustic and demanding. They shared a deep commitment to socialism and the Soviet Union. They began taking Ruth and her younger brother Ronnie at an early age to Sunday-night meetings on the Johannesburg City Hall steps where they would listen to left-wing speakers denounce Western imperialism abroad and white domination at home. Most of their friends, the people whom Ruth met at their home, were fellow socialists. Tilly always said she had no time for those who did not share her politics.

By the time Ruth graduated from the University of Witwatersrand in 1945, she was deeply involved in left-wing politics. She went to work for the city's social welfare department with visions of doing research on Johannesburg's burgeoning black population. Instead, she was assigned to help prepare the commemorative album marking the city's Fiftieth Jubilee. She was bored and sickened by the mind-numbing work. She compiled statistics, such as the number of supervisors for children in the all-white city parks, and she wrote a sycophantic account of the department's achievements for a radio broadcast by its ambitious director. But when the mine workers' strike broke out, she decided to quit without notice. The next morning she reported to work at strike headquarters instead of City Hall.

After the strike was crushed she went to work for a series of left-wing weekly newspapers whose influence within the Congress Movement—the ANC and its smaller allies representing whites, Asians and those of mixed race—and unpopularity with the government far exceeded their actual circulation. The first was the *Guardian,* which was banned in 1952. It reappeared within weeks as the *Clarion*—a new name but with the same staff and the same radical politics. Later came the *People's World, Advance* and *New Age.* She also inherited from Rusty Bernstein the editorship of *Fighting Talk,* a feisty monthly. These publications offered a formidable menu of indigestible and disingenuous Marxist fare ("Soviet and Chinese Leaders Emphasize Close Unity" read a headline in November 1960 even as the Sino-Soviet rift was deepening beyond repair). But they also contained some of the only firsthand investigative reporting on conditions among the victims of apartheid. Ruth was responsible for much of it. She worked both as an editor guiding a group of raw but talented young journalists and as a reporter herself. She did it through force of will, aggressive research and a measure of fearlessness.

When a maverick Anglican priest named Michael Scott came to her office with a small, cryptic article from a local newspaper suggesting farm workers were being mistreated in eastern Transvaal province, Ruth agreed to accompany him on a fact-finding trip. They found laborers who worked fourteen hours per day for minuscule wages and spoiled food. Those who complained or sought to leave were beaten. Ruth's reporting forced a government inquiry and a promise from the Minister of Justice to clean up conditions. She even accompanied Scott to a public meeting in the town of Bethal, where angry white farmers showered them with abuse and vitriolic threats. But Ruth was more than courageous. She set a pattern for her journalistic career of focusing on the human damage wrought by apartheid—farm and prison conditions, the daily indignities of the pass system, township squalor and inequitable legal procedures. Unlike that of most journalists, her work had compelling thematic coherence; a rare intelligence was at work.

When it came to the police, Ruth was both fearless and contemptuous. Beate Lipman, a young reporter working in the Johannesburg office of *New Age*, was at her desk one day when two white plainclothes detectives—known for their attire as the Gray Shoes—came through the door. "Is Miss First here?" one of them asked.

Lipman told them Ruth had not yet arrived. "Ag, we'll wait," said the Gray Shoes.

Forty minutes later a smartly dressed woman in heels with curly black hair and bright red lipstick marched through the door. She took one sharp glance at the two men sitting stiffly to one side, then looked at Lipman and asked coolly, "Has Miss First come in yet?"

Lipman, too stunned to respond, just shook her head no.

"That's all right," said Ruth, flashing the thinnest of smiles. "I'll catch up to her later." And she turned on her heel and marched back out the door.

Novelist Alan Paton, a prominent liberal, saw a different side of Ruth's determination on a flight from Europe to Johannesburg. He watched with grim fascination as she spent hour after hour across the aisle tearing incriminating papers into small pieces. When she accumulated a sufficient pile of fragments she would sweep them into her hands, stroll to the lavatory and flush them down the toilet. When she finished, she sat taut and motionless waiting for the arrival at Johannesburg's Jan Smuts Airport and the inevitable scrutiny of security police at Immigration. The strain showed on her face. Ruth First, Paton reflected, paid a high price for her courage.

From the beginning Ruth was a minority within a minority within a minority: a left-wing radical in a right-wing country, a white person in a black liberation movement and a woman in a male-dominated world. She felt she always had to be better, smarter and faster than her male comrades. To outsiders she projected great personal strength and self-confidence, even arrogance. But those who knew her better saw that the facade covered a profound sense of vulnerability. Despite her writing skills, her formidable intellect and her prominent place in the movement, she always felt the need to prove herself. In gatherings of comrades, she spoke in great crescendos of words, as if to vanquish self-doubt from the room. Even her most seemingly arrogant habits took on different meaning when viewed by friends. She often fell asleep at the tediously intricate meetings that were a communist hallmark. Those who did not know her saw this as rudeness; those who did understood that the sleepiness was the result of her hyperthyroid condition.

Hilda Bernstein admired Ruth's intelligence and energy, but the two women had different areas of interest. Ruth had been active in youth and student movements; Hilda focused increasingly on women's issues. "You won't always be young, but you'll always be a woman," Hilda would explain. During the 1950s, Ruth's political profile grew while Hilda's began to shrink. Because Ruth's family was more affluent, she could spend more time on unpaid activities. Hilda needed the income from the job at *Childhood* magazine. Rusty Bernstein and Ruth were often at loggerheads. Ruth treated him as one of those dreary, conventional ideologues whom she found so predictable and deserving of scorn. Still, every Monday evening, after arguing at the district committee meeting, the Slovos would join the Bernsteins for a late supper at one of their houses. Hilda watched Ruth wrestle with self-doubt and could only marvel that such a remarkable woman could be so insecure and self-lacerating.

Ruth was quite aware of the damage she inflicted upon herself with her sense of insecurity and was typically self-critical of it. "My introspection gets more and more involved as I go in for my favorite pastime of undermining me and my character and seeing my faults," she once wrote in a letter to Joe. "Trouble really is I would like to prove to myself I can produce something worthwhile. . . . But I'm too directionless and I know at heart that if direction, application and talent aren't there, it's all my own undoing and no one can overcome that . . . It's a form of masochism I suffer from; one of my afflictions, like heavy eyebrows and a mole on my nose."

She was a stylish revolutionary. She loved Italian shoes, French perfume, Greek restaurants and European cinema. She wore expensive clothes and carefully applied makeup and saw no conflict between her politics and her sense of style. She lived life in Technicolor.

She was only eighteen when she became romantically involved with Ismail Meer, the Indian law student and political activist. Indians were a small but important component of the liberation movement. While they were not treated as badly as blacks, they were restricted to certain residential and commercial areas and denied the right to vote. Like the new generation of urban blacks, young Indians like Meer were fed up with their second-class status and their own parents' docility, and they provided new energy and ideas to the movement. He and Ruth were together nearly four years, but after he finished at the university, he returned to his native Natal. The decision to break it off apparently was mutual; still, Ruth was heartbroken. Soon, however, there was a new man in her life.

Joe Slovo was a handsome but pudgy extrovert with curly brown hair and a gambler's brash smile. While Ruth's family had become affluent in South Africa, Joe's remained undeniably of the peasantry. His father, Wulfus, who left Lithuania in 1928, hawked fruit in the streets of Johannesburg for seven years to save enough money to bring over his wife and two children, including ten-year-old Yossel. The boy's head was shaved as part of the delousing process at the immigration station and his fellow schoolmates at the Jewish government school he first attended called him the "Bald Bolshie." When his beloved mother died during childbirth in 1938, Joe was not told immediately of her death, he would recall later. He woke up in the middle of the night to find the mirror in his room covered with a white sheet and an open coffin in the parlor. Inside was his mother, her blank yellow face staring vacantly. It was an image he never forgot.

After his wife died, Wulfus Slovo lost his fruit shop and earned a living driving a bread truck. Joe and his father moved to a small boardinghouse where rent was cheap and dinner consisted largely of starch and table talk of socialism. Joe learned about Marx from his teachers and his dinner companions. He was forced to leave school at age fourteen to support himself. He never properly studied English grammar; "I can't tell you what an adverb is," he would confess to an interviewer more than fifty years later. He began work as a dispatch clerk at the pharmaceutical supply firm of Sive Brothers and Karnovsky, known by its Jewish staff as "Syphilis Brothers and *Ganovim* (crooks)."

At age sixteen Joe was accepted as a probationary member of the Communist Party. Two years later, at the party's behest he joined the army. He saw no combat, but came home qualified for a veteran's scholarship to the university, even though he had never attended high school. He learned law at Wits, where he met Harold Wolpe, Nelson Mandela and many of the other future comrades with whom he would work for decades, and he immersed himself in radical politics. Joe himself would later admit that he was one of the most orthodox of Marxists in those days, dedicated to Moscow's line.

Many people of working-class background who claw their way to success and a university degree would have inevitably turned their attention to accumulating wealth and all of the comforts they had been denied in their youth. But Joe Slovo was different. Perhaps because of his immigrant origins or his early exposure to Marxism or the spirit of the decade in which he came of age, Joe possessed a sense of idealism that drove him not toward money but toward the political movement that became his life's work. While some of his comrades would question his judgment, and many—including his wife—would come to criticize his uncritical devotion to the Soviet Union, no one could doubt his commitment or his willingness to make personal sacrifices for the cause.

When Joe first met Ruth he dismissed her and her friends as effete university intellectuals whose radicalism was more affectation than commitment. But Joe had respect for intelligence and an eye for beauty. When Ruth and Ismail Meer split up, he was waiting. They were married in 1949 and, like the Bernsteins, they did so with a simple trip to the registry office. Later Ruth's parents threw a large, boisterous party with a guest list that read like a Who's Who of South African subversives.

From the beginning it was a tempestuous relationship. Ruth and Joe shared so much—a movement, a sense of commitment and, within a few years, a family of three daughters. They challenged and supported each other in the difficult and sometimes dangerous work they were engaged in. Yet there was a sad hole at the heart of their marriage.

While Joe was warm, gregarious and full of humor, Ruth often felt tense and competitive. She needed Joe's approval yet cringed at his earthy humor and his off-key, off-color singing, hated it when he ate peanuts in bed or left the dinner table with bits of food clinging to his face. She could even get furious at the way he cut tomatoes—bludgeoning them with a knife when she wanted graceful French-style slices.

They tortured and criticized each other, they cheated on each other as well, yet each relied heavily on the other. Even after conducting an affair with a local architect, Ruth wrote to Joe while he was in detention in 1960: "I feel so inadequate without you. I think of you every moment. It's no longer a matter of thinking, a conscious act. You are part of me, my life, my being and I don't know why I missed so very many opportunities to tell you so."

In return he could give her enormous emotional support. "You make me cross at your underestimation of yourself," he wrote back to her. "We are lucky people you and me. To be blessed with a deep personal relationship and at the same time to punch through life with vitality, comradeship and no regret is as much as one human can ask for. As for your self-effacement, let me tell you a couple of home truths. Your ability extends mine. You are better-looking than I am and you have a passion which if it disappeared would destroy you and a lot of me. What more do you want? Don't you change now!"

Joe also craved support, and what he did not get from Ruth he sought elsewhere. He was attracted to many women, and they to him. Few attractive women in the movement, whether married or not, could claim he had never made a pass at them. To their friends, Ruth and Joe seldom spoke of these infidelities. "You've got the wrong idea about communism," Joe told one young female admirer who was at first a bit shocked when he kissed her on the mouth one night at a particularly raucous dance party. "It isn't about making everyone miserable; it's about making everyone happy."

At the same time, Joe could be intensely possessive of Ruth. "Are you behaving yourself?" he asked her in a letter from prison. "You know me—how jealous I am by nature—but that's because I love you so very much. I'm selfish."

Despite the demands of underground political work and the turmoil of their relationship, the Slovos sought to create a normal family life for themselves. Shawn, Gillian and Robyn were born in the first years of their marriage, when the idea of a police state still seemed far-fetched. As a mother, Ruth was forced to juggle the needs of the three girls with the pressures of her work. She had much help from servants and from Julius and Tilly. Her father provided Joe and Ruth with extra funds and a new Citroën every few years. Just two months after Robyn was born in 1953, when Ruth left on a four-month study trip to China, Tilly moved in to take care of the children. Ruth's parents also helped pay for the comfortable three-bedroom bungalow in Roosevelt Park, designed by the flamboyant Arthur Goldreich. When Arthur's original plan proved impractical, Joe and Ruth turned to Rusty, who toned down Arthur's design and made it workable. Rusty also designed a desk for Ruth with a secret compartment that Julius had made at the furniture factory.

The 1950s were a heady mixture of increasingly risky political activism and middle-class pleasures. "While there was a fantastic array of laws controlling our lives it was still possible to organize marches to police stations, to Parliament, to the very prisons holding our political leaders," wrote Lewis Nkosi. "It was possible to go to the same universities as white students; there were racially mixed parties enjoyed with the gusto of a drowning people; it seemed at the least obligatory to assume an air of defiance against Government and authority."

Optimism reigned. Even levelheaded Walter Sisulu caught the bug. "As far as the National Party is concerned, any serious analysis will reveal that it has reached its high-water mark," he wrote in 1957 in the journal *Africa South*. "Already there are signs that the edge of the Nationalist blitzkrieg is blunted in the face of the determined and growing resistance of the people."

Ruth and Joe did underground political work, carried on with their careers, yet at the same time went to dinner parties, concerts, films, opera and theater, dances and weekend picnics. There were annual beach holidays to Cape Town. Joe, guzzling amphetamines to stay awake, would drive all night singing ditties like "One Little Fishy" and barking like a dog to amuse the three girls. The girls would curl up in the back—Shawn on the seat, Gillian on the floor and Robyn on the ledge under the rear window. Ruth would smile tolerantly and try to sleep.

This seductive swirl of politics and affluence was sometimes hard for the children to comprehend. Their lives were comfortable and entertaining. They enjoyed the same material benefits as their middle-class neighbors. There were servants and whites-only schools, dance lessons, horseback riding and a large Wendy house in the back yard. At the same time, there was an air of increasing danger. They were part of the white world of Roosevelt Park, yet they were different, special perhaps, but also at risk. The girls knew nothing about the politics of the matter, and Ruth and Joe never spoke of their own activities, nor of the dangers. But all three daughters had fine-tuned antennae. They could hear and smell the electricity in the air. Even when they were very young, they could sense that their parents were not ordinary people, and that they themselves could not lead ordinary lives. But what it all meant, and where it would lead, was a puzzle they could not even begin to articulate, let alone solve.

Looking back later, when the girls were grown, Joe acknowledged the impact of his and Ruth's secret political life on them. "The very nature of our activities in conspiratorial work left very little scope for intimate frankness about what we were doing and why," he wrote. "Fear and a sense of insecurity apart, our arrests and frequent absences must have seemed, in the eyes of our children, acts of voluntary preference; they must have felt that they came a poor second to the cause."

It was life on a ledge and it could not maintain its balance for long. Ruth believed in the future and in socialism. Looking to the north, she saw colonial empires collapsing and black Africa lurching toward independence. Could South Africa be far behind? But her optimism betrayed her. The liberation movement was so intent upon breaking free of the chains on its hands and feet that it failed to feel the noose slowly tightening around its neck.

Although they seldom cared to acknowledge it, the fact that Ruth and Joe were both Jews whose ancestors came from Lithuania was an important clue to their radicalism. Jews comprised a large proportion of the whites involved in left-wing politics in South Africa, and perhaps as much as 75 percent of the country's 100,000 Jews hailed from Lithuania and its immediate neighbors. Samuel Marks and his business partner Isaac Lewis, two of the Lithuanian Jews who settled early on in Sheffield, England, decamped for the southern tip of Africa in the late 1860s after hearing of great opportunities for dry goods merchants in the untamed interior. News of their success quickly filtered back to Vilna, Lithuania's medieval capital, and family and friends followed in their footsteps, part of the great migration of Jews who fled economic hardship and anti-Semitic violence in the region in the years before World War I.

Napoleon called Vilna the "Jerusalem of Lithuania" and the city was a longtime center of Jewish learning. It was home to the Vilna Gaon, one of Judaism's most renowned moral and scholarly figures, the Romm

Press, distinguished printers of the Talmud, Bible and rabbinical works, and the Great Synagogue, which dated back to 1633. But the city was also a cradle for socialist and nationalist movements. In 1902 the Jewish shoemaker Hirsh Lekert was hanged after an abortive attempt to assassinate the city's governor-general. The failed 1905 revolt against czarist rule was welcomed in many parts of the Vilna ghetto, as was the October Revolution twelve years later. It was a tradition of the Jewish Bund in Vilna to hold a Yom Kippur ball that mocked religious observances on Judaism's most solemn day. Among the Jews who emigrated to South Africa were many who had little but scorn for rabbis and religion.

It was no surprise that many of the activists were openly hostile to Judaism and Jewish causes. Jewishness quickly ceased to be part of their self-identity. Hilda and Rusty never mentioned their Jewish origins, celebrated Christmas rather than Hanukkah and were unceasingly critical of the new state of Israel and its dependence on the imperialist West. Ruth also had little but scorn for Jewish culture and for the timidity of South African Jews who did not actively oppose apartheid even when they found it distasteful. Joe lost his faith at an early age, but he retained an appreciation and nostalgia for Jewish humor, culture and cuisine that singled him out among the radicals. What none of them saw was that their alienation from Judaism and their radicalism were consistent with one wing of Jewish tradition—that even as rejectionists they were firmly within the larger family of their contentious and self-contradictory faith.

Most of the Lithuanian Jews who came to South Africa settled in cities such as Cape Town and Johannesburg, where the dominant culture and language were English, and most of their children quickly shed Lithuanian customs and their native Yiddish. Joe's family was typical in this respect: by the time he was fifteen, he spoke only English and could no longer converse with his father, who spoke only Yiddish.

But the veneer of English culture that they quickly acquired did not lead to complete assimilation. Most South African Jews were still outsiders. They were generally more liberal than other whites and they tended to be less comfortable with white domination, even though they benefited from it economically. From the 1920s through the 1950s, most voted for the United Party, the mainstream white political party led for decades by Jan Smuts, a legendary Boer War general who was a philo-Semite and fervent supporter of a Jewish homeland in Palestine.

For most Jews, Smuts was the ideal Afrikaner. They feared the National Party, the Afrikaner nationalist movement to the right of Smuts, which preached a brand of racial purity and ethnic destiny that was similar in genre, if not in murderous intent, to Nazism. National Party leaders viewed Jews at best as a regrettable but irreversible addition to the white community. Moderate Nationalists in the 1930s wanted South Africa's gates closed to further Jewish immigration; extremists wanted those already in the country expelled. *Die Burger*, the Cape Town daily newspaper that served as mouthpiece for the party, railed against British-Jewish capitalism and came to feature on its editorial pages the cartoon character of "Hoggenheimer," a bloated capitalist with grotesquely Jewish facial features.

Fear of the Nationalists rendered the official Jewish community speechless when it came to apartheid. The South African Jewish Board of Deputies, the community's leadership forum, studiously avoided comment when the government passed the Group Areas Act in 1950, which enshrined racial segregation in housing and commercial ventures. It did not join with Catholic and Protestant leaders in protesting the 1956 law that empowered the minister of native affairs to ban racially mixed religious services. A handful of Jewish liberals sought to push the community into taking a moral stance. Ronald Segal, editor and publisher of the influential quarterly *Africa South*, argued that if Jews were a race they should condemn the new racial purity laws as an echo of Hitler's Nuremburg codes; and if they were a religious community they should protest the state's attempt to interfere with the right to worship. But the Jewish establishment would not be shamed into action. Officially it argued that while individual Jews could say what they liked, there was no community consensus on what it called "political matters," and therefore nothing that could be considered the "Jewish position" on such issues. Unofficially, Jewish leaders warned that any attempt to stand against the apartheid juggernaut would serve only to reawaken the ugly neo-Nazi brand of anti-Semitism that slept within the soul of the National Party.

Among the Jewish community, those who joined the Communist Party and various liberal organizations were the exception rather than the rule, although they were often influential—and notorious—far beyond their actual numbers. The party was dominated by Jews from its founding in 1921. Government officials, quickly availing themselves of the perils and opportunities of invoking the Red Menace, blamed Bolshevik Jews for the 1922 mine workers' strike. Partly as a result, the Immigration Quota Act of 1930 reduced the flow of Jewish immigrants from Eastern Europe to a trickle. Still, of sixty active leaders of the party's Johannesburg District on a February 1946 police list, twenty-three were identified as Jewish, including the chairman, Michael Harmel. "We know that a large percentage of a certain population group devote themselves to undermining activities," stated Nationalist lawmaker C. T. M. Wilcocks before the Senate.

Many Jews shunned South African politics altogether and devoted themselves instead to Zionism. South African Jews boasted by far the highest per capita level in the world of fund-raising for Israel. There were times when even this kind of activity became politically fraught, especially in the early 1960s when Israel consistently joined with the emerging new bloc of independent African states in the United Nations General Assembly to support censure of and sanctions against the South African regime and its racial policies. In 1961 the regime even froze the transfer of funds to the Jewish homeland in retaliation. *Die Transvaler*, another of the National Party's journalistic mouthpieces, declared, "The Jews will thus now have to choose where they stand just as the Jews of Israel have chosen: with South Africa or with Israel. It can no longer be with both."

Of course, most Jews were not prepared to choose. They saw themselves as both loyal South Africans and supporters of Israel, even when that dual identity caused discomfort.

Fueled by its mineral wealth, Johannesburg increasingly became the center of South African commerce in the first half of the twentieth century, and it attracted the country's largest concentration of Jews. The "Randlords," men of finance and commerce who owned the mineral rights to the rich veins of gold under the city and its environs, numbered many Jews among their ranks, including Ernest Oppenheimer, whose Anglo American Corporation became the country's biggest company. "Joburg," which was the city's nickname, was renamed "Jewburg" by those who rued the extent of the Jewish presence there.

Among blacks, there were many who appreciated the impact of Jews on the city. Lazar Sidelsky, the lawyer who gave Nelson Mandela his first legal job, was a Jewish liberal, and Mandela never forgot the kindness. He would later write that he found Jews to be more broad-minded about matters of race and politics, perhaps because they themselves had often been victims of prejudice. Lewis Nkosi believed that Jewish interest in classical music, jazz, art and literature softened the crude, rock-hard urban landscape of Johannesburg, which was still in many ways an upstart mining camp. "It was the Jews who tempered this harsh social order of apartheid with a tenuous liberalism and humane values," Nkosi wrote. "If one was foolhardy enough to have girl friends across the color line, they were likely to be Jewish; if one had white friends of any sort they were most likely Jewish; almost eighty per cent of white South Africans who belonged to left wing and liberal organizations were Jewish; whatever cultural vitality Johannesburg enjoyed was contributed by this Jewish community."

But the very qualities that made some blacks embrace Jews made Afrikaners suspicious. "When photographs appear in newspapers of resistance processions, or of joint singing and dancing with the Africans, or of the Black Sash's slander tableaux, the Jewish facial type is in the majority," wrote one angry letter writer to an Afrikaans weekly. "When a book is published on the 'bad conditions' in South Africa, the writer is ten to one a Jew. Under petitions protesting against the Boers' policy, there always appear numbers of Jewish names. Jewish professors, lecturers, doctors, rabbis and lawyers fall over one another in order to be able to sign."

"The patience of the Boer," the writer concluded ominously, "must one day become exhausted."

Nineteen forty-eight—the year that Joe and Ruth were married and Rusty and Hilda moved into the house on Regent Street—was also the year that the National Party took power for the first time, defeating Smuts and his increasingly decrepit United Party. The Nats won far less than a majority of votes but took most of the underpopulated rural parliamentary districts. In the end, they and an allied splinter group won 79 seats in the 153-seat House of Assembly on a platform that called for total separation of the races and promised to deal forcefully with the twin menaces of black power and godless communism.

Before 1948, racial segregation was a fact of national life reflected brutally but haphazardly in the country's legal code. It was not so different from that practiced throughout much of the Western world, especially the United States. But the National Party's triumph marked the death knell for the old, paternalistic racial order and the emergence of a new, dynamic and virulent ideology. Feeding on the same crude and lethal mixture of economic despair and ethnic fear as Hitler's Nazis, the National Party's ideological architects—led by a Dutch-born newspaper editor and former psychology professor named Hendrik F. Verwoerd—set about laying the pillars of apartheid: the Population Registration Act, which required the categorization of each person by race; the Group Areas Act, which enforced residential segregation; the Immorality Amendment Act, which banned mixed marriages and criminalized interracial sex; the Bantu Education Act, which imposed inferior schools for blacks; and many more.

But apartheid was more than a means of enshrining legalized segregation. It was a total system of racial domination designed to preserve and protect the purity and special destiny of the Afrikaners, the Dutch-descended settlers who comprised the majority of South Africa's white population. To achieve its ideal, apartheid strove to seal off blacks from the white world. It seized an African at birth, strangled his chances and suffocated his dreams, stamping each phase of his life with a constant reminder of his separateness and inferiority. Where he was born, where he went to school and what he could learn there, whom he could sleep with and whom he could marry, where he could work and how high he could rise, where he could live, where he could be treated for illness, where he could die and where he could be buried—all of this and more were dictated and controlled by the state relying upon one criterion: his race.

In the pamphlet "Your Bantu Servant and You," the city of Johannesburg—more progressive than most—offered advice to whites on the care and handling of their black domestic workers. "Give orders one at a time," it advises. "Very few servants are able to follow, remember and carry out a series of instructions in the correct order, or at all, for that matter." The pamphlet suggested that live-in servants should receive between fourteen and twenty rand per month, cooks between sixteen and twenty-four. It went on to note that the city's own surveys showed that the minimum needed for a family of five to survive was forty-eight rand per month. "Regrettably very few families earn this amount, even where both parents are working," it noted blandly.

There were so many crimes, so many petty cruelties, so many families ripped apart. One thousand blacks each day were arrested for pass law violations—eventually the total would reach eighteen million arrests; three and a half million more would be uprooted from their homes and trucked further away from the white man's world. The black community of Sophiatown had started in the 1920s near a vast municipal refuse dump in western Johannesburg. It was a congested, overcrowded, ugly and haphazard slum—and a symbol of the vitality of the emerging urban South Africa. It boasted two movie houses—the Picture Palace and the Odin—twenty churches, seventeen schools, and countless shops, jazz clubs and drinking houses known as shebeens. Its inhabitants included musicians, artists, poets, shopkeepers, singers and lawyers, prostitutes, con men and gangsters. "The rich and the poor, the exploiters and the exploited, all knitted together in a colorful fabric that ignored race or class structures," recalled Don Mattera in his memoir of growing up in Sophiatown. Jazz, booze and prostitution were its singular recreations, the ANC and black trade unions ruled its politics, and life "was based on the premise that if you were black you had to live outside the law," according to Lewis Nkosi. It was, in short, an affront to the apartheid regime.

In January 1955 the first government bulldozers arrived. A resistance campaign organized by the ANC rapidly fizzled. Within months the authorities had flattened the entire community and hauled some sixty thousand inhabitants ten miles away to the sterile wasteland officially known as the South Western Township, later to be called Soweto. There they were separated by tribe and consigned to bleak ethnic subsections. After the rubble of Sophiatown was cleared away, the government built a new suburb for whites. They called it Triomf. It was indeed the first great victory for the social engineers of apartheid, and a declaration of war on the aspirations of urban blacks and the liberation movement that represented them.

The Minister of the Interior summed it all up before Parliament in introducing the Group Areas Act, when he compared human beings to the parts of an automobile. "We believe, and believe strongly, that all unnecessary points of contact between the races must be avoided," he declared. " ... If you are continually having contact between your brakes and your tires, you cause friction; the friction engenders heat, and it can lead to very grave trouble with your motorcar. Now, we want to avoid those root causes of that trouble."

For all their early enthusiasm, the Nationalists needed more than race laws to achieve their vision of a purified state. They also needed enemies to keep the *volk* solidified and disciplined, and to help ward off any political comeback by Smuts's wounded United Party. One of the very first bills that the new government presented to Parliament was the Suppression of Communism Act, a law whose purpose was far broader than its title inferred. It not only outlawed the Communist Party, but defined communism in such sweeping terms that virtually all political opposition to the government could be prohibited. It banned any doctrine aimed at bringing about political or social change "by the promotion of disturbance or disorder," or "which aims at the encouragement of feelings of hostility between the European and non-European races." The Minister of Justice could formulate a list of purported subversives in complete secrecy, with no provision for appeal. The law, said the Johannesburg bar, could be used to outlaw "many liberal and humanitarian objects which are advocated and cherished by persons who are very far from being communists."

The move against the communists was not just a tactical matter but a psychological one. For all its ideological underpinnings, apartheid was in its essence an act of fear: fear of the native, fear of the massed hordes, fear of the stranger, fear of blackness, fear of losing control. Clinging to the southernmost tip of Africa, beset not only by those they saw as black savages but by imperial interlopers from London, Afrikaners believed their survival and dignity were constantly endangered. Their first impulse was to circle their ox wagons. Inside that magical laager, every white man looked to his neighbor for military and moral support. Every man was expected to watch his neighbor's back. Any break in the wall of solidarity, any weakness, could destroy the entire encampment. And what were the white communists if not a gaping hole in the protective wall of racial unity? These people were not only unwilling to defend their fellow whites, but were actively working to undermine white rule. They were not just enemies but traitors. Distasteful as it was, many inside the government could understand black opposition to apartheid. Blacks were attempting to assert themselves as a nation just as Afrikaners had done. This was natural, perhaps even admirable, although it must be crushed. But those with white skin joining them? This was monstrous, untenable, evil. It must not only be defeated, but crushed, extirpated and buried forever deep down the mine shaft of national memory.

For the activists, the process of repression was so gradual that for a long time they did not perceive the deterioration. Partly they were victims of their own propaganda; having preached so long about the evils of the old Smuts-led regime, they were slow to comprehend that the new one was far worse. Many of them actually believed they were winning, that the National Party's victory was a sign of desperation. They interpreted the stripping away of their liberties and the increasing violence of the state as the last gasps of a frightened and dying order. Rusty and Hilda Bernstein could see that state repression was gaining in strength, but so was the liberation movement. They believed a confrontation was coming—and they believed the movement might be able to win.

Faced with the Suppression of Communism Act, the still-legal Communist Party chose to disband in 1950, despite objections from Rusty, Joe and other dissidents who wanted to defy the law. The Ministry of Justice published long lists of Reds, including people like Rusty and Hilda, Joe and Ruth, and Bram and Molly Fischer. Each year they received written notice from the minister instructing them "not to become an office-bearer, officer or member and not to take part in the activities of any of the undermentioned organizations," followed by a long list that included just about every activist antiapartheid group in the country. Special Branch also began the practice of periodic raids of their homes to search for banned literature, documents and other evidence. They and hundreds of other activists like Nelson Mandela, Walter Sisulu, Moses Kotane, Michael Harmel and Yusuf Dadoo of the South African Indian Congress faced banning orders that prevented them from meeting with two or more of their colleagues at a time or appearing at any public gathering. Plainclothes police became their constant companions, seeking to prove that the radicals were evading the restrictions imposed upon them.

Which was true, of course. The Bernsteins, Slovos and Fischers were all part of a committed core of communists, based in Johannesburg, who re-formed the party as an illegal underground movement in 1953. They created a cell structure to provide secrecy and security: few members knew who else was in the party. One person served as courier from each cell to the next level, the Area Committee. A similar courier connected the various area committees to the Central Committee. The system was rudimentary but effective. Until the party publicly declared its existence in 1960, the security police had no inkling it had been formally reconstituted and had not won a single conviction under the Suppression of Communism Act against any of its members.

When the comrades reestablished the party underground, they were embarking upon a risky course that they themselves chose, not something that was ordered by Moscow. Apollon Davidson, a Russian political scientist at the University of Cape Town, has examined the Soviet Communist Party archives on South Africa and concluded that the South African party received limited financial and ideological sustenance from the Soviet Union. Soviet-front institutions like the World Peace Council occasionally funded trips to the East Bloc by comrades. Ruth's visit to China was one such mission. Hilda went there later and daughter Toni visited Moscow on a youth mission as late as 1962. But the South African security crackdown soon put an end to travel abroad for most of the comrades. The closure of the Soviet consulate in Pretoria in February 1956 and the departure of all East Bloc diplomats cut off the last open link to Moscow. Important decisions may have been rubber-stamped in Moscow, according to Davidson, but they were made in Johannesburg.

The clandestine life took its toll. The party became less open, less democratic and more suspicious. Membership was limited, dissent frowned upon. The Soviet invasion of Hungary in 1956 sent a ripple of unease through the ranks. Some members were not prepared to accept the boilerplate explanation that Soviet troops had been dispatched to crush a dangerous fascist uprising. But most took the view that their main concern was the enemy at home, not events in a distant Eastern European capital. The Soviet Union was too important an ally in the struggle against apartheid to be doubted. When Alan and Beate Lipman dissented from this view, they felt ostracized by those who had been among their dearest friends and comrades. When they spoke about leaving the party, they were chastised—and later expelled. "No one quits the Communist Party," one of their former comrades explained. "The party quits you."

The party was like a family—the ties of mutual belief and affection that bound were strong. Even its squabbles were familylike—some of the younger activists complained about the "Northern Suburbs Clique" of the Fischers, Bernsteins, Slovos and Harmels in the same way teenagers complain about their parents. Indeed, over the phone and in conversation, comrades began to refer to the party as "The Family." The code name was a way of misleading those who were listening in but also a recognition of how many of the members felt. The party was their home. To break away was hard and painful.

Alongside the underground movement, the activists also created a new, legal organization called the Congress of Democrats, which consisted of white former party members, fellow travelers and left-leaning liberals. Rusty personally moved the resolution creating the COD and he and Bram sat on its executive committee until they both were banned in 1954. The COD took its place among a phalanx of race-based political organizations known collectively as the Congress Alliance, led by the ANC, the Colored People's Congress and the South African Indian Congress. The COD was the smallest of these organizations, but its members had experience as political organizers and access to money. People within the COD controlled several important weekly and monthly newspapers that gave the ANC and its sister organizations favorable publicity and helped spread information. At the same time, however, the presence of COD leaders on Congress Alliance platforms led to the alienation of younger, more radical ANC members who viewed whites with the same suspicions that Nelson Mandela and his peers had harbored in the 1940s.

Despite these suspicions and the government's increasingly restrictive crackdown, white radicals played an active and visible role in the anti-apartheid movement throughout the 1950s. They were involved in the 1952 Defiance Campaign in which thousands of blacks, Coloreds and Indians turned in their passes and courted arrest. The Gandhian-style mass protest collapsed after about eight thousand arrests and the passage of an act that made the breaking of a law for reasons of political protest punishable by flogging and years of imprisonment. Whites in the movement also helped organize the 1954 school boycott, a yearlong protest that failed to stop the government's drive to saddle black children with an inferior "Bantu education." Hilda, although banned, played an important but clandestine role in helping her friends Albertina Sisulu and Lillian Ngoyi found the Federation of South African Women, which staged a historic march on Pretoria in which twenty thousand women protested the requirement that African women carry passes. But perhaps their most important role was in the formulation of the Freedom Charter.

The charter was an attempt by the ANC and its sister organizations to create a document that would unite all of South Africa's freedom forces behind a set of democratic principles. It was designed to be as broadly based and inclusive as possible in order to put an end to the ideological and sectional rifts that hobbled the movement. But the charter itself became a cause for further internecine dispute because white communists played a key and visible role in its creation. As the sole writer on the working committee set up to oversee the project, Rusty was a major participant from the start. He had the task of composing a statement to launch the process. He started with a phrase—"Let us speak of Freedom." From there he set to work, eventually producing a powerful leaflet-poem, "The Call," that announced plans for the charter and exhorted ordinary citizens to participate in its birth:

WE CALL THE PEOPLE OF SOUTH AFRICA BLACK AND
WHITE—LET US SPEAK TOGETHER OF FREEDOM!

WE CALL THE FARMERS OF THE RESERVES
AND TRUST LANDS.
*Let us speak of the wide land, and the narrow strips on which
we toil.*
*Let us speak of brothers without land, and of children without
schooling.*
Let us speak of taxes and of cattle, and of famine.

Let us speak of freedom.

WE CALL THE MINERS OF COAL, GOLD
AND DIAMONDS.
*Let us speak of the dark shafts, and the cold compounds far
from our families.*
*Let us speak of heavy labor and long hours, and of men sent
home to die.*
Let us speak of rich masters and poor wages.

Let us speak of freedom.

"The Call" went on to exhort factory and farm workers, teachers and students, housewives and mothers to join in the process and volunteer to attend a Congress of the People to be held by June 1955. Such a Congress, it declared, would be "a meeting of elected representatives of all races, coming together from every town and village, every farm and factory, every mine and kraal, every street and suburb, in the whole land. Here all will speak together. Freely, as equals. They will speak together of the things their people need to make them free . . . And they will write their demands into THE FREEDOM CHARTER."

Characteristically hesitant about what he had written, Rusty took a draft of "The Call" to a late-night meeting outside Durban in a dusty school meeting room. The room was lit by a single gas lantern that illuminated the face of Chief Albert Luthuli, the distinguished head of the ANC, as he read the invocation. It was a stirring performance; afterward the committee unanimously endorsed Rusty's draft without a single change.

Thousands responded to "The Call" with notes and comments— some scribbled on the backs of envelopes and brown paper bags, others verbally transmitted to field interviewers. Rusty and his comrades on the drafting committee stored the slips of paper in a steamer trunk, then sorted them into various categories, covering the entire living-room floor at Regent Street. Rusty tried to come up with a document that would accommodate all the various piles. In the end, however, they proved too unwieldy. Although the charter was billed as a collective effort, Rusty eventually sat down and wrote it by himself.

The final document declared in sweeping Jeffersonian phrases: "That South Africa belongs to all who live in it, black and white, and that no government can justly claim authority unless it is based on the will of the people." It demanded equal rights in education, housing and employment, and Rusty purposely avoided communist rhetoric or ideology. The only real Marxist touch was added later by resolution: an ambiguous call that "the mineral wealth beneath the soil, the banks and monopoly industry shall be transferred to the ownership of the people as a whole," a section that some communists opposed for fear it would alienate some ANC members and supporters. Sure enough, the Liberal Party and many young Africanists refused to participate in adopting the charter because they claimed it was communist-inspired.

The charter was adopted during a two-day outdoor mass meeting of three thousand delegates in Kliptown outside Johannesburg in June 1955. Because they were listed activists, Rusty, Hilda, Joe and Bram could not attend, but they watched the proceedings from a grove of trees a few hundred yards away. As the meeting was wrapping up, a large contingent of police armed with Sten guns surrounded the area in trucks and mounted the platform. Detectives confiscated every document in sight as well as cameras and rolls of film, money and pamphlets, and they conducted body searches of every person on the dais. They even seized the signs from the nearby soup kitchen that read "Soup With Meat" and "Soup Without Meat." Then they cordoned off the conference square, set up a table at the exit and recorded the name and address of each delegate before he or she was allowed to leave. All of the white delegates were photographed as well.

Three months later, the government struck again, sweeping through the homes and offices of four hundred individuals and organizations and seizing an enormous quantity of books, pamphlets and other materials in the largest police raid in South African history. Police took three hundred sixty-nine separate items from the Bernstein house alone, all of them meticulously listed on eight pages of single-spaced notebook paper. The authorities announced they were looking for evidence of high treason.

It took them a year to find it. In the predawn hours of December 5, 1956, police rounded up one hundred fifty-six leaders of the Congress Movement—Rusty, Joe, Ruth, Nelson Mandela and Walter Sisulu among them—and charged them with treason. The *Johannesburg Star* was quickly on the scene at Ruth and Joe's house in Roosevelt Park, taking photographs of Shawn, Gillian and Robyn in their pajamas, eating cornflakes and smiling for the camera. "Mummy's gone to prison to look after the black people," Shawn, who was six, told the press, she and her sisters clinging to a tranquil world of breakfast cereal and pajamas inside a political maelstrom.

The state set out to prove that the ANC and its sister institutions were engaged in a conspiracy to overthrow the government. Prosecutors argued that the organization was communist and that the Freedom Charter envisaged a communist state. But the government blundered early and often. It targeted a wide and unwieldy range of defendants from all of the various antiapartheid movements: blacks, whites and Indians, liberals, moderates, clergymen, radicals and communists, including Chief Luthuli, who later won the Nobel Peace Prize, and Professor Z. K. Matthews, the country's most prominent black academic. Throwing such a varied group together increased the solidarity and friendship among them, and made it much harder for the state to prove subversive intent. The prosecution's self-assured expert witness, Professor Charles Murray of the University of Cape Town's political science department, testified that the Freedom Charter and many other ANC documents were classic Marxist works. But under questioning from defense lawyer Vernon Berrange, a devastating cross-examiner, Murray stumbled badly. Berrange read to him excerpts from three different works, all of which Murray labeled as communistic. They turned out to have been written by Abraham Lincoln, Woodrow Wilson and D. F. Malan, the first National Party Prime Minister. Berrange read another passage, which the imperturbable Murray declared was "communism straight from the shoulder." This time it turned out that the distinguished professor himself had penned the offending passage in the 1930s.

The Treason Trial dragged on for more than three years, despite the fact that the first indictment was thrown out of court. The trial became an annoying and tedious burden. Rusty's attempt to build an independent architectural practice collapsed while Joe's law practice suffered. As for Ruth, when the one hundred fifty-six defendants were listed in alphabetical order, she was placed next to Joe in the S's, rather than in the F's where she belonged. It took months to force the prosecution to recognize that she had her own last name.

In the end, the state could not prove that the ANC was either communistic or violent. When the first indictment collapsed in October 1958, the Slovos held a party to celebrate. Ruth and Joe stuffed more than two hundred people into their house and the lawn outside. With the burden of the trial lifted, she was in classic form, drink in one hand, cigarette in another, flirting with some of the guests and lecturing others. "Hutch, about that article," she addressed Alfred Hutchinson, a young black writer whom she had commissioned to do a piece for *Fighting Talk*. "I want it. Write it, man."

Alerted by the police, a reporter for the Afrikaans daily *Die Vaderland* staked out the house along with two photographers, looking for evidence of scandalous interracial fraternization. It was not hard to find. As the reporter recounted in the next day's paper, he observed "a number of White women with non-White men getting out of a car." Aroused by this unusual sight, the reporter walked through the back garden of an adjoining house to get a closer look. "In the back yard White women were jesting and talking with Native men. Glasses clinked . . . A couple walked out—a White woman in a low-necked dress and a Native man. Each had a glass. In the sultry light of evening, they leant against the mudguard of a motorcar in the back garden and talked softly."

The scandalized reporter and two colleagues entered Ruth and Joe's side yard, made their way to an open window and climbed into the crowded living room. One of them leaped onto a table, pulled a camera on a strap from around his back and started taking pictures with flash-bulbs exploding. Black and white guests, expecting that the police were close behind, poured their cocktails into the potted plants, slipped glasses under the couch or rapidly gulped the contents. And indeed, within minutes a group of armed policemen stormed through the front door. They announced that they were from Special Branch and the Liquor Squad and that they had been tipped off that alcohol was being served at a mixed racial gathering. By the time they pushed inside the overcrowded room, virtually all of the evidence had disappeared.

Nerves were rapidly fraying. "Don't push me, man, don't push me!" Fred Carneson yelled at one burly detective who was trying to force his way into the room. Joe climbed on a chair. "Friends, I ask you to be calm," he declared. "The police are here in the course of their duty."

The police confiscated liquor bottles from the kitchen and departed. The party resumed with soft drinks and chips and a mood of subdued triumph. Ruth and Joe later sued *Die Vaderland* for five thousand pounds for invasion of privacy and won a small judgment, which they contributed to the Treason Trial defense fund.

The Afrikaner establishment was not the only group that objected to this kind of sultry interracial contact. A new generation of Africanist dissidents had come to the conclusion that whites were dominating the movement, setting the agenda and seducing black leaders like Mandela, Tambo and Sisulu. Many Africanists opposed the Freedom Charter for its racial inclusiveness—its statement that South Africa belonged to all of its peoples, white and black alike, seemed to them to condone white theft of African lands—and they saw the involvement of whites as continuing the tradition of psychological dependency upon which white rule was based. Some went further, contending that whites and Indians constituted a diabolical fifth column that pretended to support black liberation yet ultimately was dedicated to undermining it from within. Multiracial parties and interracial social relationships were just another means of white domination. "Decisions were being arrived at in Lower Houghton by whites, Indians and so-called African intellectuals who were being treated to victuals and liquor and returned drunk with the sense of their self-importance to impose such decisions upon us," complained one Africanist in an interview with historian Gail Gerhart.

The Africanists formally broke off from the ANC and formed the Pan Africanist Congress in April 1959. The PAC was small and chaotically organized, but with its bitter energy and radical enthusiasm it posed a serious threat to the ANC. The competition between the two movements was another step down the road to disaster.

The Africanists were not the only ones who saw Reds under every ANC bed. African moderates were split. Some, like ANC President Luthuli, openly welcomed communist support and relied upon party leaders such as Moses Kotane and J. B. Marks, whose advice tended to be cautious and conservative even if their ideology was radical. Others believed that communists had captured effective control of the Congress Alliance and of the highly respected but physically ailing Luthuli, and were helping Nelson Mandela supplant Luthuli as the real leader of the ANC. In every ANC action, from the adoption of the Freedom Charter to the failure to effectively oppose the razing of Sophiatown to the collapse of several mass defiance campaigns, these critics saw the dark hand of communism. They fell back on conspiracy theories to explain away their own shortcomings and those of their movement—and they failed as well to take into account the handiwork of the increasingly repressive regime that harassed them all, moderate and radical alike.

Still, despite setbacks and divisions, the 1950s were a hopeful time for those in the movement. The ANC was growing in strength and expertise, becoming more adept at organizing mass campaigns. Relations between white radicals and the black leadership were cemented. Hilda and Rusty could see that the Treason Trial marked an end of an era. As it wound down, both the security police and the activists moved toward extralegal means of conflict. But the comrades believed that in the battle to come, they could prevail.

———

The year 1960 was the watershed. Nelson Mandela and the ANC planned a major new round of mass demonstrations and pass burnings to begin in late March. But the upstart Pan Africanist Congress beat the ANC to the punch, issuing a call for blacks to turn in their passes on March 21. Like everything the PAC did, its proposed mass protest was half-baked and haphazardly organized. The ANC's limited success in organizing mass campaigns in the 1950s had made glaringly clear that most Africans were not prepared for a showdown with white rule; yet the PAC's leaders were determined to launch a campaign of defiance that would trigger a full-scale uprising. It was, wrote Gail Gerhart, as if the organization had a political death wish.

Black communities in large parts of the country where the PAC was merely a rumor, ignored the March 21 call. But in the black townships around Johannesburg where the organization had most of its supporters, there were mass demonstrations and civil unrest. The authorities were keen to assert control after rioters in the township of Cato Manor outside Durban had killed nine policemen in an incident a month earlier. They furiously embraced the new challenge.

The worst confrontation took place at Sharpeville, a township south of Johannesburg. A crowd of between five and ten thousand people gathered in the morning outside the police station. Some were there to protest against the pass laws, others just out of curiosity. None were armed. With school out and most shops closed, the gathering took on a festive holiday atmosphere. At first there were only a dozen policemen inside the station compound. But as the morning wound on, dozens more arrived in armored Saracens, accompanied by senior officers. The vehicles moved easily through the crowd wihout incident. By early afternoon there were perhaps three hundred policemen on the scene. The officer in charge made no effort to peacefully disperse the crowd. Nor did he break out the tear gas and riot gear stored on the premises. Instead he ordered his men to load their Sten guns and pistols. Meanwhile, another officer ordered the arrest of two PAC leaders near the west gate of the station. This provocation agitated the crowd at the gate, and there was angry shouting. But most people were unaware of what was happening.

Perhaps someone gave an order, or maybe one of the policemen opened fire on his own. But suddenly police were pouring round after round into the crowd. People turned and fled in panic—perhaps 85 percent of the victims were shot in the back. Most of them fell in the road directly in front of the western fence or in the field to the north. The shooting went on for perhaps forty seconds. Women, children and old people fell. John Mailane, father of a large family who was distributing invoices for his firm on his bicycle, had his head blown off.

"Some of the children, hardly as tall as the grass, were leaping like rabbits," wrote Humphrey Tyler, editor of *Drum*, in an eyewitness account. "Some were shot, too. Still the shooting went on. One of the policemen was standing on top of a Saracen, and it looked as though he was firing his Sten gun into the crowd. He was swinging it around in a wide arc from his hip as though he were panning a movie camera. . . .

"When the shooting started it did not stop until there was no living thing in the huge compound in front of the police station."

When the smoke cleared, sixty-nine people were dead and one hundred eighty-six lay wounded. Bodies lay sprawled in the grass, and pools of blood formed in the road. Clothing, shoes, even chairs were scattered among the dead. Police emerged from the compound and threatened some of the wounded, ordering them to drag themselves away or be shot again. Some who sought to tend to the victims were ordered to leave.

But as bad as the Sharpeville Massacre was, the official reaction made it even worse. Police harassed and intimidated witnesses to the shooting. Those who attempted to gather independent evidence were barred from talking to victims. An official Commission of Inquiry exonerated the police, ruling that their lives had been endangered. Ambrose Reeves, the Anglican bishop of Johannesburg, who took the lead in pressing for the truth, was deported to Britain. While the massacre triggered worldwide condemnation, the government's attitude was that the victims had gotten exactly what they deserved. Carel de Wet, the National Party Member of Parliament for the area and a close associate of the Prime Minister, at first was mistakenly told that the body count was low. "It is a matter of concern to me that only one person was killed," he blithely declared.

The government proclaimed a state of emergency. Ten days later it banned both the ANC and the PAC. Using powers granted under the emergency, police began detaining activists without charge or trial. Some twenty thousand were arrested, mostly in predawn raids. Many activists vanished, fleeing to safe houses inside the country or across the border. Luthuli, in his sixties and suffering from high blood pressure and a weak heart, was slapped hard across the face by a white policeman when he slowed to negotiate a flight of steps on his way to his cell in Pretoria. When the chief stooped to pick up his hat, the policeman hit him again.

Joe knew he was on the arrest list, but he was in the middle of an important legal case and chose to remain at home. Within a few days police came for him. For some reason Ruth was not on their list, but she knew that more arrests would soon follow. She donned a red wig, packed her three daughters into the Citroën and drove to neighboring Swaziland. Julius and Tilly First soon followed. The family lived for several months in a block of flats in the Swazi capital, Mbabane, with dozens of other activists and their families.

The police came to the Bernstein house at 154 Regent Street at 3 a.m. on a Friday. The front-door bell echoed throughout the silent house. Hilda shook Rusty awake, urging him to sneak out the kitchen door. "They're here!" she cried. "Go! Go! Go!"

It was already too late. Police were pounding on the kitchen door as well and someone beamed a flashlight through the bedroom window. Rusty threw on his dressing gown and went to let them in just as Toni was coming out of her room in nightgown and curlers. Rusty thought the police had only come for him, and he returned to the bedroom to pack a bag. But this time they wanted Hilda as well. The officer in charge followed Rusty into the bedroom and asked, "Mr. and Mrs. Bernstein, what do you intend doing about the children?"

Hilda phoned their friends Archie and Yvonne Lewitton. A policeman answered—Archie was also being arrested at that moment. After the police took him away Yvonne came by to gather up the Bernstein children. Meanwhile, the police went through the familiar ritual of seizing books and documents. Wendell Willkie's suspicious-sounding *One World* and Basil Davidson's *Africa Awakening* were among the haul. So was a copy of a book on the Treason Trial, signed in front by all of Rusty's fellow accused. It took detectives three hours to complete the search. Hilda's biggest fear was that Keith, age four, would wake before they left. She did not want him to be frightened by the police—and at the same time she could not bear to see him or even go into his room. Frances was away at a friend's house. Patrick lay curled up in bed, gently weeping. Toni, excelling in the role of efficient eldest child, made coffee, took down phone numbers of family and friends from the phone pad that the police had marked for confiscation and made sure that Hilda packed such practical necessities as a warm coat and hair curlers.

Hilda and Rusty were among one thousand five hundred people arrested that night. They were separated at Marshall Square, where Hilda was put in a room with seventeen other women, including her old friend Molly Fischer. She and Molly and several dozen other women were dispatched to prisons in Johannesburg and Pretoria. It was not a bad stretch—prisoners for the most part were kept in large communal cells where they organized their own cooking, held classes on politics, economics and foreign languages and put on plays and choral recitals. The women staged a hunger strike to seek their release and protest dismal conditions in their cells. When the men found out, they, too, went on strike. The atmosphere had a touch of summer camp.

It might have been fun, except for the children. Molly spoke to Hilda constantly of her twelve-year-old son Paul, who suffered from cystic fibrosis and diabetes. Who was seeing to his daily regimen of pills and nebulizers and who was nursing him through the night attacks when mucus clogged his lungs and he felt he was drowning? One day Paul was allowed to visit her, but it only made things worse. He grabbed hold of the bars and refused to let go. "Nobody's going to take me away from here," he declared.

The Bernstein children were farmed out to neighbors. Toni and Keith stayed at the Lewittons', while Patrick and Frances were soon transferred to the Schermbruckers'. Toni became the general manager in charge of keeping track of her siblings. Patrick was unhappy away from home and deeply disturbed that both his parents were in jail, but he was, like his father, unable to articulate his feelings. "What do you want?" Toni, who felt responsible for his welfare, would demand of him. *"What do you want?"* But the question would only make him more unhappy and more withdrawn, and Toni would feel both angry and guilty.

Frances, who was eight, was the brave soldier of the family, remaining outwardly stoical even though she hated and feared the dark, strange smells and unfamiliar food when she was at the Lewittons'. Frances was a homebody. She loved her room and she loved the garden at Regent Street. In summer, when it was hot, she would start stripping down on her way home from school and march straight to the small swimming pool in the back yard and jump in. She would swim for hours or play in the back yard with her friend Moira or with her cocker spaniel Muffin.

Frances knew her parents often went out at night to do unusual things but she never knew exactly what. When she asked where her father was going, he would inevitably reply, "To see a man about a dog," and give her a big smile. She hated it when both Rusty and Hilda were away at night, even though they always left a special chocolate under each child's pillow.

From an early age, Frances knew that the police were always watching, sometimes literally. One day she and Moira were romping through the open grounds behind the back yard when she spotted a man lying on the ground peering at the back of her house through a hole in the fence. She used to play post office with an old receipt book in which she wrote the names of family friends like the Schermbruckers and the Fischers and placed stamps next to them. During one of the raids on the house, police found the book in her parents' bedroom. They looked at the names and suspicious markings and confiscated it. Frances was also aware that her parents used the old cracked porcelain bathtub in the back yard to burn books and documents they did not want the police to find. The scorched tub was full of half-burned paper and ashes.

Toni Bernstein had the advantage of being older than Patrick and Frances and more capable of dealing with the inevitable problems caused by parents who lived with one foot in the white suburbs and another in the increasingly fraught world of radical politics and police raids. Toni could recall being taken to city council meetings as a small child, bored to tears as her mother argued with the other grown-ups over housing plots, utility rates, bus fares and the other arcana of economic inequity. She could recall her puzzlement in 1953 at a memorial ceremony following Joseph Stalin's death when Joe Slovo concluded his address with the declaration "Long live Stalin!" Toni was confused: had not Stalin just died?

Early on, she formed a threesome with Ilse Fischer, daughter of Bram and Molly, and Barbara Harmel, daughter of Michael and Ray. There were times when the girls knew what their parents were doing and times when they did not, times when they took to calling each other and asking, "Are your parents in tonight?" and wondering if the Bernsteins, Fischers and Harmels were out making revolution together. But it was all done slyly, for who knew who was listening and what dangers lurked?

Still, despite the tension Toni felt Hilda was a good mother. Whatever Hilda's job, she always managed to be home by two in the afternoon when the children returned from school. She expressed interest in what the children were doing and took pride in their achievements. The house was full of interesting people and the children were always encouraged to bring home friends.

But Hilda could be dismissive when her children sought to conform to the norms they learned at school, norms that Hilda herself scorned. There were touchy moments when Toni would arrive home with a school friend to find Nelson Mandela or Walter Sisulu sitting in the living room talking to her mother. "There's a giant in the house!" Keith had exclaimed one day when he saw Mandela at the doorway. A black house guest sipping tea and talking politics in the lounge was no ordinary sight in suburban white Johannesburg. Sometimes the school friend would make a point of not visiting the Bernstein house again. It was a recurring dilemma: Toni was proud of her parents for being morally and politically different—and she was embarrassed by her parents for exactly the same reasons.

This was the dilemma that all of the children faced. How to be normal in an abnormal world, especially when it was your own parents— your supreme defenders, your protectors, those who knew and loved and cherished you best—who were the agents of your abnormality and thus the cause of your distress?

One other thing puzzled Toni: her parents never sought to recruit her to the Communist Party, even though others of her contemporaries were invited. Was it because they feared for her safety? Or because they did not believe she was smart enough to be a party member? Or was it because they needed her to look after their other children during the times when they themselves were imprisoned?

Toni was the only one old enough to visit her parents in prison that year. Her aunt or uncle would fetch her early from school once a week for the long drive to Pretoria. She could have gotten up and quietly made her way from class, but she liked to make a bit of a fuss, to let everyone know she was different, even special. So she might drop a pen or close her book with a flourish, rise up at her desk and say to the teacher, "I'm sorry, miss, but I have to go and see my parents in prison now." Anything for a bit of attention and pride in a situation that otherwise might have been humiliating.

After six weeks of visits, Toni, Ilse, Barbara and their friend Sheila Weinberg decided to do something more dramatic. Taking a page from their parents' own radical handbook, they organized about two dozen children of detainees and staged a protest on the steps outside City Hall in Johannesburg, carrying placards that read "I want my daddy home," or "I want my mama," or, in one case, "While they starve, we starve."

Toni phoned the press ahead of time, and newspaper reporters and international camera crews were at the scene as the children arrived. She, Ilse and a few friends, the oldest of the demonstrators, were invited inside to meet with Mayor Alec Gorshel and deliver a petition demanding the release of their parents. The mayor was sympathetic but pointed out the obvious: he had no influence whatsoever over the Justice Ministry or the security police, and could do nothing except promise to send a telegram to the minister asking him to respond to the children's demands. But when the delegation emerged from City Hall, the other children were gone. Toni and Ilse quickly learned that the group of twenty-two youngsters, some as young as five, had been rounded up by police and taken into custody. White children were placed in police cars while blacks were confined in a van. They were all taken to Marshall Square, where they were kept for an hour. When Ilse and Toni arrived there, Ilse asked to phone her father. "Look, I'm sorry," she told him, "but we're all in Marshall Square—can you come and get us?" Bram arrived minutes later and arranged for everyone's release.

"The children were simply removed to be handed over to their parents, guardians and relatives," Colonel J. C. Lemmer, Deputy Police Commissioner, told the press in a statement. "They had advertised that they were starving and it is the duty of the police to take care of people in want. They were taken away so that this could be done.

"At no time were they arrested," said Lemmer, adding helpfully, "One doesn't arrest children."

It was Toni's first taste of publicity and she rather liked it. Soon she became a sort of junior publicity agent for the Bernstein family. Her father and mother's banning orders made it impossible for them to be quoted in the press. But Toni could be and was.

She also liked being in charge of family visits. After weeks of petitions, the authorities finally allowed the younger children to visit their mother. Toni supervised their getting dressed and herded them into their Uncle Harold's big sedan for the drive up to Pretoria. Once there, Keith was the first to greet Hilda. "Hello, Mummy," he said, and fell into her arms. Frances wore a big shy smile, while Patrick fought back tears. Toni as usual ran the show. "Don't cry, you will upset them," she had hissed sharply to Hilda when her mother's eyes began to glisten.

It was over in thirty minutes and Hilda's pain afterward was sharp. For the seven weeks before the visit, Hilda had managed to keep thoughts of the children out of her head. Afterward, she could think of nothing else.

"Please, Pat," she pleaded with her oldest son in one letter, "do tell me how you occupy your weekends, who you go to, and so on. Are you continuing with your guitar, and do you play at all? Do you still go to Scouts? And who do you see most? Do you still go to the house sometimes to see how Fluffy and Muffin are getting on?" A few days after the visit she wrote to him again. "Perhaps you and I will have arguments when I come home—about homework, and comics and such things; but even if we do, it will be so wonderful to be with you all, I shall even enjoy the fights!"

One night Hilda dreamed she was back with the children. Keith was distant at first, but rushed to hug her. But he had a question that clearly haunted her: "You're back now, but how do I know that it will not happen again?"

After two months of detention, Rusty's brother Harold made a formal petition for Hilda's release on compassionate grounds, citing the damage to the children. While they were being well fed and looked after, Harold wrote, they had been separated and he feared they had suffered "serious and lasting adverse effects." He gave details:

"Frances—Aged 8: This girl is an extremely intelligent and sensitive child. She is now prone to frequent crying spells for no apparent reason and shows all the signs of insecurity.

"Patrick—Aged 11: This lad is subject to moods and for long periods he does not utter a word—he seems to withdraw into himself and has become a complete introvert.

"Toni—Aged 17: This girl is in her Matric [final] year at school. At this important stage in her life she has had to shoulder a burden which normally falls to the lot of a mother. . . . The time lost for study purposes cou-

pled with the other calls on her time by the children becomes material. The result will be a failure in Matric and the consequential results of such a failure.

"Keith—Aged 3½: This child is bewildered and cannot understand what has happened. He will certainly be the worst affected."

Harold requested the Justice Ministry's "sympathetic and speedy consideration" of his plea. The answer came swiftly: rejection. But two weeks later Hilda and the other female detainees were freed. They had been held without charge for three months. Rusty's release followed several weeks later.

The detentions marked the turning of an era. The banning of the ANC and its sister organizations meant black activists had lost the last quasi-legal means of protest and dissent. The PAC had already made plans to move into armed struggle. Now the ANC, frustrated by its banning and afraid of being left behind by its younger, more radical rival, was rapidly preparing to follow suit.

THREE

SABOTAGE

What we have aimed to do in South Africa is to bring
the white man to his senses, not slaughter him.
Albert Luthuli
Let My People Go

Rivonia means "between rivers." They are streams, really, the Braamfonteinspruit and the Sandspruit, so dry in winter that at certain junctures a man can leap across them without wetting the soles of his boots. The land rises between them in a rolling ridge bristling with wattle, syringa and jacaranda trees. Because it is located less than fifteen miles from the heart of Johannesburg, by the 1960s the land was filled with luxury estates and small farms. Rivonia is a mother's name, but her soil is poor. Only small fruit trees and a handful of hearty crops survive in the rugged African veld. At the top of the ridge was a crossroads with no traffic light and a thin ribbon of shops and buildings, including a police station, school, community hall and library and a red-brick post office that whites entered through one door and blacks through another.

In July 1961 a man who called himself Jacobson approached Mrs. E. Watermeyer, a local real estate agent, telling her he was looking to purchase a quiet, secluded place for his brother-in-law, a businessman who had suffered a nervous breakdown. She showed him a number of houses, all of which were a little too exposed to busy roads and prying eyes. The brother-in-law, Mr. Vivian Ezra, needed something more tranquil, Jacobson explained, a place where he could begin the long road to recovery. None of these seemed quite right. Then she took him to Lilliesleaf.

It was the perfect place. Twenty-eight acres of prime land, most of it wooded, just off the Rietfontein Road; a large, modern, shingle-roofed, one-story house with four bedrooms and a spacious living room; a series of outbuildings for servants' quarters, workrooms and storage areas, including a charming thatched-roof cottage. The price was 25,000 rand, then the equivalent of 50,000 U.S. dollars—very reasonable for a prime piece of real estate less than fifteen miles north of downtown Johannesburg. Jacobson was certain his ailing brother-in-law would be pleased.

Indeed he was. Vivian Ezra quickly came to terms with Mrs. Watermeyer and her client. Some of his conditions were a bit unusual. Ezra wanted the farm to be recorded in the name of Navian Ltd., of which Ezra was sole director. He was willing to pay the full asking price, but negotiated an agreement to pay for the property in annual installments of 5,000 rand. This proved not to be a problem. Ezra had two lawyers—Ralph Sepel, who worked in the same office building with Ezra, and Harold Wolpe, a partner in the Johannesburg law firm of James Kantor—draw up the purchase contract and on August 21, 1961, Ezra signed. Sepel received the first year's installment in cash in an unmarked envelope that a clerk hand-delivered from Kantor's law firm. The deal for Lilliesleaf was done.

But Vivian Ezra never moved into the house in Rivonia. Instead, Ezra's company immediately leased the property to a local architect and interior designer named Arthur Goldreich for one hundred rand per month. A few weeks later Goldreich moved to the property with his wife Hazel and their two young sons. The elusive Mr. Jacobson was a frequent visitor, only he was known there by his real name: Michael Harmel, a listed communist with a long police record of radical activities.

Lilliesleaf was not purchased as a refuge for a recuperating businessman, but rather as an incubator for a revolution. It was the brainchild of Harmel, Joe Slovo and Bram Fischer, who set it up as the secret headquarters for the underground Communist Party and a safe house for political fugitives. At least some of the funding was provided by Julius First, Ruth's father, who for years had been a secret benefactor and treasurer of the party. Inevitably, it became the nerve center of the sabotage campaign they had decided to launch hand in hand with Nelson Mandela and the ANC.

The decision to turn to violence had not been an easy one. For decades nonviolence had been one of the foremost principles of the antiapartheid movement. Mohandas Gandhi had spent his formative years as a young lawyer in the city of Durban, and his advocacy of civil disobedience had a strong effect not only on the Indian population but on nonwhites in general. But the Defiance Campaign and its successors had all failed to achieve what Gandhi's mass protests in India had accomplished. This was in large part because the South African authorities were prepared to use any tactics, including the large-scale violence of the Sharpeville Massacre, to smother such protests. The Afrikaners were not British colonial rulers—they could not cede power, pack up and return to Mother England. They had no place else to go; they were home and they intended to defend that home and the privileges they had amassed for themselves by any means necessary. The 1960 crackdown was only the beginning. The government's determination to crush dissent left the movement with no choice. Both the remnants of the ANC leadership and the Communist Party, moving on parallel tracks, drew the same grim conclusion.

The communists, with their far smaller and more cohesive organization, took the decision first. Operating from underground during the 1960 emergency, Michael Harmel produced a paper arguing that traditional means of nonviolence were of no use in a system that treated legitimate dissent as an act of treason or rebellion. He won swift support from some of the younger radicals, especially Joe Slovo and Govan Mbeki, and eventually almost everyone agreed that violence was the only way left. Bram and Rusty went along reluctantly. Rusty felt they had no choice—it was either turn to armed struggle or give up altogether. Bram expressed similar feelings. "Much as I don't like this, we're left with no other option," he told his oldest daughter Ruth. "We've tried every nonviolent means possible and nothing has worked." At a secret meeting in December 1960 party leaders agreed to begin setting up special sabotage units. A few weeks later, Rusty journeyed to Durban to inform district party leaders there of the decision and to help get units started there.

The ANC took considerably longer to come to a similar conclusion. Ignoring the government's banning order, the National Executive Committee of the ANC met secretly and voted to carry on its work underground. When Mandela's five-year banning order expired in March 1961, he decided to take advantage of his momentary freedom by going underground himself before the authorities could slap on new restrictions. From now on, like the organization he led, Mandela would operate clandestinely, his movements and activities concealed. He hopped from city to city, appearing briefly at meetings and press conferences. South African newspapers, desperate for an easy label, dubbed him the "Black Pimpernel." Every policeman was looking for him; every informer was eager to turn him in for a reward. Ruth and Joe were key members of his small group of trusted advisors. Joe often arranged for drivers and safe places to stay, while Ruth organized secret briefings with members of the local press and foreign correspondents.

From underground Mandela made one last attempt to organize non-violent resistance. He proposed a mass stay-at-home campaign beginning May 29, 1961, to protest the whites-only referendum on whether South Africa should break its last formal tie with the British Commonwealth and declare itself a republic. The authorities moved swiftly to crush the protest by all available means. They arrested hundreds of activists, banned meetings, seized printing presses and rushed through new legislation authorizing police to detain suspects for twelve days without charge. Two days before the strike, the government issued a military call-up and stationed heavily armed soldiers at the entrances of black townships. The strike's first day saw hundreds of thousands of workers remain home in defiance of the government. Still, the response nationwide was far less than Mandela had hoped for. Angry and demoralized, he called it off the next day. That night he met with members of the press at a safe house in Johannesburg arranged by Ruth. "If the government reaction is to crush by naked force our nonviolent struggle, we will have to reconsider our tactics," he told one of his interviewers. "In my mind we are closing a chapter on this question of a nonviolent policy."

With Walter Sisulu's expert help, Mandela set about persuading the various leadership groups within the ANC that violence was the only means of opposition left. For justification he cited an old African expression, *sebatana ha se bokwe ka diatla*—"the attacks of the wild beast cannot be averted with only bare hands." He argued that the rival Pan Africanist Congress was taking the lead and that if the ANC did not follow suit, it would soon lose support, especially among the impatient young. Better, Mandela insisted, that the more moderate ANC, which believed in restraint and racial reconciliation and would be judicious in its use of force, be in the vanguard of what was to come rather than the younger, more chaotic and more bloodthirsty Africanists.

The leader most skeptical of Mandela's argument was Chief Luthuli, still the nominal head of what was left of the banned ANC. A devout Christian with a strong commitment to nonviolence who was soon to be named winner of the Nobel Peace Prize, Luthuli at first resisted the move to armed struggle. But after a long night of discussion in which a passionate Mandela and a low-key, logical Sisulu took turns wearing him down, the chief succumbed. He insisted, however, that Nelson should form a separate and autonomous organization that would be subject to ANC control. Many other executive committee members objected, especially those long committed to the Gandhian path. But in the end they could offer no effective alternative. The National Executive Committee secretly approved the move. Fifty years of nonviolent opposition to white rule was at an end.

During this time relations between white and black activists were further cemented. Both the ANC and the Communist Party sought to maintain the appearance of separation, but the pressures of working underground under the constant threat of exposure to the police swept away whatever barriers remained between them. By now Mandela, like Sisulu, was a member of the Communist Party, in spirit if not in name. Mandela and Slovo, chosen to represent the two organizations, quickly concluded that it made no sense to form separate military campaigns, and they decided to pool their resources in a single movement, Umkhonto We Sizwe. Money began trickling in from the newborn African states as well as from the communist world. Members were recruited from the ranks of both organizations.

Mandela and Slovo became the first members of Umkhonto's National High Command, with Govan Mbeki and Jack Hodgson as their respective deputies. The High Command was to determine tactics, targets, training and finances for the organization. In turn, it appointed Regional Commands, which oversaw the work of local sabotage groups. The basic structure and terminology were adapted from the Irgun, Menachem Begin's Jewish underground movement that had fought British rule in Palestine in the 1940s. The Regional Commands had the authority to choose individual targets, but were expected to operate within the framework laid down by the High Command.

Under Mandela's guidance, the High Command considered four options: sabotage, guerrilla warfare, terrorism and open revolution. It decided upon the first, because sabotage aimed at property would inflict the least amount of human damage and leave open the possibility of racial reconciliation once the conflict ended. Mandela also argued that sabotage was the most practical means of initiating armed struggle because it required the fewest people. He laid down two immediate principles: the operations would target government buildings and infrastructure, not people. And no one was allowed to carry a weapon when he went on a mission. Umkhonto's warriors were to go into battle unarmed.

Joe could see at once that he and his comrades were ill prepared for armed struggle. They did not have a single pistol among them. While some of them had served in the army, few had any combat experience, and certainly none had ever engaged in sabotage using homemade explosives. What's more, few members understood the importance of secrecy. Too many meetings were held in open places, and many of them went on far too long. Documents were left in insecure places with fingerprints and identifiable handwriting. Everyone had a lot to learn.

The purchase of Lilliesleaf was designed in part to help provide security for the movement's wanted leaders. The first underground activist to make use of it was Mandela himself. Going by the alias David Matsamayi, he took up residence on the property as caretaker in October 1961. Tall and trim, with a boxer's build and a markedly regal bearing, Matsamayi wore simple blue overalls and spent his days preparing breakfast and tea for the African workers who were repairing the main house and extending the outbuildings for the arrival of the Goldreichs. The workers also made him run errands for them, sweep the floor and pick up the trash. Sometimes they spoke rudely to him, but Matsamayi never answered back. He was a servant while they were tradesmen, and they assumed he was lower in status than they.

But at sunset, after the workers left for home in the nearby black township of Alexandra, Mandela would change clothes and identities. Comrades like Rusty and Joe would drive to the farm in the evenings to speak with him. Rusty lent him books on Marxist thought, while Joe helped in drafting the Umkhonto constitution. So did Raymond

Mhlaba, a staunch trade unionist, ANC and Communist Party member from the city of Port Elizabeth, one of the ANC's urban strongholds.

On October 18, 1961, the National Party scored yet another electoral triumph. Capitalizing on scattered incidents of violence caused largely by PAC members and by a shadowy group of saboteurs that called itself the National Liberation Committee, the Nats promised a harsh crackdown. A skittish white electorate rewarded the party with its greatest electoral victory since coming to power. The Nats took 105 of 160 seats—just two votes short of a two-thirds majority. The dwindling United Party was further weakened by the defection of eleven liberal members who ran on a joint ticket as the Progressive Party. Ten of them were defeated, leaving Helen Suzman as the sole Progressive in Parliament.

A few weeks later, Arthur Goldreich, his wife Hazel, and their two young sons moved into the main house in Rivonia. Joe had personally approached Arthur and asked him to serve as the front man for Lilliesleaf. Few people knew of Arthur's long-standing secret membership in the Communist Party. Although he had many friends in the movement, his name appeared on no police lists. He had never been arrested. As far as most people knew, Goldreich had been a member of the Congress of Democrats until 1957 when he dropped out and seemed to lose interest in politics. Many thought of him as an ostentatious dilettante. The Goldreichs went riding every weekend, hobnobbed at the polo club and held frequent dinner parties in their new country home. Arthur affected the air of a foppish country gentleman, dressing in tweeds and riding boots. One night at Franco's restaurant, after watching him dance, drink champagne, flirt with women and talk cynically of politics, Selma Browde got fed up. "How can you go on living like this in a country like South Africa?" demanded Selma, a prominent liberal who was a friend and ally of Helen Suzman. "Why don't you do something?"

Goldreich just laughed. "I enjoy the good life," was his response.

It was all a front. Arthur Goldreich was in fact a dedicated communist and a member of the logistics committee of Umkhonto. His masquerade as an apolitical bon vivant even allowed him to travel freely abroad. While in London in 1961 he made a secret side trip to Czechoslovakia and East Germany, where he gathered expertise on running a campaign of insurgency against a conventional army and on the manufacture of armaments. Soviet Bloc countries had played no role in the decision to move to armed struggle, but they were ardent supporters, and promised money, training and some weaponry. Goldreich's cover was so secure that he was able to make a second trip, this time to the Soviet Union and China in December 1962. While in Beijing he and Vela Pillay, the party's London representative, were treated to a four-hour session with a small, intense man who launched a long and cogent diatribe against the Soviet Union. The man's name was Deng Xiaoping.

No one outside a select few in the party knew of Goldreich's secret. But Hazel's mother, Maimie Berman, figured it out. She came out to the house a few days after the Goldreichs had moved in and found Michael Harmel on the premises. "I know that he's a communist," she told Hazel. "What's he doing here?"

Hazel made up a story about Harmel's coming out to help move furniture, but Maimie Berman knew better. "Just be careful," she warned her daughter.

Jack Hodgson had fought with the British as a demolitions expert during World War II, and he was one of the few Umkhonto members with any practical military experience. Half Scot and half Yorkshireman, Hodgson was a tough-talking former mine worker and an eager saboteur. His wife Rica was a fund-raiser for the movement and one of Ruth First's closest friends. Despite being under constant police surveillance, he managed to turn their three-room flat in the Hillbrow section of the city into Umkhonto's Johannesburg bomb factory. The fledgling saboteurs hauled to the apartment sacks of permanganate of potash—used in civilian life to wash lettuce—and spent days grinding the potash to a fine powder with a large brass pestle and mortar that Rica had inherited from her mother. Soon the walls, curtains and carpets of the living room where they worked were saturated with white dust.

Hodgson mixed the potash with aluminum powder, which became unstable when a drop of acid was added as a catalyst. He constructed a primitive timing device using a piece of cardboard placed over a small bottle of acid. When the bottle was turned over, the acid would slowly eat through the cardboard, then drop onto the powdered mixture, causing it to explode. The process was supposed to take about fifteen minutes.

Armed with this makeshift explosive, the men of Umkhonto set forth on December 16, 1961, the same date that Afrikaners mark to celebrate the triumph of their pioneering ancestors over Zulu warriors at the Battle of Blood River. Joe, who was not content with letting others take all the risks, decided he would be part of the first wave of saboteurs. He took the homemade device that Hodgson had stuffed inside a tennis ball can, placed it in a canvas carrier bag and set out for the Johannesburg Drill Hall, a squat, red-brick relic from colonial times that the authorities had used for preliminary hearings during the Treason Trial. Joe had reconnoitered the building several times and had decided that a well-placed bomb would ignite the large wooden floor in the central hall and the hundreds of wooden chairs spread across it. He arrived, bag in hand, just after five o'clock expecting to find the building deserted, but was surprised to find a small army of black janitors carefully removing the chairs and painstakingly polishing the floor on their hands and knees.

Frustrated and disappointed, Joe quietly slipped out and looked for another place within the building that would be far enough from the hall so as not to harm the janitors, yet still cause enough damage to burn down the building. He settled on a deserted office with huge wooden cupboards. He turned the bottle of acid upside down to start the explosive process. But just as Joe was about to place the bag behind one of the cupboards, a man's voice called out from behind him, "Can I do anything for you, sir?"

Joe had rehearsed carefully for this moment. He turned and saw a white man dressed in a sergeant major's uniform. Joe told him he was seeking an exemption for his brother, who had recently received a notice of conscription but was about to take an important university exam. The sergeant major asked Joe to follow him to another office. Joe had no choice, although he did not know how long the acid-soaked cardboard would hold. They walked to the office of exemptions. The sergeant major tried the door handle; it was locked. The officer had left for the day, he told Joe, you'll have to come back tomorrow. Joe thanked him profusely, turned and marched briskly for the front door. Once outside he rounded a corner, reached in the bag and snatched out the bottle of acid. The Drill Hall—and Joe himself—was spared.

When he got home later that evening he learned how lucky he had been. One of his fellow saboteurs, Peter Molefe, had died that same day outside the Municipal Bantu Control Office in Soweto, and Molefe's companion, Benjamin Ramotsi, had been severely burned. Molefe had been holding a bomb when it prematurely exploded. His severed left hand was found nearby.

Rusty was not part of an Umkhonto unit, but he felt obligated to take part in that first symbolic day. That night he joined Joe and Jack Hodgson for a ride to a manhole on the Johannesburg–Pretoria road that housed the telephone cables connecting the two cities. Under Jack's supervision, they set a charge. As they raced back to town, they heard behind them the sharp report of the bomb. But the explosion did not sever the cable. Phone service was undisturbed.

Others were more successful. That same evening bombs exploded at power stations and government offices in Johannesburg, Cape Town, Durban and Port Elizabeth. In pamphlets issued in each city, Umkhonto We Sizwe declared its existence as "the fighting arm of the people against the Government and its policies of race oppression." For a self-declared revolutionary movement, Umkhonto's first public proclamation was surprisingly moderate, even apologetic, about the decision to turn to violence. "The choice is not ours," declared the statement, which Rusty had helped to write. "It has been made by the Nationalist Government which has rejected every peaceable demand by the people for rights and freedom and answered every such demand with force and yet more force!"

It went on: "We of Umkhonto We Sizwe have always sought—as the liberation movement has sought—to achieve liberation, without bloodshed and civil clash. We do so still. We hope—even at this late hour—that our first actions will awaken everyone to a realization of the disastrous situation to which the Nationalist policy is leading. *We hope that we will bring the Government and its supporters to their senses before it is too late, so that . . . its policies can be changed before matters reach the desperate stage of civil war* [author's italics]."

So there it was. The supposed radicals of Umkhonto stood self-revealed as humanists and reluctant saboteurs who believed the apartheid state could still be shaken out of its fantasy of white power and who had taken up bombs not to start a war but rather to prevent one. Even allowing for the rhetorical hyperbole of self-justification, the manifesto is a remarkable document. Almost everything about Umkhonto—its relentless amateurism, its insistence on targeting infrastructure rather than personnel and its naive faith in the power of a few bombs to bring

Verwoerd, Vorster & Company *"to their senses"*—smacked not of ruthless terrorism but of humanism at its most idealistic and naive. Taken at their word, the men of Umkhonto were not the First Communists, but the Last Humanists.

Of the leaders who oversaw the movement in the early days of the sabotage campaign, none was more influential than Bram Fischer. He had been reluctant to support the move to violence. When outvoted after a heated debate, he had argued that the underground should give the government one last warning before launching its campaign. When that motion was defeated as well, he accepted the decision with his customary sense of commitment. But he always saw the sabotage campaign not as the first step toward a civil war but as a last-ditch effort to avoid one.

In a movement dominated by English speakers, recent immigrants and Jews, Bram Fischer stood out. He was a native Afrikaner, a son of the South African soil, born in 1908 in the old Boer republic of the Orange Free State. His grandfather was the province's first Prime Minister and his father its most senior judge. Bram himself was marked for greatness from childhood. A superb scholar and rugged athlete, when he turned twenty-one he received a letter from Ouma Steyn, widow of the President of the province. "As a child and as a student you were an example to everyone," she wrote, "and I know you will play an honorable role in the history of South Africa."

From the beginning, however, Bram was too restless and independent to meet anyone's preconceived expectations. He could not avoid detecting the gap between his Calvinist ideals and the reality of racial domination upon which his society was based. Growing up on a farm, he had two African companions whom he played with daily. When his family moved to town he lost touch with them and adopted the prevailing belief that whites and blacks should remain separate and unequal. Then as a young adult serving on a local panel for racial affairs, he was introduced to Africans again. "I found I had to shake hands with them," he later recalled. "This, I found, required an enormous effort of will. . . . That night, I spent many hours in thought, trying to account for my strange revulsion, when I remembered I had never had any such feelings toward my boyhood friends."

Because he did not shy away from self-criticism, Bram quickly came to the conclusion that the fault lay not with blacks, but with himself. "What had become abundantly clear was that it was I who had changed, and not the black man," he recalled. "I came to understand that color prejudice was a wholly irrational phenomenon and that true human friendship could extend across the color bar once the initial prejudice was overcome."

From there it did not take long for him to gravitate toward the Communist Party, which was at that time the only political organization in South Africa that stood unconditionally for equal rights for nonwhites. Its members, Bram said later, "were, save for a handful of courageous individuals, the only whites who showed complete disregard for the hatred which this attitude attracted from their fellow white South Africans. . . . They were not prepared to flourish on the deprivations suffered by others."

As an Afrikaner, Bram also admired communism's hatred of colonialism and imperialism. After all, had not his people been the first African tribe to win its liberation? Who better could understand black aspirations? He could foresee a time when Afrikaners would encourage blacks as partners, not subordinates.

He earned a law degree at a local college in Bloemfontein, where he was a brilliant student and star rugby player, then won a Rhodes scholarship to New College at Oxford. He spent three years in England at a time when Europe was in the grip of the Great Depression and fascism and communism vied for youthful hearts and minds. He toured parts of Germany soon after Hitler came to power and the Soviet Union under Joseph Stalin, trips that reinforced his own growing leftist beliefs. No one can pin down the exact date when he joined the Communist Party, but by the time he returned to South Africa in 1934 he was clearly dedicated to the cause. Early the following year he moved to Johannesburg, where his brilliance as a lawyer quickly led to lucrative work for the city's big mining houses and insurance companies. Two years later, he married Susanna Johanna Krige, known to all as Molly, herself a cousin of the wife of Prime Minister Smuts.

Even as a dedicated communist, Bram was by nature an inclusive person. He never surrendered the hope that he could convert others by the sheer righteousness of his cause. In the early 1940s Bram even had lunch with Hendrik F. Verwoerd, the main architect of apartheid and ultimately his archenemy, in an attempt to convince the austere

Afrikaner newspaper editor to switch his allegiance from fascism and race politics to socialism.

Bram coupled such boundless political optimism with enormous personal empathy. He liked people and he managed to convey a sense of warmth and concern that crossed all political lines. When novelist Alan Paton helped form the Liberal Party in the early 1950s, he came in for much criticism from the radicals for not joining his movement to the left-wing Congress of Democrats. But Bram, who was one of the founders of the congress, remained personally affectionate toward Paton even while politically at odds. The author praised Bram one day at a meeting of fellow liberals. "Don't bluff yourself," one of them warned. "When Bram comes to power, you'll be the first one to have your throat cut." Paton could never accept that prophecy; he suspected that if such a day ever came to pass, Bram might instead send him a one-way air ticket with the message "Get out of here as fast as possible."

Bram's face was florid from high blood pressure and he suffered constantly from an ulcer that belied the calm exterior he presented to the world. But he had dark brown hair that turned snow white with age and clear blue eyes that twinkled with a conspiratorial sense of amusement. Women loved him deeply. He projected a sense of intimacy and concern—to men as well as women—even while keeping his deepest thoughts and many dangerous secrets well guarded.

Around the time their first child was born in 1939 Bram and Molly bought an acre of land in Oaklands, one of the northern suburbs, and built a large house at 12 Beaumont Street. Bram loved the house, especially the garden. He boasted that after the revolution, his dream was to work as a groundskeeper in the Wilds, the vast, overgrown public gardens in the northern suburbs.

The Fischers helped make all of the left-wing community of Johannesburg into an extended family. Their phone rang all day long—it was impossible even to get through dinner without two or three calls. People called for advice on their legal problems, their love lives and their financial woes. Many arrived at the Fischer doorstep and few were turned away. After the Fischers added on a swimming pool in the early 1950s, the flow of guests was so constant that sometimes for privacy Bram and Molly would pack the children in their old Mercedes and drive off for a picnic out on the veld.

In the early days their hospitality extended even to the men of Special

Branch. The police would show up for a search in their brown felt hats, open suit jackets and brown shoes and Bram and Molly would welcome them solemnly at the door, even provide them with tea as they scoured the premises. The detectives, knowing they were in the presence of Afrikaner royalty, generally were on their best behavior.

Molly was no less empathic than Bram; she had a devoted following among the comrades, especially those, like Walter Sisulu and Ahmed Kathrada, whom she singled out for special concern. But she also had a sharp tongue and an acerbic wit. She was Bram's rudder: she kept him organized, managed his schedule and made sure he kept his commitments. She, too, joined the Communist Party and ran for city council in 1944, the same year as Hilda Bernstein. For many years she taught and served as headmistress at the Central Indian High School in Fordsburg, whose staff was dominated by party members. During the Alexandra bus boycott in the mid-1950s she would set out in her small Anglia sedan each morning and pick up people needing rides even after police declared such help illegal and began harassing drivers. Molly took care of the details of life, from arranging for the dry cleaning of Sisulu's suit before he appeared in court to delivering a bottle of brandy to Kathrada on his birthday while he was under house arrest.

Within the party Bram was respected for his brain and judgment, but younger members such as Joe Slovo believed he was too cautious. He brought a lawyer's sensibility to politics, which they felt was not always appropriate. When the Suppression of Communism Act was about to take effect, he pushed for the party to disband, arguing that otherwise individual members would be compelled to publicly denounce their membership or else face stiff prison sentences. It was the correct move legally, but all wrong politically, Joe believed. Bram was not among those who pushed to form a new underground party, although once it came into existence he quickly became a member. Because of his respected position and high-paying salary as a barrister, he had more to lose than probably anyone else in the movement. But he took the same risks as the others. In 1962 as the police crackdown intensified, he became chairman of the Central Committee of the party and took control of the treasury. He traveled to Lilliesleaf almost daily, and sometimes twice a day.

Despite Bram's gentility and compassion, he was in many ways the most hard-line of all the comrades. In the 1950s, as evidence mounted of abuses in the Soviet Union, Bram dug his heels in. He would not accept Stalin's misdeeds until Khrushchev aired them himself in the famous 1956 address to the Twentieth Congress of the Soviet Communist Party. Even the invasion of Hungary caused no second-guessing. When Monty and Myrtle Berman announced they had had enough and were leaving the party, Bram pleaded with them to stay. "You're misjudging what is going on," he told them. "There must be a reason for it."

Bram was also unyielding in opposing those of his white comrades who decided to flee the country. He argued passionately that because most blacks did not have such an option—they had no money and no travel documents—whites who fled were taking advantage of their skin privilege. Nothing was more of an anathema to Bram. Besides, he was an Afrikaner. South Africa was his home—he could not abide the idea of leaving, nor could he fathom how others could do so, no matter how bad things got. Inside Bram's kindly exterior, thought Rusty Bernstein, was a core of rigid steel.

Ruth Fischer was the oldest of Bram and Molly's three children and also the most rebellious. She embarrassed her father by studying psychology at university rather than politics or economics as he would have liked. It was one of Bram's many self-contradictions—as a Marxist he said he did not believe in psychology, but as the avuncular leader of the movement, he practiced it constantly on members and their spouses.

Ilse, who was Toni Bernstein's friend and whose brown hair and blue eyes matched her father's, was more obedient and more prepared to follow in his footsteps. Then there was Paul, the youngest, born in 1948. His illness helped put a brake on Molly's political activities. It became her mission to keep him alive and comfortable for as long as possible. Paul had many doctors and a daily regimen of antibiotics, insulin shots, vitamins and digestive pills, but his life was a constant struggle to weather the suffocating attacks he suffered late at night. Paul was bright and rebellious, not unlike his father. He could be bitter about the time and attention his parents paid to their surrogate children in the movement rather than to him. He liked to be rude in public, calling his parents *"kaffirboeties"*—the ugly local equivalent of "nigger lovers." His demeanor toward blacks was always respectful; Paul's rough language was part of an adolescent's efforts to provoke his parents. But he was fiercely loyal to Bram and Molly as well.

Many of Bram's statements and beliefs had an air of unreality. More than any of the others, he maintained his optimism the longest, even when all the evidence was pointing the other way. In his mind, every police crackdown was another sign of the state's desperation, another last gasp of a tottering regime. Even the prospect of ninety-day detention did not faze him. He developed an elaborate theory that one trip to prison "immunized" a detainee so that he or she would not be affected by further imprisonment. It was a myth, as he and the party would learn through painful experience when one comrade after another was chewed up and broken by continual isolation. Yet if Bram's optimism was infuriating at times, more often it was endearing and inspiring. If this intelligent, caring man could look past the crisis of the moment and see a bright future, then surely the rest of the comrades could do the same.

A few weeks after Umkhonto launched its campaign, Nelson Mandela left the country to attend a Pan-African freedom conference in Addis Ababa—forerunner of the Organization of African Unity—and tour the continent seeking support and funding for the military training of recruits for Umkhonto. He met with the leaders of Ethiopia, Tanganyika, Tunisia, Sudan, Sierra Leone, Algeria, Mali, Senegal, Guinea, Liberia and Uganda. He also visited London and Cairo. He was dismayed to hear several African leaders express support for the Pan Africanist Congress, whose envoys were spreading the idea that it, and not the ANC, was the main engine of the South African liberation movement. Many leaders understood the PAC's brand of pure African nationalism, but were bewildered by the ANC's nonracialism and by its intimate relationship with white communists. Some swallowed the PAC's claim that Umkhonto was essentially the brainchild of the Communist Party.

Mandela sought to reassure his hosts that Africans such as himself were firmly in control of Umkhonto. But what he heard disturbed him. When he passed through London, he and Oliver Tambo, who had headed up the ANC's external mission since fleeing South Africa in 1960, agreed that the organization had at least to appear to be more independent of the Communist Party and stand as first among equals in the Congress Alliance. This led to an argument with Yusuf Dadoo, an

Indian Congress leader and communist who was working with Tambo. Dadoo accused Mandela and Tambo of violating the principles of non-racialism. Mandela contended that he was only advocating that the ANC make some minor changes in image, not policy, in order to appease the African leaders it would be relying upon for weapons, money and training. But a rift was beginning to reopen between Africans and other parts of the Congress Alliance. Then, after two months of military training in Addis Ababa, Mandela cut short his trip and reported back to a mixed committee of ANC and communist leaders at Lilliesleaf in July 1962. He repeated some of the misgivings he had heard abroad. He proposed that the Congress Alliance be reshaped so that the ANC would be seen as taking the lead. A number of participants echoed Dadoo's misgivings. They urged Mandela to go to Natal and discuss the matter with Luthuli. Despite the dangers involved in traveling around the country, he agreed to make the five-hundred-mile drive in the company of Cecil Williams, a trusted comrade.

Mandela met with Luthuli and also held a session with the Natal Regional Command, one of whose key members was a smooth and enthusiastic saboteur named Bruno Mtolo. The next afternoon, he and Williams left for the long drive back to Johannesburg. Mandela wore a white chauffeur's coat and sat up front next to Williams, who was driving. About an hour north of Durban, three cars filled with police pulled them over. Someone had tipped off Special Branch.

Soon there were government-planted stories in the South African press claiming that white and Indian communists had betrayed Mandela because of his suggestions that the ANC become more African-oriented, but he himself did not believe this. Nor did he believe a credible rumor that a CIA operative had tipped off the police. A more likely explanation, he later conceded, was that Umkhonto's security was so lax that the police could have learned of his movements in any number of ways. But the leaked reports and rumors exacerbated tensions within the movement and heightened the sense of fear and paranoia as police closed in.

Mandela's arrest came at a time when many old-guard ANC members were increasingly restive over the activities of Umkhonto. Some felt the decision to launch armed struggle had been taken without their endorsement; most were unaware that Luthuli himself had given his passive consent. They feared the police would conclude that Umkhonto was the military wing of the ANC and hold all ANC members responsible for Umkhonto's deeds. If arrested, a member could be prosecuted not only for belonging to an illegal organization but for the far more serious charge of sabotage. And again, the old issue of race came up. Who was calling the shots in Umkhonto, they wondered, African nationalists or white communists? Increasingly, some ANC members believed the Communist Party was seeking to control the movement, recruiting the best and brightest among them for secret membership in the party.

The arrest was a terrible blow to morale. To try to recoup, Joe, Harold Wolpe and a comrade named Joe Modise formed an escape committee. They met at Lilliesleaf to float ideas, finally settling upon an elaborate scheme that called for freeing Mandela when he appeared at Magistrate's Court in Johannesburg for a preliminary hearing. Modise persuaded a black police officer to leave Mandela's cell unlocked, while a member of the court staff slipped Slovo a key to the holding area. A professional wig maker produced an Indian-looking wig, mustache and beard that Slovo had sewn into the shoulder pad of one of Mandela's suit coats and smuggled in. Mandela had serious doubts about the scheme and wrote Joe a long note suggesting that the plan be postponed. The last sentence read: "Please destroy this after you have finished reading it."

Joe and Harold followed Mandela's advice about suspending the escape effort, and they were forced to abandon the scheme altogether when he was suddenly transferred to another jail. But they ignored his instruction to destroy the note. Like so many other documents that Joe and his comrades considered of historical significance, it was placed in a file at Lilliesleaf—for safekeeping.

At his trial, Nelson Mandela challenged the right of a white-ruled court to judge him. "I consider myself neither morally nor legally bound to obey laws made by a Parliament in which I have no representation," he told the court. He was convicted of leaving the country illegally and of inciting workers to stay away from their jobs and he was sentenced to five years' imprisonment. In his final plea of mitigation before sentencing, Mandela explained his decision to go underground: "There comes a time, as it came in my life, when a man is denied the right to live a normal life, when he can only live the life of an outlaw because the Government has so decreed to use the law to impose a state of outlawry upon him. I was driven to this situation, and I do not regret having taken the decisions that I did take."

At first the police were slow to react to the sabotage campaign. They used their usual methods: roundups in the black townships, beatings of suspects, and other physical abuse. But the bombs continued to explode, not only from Umkhonto but from two other organizations: the National Liberation Committee, which consisted mostly of a small group of young white radicals who had broken off from Alan Paton's Liberal Party but came to include Monty and Myrtle Berman and other former Communist Party members; and Poqo, which means "independent" in Xhosa, a rural-based movement that was connected to the PAC. Poqo practiced armed insurrection and indiscriminate terrorism; its followers murdered two whites in the town of Paarl outside Cape Town and hacked to death five white campers, including a woman and two young girls, at Bashee River Bridge in the rural Transkei.

White fear and the lack of police success in coping with the violence presented the new Minister of Justice, Balthazar John Vorster, with the opportunity to come before Parliament in May 1962 to seek new legislation. Vorster told lawmakers that his government had taken strong measures to raise the standard of living and job opportunities for all South Africans and that apartheid was working to reduce "friction" between the races. But one group of vicious troublemakers stood in the way: communists "and their camp followers." They wanted to derail "peaceful coexistence," Vorster declared, and replace it with "chaos and anarchy, which is their ultimate object."

"I believe the time has arrived, and in fact it has become high time, to devote more attention particularly to the white agitators in South Africa," Vorster told Parliament. Recent acts of sabotage were not the work of a handful of isolated wrongdoers, but rather a calculated and coordinated campaign by well-organized people. Although it had been outlawed twelve years earlier, the Communist Party, he warned, "is getting its second breath." Its goal, he said, was "totally to destroy all that we stand for on this side of the House."

Vorster proposed the Sabotage Act, a bill he said was designed to tighten the screws on the white left and its black comrades in order "to render them harmless." Clause Two streamlined the ban on dissident political organizations. Clause Four required "listed" persons to resign from subversive organizations and also banned any publication or broadcast of their writings. Clause Five effectively banned left-wing newspapers like *New Age* by requiring them to post a bond of 15,000 rand that would be forfeited if they published material deemed subversive. Clause Six provided that lists of communists be published so that no purported subversive could conceal his or her legal status. Clause Seven gave the minister the power to close off the steps outside the City Hall in Johannesburg and the parade grounds in Cape Town to political rallies where, Vorster groused, "cameramen can photograph these little scenes and demonstrate to the world what a rotten place South Africa is." Clauses Sixteen and Seventeen expanded the state's capacity to use its emergency powers.

But the key section was Clause Twenty-one. It not only made sabotage a capital offense but placed the burden on the accused to prove he did not intend to commit a political act when he destroyed property. The clause also eliminated the requirement that the state conduct a preliminary legal examination before trial; under it, the accused would no longer know the size and scope of the case against him until he entered the courtroom. "We are dealing with people who are dangerous, and who will not hesitate for one moment to get a witness out of the way," explained Vorster in justifying this unprecedented step. Finally, if a person were found not guilty of sabotage, he could be charged again with a lesser offense and retried, a form of double jeopardy that even Vorster conceded was "admittedly a new principle."

Sir de Villiers Graaff, leader of the opposition United Party, warned that the bill would give Vorster "vast new powers . . . over the liberties of the people." The party opposed the bill, as did Helen Suzman, the sole woman and Progressive Party member in the House of Assembly.

The debate over the bill constituted a coming-out party for Suzman, who took on the nastiest of her National Party opponents with undisguised gusto. Suzman loved the attention and she loved the challenge. She moved seventeen amendments to the Sabotage Act, and her biggest complaint was that she could not leave the House floor to go to the bathroom for fear of missing one of the votes. One Nationalist complained, "God, Helen, we can think of ten Progs we would rather have here instead of you—why did they pick on you?" To which she replied, "For that very reason."

Helen Suzman was in many ways the National Party's worst nightmare: an articulate Jewish woman with an attitude. Helen Gavronsky's mother died soon after her birth in 1917 and she was raised largely by her aunt. In 1937, at nineteen, she married Mosie Suzman, an eminent Johannesburg physician, a marriage that helped free her from menial household duties even while she was giving birth to and raising two daughters. For eight years she taught economic history at the University of Witwatersrand to students such as Joe Slovo and Eduardo Mondlane, who became leader of the Mozambican liberation movement Frelimo. Then she drifted into politics. She was first elected to Parliament in 1953 on the United Party list from a bluestocking, decidedly Jewish and liberal district in the northern suburbs of Johannesburg. After six years of watching the party shrink in size and stature and turn increasingly rightward in a vain effort to staunch the hemorrhaging of support to the Nats, Suzman and her liberal allies walked out. When her colleagues were all defeated for reelection in 1961, she handled her sudden isolation with a sense of bravado and defiance that became her political trademark.

Suzman was appalled by apartheid; it violated not only her belief in human rights but her sense of aesthetics. She scorned the grim, under-educated Afrikaner politicians she met in Parliament with their cheap suits and bad haircuts—as a master race they were a joke. And the human cost of their brutal and ridiculous policies was beyond calculation. They were either bullies or idiots, Helen believed, and many were both. "You might try going to Soweto yourself one day," she told one National Party mandarin who had criticized her forays into the black townships. "But disguise yourself—go as a human being."

Suzman expressed sympathy and respect for black leaders like Nelson Mandela who turned to violence because they saw no other path for dissent. "Long before the final chapter of the struggle which is going on in this country is written a great number of other people who were formerly peace-loving people will be driven to desperate acts of reckless-ness," she told the House.

"Is that a threat?" demanded one Nationalist member.

"It is not a threat," she replied. "I am in no position to threaten, but I am in a position to warn."

The spiral of violence between the government and its opponents left Suzman and her fellow white liberals in an impossible position. They despised the regime, yet they were not prepared to take up arms against it or condone violence. They were especially critical of white communists who stood alongside Mandela. Suzman feared they had their own secret agenda and were manipulating the movement. Worse, perhaps, they seemed at times like bungling amateurs.

The comrades were critical of Suzman as well, accusing her and her liberal colleagues of being elitist, armchair opponents of apartheid who never got their hands dirty or saw the inside of a jail cell. By participating in whites-only elections and accepting a seat in Parliament, they argued, Suzman was legitimizing a regime she claimed to loathe. Liberals simply had no answer to the fact that the government could not be changed or toppled by democratic means. The handful, like Peter Brown and Patrick Duncan, who were willing take a firm stand alongside blacks found themselves banned and silenced. Liberals also suffered from a deep philosophical split between those who wanted to preserve white control with a qualified franchise that would only permit blacks with education and property to participate, and those who held to the principle of universal suffrage even if it meant submitting to black majority rule.

In the end liberals were too weak and divided to ever mount a coherent challenge to the Nats. "Liberalism in South Africa had never come to terms with its circumstances," wrote Ronald Segal. "It had taught where it should have learned, petitioned where it should have campaigned, protested where instead it should have resisted." Liberals, he added, "read Exodus as though Pharaoh's heart had softened at the eloquence of Moses."

Despite Suzman's spirited and eloquent opposition, the Sabotage Act passed easily. Both sides understood that the measure was more than a new law. It amounted to legal suspension of due process, and as such, was a crucial milestone on the road to a police state.

Within weeks of its passage, Vorster published the names of 437 alleged communists for special restrictions. He placed activists such as Ahmed Kathrada and Rica Hodgson under twelve-hour daily house arrest and Jack Hodgson and Michael Harmel under twenty-four-hour restriction. Albert Luthuli, Walter Sisulu and Helen Joseph, a longtime liberal activist, were also restricted. Luthuli protested his ban, but no one could read what he had to say because the new act prohibited any publication or broadcast of his words. He was never to speak in public again.

Two members of Special Branch showed up at 154 Regent Street on a warm October night with two official notices for Rusty. The first prohibited him from writing, compiling, editing or contributing in any way to any publication. The second set the terms of his twelve-hour daily house arrest. He was allowed no visitors whatsoever, was confined to Johannesburg, and was forbidden to enter any black township or factory and to communicate with any other listed person except for Hilda. The police returned twice in two days to check up on him. Their second visit occurred on an evening when Toni had invited two friends to the house—Johnny, a young doctor, and Lorna, a friend from Toni's college. So as not to violate Rusty's banning order, the guests ate dinner in the living room with Toni and Hilda, while Rusty and the children ate in the kitchen.

This arrangement did not suit the three detectives who barged in just after the family had finished eating. They took the names and addresses of Toni's friends and ordered them to leave. When Johnny could not produce his identity card, the detectives drove him to the hospital where he worked to establish his identity. When Toni objected to their treatment of her friends—"you haven't served *me* with any notice prohibiting *me* from having visitors"—they warned her that they would be back. Not surprisingly, her two friends never came to visit again.

Hilda began receiving threatening phone calls at night, and she became uneasy about their old habit of leaving the front door open in summer. Soon they started closing and locking it. Hilda bought bamboo curtains to cover the ribbed glass on both sides of the door. The continuous stream of guests that they once knew dried up to a trickle. Soon no visitors came at all. The house grew quiet; Hilda writes that she and Rusty felt like they were becoming their own prison guards.

Freedom was drying up; so was money. Rusty could not visit building sites outside the city limits without written permission in advance from the Chief Magistrate. Each letter warned him that permission was granted "provided you proceed straight there and back in the day time during ordinary office hours. . . . Any further applications for relaxation must please be made timeously and in writing." With such restrictions in place, new architectural contracts were hard to obtain.

As a listed person, Hilda was compelled to quit her morning job working as an editor for *Amateur Photographer*, published by her old friend and comrade Mannie Brown. Her listing notice banned her not

```
81/172690
(2. 14 B)
                                          Republiek  [coat of arms]  Republic
                                          XXX VAN SUID-AFRIKA        XXX OF SOUTH AFRICA

Verw. Nr./Ref. No.   17/33/4 (8).                    KANTOOR VAN DIE—OFFICE OF THE
                                                                 MAGISTRATE,
NAVRAE/ENQUIRIES:                                               JOHANNESBURG.

        Tel. No.   835-8396.                                  7th June 1963.



               Mr. L. Bernstein,
               154 Regent Street,
               Observatory,
               JOHANNESBURG.

               Sir,

                       Permission is hereby granted for you to
               visit the building Avondale Industries Ltd.,
               2 Rand Road, Germiston, on 10th or 11th June,
               1963, in connection with your duties as architect
               provided you proceed straight there and back in the
               day time during ordinary office hours.

                       Any further applications for relaxation
               must please be made timeously and in writing.

                                          Yours faithfully,

                                          [signature]

                                          CHIEF MAGISTRATE.
```

only from working there but even from entering the premises. She could not even return to her previous job writing ad copy at a local advertising agency. Any ads she wrote could not be published.

Rusty's brother Harold and sister-in-law Vera came by the house one evening to plead with him to leave the country. They sat in the living room arguing. What was the point in staying any longer, Harold asked Rusty, when everyone in the security establishment from John Vorster on down was determined to destroy you? It was only a matter of time before the police would lock you up and throw away the key. What could possibly stop them? Rusty conceded that the situation was deteriorating. But he had come too far to turn back. He had spent a lifetime building a movement, and helping persuade others to risk their necks in the cause

81/172690
(Z. 14 8)

/MS

Republiek VAN SUID-AFRIKA   Republic OF SOUTH AFRICA

Verw. Nr./Ref. No. 17/33/4/41

NAVRAE/ENQUIRIES:

Tel. No. 835-8396

KANTOOR VAN DIE — OFFICE OF THE

MAGISTRATE,

JOHANNESBURG.

3 April, 1963.

Mrs. H. Bernstein,
154, Regent Street,
Observatory,
JOHANNESBURG.

Madam,

Your letter of the 14th March, 1963, refers.

In confirmation of the telephonic conversation to-day between yourself and a member of my staff, I have to inform you that the permission applied for cannot be granted. You must sever your connections with the firm Amateur Photography by 2 p.m. to-day.

Yours faithfully,

CHIEF MAGISTRATE

of liberation. How could he desert those people now? Besides, he had invested everything in the cause, had sacrificed his livelihood and even the security of his family. He was sorry, but he could not walk away. Hilda listened but said little. She secretly agreed with Harold and Vera, but she refused to take their side in the argument. This decision was Rusty's. She could not demand that he abandon everything he most cared about.

Two weeks after Walter Sisulu was placed under house arrest, his mother died. According to African custom, Sisulu was supposed to receive bereaved family and friends at his matchbox Soweto home. He made an urgent application to the Chief Magistrate for permission. It was refused. The guests poured in anyway while Sisulu sat in a small back room with the door closed. That evening after the visitors left, while his mother's coffin still sat in the front room, police raided the house and hauled Sisulu to jail for violating his house-arrest order.

Rica Hodgson was allowed out only during daylight hours of the work-week. With Jack banned as well, that left their son Spencer, fifteen, as the only member of the family permitted to leave their flat on nights and weekends. Jack had to quit his wholesalers job and the family fell back on Rica's small salary as a reporter at *New Age*. When that job ended, the Hodgsons followed many of their comrades slipping across the border to Botswana. Justice Minister Vorster was not displeased. He told the press he would be willing to give any of those under house arrest travel documents to leave South Africa "provided they never come back. . . . If they want to go I will definitely not stand in their way. I would be pleased if they left."

Using its new powers, the government outlawed the Congress of Democrats in September 1962. Then the authorities set out to silence the radical press, banning *New Age* two months later. Within days it reappeared as *Spark*, a name the comrades had taken pains to register before the new law took effect. Three months later, the authorities banned *Fighting Talk*. And a few weeks later *Spark* folded because so many of its staff members had been banned it could no longer function.

Ruth First's latest set of banning orders put an abrupt end to her career as a journalist. She received two notices, signed by Vorster. The first one prohibited her from traveling outside the district of Johannesburg, stepping foot in any "Native location," Colored or Asian area or factory, and communicating with any listed person other than Joe. A second prevented her from attending any social or political gathering. Like Hilda, she was no longer allowed to write articles or books, compile material for publication or even enter a newspaper office. The radical publications that Ruth had worked for over a fifteen-year period had also vanished. The noose was tightening.

As Helen Suzman had predicted, John Vorster soon came back to Parliament for yet more police powers. The enemy was still strong, he told the House of Assembly in April 1963. Not the blacks, he insisted, who were as comfortable and secure in the old racial order as children in a stable home with a stern but loving father. "We have to bear in mind that we are not dealing with a Black movement, but we are at all times dealing with movements backed by Whites and where Whites are the propelling force," Vorster declared.

The whites he was talking about were communists, Vorster told Parliament, people who "carry on in a way in which normal people do not carry on." They "do not allow themselves to be bound by any rules whatsoever." In case anyone misunderstood, Vorster named some of those he had in mind, among them: Brian Bunting, editor in chief of *New Age*; Fred Carneson, the Cape Town activist and union organizer; Michael Harmel, one of the party's best-known writers and propagandists; and Moses Kotane, former head of the Communist Party and an ANC leader. But the name at the top of Vorster's list was none other than Lionel Bernstein. "He is one of the people who have been placed under very severe restrictions in Johannesburg," Vorster assured the House.

Because these communists knew no rules, the Justice Minister declared, the government would have to suspend its own set of gentleman's rules in order to deal with them. Police had been fighting with "obsolete weapons—obsolete in the sense that they are bound to rules and laws that have not been designed for a situation such as this." But Vorster had a new and mighty weapon to propose, something that he said would contribute greatly to the battle to "exterminate this cancer in our national life." It was known officially as the General Law Amendment Act of 1963, and the key section was Clause Seventeen. It authorized a police officer to arrest "any person whom he suspects upon reasonable ground of having committed or intending or having intended to commit any offense under the Suppression of Communism Act . . . or the offense of sabotage, or who in his opinion is in possession of any information relating to the commission of any such offense." Clause Seventeen allowed the police to detain the suspect "until such person has *in the opinion of the Commissioner of the South African Police replied satisfactorily to all questions at the said interrogation*, but no such person shall be so detained for more than ninety days on any particular occasion when he is so arrested [author's italics]."

Vorster admitted that he himself was reluctant to propose such a powerful and contentious measure, but he felt he had no choice. "It is absolutely essential that we should have this clause at this stage," he told the House of Assembly. "I realize that I shall probably incur the displeasure of my own colleagues but I am prepared to do so for the sake of the security of the State, which I believe is at stake here."

Displeasure from the opposition was minimal. United Party leader Sir de Villiers Graaff, mindful of the Bashee Bridge murders, supported the measure, albeit, he said, "with great regret." Which left Helen as the sole opponent.

She was quite prepared to stand alone. She rose to speak against the measure, lamenting, as she put it, that the rule of law was being sacrificed "on the altar of the holy cow of apartheid."

"It is quite ironic," she went on, that in the so-called War Against Communism, the government should finally adopt measures "which are indistinguishable from the measures taken in totalitarian or communist countries."

"Go to Ghana and enjoy freedom there!" one Nationalist MP shouted at her. Another virtually accused her of treason. Others hooted and sought to interrupt. Anti-Semitic slurs were flung her way as well. "What does she want?" demanded Vorster when it was his turn to speak again. "Why does she use long sentences and pious words? Why does she not tell us straight out that it is the policy of herself and her party that the Black man should take over in South Africa?"

Helen fought back. Did it not occur to Vorster, she asked, that the sort of interrogation that would take place under ninety-day detention inevitably would "lead to perjured evidence and to disclosures which do not have a grain of truth in them? . . . My basic objection to this clause is that it overrides completely every single fundamental principle of the rule of law."

When it was time to vote, Helen gamely exercised her right to call for a physical division of the House. Members were required to take their seats and then the doors were locked. Those in favor were ordered to stand on one side of the room, those opposed on the other. Every member of the United Party crossed the floor and voted with the government. One hundred sixty-four men stood on one side of the room; Helen stood alone across from them, one defiant woman in a sea of empty green benches.

The government was not alone in seeking to intensify the conflict. A growing number of activists within Umkhonto believed the sabotage campaign was not working. A few toppled pylons and charred offices would never bring South Africa to its senses or its knees, they argued.

With Nelson Mandela's capture, the campaign seemed to lose momentum. Some of the bigger enthusiasts, including Joe Slovo, wanted to move to open guerrilla warfare. He and Govan Mbeki drew up an elaborate plan, using some of the data and concepts Arthur Goldreich had gathered during his secret trips to the East Bloc.

Their six-page proposal was both a sweeping policy statement and an ambitious blueprint. "The white state has thrown overboard every pretense of rule by democratic process," they began. "Armed to the teeth it has presented the people with only one choice and that is its overthrow by force and violence."

In the midst of the biggest security crackdown in South African history, Slovo and Mbeki managed to detect what they called "two important ingredients of a revolutionary situation": disillusionment with constitutional forms of protest and a readiness to follow the lead into a more militant approach. They conceded that "objective military conditions" made the prospect of a general uprising "unlikely." They also acknowledged that the white state was powerfully armed, that the black majority lacked modern weapons or military training and that the country was surrounded by colonial neighbors—Portuguese Mozambique and white-ruled Rhodesia—who would be hostile to any hint of revolt. Nonetheless, they insisted that guerrilla warfare could succeed because of the disaffection of the black masses, South Africa's international isolation and support from other African states and the socialist world. Joe and Govan cited successful guerrilla campaigns in Algeria, Cuba, China, Cyprus and even South Africa itself during the Boer War at the turn of the century. "As in Cuba," they wrote, "the general uprising must be sparked off by organized and well-prepared guerrilla operations during the course of which the masses of the people will be drawn in and armed."

In keeping with the spirit of the venture, Slovo and Mbeki even devised a code name. They called it Operation Mayibuye—"The Return." "The time for small thinking is over," they grandly concluded, "because history leaves us no choice."

No one could accuse the leaders of Umkhonto of small thinking. Their six-page blueprint called for military units totaling 7,000 men in four regional operational areas. It stipulated command structures, military targets, goals and amounts of weaponry and supplies. It also called for 210,000 hand grenades, 48,000 antipersonnel mines, 1,500 timing devices for bombs, 144 tons of ammonium nitrate, 21.6 tons of aluminum powder and 15 tons of black powder. Acting at the High Command's behest, Arthur Goldreich dispatched Denis Goldberg to research what it would take to produce such an arsenal. The young civil engineer came back saying they would need a 40-foot-high furnace, 260,000 detonators, 48,000 batteries, 270 tons of ammonium nitrate, huge amounts of timber for land-mine casings, workshops, machine tools and a workforce of 200 men. It was the kind of midsized factory that would be hard to conceal in the Ruhr Valley, let alone amidst the rolling hills of Rivonia. Goldreich commissioned Goldberg to lease the second, smaller property at Travellyn in nearby Krugersdorp for this purpose.

To Rusty, who was wary of the entire plan, Operation Mayibuye had an eerie *Boy's Own* quality that was typical of Joe and Govan's flamboyant, adventure-loving personalities. What was more alarming was the fervor with which it was embraced by other members of the High Command. They insisted that Operation Mayibuye was realistic. After all, argued Joe, had not Fidel Castro started the Cuban revolution a few years earlier with just a handful of ragtag followers who had at first failed miserably in their assault on the Moncada Barracks? All of Africa was in the process of shedding colonial rule. Who was to say what might spark off the rebellion that would cause white rule in South Africa to crumble? Oliver Tambo and other leaders in exile were pursuing the campaign that Mandela had begun, to raise funds in the newly independent states of black Africa and among sympathetic regimes in the Soviet Bloc as well. Dozens of young black recruits had already left South Africa to receive guerrilla training in China, Ethiopia and Algeria. As far as its supporters were concerned, Operation Mayibuye had already begun.

Rusty agreed that the original sabotage campaign was not developing as they had hoped, but Operation Mayibuye appeared to him to be an exercise in sheer fantasy. He argued that guerrilla warfare had no real chance of succeeding in the current political climate. He and his fellow rebels might have struck fear in some white hearts and they had certainly goaded the government to new police-state measures, but they had not managed to stimulate a spirit of resistance in the vast townships and tribal homelands where most blacks lived. Blacks had many longstanding and bitter grievances; many may have hated the government. But very few seemed inclined to risk open rebellion. And without a sea of popular support to swim in, the guerrillas would be left high and dry, in Rusty's view, easy targets for the police and army to pick off. Bram Fischer and Walter Sisulu agreed with his reservations.

Rusty feared that his comrades living underground had built for themselves a dangerous illusion of safety, that Lilliesleaf had contributed to a childlike naiveté among the activists that could destroy them all. Things had grown far too lax and there were too many pieces of potential evidence lying around. After Mandela's arrest, his comrades did not destroy his incriminating diaries and notebooks, but instead decided to preserve them by burying them in a metal trunk in a coal pit at Lilliesleaf. When Govan Mbeki wrote to the various regional chairmen of the ANC updating them on events, he included a demand that each copy of his letter be destroyed as soon as each chairman had seen it. Yet Mbeki kept the original in his file. He figured he was safe because he was underground. This feeling of invulnerability made for recklessness in personal security and in politics. Fantasy fed upon fantasy. No one who had been living in the real world could have given credence to Joe and Govan's outlandish document, Rusty felt. Yet here they were debating it as if it were something in the realm of fact.

An ugly rift began to develop within the movement over Operation Mayibuye. In one rancorous debate session, Joe and others in Umkhonto's High Command argued that the plan was already operational and implied that those who opposed it lacked the requisite nerve. Rusty and Walter Sisulu argued just as vehemently that the plan could not go forward until it received endorsement from the underground leadership of both the ANC and the Communist Party. When Joe insisted at a party Central Committee meeting in early June that he go abroad to present the case for Operation Mayibuye to the ANC in exile, his comrades reluctantly agreed. Rusty argued that the steering group was being maneuvered into a fait accompli, but he was overruled. Joe had no travel documents—activists like him had long been denied passports—so he slipped over the Bechuanaland border in a car, along with J. B. Marks, a longtime comrade and labor union organizer. The trip was supposed to be a secret, but the South African press soon learned of Joe's departure and published articles about his itinerary. He would undoubtedly face prosecution immediately upon his return.

Soon July rolled around, the heart of the dry but mild South African winter. In the rest of the world, racial barriers were beginning to crumble. In Kenya, black leader Jomo Kenyatta announced that *Uhuru*—independence—would take effect by year's end. In the United States, Martin Luther King and his followers were making preparations for the historic March on Washington that August. But in South Africa, the government was moving in the opposite direction. The Transkei Constitution Act had taken effect in May, and by December the region was to become a semi-autonomous "homeland" for blacks. It was the beginning of an elaborate scheme to create a network of phony bantustans so that blacks could be permanently deprived of political rights inside South Africa itself. The government was at the height of its arrogance. On the Fourth of July the United States embassy in Pretoria held two Independence Day celebrations, one for whites only and the other multiracial. South African officials, insulted by the latter, boycotted both.

Meanwhile, the sabotage campaign went on, as did the seemingly endless succession of meetings and debates. Cautious man that he was, Rusty came to fear meeting at Rivonia. Each time he went, he promised himself it would be the last. His misgivings were heightened in late June after police captured Bartholomew Hlapane, Patrick Mthembu and Brian Somana, three activists who had been to Lilliesleaf and knew what was going on there. Still, Rusty kept going there for meetings, as did Ruth, Walter, Bram, Harold Wolpe and many other leaders and activists, sometimes twice a day, all through June and early July. Finally, Rusty and Ahmed Kathrada laid down an ultimatum. Lilliesleaf was no longer secure, they argued, and they demanded that it be abandoned as a meeting place. Everyone agreed. But the debate over Operation Mayibuye still raged. Both sides needed to sit down and hash it out together, or risk the prospect of a permanent split between the military and political wings of the movement. Lilliesleaf was the only venue where such a meeting could be called on short notice. Bob Hepple, who served as secretary to the group, pleaded with Rusty to come to Lilliesleaf one more time. This will be the last time, Hepple promised.

Which was why Rusty Bernstein, Bob Hepple and their comrades were sitting in the thatched cottage on the afternoon of July 11, when the dry cleaning van carrying Willie van Wyk and the men of Special Branch came down the drive of Lilliesleaf farm.

FOUR

THE ESCAPE

As a prisoner, I always contemplated escape.
Nelson Mandela
Long Walk to Freedom

AnnMarie Wolpe, wife of Harold and mother of Peta, Tessa and twelve-week-old Nicholas, heard about the Rivonia raid the next morning at her cousin's farm in Rustenberg, fifty miles northwest of Johannesburg. It was a calm, lazy Friday, a perfect South African winter's morning, as AnnMarie recalls in her memoir, not a cloud in the sky, the air as clear as crystal, its chill subdued by the hearty winter sun. The kind of day that offered no warning that her world was about to cave in.

The last few weeks had been harrowing and traumatic. AnnMarie's father had died suddenly of an aneurysm. Nicholas had been stricken with pneumonia and had come close to death as well. But after five weeks in the hospital, he was recovering nicely and would be home in a few days. For the first time in months, AnnMarie felt she could relax. She awoke refreshed and looking forward to a long, quiet weekend. After a huge breakfast, the girls wandered outside to enjoy the rustic pleasures of the farm, making their way from the stables to the jam factory.

Left to herself, AnnMarie eased into a comfortable chair and started on the bright red cardigan she was knitting for Peta. Then she switched on the radio for company, coming across a recital of the Chopin études that her mother used to play in the halcyon days when the family still had a grand piano and an accompanying sense of prosperity.

The news bulletin came on the hour. AnnMarie got up to turn off the radio, but she stopped when she heard the news reader announce that security police had raided a Rivonia farm estate the previous evening. Six whites and a number of Bantu had been arrested, including Walter Sisulu, a banned leader of the African National Congress, and the owners of the property, Mr. and Mrs. Arthur Goldreich. Police claimed to have gained a major success in their war against terrorism.

AnnMarie had known about Rivonia for months. She knew Harold spent much of his time there and that he was responsible for drawing up maps of potential sabotage targets for Umkhonto We Sizwe. She understood that if the police had managed to seize the cache of written materials kept by the movement, Harold would be deeply implicated. But she did not know whether he was among those arrested. They had not spoken by phone since Harold had sent her off to Rustenberg the previous afternoon. He had remained behind in the city to work. She knew he often left the office early to attend meetings at the farm. Had he been there when the police arrived?

The first thing AnnMarie did was phone the law office that Harold shared with her older brother, James Kantor. After several busy signals, she reached the receptionist, who told her, "Mr. Wolpe is out of town, but I'll reach Mr. James for you."

Within seconds Jimmy was on the line. "Harold asked me to tell you that he has had to go out of town for a couple of days and will phone you," he told her. "Not to worry. We had some urgent case come up, and he had to go and interview the client." Everything seemed all right.

AnnMarie was concerned that she could not speak to Harold right away. At the same time, she felt relieved to hear her brother's confident, reassuring voice. Jimmy was her rock. She could always count on him to fix things. He knew everyone who was anyone in town—his clients ranged from some of Johannesburg's most notorious hoodlums to Colonel George Klindt, head of the Johannesburg branch of the security police. Whatever happened, Jimmy would be there to protect her and the children.

Harold phoned a few minutes later. He said he was calling from a pay phone, and he asked if she had heard the news. She said yes, and Harold was silent for a moment. Then he said, "I will be in touch with you again today." He hung up, leaving AnnMarie to wonder if the terrible day she had long dreaded had finally arrived.

In the dangerous game of cat and mouse that the Rivonia activists played with the security police, AnnMarie Wolpe was the closest thing to an innocent bystander. Like Arthur Goldreich's wife Hazel, she had made a vow early on to stay out of the movement in order to protect herself and her three children. But she was married to one of the movement's key figures. She loved Harold and she agreed with him that apartheid was evil and that it could not be brought down by any means short of violence. She acquiesced in his increasingly dangerous activities. While Harold told her little, she knew enough about the underground to lock up him—and many of his comrades—for a lifetime. Hazel was already in jail because of her husband Arthur's activities. AnnMarie feared that, for herself as well, passive compliance would no longer provide her with immunity.

AnnMarie and Harold tape-recorded their memories of the Rivonia era several years later, but she waited for nearly three decades to write *The Long Way Home*. Part of the long delay was because of their fear that divulging the story would endanger participants still living in South Africa, and part was because Harold did not trust AnnMarie to put the events in what he felt was a proper Marxist context. When they finally started writing it together, Harold's prose was stiff and inanimate, and eventually he deferred to AnnMarie. Some of Harold's comrades felt the book overestimated AnnMarie's role and downplayed the help that she and Harold received from others. They, after all, were working hard to keep the movement alive and felt strongly that they did what they could at a time of crisis for everyone. But what makes AnnMarie's account so powerful and what rings true is its depiction of her feelings as she sought to rescue her husband from a police state that was ruthlessly determined to destroy him. In the end, her book is not about the movement so much as about the devastating impact of the Rivonia era on the wives and children of the activists.

When Harold Wolpe married AnnMarie Kantor in 1955, his comrades in the Communist Party went into a prolonged state of mourning, or at least it seemed that way to her. They saw AnnMarie as a spoiled, status-conscious Jewish princess from the northern suburbs who would drag Harold down to her bourgeois level. But in their rush to judgment they underestimated her. Yes, she bore many of the trappings of the bourgeoisie, but her life was far from standard. During her childhood, her family had flitted in and out of bankruptcy, thanks to her father's inveterate scheming. Abraham Kantor was a lawyer and a dreamer; he wore spats during winter atop his handmade English shoes and he was a man of big ideas that had an unfortunate tendency to go astray, leaving himself, his wife Polly, and his three children high and dry. After her first year at Wits, AnnMarie had to take out a loan to pay her own way through college—not very typical of suburban middle-class females of that era. Once married to Harold, she would pin back her dark, curly hair, roll up her sleeves, tie her blouse around her small waist and do her own cooking, wallpapering, decorating and furniture stripping. She also made her own clothes. She might complain bitterly at times about her straitened circumstances, but that was AnnMarie: never the stoic, but nonetheless someone who did what had to be done.

She had met Harold at a University of Witwatersrand statistics class, which he managed to fail despite the fact he was easily the most brilliant person in it. Harold Wolpe had been involved in the movement since he was a teenager in mid-1940s Johannesburg. While a sociology student at Wits, he joined the Young Communist League and a coordinating body known as the Progressive Youth Council. He and Ruth First, whom he had known from childhood, became joint delegates to left-wing student conferences held in 1946 in London and Prague. He and Joe Slovo soon became best friends. They shared a love of rugby, cricket, snooker and Marxism. Harold was a fine public speaker and, after he got his law degree, an increasingly important figure in radical politics. He became, in effect, the movement's main lawyer. Anyone who needed legal counsel—and as the years went on and the state tightened down, an increasing number of activists did—turned to him. He once estimated he had handled more than a thousand cases.

Harold was not exactly AnnMarie's ideal man. His mother and father were Jewish immigrants from Lithuania with hopelessly thick accents; AnnMarie's family, by comparison, were sophisticated old-timers. Harold did not know one wine from another or how to order in a restaurant. He had none of the panache of her father or her brother. He was awkward and shy, but he was also gentle, funny and intellectually adept and he pursued her with a single-minded devotion that she found hard to resist. Nonetheless, resist she did for seven years. He was thirty and she twenty-five when they finally married. If it was not the grand passion she had imagined for herself, it was sufficient. Harold was steady and reliable, but not romantic. Too often, he kept his feelings in check. And AnnMarie was easily slighted. On their honeymoon, when AnnMarie said, "It's a beautiful night," and Harold failed to reply, she did not talk to him for two days.

There would be other times when AnnMarie needed Harold but got no response. When, after a miscarriage, she became pregnant with their third child, AnnMarie planned for an abortion but got cold feet. When she turned to Harold for advice, he was not forthcoming. "It's your decision," he told her, "whatever you do is okay." In a sense, Harold was saying it was AnnMarie's body and her right to choose. But AnnMarie wanted more. It was Jimmy who insisted that she keep the baby. That was what she had needed to hear. And so Nicholas came to be born.

From the beginning, AnnMarie resented the hold his comrades had over Harold, yet at the same time she longed for their respect. She felt that Joe and Ruth and the others were constantly judging her and finding her wanting. When so many of the comrades were locked up during the 1960 state of emergency, AnnMarie made a point of keeping contact with their teenaged children, inviting over a group of them for dinner every Friday night. During her visits to Harold in detention, she risked her own freedom by smuggling out messages, and took news of the prison hunger strike to the newspapers. That helped ease some of the tensions between her and the comrades. But the move to armed resistance frightened AnnMarie. She hated violence and she feared her husband and his friends were heading toward disaster. She admired their courage, but was wary of their naiveté. "Harold, this is crazy," she told him. "You're all amateurs and you're sitting ducks. They're going to catch all of you."

Harold's commitment to the movement was total. He would not consider her pleas that they leave the country. The movement was his guiding principle. "You can leave if you feel you must," he told her. "I have to stay." AnnMarie admired his sense of duty to his comrades, but resented when it overran his other responsibilities—to her and the children.

When she was pregnant with Nicholas, her fears and anxieties swelled again. She again raised the possibility of emigrating, begging Harold to reconsider. She was afraid to stay in South Africa—she knew he could be picked up for detention at any time under the new Ninety-Day Act. At the same time, she was afraid to go, to leave her family for cold, damp England where Harold might have trouble getting work, and life would be so much more difficult. And she knew that if she tried to force him to leave, she could lose him altogether.

Finally, Harold decided they should discuss the matter with Bram Fischer, a father figure for Harold as he was for many in the movement. Bram was devoted to the cause, but his avuncular manner and sense of concern made him easy to talk to. He came out to Jimmy's cottage at Hartebeespoort Dam northwest of Johannesburg one Sunday afternoon to see them. Bram did not attempt to minimize the risks or the strain of doing political work, and he acknowledged that things might soon get worse. But he said it was crucial for people like Harold to carry on.

Harold, he noted, was one of the few attorneys willing to take political cases. "He is playing an extremely significant role in the struggle," Bram told AnnMarie. Leaving the country, he argued, was out of the question. Those few whites who sided with the black majority needed to stay and show that they, too, were willing to make sacrifices. Bram implored AnnMarie to put aside thoughts of moving for now. "If the time comes for Harold to leave, the movement will provide every assistance, as it has done with other people," he told her. Coming from Bram, Ann-Marie felt it was a promise she could rely on.

There was one other person AnnMarie knew she could always count on. At thirty-six, Jimmy Kantor was one of Johannesburg's best-known lawyers. He had his own firm, James Kantor & Partners, a seven-room suite of offices on the second floor of the President Assurance House on the corner of Commissioner and Simmonds streets in the heart of downtown, and a finger in every tasty legal pie. He defended some of the city's biggest crooks and he did it with flair. He loved the work, the publicity and the money. Often, when he knew he had an interesting case, he would stop by the pressroom at the courthouse and invite reporters to tag along. He would even interrupt his own cross-examinations to inquire in a stage whisper if there were any questions the reporters wanted him to put to a witness. But Jimmy's real métier was divorce. He usually represented the wife and, at a time when women were second-class citizens at best, he invariably won for his client a decent share of assets. The chief attributes for such work, he boasted, were an ability to negotiate and make outrageous demands without blushing.

Jimmy was a swinger and his flamboyance thrilled and amused his younger sister. He wore his dark brown hair swept back dramatically from his high forehead, and below it, he kept a meticulously trimmed goatee. His suits were made in England and his car came from America—a powder-blue Cadillac convertible that AnnMarie and the children loved to ride in. He kept as pets a large and ill-tempered chameleon and a bull terrier named Greta. He had a grand house on Donaway Road with a large pool, fabulous gardens and a Portuguese chef. He was, perhaps, the first South African to own one of the new Polaroid cameras that were the rage in America and he never seemed to go anywhere without a silk cravat around his neck and a gold cigarette case in his pocket. By his own reckoning he had no use for the "squirrel temperament." He spent every penny he earned. He devoted his weekends to the cottage at Hartebeespoort (a *hartebeest* is a kind of antelope; a *poort* is a gulch or gap in a mountain range). There he bought a boat, learned to water-ski and brought an array of women who looked extremely good in bathing suits. One of the most alluring was Barbara, a part-time model and actress who had two sons from a previous marriage and with whom Jimmy was immediately smitten. They married in 1962. His playboy days were over, or at least severely curtailed.

One of the many things Jimmy did not much care about was politics. He did not like the thuggishness and arrogance of the new Special Branch men he was meeting. As a Jew, he was aware of the anti-Semitism rampant in their ranks. He also was not a racist. When Nelson Mandela became a lawyer, Jimmy was one of the first to greet him and shake his hand. He was not making a political point that day, just following his instincts. But Jimmy was no radical. He worked hard at cultivating the security police, starting at the top with George Klindt himself. Jimmy was content to live within the rules. After all, the system had been very good to him. Why rock the boat?

But Jimmy made one important political error. He invited his brother-in-law Harold to join him as a partner in 1959. It was a natural marriage. Jimmy was a flamboyant front man and legal performer who got lucrative cases and big-name clients, but he was a poor administrator and sloppy researcher. Harold was a skilled lawyer who hated to appear in court. He knew the law and he knew how to keep the books. Harold made it clear that he planned to devote large chunks of his time to defending his political comrades. Jimmy admired Harold's idealism and his integrity. His brother-in-law, he would boast, seemed impervious to the urge to make money. He agreed that Harold could go on defending political cases pro bono, but he insisted that Harold agree not to take unnecessary risks or do anything that would jeopardize Jimmy's position as senior member of the practice.

Was Jimmy naive, or was he a secret sympathizer of the cause? Most likely he was both. In his memoir he insists he had no notion that Harold's work extended to illegal activities or that his partner was involved with Umkhonto We Sizwe. Nor, he writes, did he realize that Harold had used the firm to set up the dummy company and launder the funds that paid for the purchase of Lilliesleaf. "Don't you have any idea what you're signing?" Jimmy's sister Betty asked him one day as he put his name on a series of checks and documents drawn up by Harold and the staff.

"None whatsoever," Jimmy replied with a smile. "That's what I pay other people to do."

At the same time, however, Jimmy was a secret financial contributor to the movement, someone whom Ivan Schermbrucker—a neighbor and friend of Hilda and Rusty Bernstein who helped raised money for the cause—could count on when someone needed to make bail or when relatives of a detainee ran short. Jimmy made a point of knowing things—it was one of his passions and something he was good at, a useful trait for a lawyer on the make, and for a concerned brother whose sister's husband was getting in over his head.

Harold heard about the Rivonia raid early Friday morning from a distraught Molly Fischer, who stopped by his house to show him the report in the Afrikaans newspaper *Die Transvaler*. He immediately understood its import. He went to a coin box and placed a series of phone calls to comrades, warning them that the network was blown. Then he headed to the office and asked Jimmy to step out for a cup of coffee.

At a coffee shop around the corner, Harold told Jimmy of the depth of his involvement with Rivonia. He said the police had discovered enough information to destroy the resistance movement throughout the country, and that it was simply a matter of time before they tied him in with the network. The evidence was irrefutable—there were notes in his handwriting about guerrilla warfare, and a duplicating machine that he had repaired just a few days before was probably overflowing with his fingerprints. "I've got to go into hiding immediately," he told Jimmy.

His only choice, Harold said, was to leave the country. He would try to sneak across the border to the British protectorate of Bechuanaland. AnnMarie and the children could follow later.

All of this shook Jimmy, who knew that once Harold left he could not return without facing imprisonment. Jimmy would lose a law partner whom he relied upon, and his beloved younger sister and her children as well. He was too stunned to say much. Harold told him he would hide out at a friend's flat in Hillbrow for a few days before making a break for the border. Jimmy offered Harold use of the cottage at Hartebeespoort instead. "You'll be all right there," he said.

Harold did not come back to the office. The two men did not shake hands as they parted. Jimmy wished Harold good luck and joked lamely that if he got caught, he should be sure to get himself a good lawyer.

Later that morning, Jimmy got a phone call from Hazel Goldreich's mother, Maimie Berman. She had asked to speak to Harold, who was her son-in-law's lawyer, and had been put through to Jimmy instead. She told him that both her daughter and Arthur had been arrested and that she was worried about their two sons who were still at Lilliesleaf. Police were in control of the property. Jimmy agreed to accompany her to the house to fetch the boys.

Jimmy had never been to Lilliesleaf before. There were a dozen assorted vehicles in the driveway in front of the whitewashed estate house, and the place was swarming with Special Branch officers. Before they could even park the car, Jimmy and Mrs. Berman were approached by a plainclothes detective.

"Don't get out of the car," he ordered Jimmy in Afrikaans. "What do you want?"

Jimmy ignored the order and climbed out. "Who is in charge here?" he demanded.

"Mr. Dirker, sir," was the reply.

"Get him," Jimmy said, "and don't you bloody well speak to me like that again."

While waiting for Dirker, Jimmy spotted Arthur with three burly detectives standing on the lawn perhaps one hundred feet away. Arthur wore a duffel coat and his hair was disheveled. He kept his eyes trained to the ground. He was not handcuffed, but the Special Branch men stood around him. Jimmy surmised that Arthur had been brought back to the estate to witness the police search of the premises, as required by law. He made no acknowledgment of Jimmy's presence, and Jimmy made no attempt to communicate with him.

When Dirker arrived, Jimmy told him that Mrs. Berman had come to fetch her grandsons. Dirker told Mrs. Berman she could enter the house with police supervision, get the boys and pack some clothing for them. Jimmy would have to wait outside. He leaned against the car, chatting with one or two of the detectives whom he knew from his legal work. Jimmy tried to pump them for information on what they had discovered so far, but no one would talk about it. They did let out that it might take a week to sort through all the material they had found.

"What about the animals?" asked Jimmy, who was always solicitous of pets. He was referring to the dogs, chickens and geese he saw wandering the property.

One of the detectives said a guard would attend to the dogs but that no one was concerned about the chickens and geese. Jimmy said he would have Mrs. Berman arrange for someone to come out daily to feed them, and he offered to do it himself that day. Hazel and Arthur's son Nicholas pointed to the outbuilding where the seed was stored, and Jimmy walked over, pulled a bag of feed from the storage area, fed and watered the birds. It only took a few minutes.

All this time Lieutenant Willie van Wyk was standing alongside Arthur Goldreich and focusing on the search he was supervising. He looked up at one point to see Jimmy, whom he knew, marching across the open yard to the outbuilding and feeding the fowl. It looked to van Wyk as if Jimmy was so familiar with the property that he knew exactly where he was going. Clearly, van Wyk surmised, Jimmy had been here before, perhaps many times.

Jimmy's visit to Lilliesleaf had taken less than one hour. But it had lasted long enough to plant a seed of suspicion in van Wyk's mind.

After more phone calls of warning to his comrades, Harold headed to Hartebeespoort. Early the next morning, Bram and Ivan came by to talk about escape plans. They had little help to offer. AnnMarie describes the disheartening scene in her memoir.

Usually the most ebullient of men, Bram looked sad and defeated. The network that he and his fellow activists had carefully constructed was in the process of being smashed and there was nothing he could do. Already the police, working from information they had seized at Rivonia, were starting to make arrests. "We've taken a helluva beating," Bram told Harold. "You must leave the country. There's no way we can protect you underground. Our organizations are in total disarray. You'll have to find your own way out."

The two men left Harold to think through his next move. He had no passport and little cash. His face and his résumé were well known to the police. It would not take long for Special Branch to come knocking.

That evening he drove out to Rustenberg to see AnnMarie and the girls. After a tense dinner with her relatives, she and Harold went into the bedroom to talk. He told her he had to flee the country and that he was on his own.

"This arrest has been absolutely catastrophic," he said. "We don't know what has hit us. They've got our radio transmitter, they've got lists, they've got extraordinarily incriminating documents. They've got the whole fucking works. It's just a matter of time before they start with other arrests. Nobody is able to help me at all. I've been told that I've got to make my own way. Every man for himself."

AnnMarie felt ill. She was shocked to learn how bad things were. She felt angry with Harold for getting himself into this predicament and she felt betrayed by the movement that had promised them its protection.

Harold went back to Johannesburg early the next morning and hid out at the flat of a friend. Within a few minutes, Harold recalled later, Barbara Kantor came by carrying a large cosmetics case. "I've come to give you a new look," she told Harold. "Jimmy thinks you had better change your image."

Over the next two hours, Harold cut off and shaved the beard he had worn since college days. Then Barbara dyed his hair an auburn red. Jimmy arrived later with one hundred rand in cash and a compass. When Harold came back to Rustenberg that evening, he had a new look and a scheme. Mike Michaelis, husband of AnnMarie's cousin, had made plans to take two Norwegian guests on a picnic to a friend's farm in the border region the following day. He proposed that Harold come along as part of the group, then cross into Bechuanaland on foot during lunch. Once safely across, Harold could make his way to Lobatse, a border town where many ANC exiles were camped out.

Only Harold never got there. Mike got lost trying to find the farm and drove straight into a group of black workers led by two white overseers. One of the white men approached the car, identified himself as a border policeman and asked to see everyone's papers. Mike and Harold had none, and so the sergeant ordered them to drive to a nearby police station. There Harold made a crucial mistake. He gave the sergeant at the station a false name and address—something he had always warned his legal clients never to do—but he also told them he was a lawyer from Johannesburg. Soon the police were on the phone with their counterparts in Johannesburg.

By evening the security police had arrived, led by the ubiquitous Sergeant Dirker, who took one look at Harold's dyed hair and clean-shaven face and burst into laughter. "Ag, Herold, it's really you, man. Look at you. You're yellow, man. Trying to run away like this."

AnnMarie found out about Harold's capture when two detectives from Special Branch came to search the farmhouse. Afterward, they agreed to take her to see Harold at the local jail. He looked unwashed, exhausted and despondent. He told her what had happened, and said they were charging him with giving false information and taking him back to Johannesburg to be detained for ninety days. Get hold of Jimmy as soon as possible, he pleaded.

"Say goodbye to your wife, you won't be seeing her for a helluva long time," said one of the officers. And with that, they marched Harold to a patrol car for the ride to Johannesburg.

AnnMarie's relatives suddenly seemed cold and distant. Mike had returned from his day at the police station and had nothing to say to her. AnnMarie's mother and aunt had also arrived at the farm, but huddled with the cousins, leaving AnnMarie on her own. The next morning, she bundled the girls into the car and sped home to Johannesburg. The police had already searched the house, making off with boxes of Harold's books and papers.

The first place she went that afternoon was to Jimmy's law office. She found little sympathy there. "Well, what do you expect?" Jimmy asked her. "If Harold insists on being a bloody communist then he will get into trouble. He should expect to be arrested."

But Jimmy was quickly on the phone to George Klindt. First they spoke about the will that Jimmy was drawing up for him, then Jimmy gently steered the subject to Harold. Klindt confirmed that Harold was being held at Marshall Square under the Ninety-Day Act and that no one, Jimmy included, would be allowed to see him. But AnnMarie could bring food and clean laundry to the jail every day and receive dirty laundry to take home and wash.

That evening, AnnMarie paid her first visit to Marshall Square. She recalls that the streets of downtown Johannesburg felt eerily deserted, with the only sign of life the glowing charcoal braziers of black night watchmen who huddled around them to keep warm. AnnMarie pulled on the old-fashioned bell outside the thick double doors and was greeted by a young Afrikaner warder, who led her inside.

For AnnMarie, Afrikaners were a breed apart. She had known very few of them while growing up, and had come to identify them with the worst crimes and abuses of the apartheid era. She feared and loathed many of them. Such feelings were widespread among South Africa's English-speaking minority—and heartily reciprocated by Afrikaners themselves. English speakers saw Afrikaners as uncouth, lazy and brutal. Apartheid, many English speakers believed, was little more than a design to protect Afrikaners' jobs and social standing by suppressing black aspirations. Afrikaners, in turn, saw the English as disloyal and unreliable hypocrites who benefited from white domination even while deploring it. Many Afrikaners particularly disdained Jews like AnnMarie, a subspecies of the English-speaking community that was markedly liberal, cosmopolitan and, in their view, unreliable.

Now, as AnnMarie sat in a waiting room near the front door, two young Afrikaner warders scrutinized her with undisguised interest while a third took the food basket to Harold. She felt uneasy. But she had no choice but to come here night after night. After all, Harold was in jail, and it was her duty as his wife to help him in any way she could.

Isolated in a small, dank cell with no cot or chair and a bucket for a latrine, Harold reacted to that first basket of food and clean laundry as if it were a gift from heaven. He eagerly wolfed down the homemade meatballs and salad, his first real meal in three days. He felt his spirits begin to lift. The next morning he insisted that he be transferred to a better cell with a bed and toilet facilities. To his amazement, his keepers complied with the demand. But the surprises were just beginning.

There was a hierarchy of discipline in the South African prison system. The prisons in Pretoria, under the watchful eye of the Justice Ministry, were by far the strictest and most regimented. Guards there knew what they were about; they did not have to be told how political detainees were to be treated—that they were to be isolated, harassed, their needs and grievances belittled or ignored. These detainees may have looked harmless, with their wire-rimmed glasses, their soft, fleshy, middle-aged bodies and their endless medications for ulcers and high blood pressure; in fact, they were far more dangerous than common criminals. They could contaminate an entire society with their subversive ideas. But some of the warders at Marshall Square took a much more relaxed approach. They were inclined to treat the detainees as wayward intellectuals who seemed out of place and slightly ridiculous among the youthful hard cases, weekend drunks and prostitutes who occupied most of the cells.

It was to be expected perhaps that the black warders quietly did favors for the detainees out of sympathy and respect—an extra pack of cigarettes here or a smuggled book there. But even the young white Afrikaner warders were known to do a favor or two, bend a rule or close an eye. Besides, there was no love lost between the warders and Special Branch. It was felt among the warders that the security cops were a little too arrogant and pleased with themselves to merit anything other than quiet contempt and the occasional bit of quiet defiance.

That evening, a black warder named Ben came by after dinner, unlocked Harold's cell and gestured for him to come into the corridor. There Harold was stunned to find Arthur Goldreich and three Indian prisoners—Laloo Chiba, Abdullah Jassat and Mosie Moola. Abdullah and Mosie were foot soldiers in Umkhonto and former clients of Harold's who were being held on sabotage charges. The men talked about their arrests. Unlike the white detainees, the Indians had been tortured by the police. Chiba had been especially brutalized—his head placed in a wet burlap sack, his hands and feet wired to a crude battery that his interrogators switched on when he refused to answer questions. The prisoners also talked about their families, but most of all they talked about escaping. Harold and Arthur both knew they would probably be tried with the other Rivonia suspects. Life imprisonment was a likelihood, hanging a possibility. Everyone quickly agreed that they had better take advantage of their time at Marshall Square to plan a break-out. They came up eventually with three possible means of escape: bribing one of the warders, shooting their way out with weapons somehow smuggled into the jail or cutting their way out of their cells by filing through the bars. To pull off any of these, they knew, they would need outside help. But who? Arthur's wife Hazel was in jail; Mosie's wife Zubeidah was seven months pregnant. Bram, Ivan, Hilda and their other comrades were being closely watched by Special Branch. Ann-Marie was their last best hope.

That night, AnnMarie put a newspaper photograph of Nicholas's homecoming from the hospital in Harold's food basket. He put the photo in his shirt pocket as a good-luck charm. But they soon developed other means of communication. When Harold's aunt was killed in a car accident, Jimmy pulled strings and arranged for Harold to be allowed to attend the funeral. AnnMarie tried to get a moment alone with him, but could not get past his two burly Afrikaner police escorts. Then Jimmy intervened again. "Have you been to a Jewish funeral before?" he asked the policemen, launching into a detailed explanation as he walked the guards toward the grave site. That left AnnMarie and Harold alone together just long enough for him to explain a new way of sending and receiving messages.

She rushed home that night from Marshall Square with Harold's dirty laundry and carefully pushed at the narrow seam of one of Harold's handkerchiefs. Out came a note on a small piece of rolled-up toilet paper. She had hoped for some words of affection. Instead, Harold asked for a copy of *Macbeth*.

In her note of reply, AnnMarie wrote that all was well—she and the girls and Nicholas were in good health. She did not write about how miserable she truly felt. AnnMarie had not bargained for a life of smuggling contraband to a husband in jail, of being ostracized by her own family and friends, of being isolated and alone. She felt more than betrayed; she felt orphaned. Her father was dead, and her mother was acting like she did not exist. Even the doctor who had helped save Nicholas's life, a man she respected intensely, seemed horrified and indignant at what Harold had done. No one but Jimmy and Barbara stood by her. At the same time, others were suffering more than she, Harold included. What right had she to complain?

To fill the void in her life and maintain some contact with the written word after she was banned from journalism, Ruth First enrolled in a librarianship course at the University of Witwatersrand. The fast pace and passion of her newspaper work were gone; she was forced to give up reporting on labor conditions, strikes, demonstrations and political campaigns and take up instead book cataloguing and reference materials. Each day she would drive to town and park behind the distinguished brownstone Cullen Library. But after the Rivonia raid, she knew it was just a matter of time until the police would come for her. "Am curiously calm and collected in this shattered life and don't want you to worry," she wrote to Joe in a letter the day after the raid. "It doesn't help. We'll come through and it will be magnificent."

Absence always brought them closer together. Later that month she wrote to him, "I just need to know you're all right, swell, looking after yourself and that you feel for me like at the best of our times, which is really all the time, because we're too good together to let anything interfere. *Anything.*"

They came for Ruth just after lunch on Friday, August 9, two men in hats, tall and gangly in ill-fitting suits with baggy trousers. They stopped her in the corridor between the main reading hall and the library studies room.

"Will you come with us, please," one of them announced. "Colonel Klindt wants to see you."

As Ruth describes it in *117 Days*, they took her first to the Grays, where they booked her and seized her purse. She watched with disgusted fascination as they leafed through every page of her checkbook. Then they drove her to her house in Roosevelt Park, where five detectives spent three hours searching every room. They insisted that her mother wait outside. Ruth could see Tilly circling the house, hovering at the windows like an anxious bird.

The police found little of importance—Ruth had long ago destroyed or buried anything incriminating and the detectives failed to discover the hidden compartment that Rusty Bernstein had built into her desk. But they did come across an old copy of *Fighting Talk* that had sat long overlooked at the bottom of a pile of magazines. Under the new law, possession of even retroactively banned literature could get her a year in jail. She was annoyed at her own carelessness.

Toward the end of the search, Julius arrived with her three daughters. Shawn rushed out to the garden so that Ruth would not see her cry, but Gillian came in and reported directly to her mother. The girls took turns hugging Ruth as the detectives escorted her to the unmarked, American-made car. Before it left, Ruth and Tilly lit into the detectives for seizing the family telephone pad. "It's got the children's friends in it—what on earth do you want this for?" demanded Tilly.

The men made no reply. They drove off to Marshall Square, telephone pad and all, with Ruth sandwiched in front between two burly detectives.

On the way, they started needling her. "If you're interested in your children, why didn't you think of them before?" one of them demanded.

"We know all about you," he added. "You'd be surprised at what we know."

At Marshall Square the warders opened her big red leather suitcase and scrutinized each item inside. They allowed in a set of sheets, a small pillow, a towel and pajamas. But no belt. No necklace. No nail scissors. And they took away Stendhal's *The Charterhouse of Parma*, the one book she had packed. No books, no pencils, no paper.

The cell was dark. Even with the light switched on, it looked to Ruth like the gray insides of a steel trunk.

From the start, Ruth was determined to outwit her interrogators. They wanted information from her, but at the same time she was seeking it from them. They had solitary confinement and all of the brutal tools of state power. All she had was her formidable intellect and an iron will. It was an uneven contest, but a contest all the same.

She did not know why she had been detained. Had they found documents or informers who had placed her at Rivonia? She had gone there almost daily for months. Had she been tailed? Were they planning to charge her? Or were they hoping to compel her to divulge what she knew about her comrades? Either way, she decided early on not to dig in her heels and say nothing, but rather to play them along and try to find out what they knew. She especially wanted to find out how they had learned about Rivonia. Who was responsible for the leak?

Ruth's lead interrogator was Warrant Officer Nel, a lanky man in a drab gray suit, with stringy hair and a toneless, measured voice. He and a sergeant named Smit ushered Ruth into a small room with a table and two chairs. She was offered the better chair, while Nel perched on the edge of a chair with a torn seat and Smit leaned against the wall.

Did she know why she was being detained? Nel asked. He read to her the relevant section, Clause Seventeen of the General Law Amendment Act of 1963. Was she ready to answer questions? he asked.

Ruth was well prepared for this opening session. How could she decide whether to answer, she asked, until she knew what the questions were? But she was being detained to answer questions, Nel replied. But for what purpose? she asked. Were they gathering evidence in order to prosecute her?

Nel would not tell her. Obviously they were fishing for information and had not yet decided what they might do. He reluctantly gave her a small sampling of what they wanted to know. "What were you doing at Rivonia?" "Why did Joe leave the country?" And later: "Why did you hold mixed parties?"

The last one was easy. "To mix," Ruth replied.

"She thinks she's clever," Smit said to Nel. "She's just trying to probe."

And with that, they dispatched her back to her cell. But Ruth had found out something important and frightening. They knew she had been to Rivonia.

Smuggling in *Macbeth* proved easy for AnnMarie. A young, blond-haired Afrikaner warder took the basket with the book underneath the food without comment. "There's something special for him in there," said AnnMarie, not knowing whether the warder was in on the smuggling arrangement or not. Nonetheless, the basket came back with dirty laundry and empty containers from the previous night's meal. The method had worked.

A few nights later Harold sent out another message. The way Ann-Marie recalls it in her book it read like blank verse:

> *Contact D whose cousin A*
> *will give you information*
> *about gas guns we're going*

to try and escape get as much
information as possible about
guns. This must be done quickly.

AnnMarie was stunned. Sneaking in a volume of Shakespeare was one thing, smuggling in weapons was something very different and very dangerous. She surmised that D was Arthur's sister Doreen, and got in touch with her at once. But none of Arthur's contacts were eager to get involved with weapons. AnnMarie got nowhere.

At a Chinese restaurant that night, AnnMarie told Jimmy they needed to talk. Jimmy was beginning to wise up to the danger they were in. "Oh, I've got something for you in the car," he told her. "Come and collect it, otherwise I'm likely to drive off with it."

Once inside the car Jimmy turned on the radio to muffle their conversation. She told him of Harold's plan to escape. "My God, he's crazy," Jimmy replied. "He must stand his trial like a gentleman."

AnnMarie was aghast. Was her brother so naive?

Jimmy raised a possibility that AnnMarie had not even considered. "You know if he escapes, or even tries to do so, you will land up in jail."

Later that night she dropped by Marshall Square with takeout food from the restaurant. This time she was met by Ben, the black warder, who gestured to her to follow him up the stairs. To her amazement, there were Harold and Arthur, lounging quietly in the hallway outside their cells. "You'll have to be quick," said Ben.

AnnMarie told them she had learned that a gas gun would be noisy, dangerous and difficult to use. Harold and Arthur seemed relieved. Instead, Harold asked her to smuggle in steel filing blades so that they could try to cut their way through the bars. The next night she shoved a pair of steel cutters with red handles into the cavity of a roasted chicken, then wrapped the bird in paper. Mimicking the Peter Sellers film *Two Way Stretch*, which she and Harold had once seen, she stuffed twenty tungsten blades into a loaf of French bread. It weighed a ton—AnnMarie had to use both arms to haul the basket into Marshall Square that night. She handed it to Ben, who said not a word. To her amazement, it all reached Harold undisturbed. But to no avail. After hours of filing, Harold and Arthur barely made a dent in the bars. They shoved the blades under a mattress in an empty cell and started thinking about their last alternative—bribing a guard.

The perfect candidate was a young blond Afrikaner warder with a fascination for fast cars and pretty girls. Arnoldus Johannes Greeff was eighteen and had spent only a few months on duty at Marshall Square. He wanted to be a regular cop, but had flunked the police exam and was languishing on the night shift at the jail while waiting for another chance. He spent most of his nights in his small office smoking cigarettes and talking on the phone to girlfriends. Greeff did not understand that the purpose of political detention was to isolate prisoners until they cracked. He let detainees out of their cells so that they could speak to each other. He even brought back food and cigarettes from Jassat's house. In turn, Chiba, Moola and Jassat arranged for friends and relatives to supply him with a suit, shoes and new tie for a court appearance. Harold gave him a tobacco pouch, Arthur a pipe.

Arthur was especially charming to the young warder. Soon he had Greeff taking him out for haircuts. And when Greeff told him he needed one hundred rand in a hurry to pay for damage he had done to a friend's car, Arthur wrote a note to his brother-in-law and sent Greeff around to collect the cash. Consider it a gift, Arthur told him.

This was the guy who would let them escape, Arthur insisted to his comrades. But Chiba refused to allow his fellow prisoners to put Greeff in jeopardy. He had grown closest to Greeff and understood how childlike and vulnerable the warder was. They would have to find another way. But one day Chiba was released unexpectedly. Suddenly the constraints on using Greeff were gone. Time was running out—Harold and Arthur were certain they could be transferred at any time to Pretoria, where conditions were much more restrictive. If they were going to go, they had to go now.

They needed to persuade Greeff to help them and, here again, Ann-Marie proved crucial. Diane Schneier, a friend of hers who was leaving South Africa for the United States, told her she was leaving behind a trust account worth six thousand rand with Jimmy's law firm. Diane said AnnMarie should feel free to use the money to help Harold. Arthur and Harold realized that they could use the money to buy their freedom.

Mosie Moola approached Greeff and offered him two thousand rand to help them escape. It was too dangerous, Greeff replied. Mosie doubled the offer to four thousand. That was the equivalent of eight thousand dollars—enough in those days to buy the new Studebaker Lark that he had been eyeing and have plenty left over. Greeff said yes. He even came up with a plan. He would enter Arthur's cell and Arthur would knock him out with a small iron bar, tie him up and take his keys. By the time Greeff came to, the men would be safely on their way. He could collect the money at Chiba's house in nearby Fordsburg after the escape. No one would ever know. The rest of the money would go to help pay for hiding and transporting the fugitives after the escape. Arthur's family also contributed.

There were other detainees in Marshall Square whom Harold and Arthur wanted to help escape. But Greeff was unwilling to provide the keys to release black detainees held in a different wing of the jail. It was too risky, he said, and would take too long. One person he was willing to consider, however, was Arthur's wife Hazel, who had been held in the women's lockup ever since the Rivonia raid.

Like AnnMarie, Hazel had played the role of loyal wife, and now she was paying the price. Thin to begin with, she had grown so gaunt in prison that she had to hold up her pants with her hands when she walked. She had not seen her two young sons in nearly a month, and she had long ago lost her appetite. But she had told her interrogators absolutely nothing, not even after they showed her evidence of Arthur's alleged infidelities. The warders would allow Hazel to spend long stretches of time in the courtyard, where she could shout up messages to Harold and Arthur. One night, sympathetic warders even arranged for them to meet. That is when Arthur told her of the escape plan and asked her to come.

"But if we escape," Hazel asked, "when will I see the children again?"

Arthur said he did not know. He and Hazel would have to flee across the border. It might take weeks or months before the boys could follow.

"You have to go," Hazel replied. "You could be hanged. But the police have nothing on me. I've got to sit here for however long. I'm not going without the children."

Having obtained the escape money, AnnMarie now needed to find a car. She went to Mannie Brown, a member of the small escape committee that Bram and Hilda had set up. Mannie was a confident, unruffled conspirator, but he could not find an extra car on short notice and neither could AnnMarie. She even went to friends at the *Rand Daily Mail* newspaper building to see if they would help her "borrow" a car from the car park there. It was no good, they told her, because a guard was always on duty. The Wolpes' own Volkswagen would have to serve as the escape vehicle. When AnnMarie met Mannie that Friday night at the Blue Moon, a Greek restaurant, she handed over both the cash and the keys.

Mannie acted unperturbed, but the fact was he was also having trouble locating a place to hide the men when they came out. He made a list of twelve sympathizers who he thought might be willing to help. The first eleven turned him down flat, while the twelfth, a budding writer and playwright named Barney Simon, was out of town. Mannie was sweating. In pleading for their help, he had felt compelled to tell all eleven about the escape plans, and he feared it was just a matter of time before the information would leak to the police.

Nothing happened that first night. Late in the evening, Ivan Schermbrucker showed up at AnnMarie's door to return the keys. "I think we may have to borrow your car again tonight, if that's okay with you," he said matter-of-factly.

On Saturday, August 10, AnnMarie arranged for Tessa and Peta to stay with friends. That afternoon she and Mannie hopped in his car for a drive and a chance to go over the plans again. He could see how nervous she was. At one point he pointed to a block of flats, saying "That's where we'll take them tonight." It was a bald-faced lie, designed to reassure her. But it only made her more anxious.

Later that evening she took another food parcel to Harold. As she waited, hoping to see him, she was confronted by a journalist named Gordon Winter, who worked for the *Sunday Express*. No one in the movement trusted Winter, and with good reason. As he himself later revealed, he was secretly on the payroll of Long Hendrik's security police, one of several pet journalists who wrote what they were told and reported back to Special Branch everything they heard.

"What's doing, AnnMarie?" Gordon asked. "What can you tell me?"

"Oh, Gordon, come on," she nervously replied. "I'd love to know what's happening. My life is just one long run of hauling to and from this lousy place. I'm waiting to collect the dirty washing and get my basket back."

An ordinary housewife. Gordon saw no scoops here. He handed her a copy of the early edition of the next day's *Express* and left abruptly.

Ben the warder returned and led AnnMarie down the usual corridor to where Harold was waiting.

"Listen," he told her, "it's going to be tonight. We've sent out a message on the signals that we'll make. Just please make sure that the car is where it was last night." He gave her a quick hug and then sent her back downstairs. AnnMarie left the jail dazed, the *Sunday Express* still under her arm.

On the way home AnnMarie thought about the consequences of what was about to happen. Who would take care of the children if she were arrested? She knew she could not count on her mother, who was coping with her recent widowhood, or her sister Betty, who lived hundreds of miles away in Natal province. Jimmy and Barbara would surely help, and she was confident that her daughters, Tessa and Peta, would be all right. But she needed to be sure that Nicholas would be cared for. In her memoir she describes arriving home to find Marlene, Nicholas's white live-in nurse, smoking a cigarette in the sitting room. AnnMarie decided she had to take Marlene into her confidence.

"Marlene, I'm going to tell you something, and I have to trust you completely," she said. "Harold's going to escape from jail tonight."

Marlene could have destroyed those plans by phoning the police. Instead, she just laughed. "I don't care what the hell he does," she said. "It makes no difference to me at all. If he wants to escape, that's his business."

But, AnnMarie continued, "you see, I'm likely to be arrested as well. They'll be furious if it happens, and they could take me off to jail. I've got to know whether or not you will go on looking after Nicholas."

Marlene answered immediately. "After all we've been through—you're crazy to think that I would abandon him. He's got nothing to do with his father's politics. I would never leave this child."

And there it was. AnnMarie's husband might be on the run, her family might isolate and ostracize her. But Marlene, who was almost a stranger, would be there.

After AnnMarie left the jail, Harold took up his position on a bench next to his cell window to watch for the car. It arrived just after 8:30 and parked in the same spot as the night before. Harold then switched the cell light off and on four times. That signal meant yes, tonight was the night.

Greeff had agreed to come for them at midnight, and the minutes crawled by with oppressive slowness. At 11:30 he came up to say that things would have to be delayed because three young white men, arrested for drunkenness, had been dumped in his lap. They would have to be tested for blood alcohol levels at the local district surgeon's office and then returned to the jail to be booked. Greeff would have to remain at the front desk to provide immediate entry when they returned. It could take an hour or more, he warned, so just sit tight.

Just after midnight, Harold saw the escape car drive off. He was not alarmed; the plan had called for Mannie to drive the car around the corner and wait another hour or so. But if it took longer than that for Greeff to return, Harold and his partners might find themselves with no means of flight once they got out of the building.

Twelve-thirty came and went. Still no sign of the three young arrestees. The four conspirators began to reconsider their plans. Everyone agreed they could not wait another day—Harold and Arthur might be shipped out at any time. "If we don't go tonight I think we'll never get out," said Arthur.

It was Greeff who came up with the answer. "I'll unlock the back door, let you out, then relock it," he said. That meant there would be no chance to knock Greeff out upstairs in Arthur's cell to give him an alibi, one of the men pointed out.

"I've thought about that," Greeff replied. He said that after they left he would take himself up to Arthur's cell and knock himself out against the bars. "I'll say that Arthur called me into the cell and then knocked me out when my back was turned."

Each of the prisoners knew this was a harebrained scheme that would probably leave Greeff defenseless. But time was running out. It was already ten minutes past one. If they were going, it had to be now.

Greeff led them down a flight of stairs. Someone kicked over a bottle, which clattered down the steel steps like a metal bell. Greeff unlocked a door and they followed him into a storage room. At the other end was another door. It opened onto a courtyard. There were at least a dozen standard-issue police Volkswagens parked there. The cars all seemed empty, but Harold was certain someone would open fire the minute they stepped outside. There was only silence. Each man touched Greeff on the shoulder in gratitude as they headed out the door.

Suddenly Harold pulled up short. An attack of gout gripped his foot. The pain was intense, but he had to keep walking. Freedom was just a few yards away.

The four men slipped silently out the courtyard gate, headed down Main Street and crossed Sauer. They turned onto Fox Street and reached the car they thought was waiting for them. There was no driver and all the doors were locked. They had lost their means of escape.

It was too late to go back, and the streets could be swarming with cops at any minute. During the long days and nights in jail, they had discussed many contingencies and had agreed that in case of trouble, they would break into two groups. Abdullah and Mosie would head for Ferreirastown, an Indian ghetto close to downtown where they both had friends and relatives. Harold and Arthur would set off for Hillbrow, one of the city's most Jewish neighborhoods, where a number of people sympathetic to the movement lived.

Harold had no time to think about his foot as he and Arthur headed north up Rissik Street in the glistening darkness. First they tried the flat of Harold's friend Stan Goldstein. No answer. Either Stan had gone away for the weekend or he was sleeping so soundly he could not hear Harold's knocking. In any case, Harold did not want to risk waking the neighbors.

The other possibility was Barney Simon, whose flat in Highlands was perhaps another half hour's walk. Barney had allowed the comrades to use his place for meetings and Harold knew Barney kept a key on the ledge above the front door. The streets were still silent. No police sirens. But soon they were traversing Harrow Road, which was too main a thoroughfare to remain empty for long. The pain in Harold's foot was excruciating. He and Arthur turned off onto a darkened side street, and walked toward a double-parked Renault sedan. Suddenly its rear lights came on and someone started the engine. Harold took a quick peek at the driver. "I don't believe it!" he cried. "It's bloody Barney!"

Barney Simon was just as amazed. As the two men piled into the car, he told them he had spent the evening at a girlfriend's house and was on his way home when he was overcome by the urge to urinate. He had pulled over and gone in the bushes. Barney's weak bladder had come to Harold and Arthur's rescue. He took them to his flat.

Willie van Wyk was sound asleep at home when the phone rang. He got dressed and rushed to Marshall Square, where he was given a full account by the duty sergeant. Wolpe and Goldreich, two of the biggest fish in van Wyk's tank, were gone. They and two other detainees had attacked and overcome a young constable, knocked him unconscious and stolen his keys. "Apparently this was the weapon they used," said the sergeant, producing a small piece of pig iron. Goldreich had bound Greeff's hands with a nylon cord and left him lying on the floor of his cell. When Greeff came to, he had freed his hands by using broken glass from one of Goldreich's eyeglasses and sounded the alarm.

Van Wyk gripped the iron piece skeptically. It weighed no more than a few ounces. He asked to see Greeff. He invited the nervous young constable to the police cafeteria. It took just one cup of coffee to get the truth.

"I was in bad trouble, sir," Greeff told van Wyk. "I'd borrowed a friend's car and smashed it up. The repairs came to a hundred rand and he was pressing me for the money. I hadn't got it and I was getting desperate."

The detainees had been so understanding. They had done Greeff so many small favors. Helping them in return just seemed natural. But they had duped him, taken advantage and left him holding the bag. He said he had allowed in Mrs. Wolpe late that night to talk to her husband. Later, after she left, he had received a phone call from a woman telling him that the money was ready and that he should go through with the job. He believed it was Mrs. Wolpe who made the call. Half an hour later, Greeff had let the prisoners out the back door.

Van Wyk had heard enough. He ordered two teams of men to go immediately and arrest Mrs. Zubeidah Moola and Mrs. Harold Wolpe.

AnnMarie was feeding Nicholas from a bottle a little after seven that morning when Marlene came in the bedroom, followed by a young man with a large mustache. "Get your clothes on, Mrs. Wolpe, and come with us," he said.

Marlene came over and took Nicholas in her arms. "They've got away," she whispered.

AnnMarie threw on a gray shift dress, swallowed a Valium and stuffed a pack of cigarettes into her purse. She was terrified, but she knew she had to act nonchalant. She was shoveled into a back seat between two detectives. Two more sat in front. One of them launched into a nonstop tirade, cursing her and her terrorist husband. He said they knew she had organized Harold and Arthur's escape and that she had ruined the life of young Greeff. She insisted she knew nothing, but all of her disclaimers just seemed to make him angrier.

He knew she had been out all night. She had been seen in the evening at the jail, and police had found a copy of the *Sunday Express* on the back seat of her car. The newspaper did not hit the newsstands until 2 a.m. The detective cut off AnnMarie's attempt to explain. "You know where they are, and you're going to tell us sooner or later," he declared. AnnMarie's heart was racing.

Usually on a Sunday morning, the seventh-floor offices of the Grays, Johannesburg headquarters of the security police, were as silent as a cemetery. This morning they were throbbing with nervous activity. Policemen were rushing up and down corridors. Teletype machines rattled incessantly and phones rang. Officers barked commands. No one dared not look busy even though they had few ideas where to begin their manhunt for South Africa's most wanted fugitives.

Two men started AnnMarie's interrogation, taking turns yelling at her in English and Afrikaans. "We know exactly what you have done. Greeff has told us everything. You organized the whole thing."

Then they awkwardly switched tactics, lowering the volume and pleading with her to be sensible. "All you have to do is tell us, and you can go home again," said one. But what they really wanted to know— where Harold and Arthur were hiding—AnnMarie could not tell them.

Her interrogators cajoled, threatened, bullied and soothed her. Nothing seemed to work. Then two other men came into the room. One of them went to close the curtains, while the other stood before her and glared.

His name was Lieutenant T. J. Swanepoel and he had a reputation as the most brutal of Hendrik van den Bergh's wolf pack. AnnMarie could not stop looking at him. His crew-cut head and bulldog face, bright red in color, sat atop a thick neck. His beefy arms bulged from his short-sleeved shirt. His fingers seemed like blunt stumps. His nails were dirty. "I want to deal with her myself," he said in Afrikaans.

AnnMarie was smoking a cigarette when he came in. "Put out that bloody fag!" he screamed.

She burned her fingers as she nervously stubbed it out. "Look at me when I am speaking to you!" he demanded. She could see the thick swelling of veins in his forehead and saliva forming in the corners of his mouth. He fired off jagged bursts of obscenities. Then he took the arms of her chair and shook it as he talked. His partner, who looked like a junior version of him, ringed his hands around AnnMarie's throat and left them poised within inches of her skin. But they did not touch her. The old rules—no violence to white women—still applied.

Then as suddenly as they had arrived, they stormed out of the room. Swanepoel had one parting shot for her. "I'm going to get them. I'm going to fucking kill them."

The next appearance was by Willie van Wyk, who was as debonair and friendly as Swanepoel was crude and hostile. AnnMarie had seen van Wyk on several police raids, and she knew that people like Joe and Ruth considered him a decent man. She started to cry, then caught herself. "Why do you have to have people like that in the police force?" she asked plaintively.

"Well, the police force is like a marriage," he replied. "You get all types. Some are good, some are bad; you get the rough with the smooth all mixed up together."

"If you let those men near me again, I'll jump out of the window," she told him.

Van Wyk granted her request to call home and check on Nicholas. "Listen, Marlene," she told her nanny. "For Christ's sake make sure Jimmy checks with the police tomorrow to see if I am still alive. I'm frightened they may do something terrible to me."

AnnMarie was exhausted. She was frightened by the police and she was angry at Harold and his comrades. She decided it could do no harm to admit this to van Wyk. "You know, I am really very angry with Harold for landing me in this mess," she told him. "All I want to do is look after my children, and now here I am being threatened by such horrible people."

She went on to explain how she had received a message from Harold by phone one day and had smuggled some blades to him. Other than that, she claimed, she knew nothing. Whether van Wyk believed her or not she could not tell.

Eventually six more policemen came in. One of them was a good-looking, muscular man with luminous green eyes. They made her tell her story again. The man stared at her. When they made eye contact, AnnMarie felt as if he could see into her mind. "She's a bloody good actress," he finally said. "She knows absolutely everything. Don't believe a word she says."

It was 9 p.m. Fourteen hours had passed since AnnMarie's arrest, Harold and Arthur were still on the loose and the police had had enough. They stood up and prepared to bundle her off to Marshall Square for the night. Harold's former prison was about to become her own. Before she was taken away, a number of detectives came into the room. One of them pulled open a file cabinet drawer. To her surprise it was filled with handguns. Each man took one.

"Those guys are going out to hunt down and shoot those two bastards," one of her interrogators told AnnMarie. "We're sorry for you, Mrs. Wolpe, because you're going to be a widow by tomorrow morning."

Hilda Bernstein and Bram Fischer had both opposed the escape from the moment it was proposed. "They're crazy and they'll get caught," Hilda said to Ivan Schermbrucker. "We've got to discourage them."

Still, the escape's success elated those activists still on the loose. It was the first good news they had had in months. But there was much to be done. Jassat and Moola were no problem. They had their own friends and contacts among the close-knit Indian community who would protect them and see them safely across the border. Indians were a natural constituency for antigovernment activists; even the most conservative members of the community felt the sting and humiliation of the second-class citizenship apartheid imposed upon them. Besides, the police were only searching for Jassat and Moola halfheartedly. It was the white "masterminds" the state was really after. And with their networks crushed, it would be no easy task for Hilda and the other members of the escape committee to hide Harold and Arthur and ferry them safely from South Africa.

As a first step, Mannie drove the two fugitives from Barney Simon's flat to a house in the nearby suburb of Norwood, with Arthur crouched low in the front passenger seat and Harold crammed against the floor in the back. But they soon had to be moved again and the prospects were few. Hilda was forced to take a risk. She went to see Jimmy at his office.

Suspecting that the place was bugged, Hilda launched into a long-winded explanation of a legal problem she was supposedly having with a neighbor. While she spoke, she reached over, took a slip of paper off Jimmy's desk and started writing furiously. When she finished, she handed him the paper.

Jimmy read: "*We have Harold and Arthur, but must move them. They are not safe. Can you or any other members of the family find a place?*"

Jimmy looked up. Hilda, still chattering about her neighbor, motioned for him to reply on the same paper. He wrote: "*I don't know of any place, but will try to think of something.*"

Hilda droned on, while she kept writing: "*How soon?*"

Jimmy wrote: "*Come tomorrow morning.*" If they needed money, Jimmy added, he could make cash available.

As she got ready to leave, Hilda lit a match and burned the note in an ashtray. Then she crushed the remains into a fine powder. With a wan, apologetic smile, she got up and said goodbye. She had left behind no evidence, but something even more dangerous. Jimmy, a man with no personal involvement in the movement, now knew that Hilda was one of the prime conspirators in the escape.

The first Sunday after the escape was pandemonium inside Marshall Square. Three warders swung open Ruth First's cell door early in the morning and stared at her in disbelief, as if surprised to see she was still there. She heard prolonged shouting and the repeated banging of doors overhead. No one told her what had happened, but she knew. She had known before her arrest that Harold, Arthur and others were planning to escape. That evening she caught a brief glimpse of Ann-Marie in a nearby cell looking haggard and pale. AnnMarie was complaining to the wardress that she was about to have her period and needed cotton wool. Ruth dispatched some from her own supply. She called out to AnnMarie but got no reply. Still, if AnnMarie was under arrest, Ruth reasoned, then the escape must have succeeded. She quietly celebrated.

Jimmy Kantor came up with one possible hideout that Hilda and Bram rejected as unsafe. Instead, they moved Harold and Arthur to a cottage in the remote and exclusive suburb of Mountain View, a property owned by Leon and Maureen Kreel, a young couple who sympathized with the movement. Both Denis Goldberg and Ahmed Kathrada had stayed there previously, and both were now in custody. By any rule of underground work, the cottage should have been declared off-limits for further use. But Hilda was desperate. The escapees could not remain in a flat in the middle of town—too many photos of them had appeared in the newspapers. Besides, the comrades had yet to realize the destructive impact that ninety days of isolation would have in turning even the most loyal of members into quivering informants.

Harold and Arthur hid for eight days at the cottage. They spent the time playing chess, reading newspapers and smoking cigarettes. During the day they could not flush the toilets, run the taps or even talk to each other for fear of alerting the black caretakers of the estate or the Kreels' little girl, who arrived home from school at two each afternoon. At night, they could turn on a light, chat and bathe. The Kreels would have them over for drinks, along with Maureen's sister Minnie and her husband Ralph Sepel, who were committed activists. Still, the days were painfully boring and nerve-wracking.

Hilda and Bram went to see Harold and Arthur one night. She put on a long skirt and old-fashioned hat, padded her bra and her shoulders and carried a string bag with parcels, turning herself into an elderly woman. She drove her car to another suburb, parked and boarded a tram and rode halfway back to her own house, got off and walked around the corner to Bram's waiting car.

"Did you recognize me?" she asked.

"As soon as you turned the corner," he said with a smile.

On the evening of the eighth night, Mannie returned to the cottage. He told Harold and Arthur he had bought a red Ford Fairlane to transport them to Swaziland. There would almost certainly be police checkpoints along the way. Mannie brought a bag of women's clothes for them to disguise themselves. Harold and Arthur spent an hour going through the wardrobe, trying on clothes and prancing around, driving Mannie, the Kreels and the Sepels to fits of laughter. It was hilarious, but hopeless. Neither man could begin to pass for a woman.

Their only alternative was to stow away in the roomy Ford trunk for the six-hour drive. A young man named Crawford would be behind the wheel. Mannie said he could be trusted. They left after midnight. It was two hundred thirty miles to the Swazi border. Harold and Arthur lay on blankets in the trunk, while Crawford carried on a monologue to let them know where they were and how far they had to go. Amazingly, they did not come across a single checkpoint. Crawford let them out at a remote border area, where they were met by a guide arranged by Mannie.*

The guide steered Harold and Arthur across the border to St. Michael's Mission School, which was run by the Reverend Charles Hooper, an ardent foe of apartheid who had fled South Africa himself three years earlier. Hooper hid them until Tuesday, August 27, then put them aboard a small plane that flew them back across South African territory to Lobatse, Bechuanaland. He dressed them in priests' garb and introduced them to the pilot as two visiting English missionaries. It was an anxious flight. The plane passed directly over Pretoria. Harold and Arthur both carried pocketknives, and they vowed to each other to use them in case the pilot suddenly tried to land. Their faces were in all the newspapers and there was a ten-thousand-rand reward on each of their heads. But the pilot flew on.

Once safely in Lobatse, Harold and Arthur revealed their true identities to the British officer in charge at the airport and demanded asylum. The official was outraged that they were wearing clerical collars, but he agreed to their asylum request, provided they left the area as soon as possible. Later in the day they were reunited with Jack and Rica Hodgson in town, and by midnight they were on their way to Francistown to a quiet rendezvous with an East African Airways Dakota passenger plane that was due to take them and other political refugees to Tanzania.

Only it did not quite work out that way. Within a few hours of Harold and Arthur's arrival, a large pack of South African and foreign journalists descended on Francistown looking for them. The celebrity escapees tried to hide in their hotel room, but Francistown was no great metropolis and the pack was soon camped out in the lobby and the bar. No doubt the South African government and its agents knew exactly where the escapees were as well, as did white farmers living in the area,

---

*It turned out that Harold and Arthur had left Mountain View just in time. A few days later the police, working on a tip, raided the cottage. They found plenty of incriminating evidence, but no fugitives. Later they also found the Fairlane and traced it back to the used-car dealer who had sold it to Mannie Brown. Soon after, Mannie fled to England.

most of whom were loyal South African citizens. Cross-border kidnappings were not uncommon. Still, Arthur could not help goading the South African police when *Rand Daily Mail* journalist Allister Sparks chatted with him at the hotel bar. "At no time did the police get anywhere near us," Arthur told Sparks. "All those police statements about the net closing in were so much nonsense."

Perhaps so, but South Africa had one more unpleasant surprise in store for Harold and Arthur. They were awakened at five the next morning to learn that the Dakota had been gutted by fire on the Francistown runway. Someone—and it was obvious who—did not want them to leave. The local chief of police insisted that they spend the next night as his guest in jail, a much safer proposition than the hotel. There they could wait for East African Airways to try again.

But the airline and its insurers were not keen to risk another plane. None arrived the next day, nor the day after, nor the day after that. Harold and Arthur were beginning to panic. It could only be a matter of time before the South African government made another bid for them. If kidnaping proved too difficult, assassination might be easier. Few voices would be raised in protest back in South Africa, where Harold and Arthur had been portrayed as rabidly dangerous radicals working to foment a military invasion of the country.

Then an NBC correspondent named George Clay came to the rescue. Clay, a South African by birth who was based in Dar es Salaam, said the network would pay for a charter flight north provided that Harold and Arthur gave NBC an exclusive interview once they reached safety. The next morning they took off in a small chartered craft from Palapye, a dirt airstrip about one hundred miles south of Francistown. By nightfall they were in Elisabethville, in the United Nations-controlled area of the Congo. Two days later they landed in Mbeya in western Tanzania, where Clay met them with a camera crew. Clay got his interview, Harold and Arthur their freedom. In the chest pocket of Harold's shirt was the article on Nicholas. He had kept it as a good-luck charm throughout his monthlong odyssey. Harold, despite his single-mindedness, had not forgotten the family he had left behind.

Much to her relief, AnnMarie was able to follow the saga of Harold and Arthur's escape from home. The authorities let her go after a night and a day in Marshall Square. They had run out of questions for the time being, and meanwhile, Jimmy had filed a writ in court alleging she had been beaten. He based the allegation on a frantic phone call from Marlene, who had misunderstood what AnnMarie had told her during their own phone call earlier. When Jimmy picked up AnnMarie on Monday evening, she was tired and filthy and ready for a drink, a bath and a night in her own bed. But Jimmy was furious at the police, and he insisted on stopping at the Grays to file a formal complaint. She waited in the car while he stormed in and confronted the night desk man with a string of obscenities. It was a performance he would later come to regret.

Jimmy then took AnnMarie to his house. First to arrive were a reporter and photographer from the *Rand Daily Mail*, who wanted a story on her treatment in detention. Soon after they left, Bram and Molly stopped by. They were jubilant over the escape. "We've beaten them for the first time in ages," said Bram. "The townships have gone wild. People are absolutely thrilled."

AnnMarie did not know what to say. Bram and Molly did not seem to hear her when she talked about how horrible jail was. Again she got the message from Harold's comrades that her personal plight was unimportant. What mattered was the movement.

Although she was free, AnnMarie did not feel safe. There were hate phone calls. One female caller described herself as a nurse at Florence Nightingale Hospital, where Nicholas had been treated, and asked after the baby's condition. When AnnMarie told her how well Nicholas was doing and what a miracle it was, the caller suddenly changed her tone. "It's a pity he has such vicious parents," she said. "For my part, I think he would have been better dead."

A few days later, AnnMarie's sister Betty came by with more bad news. Jimmy had been arrested. AnnMarie's last safe haven, the person she relied on most of all, was now in the clutches of the police. If they could not have Harold, they would take another member of his family. Jimmy was their hostage. AnnMarie felt frightened and she felt guilty.

A few days later, Justice Minister John Vorster waxed philosophical about the escape. "There can be no doubt that two of the big fishes have got away, but some very important ones still remain in our net," he told reporters. The prosecution of the others would proceed. "It will be more or less like producing *Hamlet* without the Prince—but the show will go on just the same."

FIVE

NOTES FROM UNDERGROUND

Pain is truth; all else is subject to doubt.
J. M. Coetzee
Waiting for the Barbarians

The police escort deposited James Kantor at Pretoria Local prison jail at 2:45 a.m. He was quickly processed and dispatched to a cell after the warders had taken away his belt, shoes and wristwatch. Inside the cold cubicle, he huddled under matted blankets and fell into a restless and troubled sleep, only to be jarred awake a few hours later by a bell that served as the wake-up call for prisoners. It was still dark outside, with only the first tentative pale fingers of predawn light poking through.

Jimmy was not a skilled writer and the one-dimensional characters and wooden dialogue in his memoir, *A Healthy Grave*, betray him at times. But when he writes about his experience in prison, and especially about his feelings as the walls begin to enclose his spirit, his prose becomes powerful and credible. We join him in his cell.

Breakfast was served on a metal tray shoved under the cell door. It consisted of a pasty white corn porridge with a tablespoon of milk on top, and a small hard loaf of coarse brown bread known in prison as *kat-kop*—"cat's head." The bread was dry as sand and the porridge revolting. There was coffee in a stained enamel mug, but it was cold and greasy. Jimmy, a man long accustomed to rather finer comforts, shoved the tray back toward the door and contemplated his first day in captivity. Many of his clients were experienced jailbirds and over the years he had gleaned lots of advice on how to deal with confinement. The main thing, they all had told him, was to find ways to fill the time so that you don't drive yourself crazy.

He proceeded to lay out a regimen. He carefully made his bed, pulling taut each corner and carefully smoothing out the wrinkles, just as he had learned to do in the air force eighteen years earlier. He neatly refolded and packed the clothing he had been allowed to bring in with him. Then he took the measure of the bleak rectangular cell. It was four paces in length and two paces wide. The door was on one end, with a filthy wire-mesh window on the other. Not very palatial, but Jimmy was not planning to be here long. Surely the police would come to their senses and let him go within a few hours or a few days at the most. Meanwhile, he craved a cigarette and wrestled with a sudden urge to pee. Just as he was wondering what to do about both these needs, a warder named du Preez came to the cell door.

Du Preez took Jimmy to the exercise yard, where he was allowed to use the toilet and to have a cigarette. Then he had half an hour to troop up and down the yard. Two other detainees joined him: Bob Hepple, a fellow member of the bar, and Rusty Bernstein. Du Preez had warned Jimmy not to speak to either of them, but as they passed each other in the yard, they whispered a few words. "Hi, Bob, how are you?" Jimmy asked softly. Hepple gave no indication of having heard him, but the next time they filed past each other he replied, "Fine, thanks, Jimmy, considering that I've been here six weeks already." Before they could say much more, du Preez blew his whistle and ordered everyone to fall in. Exercise time was over.

On the way back to the cell, Jimmy, an inveterate clock watcher, asked du Preez for the time.

"What's the hurry?" the warder replied with a smirk. "You got a train to catch?"

Back in the cell, du Preez presented Jimmy a handful of filthy rags and a large dollop of black shoe polish smeared on a scrap of brown paper bag. "See that this place is kept clean," he commanded.

Polishing the chilly concrete floor was hard work, but it gave Jimmy something to concentrate on. Soon enough, lunch arrived. This time the tin tray bore one lump of steaming mashed potatoes and a second of cold, soggy boiled beet. A third, smaller gray lump appeared to be minced fish—head, skin, bones and all. On the side of the tray was another *kat-kop*, at least as hard and dry as the one from this morning. Jimmy was so hungry he devoured the mashed potatoes, but the beet and the fish were beyond contemplation. Instead, he chipped away at the hard bread loaf. He capped off the meal with another half hour or so of pacing, then sat down on his cot and immediately dozed off.

He had no idea how long he had been asleep when another guard appeared at the cell door to take him back to the exercise yard for another trip to the toilet. Jimmy could not see the warder's wristwatch at first, but estimated the time was probably around 4 p.m. The first day seemed to be moving along well.

After he flushed, Jimmy lined up behind the warder. Now he could notice the face of the guard's wristwatch. It read eleven-forty.

"Is that the right time?" Jimmy asked.

"Yes, why?"

"But it can't be. We've had lunch already."

"Lunch is at ten forty-five and supper at three."

Jimmy felt crushed. He had thought he was coping beautifully, gliding swiftly and smoothly toward the end of his first day of captivity, only to discover he was not even halfway there. Time was not just dragging; it seemed to have stopped altogether, leaving him stranded in a world with no beginning and no end. Jimmy suddenly felt nauseous. The cell was no longer a temporary inconvenience in a busy man's life. It was a trap, a monstrous hole from which there was no escape. Between dinner at 3 p.m. and breakfast the next morning at six, Jimmy faced fifteen hours of isolation and silence.

There was one possible way out. Although Jimmy was innocent of direct involvement in the escape of Harold Wolpe and Arthur Goldreich, he had incriminating knowledge. He knew of AnnMarie's role, of course, but he could never betray his younger sister, no matter how bitter he might feel toward her reckless husband. But Jimmy also knew that Hilda Bernstein was involved. The authorities wanted names of people they could arrest and squeeze, networks they could smash. They had been infuriated by the successful escape and were eager to find scapegoats. If Jimmy gave them Hilda, he could walk free. And who could blame him? Harold and Hilda and their comrades were rank amateurs whose dangerous games could destroy Jimmy's life as well as their own. He felt that they had always looked down their noses at liberals like himself. He owed them nothing. They had made their choice. Now he would have to make his.

Hilda had learned of Jimmy's arrest the same day it happened, and she knew she was vulnerable. But she had other, more pressing problems to cope with. The underground structure had been decimated by the Rivonia raid and subsequent arrests. Bram took over as chairman and Hilda became secretary of what was left of the Communist Party. They worked at rebuilding the Umkhonto High Command in Johannesburg, recruiting a new group of leaders—Mac Maharaj, Dave Kitson and Wilton Mkwayi, among them—from the movement's depleted ranks, while seeking also to reestablish links to other units in Cape Town, Port Elizabeth and Durban, all of which were under siege by the security police. Hilda also set up a new communications link with her comrades in exile in London, who attempted to smuggle money into the country to keep the network alive. Her main contact there was the longtime activist Vela Pillay, who had fled South Africa in 1960. In her written messages to him she used a secret code involving the Graham Greene novel *Ministry of Fear*. The code consisted strictly of numbers—page, line and word from the Penguin paperback edition. It was laborious and painfully dull work.

She could hardly have chosen a more suitable or depressing book. *Ministry of Fear* is a paranoid thriller, set in London during the Blitz. The protagonist is middle-aged Arthur Rowe—a wistful, innocent, helpless and deeply sad man who was once sent to prison for the mercy killing of his terminally ill wife. "There was something threatening, it seemed to him, in the very perfection of the day," Greene writes. Everything innocent and commonplace in Rowe's shattered life holds some secret terror. At a Saturday fete in Bloomsbury Square he wins a cake that turns out to contain secret microfilm of great importance to British national security. Nazi agents stalk him to get it. No one is what they seem. A doctor turns out to be a killer. A dead man comes back to life. Rowe survives two murder attempts, tracks down the villain, retrieves the stolen microfilm and gets the girl. But it all seems empty and futile, and Rowe remains filled with guilt and remorse.

Rowe's new love tells him that the enemy are those who, like the

Nazis, feel nothing. "They are the same everywhere," she says. "You think you are so bad, but it was only because you couldn't bear the pain. But *they* can bear pain—other people's pain—endlessly. They are the people who don't care."

Hilda could say the same for the enforcers of apartheid. *They* were creating a police state in the name of racial purity, condemning millions of black people to a life of suffering. Still, Hilda learned to hate *Ministry of Fear*. Turning page after page in search of the correct word for her secret messages was like wandering through the pages of a nightmare. The bleakness of the book—the sense of normalcy forfeited and irredeemable—was mirrored in her own life. It did nothing to ease her desperation or her sense of hopelessness.

Many days it was Bram who kept her going. After the Rivonia raid, Hilda had tried to persuade him to flee, fearing he, too, would soon be arrested. But Bram refused to even consider it. Instead he seemed to take on even more responsibility, adding the work left by his imprisoned comrades to his own heavy load. He helped fund the new Umkhonto High Command from the small amounts of cash that trickled in from London. He attended Central Committee meetings and High Command sessions, even though these had become highly dangerous, given the likelihood of informers and surveillance.

Despite the dangers, Bram never seemed to lose his sense of optimism or his determination to carry on. At night, he and Hilda would walk the streets near his home in Oaklands to get away from the listening devices and review what scraps of information they had picked up during the day and where things stood. One evening they sat under the grapevine in his garden watching a fingernail moon in the clear, crisp winter sky. After they had talked over everything yet another time—who had been arrested and who was still at large and what they should do next—he looked at her, and the perpetual smile he wore was gone. He spoke with vehemence of the regime, its hatreds and its cruelties. "Oh, Hilda, it can't last," he said. But it was more a plea than a declaration of faith. "*It can't last.*"

Hilda realized that she loved Bram—not in a sexual way but in the sense of a deep and abiding affection and concern. She had known him for two decades and had watched him weather every storm. His faith and commitment never seemed to waver; even at the worst of times he had the ability to project total belief in the movement. Hilda's own loyalties remained firm, but her faith was flagging. She doubted herself and her ability to withstand the pressure she was under. At the same time, she was beginning to have doubts about the movement. For years she had assumed that the men who ran things—Rusty and Bram included—knew what they were doing. She had deferred to their presumed intelligence, which she believed was greater than her own. Now that so many of them were in prison or had fled the country and she had stepped into their place, she could see more clearly their mistakes and miscalculations. And she wondered if there was any way they could recover from the blow they had been struck. She felt as if she were walking in dead men's shoes.

Then there was Rusty. Like Jimmy, he was locked away somewhere in Pretoria Local, isolated from any contact with other prisoners. She had only seen him twice in the last two months. The first time was the morning after the Rivonia raid, when the police brought him to the house unbathed, unshaven and heavy-lidded to witness their search of the premises. She and Rusty had embraced briefly at the door. "We were so anxious," she told him.

"I asked them to phone and tell you," he replied. "They said they would."

Some of the conversation was mundane. Hilda wanted to know where Rusty had put a second set of car keys. But Rusty needed to warn her about the copy of his critique of Operation Mayibuye that he had stashed in the garage, a document that would have substantiated his role as a conspirator in Umkhonto and sealed his fate. He could not pull her far enough away from a lurking detective to tell her.

Keith was in the bedroom while the detectives searched the premises. After they finished, they told Rusty to pack a bag. They allowed him a change of clothes, pajamas, toiletries, but nothing else. No books, no magazines, no diary, no writing paper, no pens or pencils, they told him. But while they were busy elsewhere, Keith grabbed a book from the shelf and slipped it into his father's bag. Rusty saw it there, looked at Keith and struggled to hold back his tears.

The police spent two hours at the house, carrying off box after box of books and documents. But even though they searched the garage, they failed to find the incriminating document. After they left with Rusty in custody, Keith, who had watched the entire scene with quiet, wide eyes, took a pencil and paper and wrote his father a note.

Dear Dad,
If they won't give you any books to read let me know and I will send you
some,
love keith

At Keith's insistence, Hilda took the letter and promised to send it. She did not tell him that his father was not allowed to receive mail.

The weeks passed slowly. Hilda spent much of her time on the endless domestic matters that she once had shared with her husband: How to discipline the children, what to do about schooling, allowances and evening curfews. Where to take the car for repairs. How to get the record player fixed. During house arrest, Rusty had been home almost full-time. Now his absence was all the more glaring. She was truly on her own.

Patrick, age fifteen, was the hardest of the children to deal with. Patrick was his father's son; he had Rusty's red hair—which he wore greased back in a hoodish semi-pompadour that he always checked in a mirror in the front hall before going out—and long, handsome face. He had Rusty's silent, introverted disposition as well. He was away at camp when his father was arrested, and Hilda did not write or phone him about it because she did not want to spoil his vacation. But he found out anyway from a friend who received a letter from home mentioning it, and the fact that Hilda had not told him first became another entry in Patrick's catalogue of grievances. His parents never told him anything, not even this. He came home angry—Patrick's most familiar emotion—and retreated to his room, where his practice karate chops and judo kicks shook the plaster. He spent hours plucking away at a guitar, modeling himself after Hank B. Marvin of the Shadows, the British pop group. One day without asking, he drove off in a neighbor's car that had been loaned to Hilda while she waited for permission to retrieve the Chevy from police custody. Hilda also suspected that Patrick was skipping school on a regular basis. His grades, never good, sank to new lows. And all the time, the thing he was coming to fear most—that his father might be hanged for treason—sat like a dead, evil weight atop his shoulders. He could not talk about it to anyone, not to his mother and not to his shrinking list of school friends. No one had come out and told him about the death penalty. But Patrick knew—*Patrick always knew*—and it ate at him.

Hilda was suffering as well. Because she could not sleep at night, she would go to bed late, taking with her a book, the newspapers, an apple or an orange. She would spread the papers and fruit over Rusty's bed and use his pillow to prop herself up. She would read until her eyes burned, then switch off the light and quietly cry herself to sleep.

On the first weekend after the raid, Hilda, Shirley Hepple and Iris Festenstein visited the seventh floor of the Grays to meet with Colonel Klindt to seek permission to visit their husbands. The Grays was enemy headquarters, nerve center of the gathering campaign to destroy Hilda, her comrades and the movement she cherished. When police came to the house, they came as intruders. No matter how rude or intimidating they tried to act, she had the psychological advantage of being on her own ground. But when she came to the Grays, she was entering their territory, with no defenses and no protection. The fact that she came as a supplicant seeking favors only made matters worse. She was no innocent housewife victimized by her husband's misdeeds, but an active participant in his political crimes. The police had studied her file and her photograph, they knew her movements and her beliefs. She was a target, a name on some future list they were even now compiling, and by coming to the Grays she had delivered herself directly into their midst. They could swallow her whole, make her disappear, add her to the roster of the silenced. Who could stop them?

The scenes at the Grays, including her meetings with Klindt, are among the most heartfelt and harrowing of Hilda's memoir. They crackle with authenticity. One thing Hilda frequently points out: Klindt may have given hard-boiled answers and lost his temper, but he always agreed to see her and the other wives. He did not have to; other Special Branch senior officers would simply have refused. But he felt some sort of obligation—to himself or to the law as he believed it should be or to his sense of common decency. Hilda will never know. She remembers Klindt not with admiration, nor even with respect, but with the recognition that inside him, somewhere, was a human being.

She devised a strategy for the first meeting. She told Klindt that she needed to see Rusty to obtain his power of attorney, discuss repayment of the bond on their house and other financial matters and review his various clients and architectural work. She also asked if she could bring Rusty his unfinished drawings.

"No! Definitely not!" Klindt proclaimed. "You know your husband is under Ninety Days? It is not permitted."

Klindt laid down the rules. Hilda could pick up Rusty's dirty clothes and take him clean laundry once a week. And Klindt would grant her a ten-minute visit with him—not a minute more—to discuss family and business matters only. Any mention of politics or legal matters and the security man monitoring the visit would immediately end it, and Hilda would never have another.

The following Monday she made the first of many drives to Pretoria. Up Louis Botha Avenue, the main road north from Johannesburg, past whitewashed shops and grimy garages, squat roadhouses like Pickin Chicken and Dairy Den and the drive-in cinema that Rusty had designed, past the teeming black township of Alexandra and the luxury estate houses of Kelvin and Buccleugh, past the Snake Park and Halfway House, the bristling air force training headquarters at Voortrekkerhoogte and, finally, the granite Voortrekker Memorial, the dour shrine of Afrikanerdom standing guard on the outskirts of Pretoria. It took more than an hour to make the thirty-six-mile trip.

Pretoria Local prison was the very first building in Pretoria proper, a red-brick fortress along the left-hand side of Potgieter Street. Behind thick mesh and glass in the unheated visiting room, Rusty looked haggard and red-eyed and he seemed to have trouble concentrating. Hilda asked about his clients—especially those who might owe money she could collect. There was so much else she wanted to say. She wanted to reassure him not only that she and the children were well but that the movement that was so much a part of both their lives was also surviving. But with the Special Branch man standing alongside, his eyes fixed upon her face as if her very expression might reveal some important piece of information, she spoke only in the most guarded, businesslike fashion.

After that she came once a week to bring clean clothes, but she was not allowed to see him. Everything was thoroughly checked, and any violation of the rules—an attempt to smuggle in a message or a newspaper clipping—would mean immediate and permanent suspension of these meager privileges.

Still, she was certain that Rusty would find a way of communicating with her. Every week, after she collected his dirty laundry, she examined each piece carefully, holding it up to the light and feeling along the seams, looking for something, even though she did not know what. Then, during the third week, standing in front of the washing machine in the kitchen, she noticed that the collar of one shirt had a corner through which light came. She laid it on the counter, gently ripped the stitches with a needle and pulled out the placket from inside. There, on strips of a torn handkerchief that had been laid flat to match the collar shape, was a message in pencil in meticulously tiny handwriting.

Rusty had found a way.

As Ruth recalls in her book, her interrogators would come about once a week, always at a different time and day so that she could never prepare herself in advance. Mostly it was Nel, with his glassy stare and cold, mechanical voice. But one week it was Swanepoel and his anemic sidekick van Zyl. Swanepoel immediately went after Joe, saying he knew Joe had been smuggling money into the country to support Umkhonto. When Ruth denied any knowledge of it, Swanepoel called Joe a coward and alluded to love affairs Joe had conducted with other women. Ruth was unimpressed. "Do you really think you can tell me anything about Joe?" she asked.

"You're an obstinate woman, Mrs. Slovo," Swanepoel told her. "But remember this. Everyone cracks sooner or later. It's our job to find the cracking point. We'll find yours too."

Ruth was a professional journalist and a Marxist. Much of her writing is passionate but impersonal. But *117 Days*, her account of her time in detention, is very different. In it she comes alive as a three-dimensional woman who is both dedicated and vulnerable, brave yet deeply frightened. The writing is full of personal observations, grim humor and long, self-conscious descriptions of her own shortcomings. It took courage to survive in prison. But it also took courage to write such an unsparingly honest account of what happened there.

For weeks Ruth remained defiant and contemptuous, mocking the inept attempts of her captors to trick her into confessing and raining insults upon their stiff Afrikaner necks. She worked hard to keep up the appearance of indomitable normality. Every day she carefully applied makeup, put on earrings and brushed the wiry, jet-black hair that she normally had straightened weekly at the hairdresser. Each afternoon when she pulled herself up to peer out the small grimy window at the top of the cell wall for a glimpse of the world outside, she wrapped a tissue around each of the bars so that her hands would not get dirty. Still, she felt deeply deprived without a mirror to perform for each morning, and she was afraid that at the age of thirty-eight she was losing her looks.

The first week after Harold and Arthur's escape was a frenzy of activity at Marshall Square. High officials and inspectors armed with clipboards came and went. Acetylene torches blazed as more locks were added to cell doors and hallway gates. The laxness that had pervaded the prison earlier was transformed into a rigorous web of strictly enforced rules and restrictions that meant Ruth was even more isolated in her cell.

The cell itself seemed filled with a series of random insults—a narrow, lumpy straw mattress that always felt damp; gray burlap blankets that smelled like moldy potatoes; a single naked lightbulb in the middle of the ceiling that fiercely illuminated the cold concrete walls; and a soot-covered window with two sets of bars and a mesh screen that served not as an opening but more like a closure.

But the worst was the incessant clang of the heavy steel doors throughout the day and night. The doors had no handles; they were pulled open by a key, then slammed shut with the shove of a hand, and they echoed throughout the gunmetal halls and stairways like bells tolling in a lost cave. The sound raced up Ruth's spine to her neck and shoulders, a jarring punctuation to each flat, endless day, and a bleak reminder of where she was. It was cold during the winter months, so she spent most of the day lying on the bed with the blankets pulled up to her chin. The walls were painted black two-thirds of the way up. The last third had once been white. Now it was covered with a permanent brown film. There was a peephole in the cell door that allowed the wardress to peek in. Ruth was isolated, but she had no privacy. Even her bodily functions were a matter of public record. When she needed the toilet, she had to shout or bang on the door.

Ruth nicknamed her wardresses Raucous, Shrill, Pained and Competent. In her book, she describes passing much time studying their characters, as well as observing the habits of the prostitutes, petty thieves and drunkards who made up most of the women's section of Marshall Square. While she was not allowed to share a cell with her fellow inmates, she could overhear their conversations and complaints, and she occasionally caught a glimpse of them during the hour she was let out each day for exercise and toilet.

Each morning the wardress would cruise the African cells, picking out five or six awaiting-trial prisoners for cleaning chores. They would be issued blankets torn into strips and filthy rags and set to work on the concrete floors. First they would sweep using the blanket strips. Then they would rub each surface to a shiny gleam with cheap red polish. The prisoners were required to put a rag under each foot and do the cha-cha or the twist at the wardresses' command. Although she was a political prisoner, Ruth was treated like a white madam for this exercise in petty sadism. The racial privileges she had scorned and bitterly fought against in the outside world were involuntarily hers by right here in this catacomb. She would sit on her bed with her feet propped up while an African prisoner polished her cell floor. When the inmate finished, she would be handed a large aluminum bucket and told to fetch hot water for the "missus."

There were many days when Ruth cried silently in her cell, panicked by the prospect of spending years in a place like this. She was worried sick about Joe and the children. Ruth knew that Tilly was in no shape to deal with three young girls or with police pressure. One thing Ruth intuited from the questions of her interrogators was that the police were interested not only in her father, Julius, who had been involved in raising and dispersing money to the Communist Party for many years, but also in Tilly. Julius fled the country in October, crossing the border into Bechuanaland with several comrades. Special Branch then detained Ruth's brother Ronnie, one of the world's most apolitical of creatures, so why not Tilly? Ruth knew her mother had an iron will but a fragile psyche. How would she survive in the grime and filth of a detention cell? And what would happen to the girls? They had lost their father in June, and their mother in August. To be deprived of their grandmother as well would leave them well and truly abandoned.

Slowly but surely she could see the children being dragged into the line of fire. She was willing to pay the price for her own activism. But the children? She tried to put them out of her mind, but of course she could not. Their fate seemed as fragile as her own.

Rusty's first notes were in pencil. Then Hilda thought to smuggle in ballpoint pen refills by shoving them into bananas. Rusty hated bananas—just the smell of them made him gag—and he would know to look inside them. She bought the straightest ones she could find. She also shopped for fresh handkerchiefs and shirts with the widest possible collars.

The notes provided Hilda with a detailed look at life inside Pretoria Local. They also charted the slow deterioration of Rusty's spirit. Interrogation was not the problem. The police had decided early on that they had enough evidence to hang Rusty and they spent little time pressuring him for more. But the lonely weight of solitary confinement pressed against him. At first, he was optimistic and cheerful, as if trying to convince her and himself that everything was okay.

I have been keeping a record and find that I am averaging eighteen spoken words a day. "Thank you" three times for meals. "May I have a match, please?" twice at exercise times. I keep my vocal cords exercised with an evening song session, taking advantage of the captive audience, Bob and H, and the two warders outside, and the quite remarkable bathroom-type acoustics of the cell which enable me to go from basso profundo to mezzo-soprano! Aided of course by the fact that I've cut down smoking to two a day for the second thirty days and intend to drop it entirely for the third. Just one of the gimmicks I'm trying out to ensure that I stay strictly non-obsessional and as non-neurotic as possible in circumstances specially designed for neurosis.

Twice a day the prisoners would be allowed into the small gray yard to wash, exercise and smoke. Political prisoners were not allowed to talk to each other. In the middle of the yard was a waist-high brick wall enclosing a toilet, sink and shower tap. The detainees took to calling the enclosure "the Battleship Potemkin" because it was painted gray. The wall was high enough so that they could sit on the toilet and not be seen. Someone came up with a pencil stub and the men took turns passing it around, leaving it on the floor behind the toilet. It was the only means they had to pierce their isolation.

. . . I am finding the nights worse than the days. Lights go out at eight p.m. I try to find exercises to keep me up till eight-thirty. But then I wake too early and from dawn to five-thirty is spent turning and tossing and having fearful nightmares. . . . I recount to myself memories of childhood, not in full, but try and discover what makes a nice Jewish boy twice face trial for treason in the matter of seven years.

Spurred by Rusty's notes, Hilda went back to Klindt time after time to try to wrest some meager privileges for her imprisoned husband. As she recounts in *The World That Was Ours*, the meetings began to take on a pattern. She learned never to accept his first fierce "No!" as final. She would continue to argue and plead, and sometimes he would give way. He looked like such a troubled man—his gray face, hair and suit matched the gunmetal desk and filing cabinets in his office. Only his pale blue eyes betrayed any hint of color. He looked ill: Hilda was not surprised to learn later that he was suffering from cancer. To Hilda he looked like a man out of time. He did not make the rules; perhaps he did not even believe in them. But he demanded that they be followed and he exploded in righteous anger whenever Hilda questioned them. Besides, Klindt was on a short tether. Every move he made was subject to the scrutiny of Long Hendrik and the bureaucrats in Pretoria, who believed white communists were vermin and race traitors and should be treated accordingly.

How was it, Hilda asked him one day, that prisoners at Pretoria Local could not receive food from outside, while those at Marshall Square could? Because each facility made its own rules, Klindt wearily replied. Yet after a month he relented and allowed Hilda and the other wives to take in food once a week when they went to collect laundry. Then one day Hilda asked Klindt for permission to visit Rusty to discuss whether to sell the Chevy. This was a white lie; Hilda had already arranged for the sale. Still, she desperately needed to see Rusty and reassure him after the harrowing messages he was sending out.

Klindt at first said no, as always. But eventually he relented. The doors of Pretoria Local swung open once again.

Willie van Wyk was convinced that Jimmy Kantor had played a major role in Umkhonto We Sizwe. Police had seized financial records from Jimmy and Harold's law firm that showed thousands of rand had been channeled through the firm to radical activists, including the money that had gone to pay for Lilliesleaf. Jimmy insisted to his interrogators that he knew nothing about the transactions, all of which he claimed were handled solely by Harold. Jimmy also insisted he knew nothing about Rivonia, and had never even been to Lilliesleaf before accompanying Hazel Goldreich's mother to the site the day after the raid. But van

Wyk had seen Jimmy confidently stroll his way to the outbuildings to feed the chickens. Jimmy, he was convinced, was lying.

"You can't make war without money," van Wyk told his fellow investigators. "And Kantor handled the money. He must be one of the High Command."

Jimmy's chief interrogators, Swanepoel and van Zyl, were also convinced that he had masterminded Harold and Arthur's escape. They brought him up to Johannesburg for questioning, then took him back to Pretoria. Week after week they would interrogate him. When he would plead "I don't know," they would bark back, "We don't believe you!" But he would admit to nothing, nor could he bring himself to implicate Hilda. He wanted to get out of detention, but he was not willing to send someone else to prison in his place. He resolved that he would do what he could to help himself, but he would not betray anyone else. Finally, at the behest of his lawyers, he was transferred to the Fort in Johannesburg and allowed to spend several days at his law office, sorting through case files and tying up loose ends, always under the watchful eyes of a police escort.

In the past, the office had always had a soothing effect on him. He would sit in his rich leather chair and admire the fruits of his financial success: the double-glazed windows that muffled traffic noise, the oak-paneled walls, the plush, wine-colored carpet, the expensive oil paintings. But now even the office offered no solace. His law practice was disintegrating at alarming speed. New clients had stopped coming, while many old ones were deserting. The monthly cost of rent and salaries quickly drove the firm's bank balance deep into the red. Jimmy knew he had little cash reserves. He had spent freely and lavishly over the years and had tied up much of the rest in a disastrous local movie project. Joel Joffe, a former partner who was about to leave the country to settle in Australia, stepped in and agreed to oversee Jimmy's cases until he could return. But Jimmy had already decided he would never practice law again. He had lost all respect for the legal system; what's more, he could see that being a lawyer no longer afforded him any real protection. In a police state where the rule of law was effectively suspended, lawyers at best were ornaments. He could no longer honestly defend clients. He could not even defend himself.

As he recalls in *A Healthy Grave*, the deciding blow occurred one morning when a prisoner in a nearby cellblock received eight strokes. Jimmy was close enough to hear it all. "First [came] the whistle of the cane through the crisp morning air, and the sound of it connecting with human flesh, followed immediately by a shout of agony from the recipient. It was all over very quickly . . . a matter of seconds. But that brief slice of time will remain with me for the rest of my life." Jimmy did not know if the victim was white or black; he had no idea what the offense was. But he felt sick to his soul.

There were days when Jimmy wallowed in complete despair, certain that he would be left forever to rot in prison; there were nights when he would weep uncontrollably. He found himself becoming more and more dependent on his warders. One day when Bennett, the chief warder, allowed him to remain in the sunny exercise yard for a full hour, Jimmy stammered his gratitude in a fawning and abject way that he hated himself for. But each privilege had its price. After an hour of glorious sunshine, his cell seemed even darker, colder and more claustrophobic.

Jimmy was losing weight and peace of mind as well. Even though he was able to smuggle in cigarettes, notepaper and a pencil, he could not get comfortable in jail. Each day was a struggle. And each week his interrogators added to the load with threats and bullying. Van Zyl told him he was "a tough little Jew" and warned that if he did not divulge what he knew, they would keep him in isolation for years, ninety days at a time.

That night Jimmy could not eat or sleep. He started drifting off just as morning came, and he was late getting ready for washing and breakfast. Bennett was in a foul mood and refused Jimmy his usual cigarette in the exercise yard as punishment because he had overslept. Back in the cell Jimmy could not help himself. He reached up and grabbed the pack he kept stashed in an air vent beneath the ceiling and lit up. Suddenly Bennett was there, his hand sternly outstretched. Jimmy sheepishly handed him the butt and Bennett began to shake down the cell.

"Where are the others?" he demanded.

Jimmy pointed to the air vent.

"Stand outside," Bennett ordered.

Bennett found all of Jimmy's cigarette packs and matches and a cheap Western novel. He tore through clothing, bedding and Jimmy's precious private food packets, flinging all of them on the floor. Everything Jimmy had smuggled in or collected to make life tolerable was taken away or destroyed.

When Bennett left, Jimmy's head ached furiously. The tangled mess before him on the floor was his shattered life. He knew he was breaking.

In a sudden moment of clarity, he decided to take his razor and slit his wrists. But before he could find the toiletries among the heap of belongings, things grew hazy. The walls were moving. First there was just a faint ripple, and then they started closing in. The bastards were reading his mind! They had found out somehow that he was going to commit suicide and had decided to crush him instead. He crumpled to the floor in defeat. Which is where Bennett found him later that morning, shaking and crying uncontrollably.

A police doctor examined Jimmy and pressed to have him admitted to the prison hospital. Special Branch refused. Max Feldman, a leading Johannesburg psychiatrist, came to see Jimmy and recommended to prison authorities that he be allowed books and regular recreation.

The recommendation was ignored.

AnnMarie Wolpe was shattered by the news of Jimmy's arrest. He had been her rock, her island of stability and protection against any storm. Now he himself had been swept under and she felt a terrible sense of anger and guilt—anger at her husband Harold, who had left all of them behind to deal with the consequences of the mess he and his comrades had made; and guilt over her own role in dragging in her beloved older brother.

There was little she could do to help. Jimmy was allowed no visitors; in any event, she was probably the last person he wanted to see. He had influential friends in the legal establishment who were trying to help him. AnnMarie could only stand aside and worry. Worse still, she was hearing rumors that she herself was in jeopardy again. Maggie Smith, a sympathetic journalist with the *Sunday Times*, came by the house to warn that stories were floating that the police were planning to arrest AnnMarie again. If they did, this time it would be no one-day affair to frighten her, but a full-fledged ninety days in a cell like Ruth First's or Hazel Goldreich's, perhaps with a criminal charge to face at the end of it.

There was only one way out. AnnMarie knew she had to leave the country. She still possessed a valid passport but she feared Special Branch would never let her board a plane. She traveled to Durban in hopes of gaining passage on a freighter by bribing a Customs official. She paid him two hundred rand but she did not board the ship after learning it would stop in neighboring Mozambique, a colony of Portugal, because she feared the Portuguese secret police would turn her over to their South African counterparts. She returned to Johannesburg feeling even more frantic and terrified. She phoned Joel Joffe at Jimmy's office. He listened sympathetically and suggested she go immediately to see a psychiatrist and get a written assessment confirming her state of anxiety. Meanwhile, he promised to take up the matter with George Klindt.

Joffe phoned back the next afternoon. "They have reached a decision," he told her. "You can go. But go now, go tonight."

There was so much to do. She made arrangements to pay the bills and sell the house, and scraped together money for the airline ticket. And then there were the children. Angelina, AnnMarie's African housekeeper, and Marlene, the live-in nurse who was looking after baby Nicholas, agreed to stay on until the children could be put safely on a flight to London to follow their mother. AnnMarie could not afford to wait. She persuaded Joffe that she needed one more day, which she spent frantically organizing matters. The next day she headed to the airport.

AnnMarie's mother drove her. Her cousin drove a second car with Angelina and the girls, Peta and Tessa. In the departure lounge waiting to say goodbye, Angelina had to stand because all of the benches were marked with signs reading "Whites Only." AnnMarie hugged everyone, then rushed on board. She was leaving behind her country, her home and her children. As she recalled later on in her memoir, she dared not look back as she climbed the narrow portable stairway onto the plane for fear her heart would break.

To further tighten the screws, Ruth First's interrogators shipped her to Pretoria Central prison early in October. She suspected that this was done to prepare her for being charged with the men who had been captured at Rivonia. Tilly even brought her navy blue frock and matching coat so she would have something to wear to court. But the charge never came. Perhaps the government did not want a white woman in the dock facing the possibility of hanging at the show trial they all feared was coming.

Ruth's cell in Pretoria was larger, cleaner and sunnier than that in Marshall Square. But her isolation was almost complete—the cell was far from those of other prisoners. She became more and more subdued and found herself sinking into inertia. She meticulously made her bed several times a day, folded and refolded her clothes, unpacked and repacked her suitcase, cleaned the walls and dusted the room. She filed her nails, plucked her eyebrows, searched her head for gray hairs, which she ruthlessly pulled. She unstitched the seams of her pillowcase, towel and dressing gown, then stitched them again. Her life, like the walls of the cell, was slowly closing in on her.

As Ruth recalls in *117 Days*, Nel seemed to take a certain dry pleasure in her discomfort. When she complained about having nothing to read except the Bible, he replied, "If you have something to read you will not think about my questions, Mrs. Slovo." When she expressed anger over being held indefinitely, his answer was standard Special Branch dogma. "We're not holding you, you're holding yourself. . . . Make a statement and in no time you will be back with your children."

"We're not holding you, you're holding yourself." What better summary could there be of the secret policeman's mind-set? Ruth wondered. As Nel expressed it, he was the passive observer of someone in the midst of self-destruction. No blame or responsibility attached to him. It was, incredibly, all her own fault.

Six days before she was due for release, she was told to pack her things. Two detectives awaited to take her back to Marshall Square. On the drive, one of them, a man with wispy blond hair named Johan Jacobus Viktor, turned to her with a smile and asked, "How's Joe?"

Viktor went on to recount how he had once rescued Joe from a band of angry prostitutes after a court hearing in which Joe had revealed complicity between their madam and certain corrupt police officers. The vengeful whores had come looking for Joe in the corridor brandishing umbrellas and stiletto-heeled shoes, but Viktor had ushered him to safety through a private exit.

Viktor explained that neither he nor his partner van der Merwe were Special Branch men. They were temporarily on loan from the fraud and murder squads. Ruth made as if she could care less, but she and Viktor were soon arguing over the cruelties of solitary confinement. From there, they somehow got into a discussion of brandy, and Viktor wrote down the name of a brand she recommended. Later when the men deposited her back at Marshall Square, she turned to Viktor and said, "If you come again bring a bottle of that brandy."

In many of the accounts of South African political detainees in the early 1960s, J. J. Viktor plays a role. When dealing with women prisoners he could be gentle and solicitous. Stephanie Kemp, a young detainee in Cape Town, said he harangued her aggressively for hours, angrily challenging her politics. Yet when she told him that not only did he speak like a Nazi, he looked like one, he smiled and relaxed a bit. When another officer struck her in the face out of Viktor's presence, he feigned anger. Later, however, he told her mockingly, "So it took only one clout to get you to make a statement."

With men he could be more brutal. Detainee Hugh Lewin recalled Viktor standing by unperturbed as his partner van der Merwe systematically assaulted Lewin one night. "Have a smoke," said Viktor at the end of the beating.

Ruth was too intelligent to be deceived by Viktor's calculated show of sympathy yet too vulnerable not to welcome it. As she describes it, they engaged in a prolonged act of mutual seduction, each of them with a not so hidden purpose. She wanted a sympathetic ear inside Special Branch; he wanted her cooperation.

She saw him again the day after she was returned to Marshall Square when she was brought to the interrogation room. He handed her a small bottle, not of brandy but of eau de cologne that had inadvertently dropped out of her handbag in the back seat of the police car. He talked a lot about himself; he was thirty-four and already a lieutenant. He was eager to return to the fraud squad, he told her. He did not feel at home in Special Branch.

Ruth obviously did not belong here either, he added, anyone could see that. Why didn't she get herself out of this mess by making a statement? Ruth replied with another tirade against the police. They had followed her around, tapped her phone, raided her house and destroyed her privacy, and now they were acting like judge, prosecutor and jury, she told him. She would never, ever cooperate with them.

Viktor made her an offer. She was certain to face prosecution for possession of banned literature—that sad, neglected copy of *Fighting Talk*. It was up to the Attorney General, but if she cooperated, Colonel Klindt would put in a word for her. When she challenged how a junior officer such as Viktor could make such a commitment, he promised to check it and get back to her.

Two days later he brought back word that Klindt would indeed intercede in return for her cooperation. "No," she said firmly. "I am not interested in any deal."

Think it over carefully, Viktor advised her. After all, your ninety days are coming up, but no one has promised that another might not follow.

Reading the latest of Rusty's smuggled notes, Hilda could feel the isolation of his prison cell eating away at his sanity.

> *The thought of being in prison for a long time is awful, but tolerable for a man like me. The discomforts and privations mean very little to me. The worst of it is the separation from you and the kids and knowing that all the time I am here they are growing out of childhood, the years in which I love them best, and I can never recapture that . . .*
>
> *It is hell, not just the loneliness and solitude of tedium but the devilish neurotic fears, anxieties and tensions with only one's mind for company and nothing to move it to think except one's own troubles. You can't imagine what this does to you. You become not just the center, but the whole of your universe, your own fate, your own future. Nothing you can do or say can possibly affect the life of anyone else, or so it seems. What little courage I have gradually erodes in loneliness with no one near to sustain me.*

Going to the Grays made her physically ill, and pleading with Klindt was distasteful at best, but Hilda had no choice. She felt she was hanging on to Rusty's sanity as if it were her own. She arranged another meeting and demanded that Rusty be allowed books. This triggered a major stand-up row. "It is not permitted!" Klindt stated over and over again. "It is not in the regulations!"

Hilda pointed out that the regulations did not specifically ban books and writing material. Surely it was within his power as the officer in charge to interpret the regulations as he saw fit.

Klindt stood up and banged his fist on his desk. "I don't make the law!" he shouted. "I am merely here to see that the law is carried out!"

He spoke of Rusty's refusal to cooperate with his interrogators. "If you would persuade your husband to be more reasonable, then we would be more reasonable as well," he said.

But Hilda would not budge. "My husband will decide for himself what he thinks is right," she replied. "I am not going to tell him to do anything he thinks is wrong."

> *Nothing gives me worse torments than the fear that something might happen to you or that you may be dragged into this nightmare situation. This tortures me almost to distraction. On the days when I expect you to bring clothes and food, I age a year with every hour that passes. I keep telling myself that this is madness, but reason doesn't help against unreasonable fear. Yesterday clothes arrived as usual in the morning, but no food until the afternoon—left in some office, I suppose. I spent the morning worrying where were you? Why did someone else have to bring the clothes? And then the food arrived, and somehow it looked more Shirley's style than yours and for a while this gave me ulcers. I know this is crazy, but it destroys what courage I have; darling, please, I beg of you, don't get into danger.*

Rusty was not the only Bernstein who worried about Hilda's clandestine activities. One evening she went to say good night to twelve-year-old Frances before going out to a secret meeting. "Where are you going tonight?" her daughter asked.

Hilda responded with the same jocular answer she and Rusty had always given the children. "To see a man about a dog," she said with a smile.

"Don't give me that, Mum," Frances said.

"I'm only going out for a little while."

"That's what Daddy said—and he never came back."

When United Party lawmakers had agreed to support the Ninety-Day Act, they insisted upon adding a provision to salve their consciences: detainees must be visited once a week by a magistrate who was to check on their condition and duly record their complaints. And so a bland man with a notebook and pencil made the rounds of Pretoria Local each week asking, "Any complaints?"

One week Rusty replied, "Yes. I want to know what happened about the complaints I made to you last week."

The magistrate started to write in his notebook. Reading upside down, Rusty saw he was writing, "I want to know what happened about the complaints I made to you last week."

When the magistrate finished writing, he looked up. "Anything else?"

"Don't I get an answer to that question?"

The magistrate wrote, "Don't I get an answer to that question?"

Later, Rusty learned that the complaints went into a central file that eventually made its way to the Commissioner of Police. In other words, the official responsible for imprisoning and interrogating him was also responsible for policing the conditions under which he was held. No judge or lawyer could intervene; no writ of habeas corpus was possible.

Cruel as it was, ninety-day detention was proving remarkably effective. Some five hundred people were detained during the first six months of the new law, and virtually every one of them reported experiencing some kind of emotional or psychological damage. Dozens broke under the pressure, providing police interrogators with the information they were seeking. In December, sixty leading psychiatrists, psychologists and medical specialists signed a statement condemning detention as "inhuman and unjustifiable. . . . The exposure of individuals to acute suffering and mental impairment for indefinite periods of time is no less abhorrent than physical torture," they stated. The signers also pointed out the obvious—that any testimony obtained from those subject to such treatment "is no longer reliable" because of the mental damage done and the degree of coercion involved.

But the authorities did not seem to care. Despite what they said publicly, detention was clearly designed not just to extract information but to punish the detainees. The government had no intention of surrendering what Swanepoel called in court testimony a "mighty weapon in the hands of the police." After five detainees, including Jimmy Kantor, were examined by psychiatrists and two were committed to a mental hospital for observation, an anonymous Security Branch officer told Gordon Winter of the *Sunday Express*: "All these people you have named were shamming mental illness. It is all part and parcel of a clever communist-inspired campaign to discredit the ninety-day detention clause and, in some cases, to facilitate escaping."

In many ways the white detainees were lucky. They may have been battered psychologically, but their black and Asian counterparts faced physical assault as well. When Abdullah Jassat—one of the Marshall Square escapees—was seized during a predawn raid after the attempted bombing of a deserted railway station, he was taken to a large room in the station in which nearly twenty policemen had been gathered in a circle. In an affidavit, Jassat later described how, after he refused to confess to involvement in the sabotage, he was passed from man to man, each one hammering him with blows to his head and face. When he fell they kicked him, beat him on the soles of his bare feet, clipped electrodes to his toes and shocked him until he lost consciousness. Then they shoved a wet sack over his head and swung him by his ankles.

But even Jassat's case paled next to that of Looksmart Solwandle Ngudle. A well-liked Cape Town political organizer, Ngudle became one of Umkhonto's regional leaders. He was arrested in mid-August as part of the crackdown following the Rivonia raid. Sixteen days later he was found hanged in his cell. His mother was not informed of his death for ten days. When she arrived at Pretoria to claim the body, she was told he had already been buried. An inquest was delayed for weeks. Meanwhile, in late October, seven weeks after his death, the *Government Gazette* announced that Ngudle had been banned under the Suppression of Communism Act.

"Dead Man Banned" read the headline in the *Johannesburg Star*. From the window of her prison cell Ruth saw it displayed by a news vendor one day and wondered what it meant.

Despite the government's best attempts at suppression, information on Ngudle's treatment slowly trickled from the catacombs of the detained. Defense lawyer Vernon Berrange, one of a handful of attorneys known for his willingness to pursue human rights cases, decided to turn the inquest on Ngudle's death into a forum on police torture. He called as a witness Isaac Tlale, a fifty-year-old businessman from Alexandra Township who had been held for ninety days as an alleged recruiter for Umkhonto. Tlale described how he had been taken to Pretoria Central, handcuffed to a chair and assaulted by a man he knew only as "Baas Kappie." A leg of Tlale's chair had broken and Baas Kappie had used it to beat him on the head. Tlale said he was also choked and kicked, then taken to another room where three white men told him to undress. He testified that he was handcuffed and forced to sit with a broom handle between his knees and a wet bag placed over his head. The men clipped electrodes to his fingers and shocked him twice until he lost consciousness. "The next thing I remember was standing next to a table signing a document," he testified.

"And thereafter where did you go?" asked Berrange.

"They said I should go and clean myself."

"Why did you have to go and clean yourself?"

"I had messed myself up."

Tlale said he was later taken to a room where Ngudle was sitting. A constable came in and called out, "Looksmart, come," and took the other detainee to the interrogation room.

"He was away for quite a time, approximately thirty minutes."

"And when he came back, how did he look?"

"When he came back he was full of sweat in his face."

"What was the color of his face, had the color undergone any change?"

"His color had changed to green."

"He looked green and did he look well or did he look sick?"

"He looked sick."

"Did he eat any food?"

"He did not eat."

"Did you ask him why?"

"I asked him why and he said this electric gave him some pain. . . . 'It's hurting me very bad.' "

After that, Tlale said, he never saw Ngudle again.

The court ruled inadmissible all of the evidence from Tlale and other detainees, agreeing with the prosecutor that none of it bore directly on Ngudle's case. Berrange then withdrew from the proceedings in protest. The magistrate later formally concluded that Looksmart Ngudle had committed suicide by hanging himself, and that his death was not due to "any act or omission involving or amounting to an offense on the part of any person."

The inquest was adjourned.

With the courts reduced to complicit silence, Parliament was left as the only public forum for accusations of torture and Helen Suzman as the only elected representative willing to use that forum. Suzman challenged the ninety-day detention clause in the next parliamentary session, calling it "a disgrace to any so-called civilized country." She repeated Berrange's charges of torture concerning Looksmart Ngudle and other cases. "There are allegations about hitting with sticks, with bare fists, with hose pipes, of people being punched and kicked, of people being beaten with straps and batons," she declared. "And there are many allegations about the giving of electric shock in order to induce people to make statements."

When Nationalists objected that she was merely repeating the lies of communists, she responded, "I think it is impossible for any reasonable person to read these statements and to believe that all of them are phony, that they are simply concoctions of neo-communists and so forth. All of them make the same sort of allegations, yet these people were kept in solitary confinement, away from each other."

Suzman also spoke of the psychological torture of solitary confinement and she implicitly compared Verwoerd's government to the Nazi regime, quoting from *The Royal Game* by Stefan Zweig, an account of solitary confinement under the Gestapo:

> *This simply indescribable state lasts four months. Well, four months; easy to write. . . . Easy to say, too. . . . But nobody can describe or measure or demonstrate, not to another or to himself, how long a period endures in the spaceless and timeless, nor can one explain to another how it eats into and destroys one, this nothing and nothing and nothing.*

Suzman's opponents in the National Party were infuriated. Some hurled anti-Semitic comments her way from the backbenches, while one member called her a communist and—worse, perhaps—a humanist, and another simply yelled that she was a liar.

Helen Suzman was not fazed, nor would she back down. "The task of all who believe in multiracialism in South Africa," she told a meeting of her constituents, "is to survive."

Rusty was losing control. His hands began to shake. The warder had given him a roll of toilet paper and warned, "You won't get another one for thirty days." Desperate for anything to occupy his time, Rusty found himself constantly unrolling and rolling the paper and counting the perforated sections to see how much he had left. You're going bloody mad, he told himself, what are you doing this for? But a day or two later he would be back at it again, counting the sections as if his life depended upon it.

> *I feel as though here I am down amongst the dead—the walking dead. But really my main feeling here is a vast love for you and the children which is slowly breaking my heart, because involved in it is tremendous*

sorrow for the awful mess I have made of all your lives. There should be heroic and noble thoughts in a time like this to sustain me, but there are not. Just a great pitying for the utter mess I have made at life. . . . Sometimes when I look at this mess and wonder what I would do if I had my time over, I still think I would travel much the same path again—in its essentials anyway. I must have been born for trouble. So, darling, when I say that all I want of life now is your happiness—all of you at home, I really mean it. I want more than anything else that you all should seek your happiness as best you can regardless of me, my troubles, my mess. I just don't want any of you to carry my mess like a millstone around your own lives. I really don't. Please remember that is utterly true. No heroics—if the worst happens in the weeks ahead of us.

One thing Rusty had in endless supply was time—time to think about what had happened and time to consider what to do next. For years he had been part of a collective movement where his personal needs had been secondary to the great historic cause he served. This had suited his personality and his idealism. But deep in the bowels of Pretoria Local, there was no cause and no community to support him. Even Hilda could not reach him. He could see that prison was crushing his spirit. And he could see clearly the price that his family was paying. Thinking about it was sheer torture. He paced the cell endlessly like a hamster in a wheel seeking to drive away his own thoughts. He knew if he began to succumb to self-pity he would be lost forever.

I now really worry about what will happen to me if I am not charged by the ninetieth day, but put back in here for another stay. . . . I don't know how long I will survive it without being reduced to complete jelly.

I am only now, I think, beginning to realize what a beating my nervous system has taken over the last four years—ceaseless tension made worse by the strain of house arrest when everyone who set foot in the house caused me to tighten up. . . . I did think that, if it got to this stage and I seemed likely to be held for another stretch, that I would try and bargain for an exit permit against a statement of the kind I once sent you. But now I know that even here there is no hope.

Curiously enough, the incident that finally put Rusty over the edge did not involve himself but rather Denis Goldberg. Denis had undergone a rough haul in detention. His wife Esme and their two small children lived in Cape Town and he had only been allowed to see her once. Then he had been transferred to another prison south of Johannesburg, where police had hoped to complete his isolation from his fellow detainees and pressure him into making a statement. Shirley Hepple and Hilda took turns delivering food and clothing to Goldberg's new location. Shirley phoned one day to say she had found bloodstains on Denis's clothing. She brought the clothes to Hilda's house: a jacket with two large holes torn in the back, a pair of pants with gashes in the bottom and bloodstains, a ripped shirt and a handkerchief soaked in blood.

Only Esme could ask to see her husband, so she flew up to Johannesburg to request a visit from Klindt. At first he said no, but then she brought him the clothing. Klindt looked alarmed. The colonel assured her that Denis was all right and told her that he had tried to escape and had been recaptured by police dogs. Still, Klindt relented and allowed Esme a visit.

Denis, who sounded in good spirits, confirmed his escape attempt. He had scaled a fourteen-foot wall and was running for cover when a fellow prisoner sounded the alarm. By the way, Denis added, don't bother to send in clean pajama trousers for a while, just the tops. His ankles had been manacled as punishment for the escape attempt and there was no way for Denis to pull the trousers over them.

The police brought Denis Goldberg back to Pretoria Local bruised and in chains. Rusty saw him in the exercise yard and almost collapsed in shock. *"I think the day he was brought back here I nearly wept,"* he wrote to Hilda. *"This is really the saddest sight I have ever seen, really the saddest sight ever. . . . "*

Hilda waited that evening until the children were in bed and the house was quiet. She could not let anyone, even the children, know that she was communicating with her husband. She sat at the desk in the front room and started to read the note. After describing Denis's condition, Rusty went on to say that he had finally had enough. He was ready to leave South Africa. If by some miracle he ever got out of custody, he told Hilda, he would head for the border and never look back. Knowing how strongly Rusty had felt about staying, Hilda wept when she read of his change of heart. Rusty had always been so strong and confident in what he believed. They had finally broken her husband's spirit.

Hilda dreaded going back to see Klindt. She learned from Shirley

Hepple that the colonel knew she had lied about the Chevy. Klindt had told Shirley he would never allow Hilda to see Rusty in detention again. But Hilda knew she had to try. In her book she recounts her visit to the security chief's office.

"Colonel Klindt, I want to see my husband," she told him.

Clearly Klindt had been waiting for this moment, and he fully intended to make her pay for her previous deception. She had lied to him, he said. He had tried to be helpful and she had taken advantage. He should have known better than to trust a communist. You are all liars, he told her.

Hilda denied having lied and tried to explain, saying she had needed to discuss the car sale with Rusty to make certain he did not object. Klindt cut her short.

"It is not so! Those are not the facts! The sale was completed before you came to me. I try to be reasonable to you women. I've let you have visits; it is a privilege, not a right. If this is how you abuse the privilege, you're not having it again."

Round and round they went, with Hilda pleading while Klindt paced the room denouncing the Rivonia men, accusing them of plotting against the government. He swore bitter oaths at Harold and Arthur as well. A day of reckoning was coming, he warned. They would all be caught, and all would face their just punishment. You communists will be taught a terrible lesson, he said.

Finally, Hilda could endure no more. She began to weep softly. She hated herself for it, but she could not stop. She could not tell him of Rusty's desperate notes, but somehow she had to make this man understand. She turned to face Klindt so that he would see her tears, and for the first time that day she raised her voice. "Listen to me, Colonel Klindt, just listen to what I have to say!"

The tears and the anger stunned Klindt into silence. He had never seen Hilda break down before. He stopped pacing, sat down at his desk and looked at her. "Well?"

Suddenly the games were over. She looked at this man and decided she had to talk to him not as a supplicant or an activist, but as one human being to another. This time she gave him the exact truth. "Colonel Klindt," she told him, "when we come to you to say we want to see our husbands, because we want to discuss the sale of a motorcar, or something about the children's education, or rent payments, or what to do about the insurance—don't you understand? Don't you realize that if our husbands were dead, or if they were ill in hospital, we would manage these things quite easily ourselves?

"When I say to you I want to see my husband, it's because I want to *see* him. I don't want your men taking messages and bringing me a reply. I want to see that he's still standing on his own two legs, that he's still able to walk and talk . . . "

"Mrs. Bernstein, I assure you, nobody has touched your husband, he is perfectly . . . "

"I don't want your assurance! I don't want to be told by the Special Branch! I want to see for myself. Even if I don't say one word to him. *I want to see my husband!*"

There was silence. Klindt got up, walked to the window, returned to his desk, fiddled with a pencil. He pulled a small pad of paper from a drawer. Without looking up, he started to write something down.

"All right," he said finally. "When do you want to go?"

On the morning of Ruth's eighty-ninth day in prison, the doors clanged open again. It was the wardress, come to fetch her to the airless, windowless waiting room. She was surprised to find her mother and three daughters sitting there. Three brightly scrubbed faces surrounded her, three sets of arms hugged her excitedly. Each girl took turns sitting on her lap with their arms clasped tight around her neck. Robyn gushed at the thought that her mother would be home in time for her tenth birthday. But Tilly whispered disturbing news: rumors were flying that Bob Hepple had given some kind of statement to the police. Bob knew everything. He had attended many meetings with Ruth and others at Rivonia, knew why she had gone there and whom she had met with. If Bob agreed to give evidence, she could wind up sitting in the dock with the Rivonia defendants facing treason or sabotage charges.

After her family left, Ruth had little time to digest this information. Within minutes, she was called out of her cell again, this time by Nel. Ruth stared into the flat, expressionless face and the cold blue eyes she had come to despise, waiting for him to launch another futile round of questions. But today Nel had none. "I've come to tell you to pack your things," he said. "I'm releasing you."

These were the words that Ruth was longing to hear. She knew she was close to the breaking point. But she also knew her jailers would not be deterred by a mere legalism. While the ninety-day term could not be technically extended, she could be arrested again immediately after her release. She did not want to be humiliated by her own false hopes.

"I don't believe you," she told Nel. "You're going to rearrest me."

"I mean what I say," he replied. "I've come to release you this morning."

"Don't bluff me," she said. "Don't tell me one thing and do another. Don't make a farce out of this thing. Don't talk of release if you mean something else."

Nel denied that he was bluffing. "I've come to release you," he insisted.

The wardress, who had been listening, intervened. "Don't be like that, Mrs. Slovo," she said. "Here is your chance to go home. Come, I'll help you pack."

Ruth let the wardress escort her through the chilly maze of bars, iron doors, stairs and hallways back to her cell. There they set to work. First Ruth changed from her slacks and sweater into the navy frock she had kept carefully folded in the bright red leather suitcase under the cot. Then they stuffed her other clothes into the suitcase, and loaded a basket with dishes and her thermos. Against her will, Ruth could feel the excitement building deep in her stomach.

She handed a box of dried fruit to the wardress as a present, then picked up the suitcase, basket and thermos, and staggered through the cell door. At the charge office, Nel hovered silently as a jovial desk sergeant filled out the release form. The sergeant made sure the carbon had worked properly, then stamped both sheets, ripping out the bottom copy with a flourish, and handing it to Ruth with a slight bow of the head.

Someone gave her a property bag that contained her purse and the other possessions that had been seized when she was first arrested. She asked the sergeant if she could use his phone to call her mother to come pick her up. The rules did not allow it, he replied, but there was a pay phone on the sidewalk just outside. She fished through her purse until she came up with a threepenny piece for the coin box. Triumphantly she headed for the door.

She was on the sidewalk, halfway to the phone booth, five more steps to freedom, when two men in dark suits intercepted her. "Just a minute, Mrs. Slovo," one of them said.

"What do you want now?" she demanded. But she already sensed the answer. Her head was swimming and she heard little as the man rattled off the official notice of detention, ending with the words "another period of ninety days."

Inside the charge office again, she stood silently while the desk sergeant, now grim-faced, filled out a new set of papers. Nel had vanished, but the two plainclothes detectives stood on either side of her. She left the suitcase, basket and thermos in the middle of the floor, and marched briskly back to the women's cellblock with the two detectives right behind her. The wardress sighed as she gestured to Ruth to come inside. When she did, the detectives slammed the iron gate behind her and crisply snapped the lock in place.

For hours Ruth sat frozen on the edge of her cot, still in her navy blue outfit, as wave after wave of self-pity washed over her. She had wanted to be so strong, and she had failed. They had stolen her hope, and her dignity. She knew now she would have to do something. She could not bear to face another ninety days of agony and stalemate, followed by perhaps another and yet another. She had lost a test of will, but now she decided to engage her captors in a different test. She would offer them crumbs of useless information to see if she could provoke some response—either her release or a formal criminal charge that would allow her to see a lawyer and end her time in solitary confinement.

She did not have long to wait. The next morning, Nel came to her cell. "You see, Mrs. Slovo," he said, "we are persistent."

Ruth felt drained. After a moment's silence he asked if she was willing to go to the Grays to answer questions. She said yes.

Viktor met her there on the seventh floor. "Don't lose your nerve," he told her. "Come on now, hold on."

It was to be a full-fledged statement. She reviewed her life history as an activist and journalist, the years of commitment and harassment. She confessed that she had attended meetings at Rivonia, but claimed to know nothing about sabotage. She could not tell them what Joe had been up to. He had always protected her by not talking about it. As for names, she had only a handful of well-used ones to offer.

The ploy did not work. "It's a funny thing, isn't it?" said Viktor. "But every name you've given us is the name of someone who has left the country." He stalked out of the room. Swanepoel was furious. "You've told us nothing, absolutely nothing," he said.

He rattled off the names of comrades whom she knew and had worked closely with. "What about Schermbrucker?" he demanded. "What about Beyleveld? What about Fischer?

"I know you communists by now," Swanepoel declared. "I've dealt with dozens of your kind. And I've learned that they have to be put against a wall and squeezed, pushed and squeezed, into a corner. Then they change and talk."

Ruth's head was reeling. It was crazy for her to think she could fabricate, probe and improvise on the spot with these people. They knew too much and they gave nothing away.

The next day her mother was allowed to make another visit. For the first time since her arrest, Ruth neglected to put on lipstick and makeup. "Are you cracking up?" Tilly whispered. Ruth nodded. "We're depending on you," Tilly told her.

Every day for a week—sometimes for two sessions in the same day—her interrogators called her in again, interspersing their questions with threats and promises. Ruth refused to complete her statement. She would tell them nothing more. But she had already said too much. They could use even a half-statement to bludgeon other detainees. She felt a wave of intense guilt and despair. Her mistake could destroy her standing with one group of people whose love and respect she most depended upon—her comrades. If she lost them, she would lose everything.

She could not sleep. She had nausea and diarrhea. Her ulcer, always a problem, was acting up again. Her doctor was summoned and prescribed medicine for the ulcer and a vial of sleeping pills.

The days were gray. Ruth berated herself over and over. Joe had always told her that her greatest weakness was her craving for acceptance and her fear of rejection. Is that why she had made a statement? Or was it arrogance? Did she really believe she could outwit these thugs? She felt like a spider trapped in her own web. The centrifugal pull of her friends, relatives and comrades was slipping away. There was nothing to hold her down, no one to keep her intact. She was, at last, totally alone.

She reached for the sleeping pills and swallowed them. All of them.

With no success. When she awoke she was lying on her cot with the commandant and the wardress beside the bed. "Do you want a doctor?" he asked.

Ruth began weeping uncontrollably. The prison doctor came, examined, and went. Viktor stopped in and left his handkerchief on the bed.

Ruth lost track of time. Her own doctor visited her again. She told him what she had done.

"You don't think I'd be so foolish as to leave you with that size dose?" he asked her.

He recommended that she see a prison psychiatrist, but she said she would not disclose to anyone on the prison staff what she had done. The police would find out immediately and only use it as further ammunition to destroy her.

"I'm heading for a crackup, aren't I?" she asked.

"You've had one already."

A few days later, Helen Suzman received a phone call from Violet Weinberg, one of Ruth's comrades. Normally the two women would have had nothing to say to each other. Weinberg was a communist, Suzman a liberal. There was much political mistrust and rivalry between the two groups. But the comrades had decided to come to Suzman because there was no place else to turn.

"I am asking you as one woman to another to intervene in Ruth First's case," Violet told Helen. "We hear that she is in a very bad way mentally. Won't you ask Mr. Vorster to release her and let her leave South Africa on an exit permit?"

Suzman replied that she would be glad to raise Ruth's case when she visited the Justice Minister the following week. Soon after, however, Tilly First phoned to demand that Suzman back off. Many blacks were suffering much more than her daughter, Tilly told her, and they must see that there were whites prepared to suffer as well. Tilly's imperious tone angered Suzman, who replied that she would drop the matter immediately. "I have more than enough work on my hands," she told Tilly.

But soon another phone call came, this one from Bram Fischer. Suzman had known Bram for years, enjoyed his company and admired his integrity, although not his politics. He also knew how to turn on the charm. "Is that my favorite MP?" he asked.

"Come off it, Bram," replied Suzman, who liked to convey the impression that she was impervious to such flattery.

Bram begged Suzman to ignore Tilly's phone call and to proceed with pleading to Vorster on Ruth's behalf. The next morning, Suzman met with both Bram and Tilly, who reiterated the request for help.

A few days later Helen Suzman drove to the Union Buildings, the ornate sandstone government complex overlooking Pretoria. She was surprised, as always, by the lack of security. She walked straight past the only guard, a dozing war veteran, and headed up the steps to Vorster's second-floor office.

John Vorster respected Suzman's brain and talent but despised her liberal views. "That woman is worth ten United Party MPs," he was once quoted as saying. When she heard about it, Suzman replied that Vorster had underestimated her worth.

The private interview was short and formal. Vorster addressed her as "Mrs. Suzman" and offered her coffee. She called him "Minister." There was no small talk. Suzman got right to the point. "I've come to discuss some cases with you," she told him. She said she had been informed that Ruth First was in a serious state of depression because of her time in solitary confinement. "I hear she's in a very bad way," Suzman told Vorster. "I am sure you don't want a suicide in prison."

Suzman said Ruth's family had indicated to her that Ruth would be willing to leave South Africa on a one-way exit permit if she were released. Vorster had often said publicly that he would be happy to ship radicals out of the country, provided they agreed never to return. In essence, Ruth's family was offering him such a deal.

"I will look into the matter," Vorster told Helen Suzman.

Every day after her suicide attempt, Viktor came to visit Ruth. He arranged for her to receive *The Charterhouse of Parma* from her mother. When she said she would answer no more questions, he promised not to press. He talked more about himself, his childhood ambition to be a policeman, his parents' frustration when he chose police work over studying music at a university. He told her he hoped to study law someday. He joked and bantered with Ruth, shared cigarettes with her in the interrogation room. When she told him she did not want to see him anymore, he replied that he did not believe her. "I've watched when you walk out of here back to your cell, and your head drops and your shoulders slump as you go in."

He asked her again about making a statement. No, she said, they were out to trap her. "But how can we trap you if we don't have evidence?" he asked. "You'll make it up," she replied. He grew angry and clenched his fist. She mockingly raised her chin as if to accept the blow. "I'd rather kiss it," he said.

Ruth hated herself for participating in this bout of flirting. But she needed the human contact, longed for someone to talk to. Viktor was all she had. The visits went on for two weeks. Then on a Saturday, she mentioned that the next day was Robyn's tenth birthday party. I know, he replied. Would you like to be there?

Of course not, she said. She did not want to be escorted home, then dragged back to prison. Never.

No, he said, she had misunderstood. If she would just make a statement, he could have her out by tomorrow. Home for good.

She refused. No statement, no cooperation. But the weekend dragged interminably. On Monday, to her great surprise, he came to tell her she was being released. At first she did not believe him. "Don't try *that* again," she told him.

But this time it was for real. She had no idea why they were letting her go, but they were. It took several hours for the paperwork to go through. Then he and van der Merwe drove her to the house. He warned her not to try to evade her banning order or to make a dash for the border. "I'll be there to catch you," he told her.

As Viktor and van der Merwe pulled away, Ruth had the awful feeling that she was not done with them. Someday, somehow, she feared, they would come for her again.

Ruth was not the only detainee in Marshall Square with whom Viktor came in contact. Jimmy had known him for years, and occasionally Viktor and his partner were pressed into service to escort Jimmy on his various trips back and forth between prisons in Pretoria and Johannesburg. But all the charm and pretense that Viktor displayed toward Ruth vanished when he spoke to Jimmy. Instead, there was a hard, ugly edge and a rancid anti-Semitism that seemed designed to frighten Jimmy into submission.

Early in October, Viktor and van der Merwe took Jimmy back to Pretoria Local. On the way, Viktor discoursed on a topic that seemed to be one of his favorites: Jews and Their Crimes. It sounded straight out of the Nazi handbook. He talked of their alleged cunning and their parasitic nature, of how they always waited until a country had been settled and established and then moved in to take it over. He also offered a few kind words about Hitler. Perhaps he meant all of it—other detainees later would recall Viktor expressing similar sentiments during their interrogations. Or perhaps he was seeking to goad Jimmy into an explosion. Jimmy tried to keep his cool. In his book he recalls responding: "You know, Vic, I've always known that you had no manners, but for the first time I realize that you are also stupid." Maybe Jimmy said it that way, or maybe he later wished he had.

The next morning Jimmy was taken to a prison reception room. Viktor came in, put his hand on Jimmy's shoulder and said, "I hereby release you from detention." He lifted his hand, took a breath and put it back on the shoulder. "James Kantor, I arrest you on a charge of sabotage. You will appear in court tomorrow." Jimmy asked for a charge sheet, but Viktor walked out the door without further comment.

During afternoon exercises, Jimmy was brought to the yard where the other white prisoners trudged in silence. The men had never been allowed to talk to each other while in the yard as detainees. Now, however, their status had changed to awaiting-trial prisoners with rights and privileges far more extensive. Technically their isolation was over. As one of the lawyers among them, Jimmy knew the rules.

"Good afternoon, gentlemen! I trust you are all well?" he called out cheerfully. Bob Hepple dropped his toilet bucket with a crash, turned around and stared at Jimmy. Rusty Bernstein and Denis Goldberg stood stock-still, as if waiting for the sky to fall. Suddenly they realized what had happened, and they all began to talk, slowly at first, but then in loud happy bursts of sentences and ideas.

Rusty and his comrades had been held for eighty-eight days in solitary confinement. Now, at last, they would face trial. Like Jimmy, ten of them—Rusty and six other Rivonia detainees, plus Nelson Mandela and two other activists—had been released from detention, then immediately rearrested and charged with organizing sabotage and armed rebellion against the state.

The maximum penalty, for those convicted, was death by hanging.

SIX

ON TRIAL

Everything belongs to the Court.
Franz Kafka
The Trial

T he first to arrive at the Palace of Justice in Pretoria on the morning of October 9, 1963, were the eleven defendants. Shortly after
breakfast, while the sun was still negotiating with the retreating
darkness, they were manacled and herded into an armored police van at
Pretoria Local. The van was divided by a steel partition—the four white
prisoners sat in front, the seven blacks in the rear. The van and its
human cargo then joined a protective convoy of a dozen police vehicles
led by a limousine that carried the prison commandant and two senior
police officials. It was followed by riot trucks filled with uniformed men
bearing Sten guns, dog handlers and Alsatians. Armed police lined the
route to the courthouse.

The ornate, neo-Italianate brownstone structure, finished in 1902,
looked like a castle under siege. Officers cradling machine guns ringed
the outside. Another unit of police, carrying handguns and tear-gas
canisters, was posted nearby. A large crowd of the defendants' supporters was already forming in front of the steps on the lawn of Church
Square, the stately heart of old Pretoria. Many had traveled from distant
black townships, spent hard-earned money to take smoky buses and
rickety, overstuffed taxis to this strange place, where they stood under a

Meeting of the Communist Party of South Africa, Johannesburg District.
From left, Ruth First, Bram Fischer, Joe Slovo, and Rusty Bernstein

Ruth First

Joe Slovo

The Rivonia Trialists and co-conspirators.
Top center photo is Nelson Mandela

Lilliesleaf farm, July 11, 1963

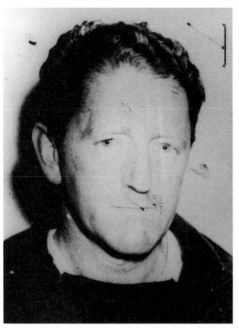
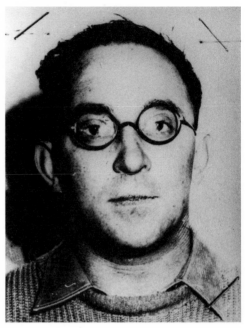

Rusty Bernstein, July 11, 1963   *Dennis Goldberg, July 11, 1963*

James Kantor and Harold Wolpe

Lt. Willem Petrus Johannes van Wyk and Arthur Goldreich watch police search Lilliesleaf grounds, July 12, 1963

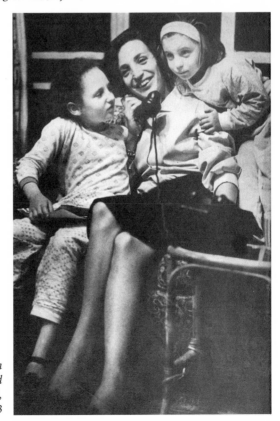

AnnMarie Wolpe and daughters Peta and Tessa receive news from Harold that he is safe in Bechuanaland, September 1, 1963

*Jimmy and Barbara Kantor
leaving the Palace of Justice after
his release on bail, December 1963*

*Ruth First and daughters Gillian
and Robyn leave Johannesburg
for London, March 13, 1964*

Rusty and Hilda Bernstein leave courthouse
after Rusty's release on bail, June 13, 1964

Bram Fischer

Percy Yutar

Nelson Mandela greets Percy Yutar on the day the State President invited his former prosecutor to lunch, November 23, 1995

handful of brown, forlorn palm trees and the dour bronze gaze of the statue of Paul Kruger, the wily Calvinist who had been the first and last President of the old Transvaal Republic. Members of the crowd hoped to catch a glimpse of their imprisoned leaders. But the police convoy avoided the gathering by pulling into the palace's rear courtyard, whose iron gates were then slammed shut and locked. The prisoners were bundled into the basement of the courthouse and locked into two separate cells, divided once again by race. Most of them immediately lit cigarettes, filling the small rooms with thick smoke.

Hilda and Toni Bernstein arrived early as well, making their way through the crowd. They had to pass three different security checks before they could enter Court Three, where they sat on backless wooden benches in the public gallery, which had barriers running down the middle separating the audience by race. Hilda could see Winnie Mandela and Albertina Sisulu on the benches opposite. Winnie was banned and could not speak to Hilda or anyone else. Albertina had just been released from detention. When Hilda started over to speak to her, a young policeman stepped in her way. She was not allowed to enter the Africans-only section, he explained, and insisted that Hilda return to the white side of the room. Even though she and Albertina had worked together for two decades, even though their two husbands were on trial together for their lives, the two women could not sit side by side.

Moments later Rusty Bernstein and the other defendants entered the courtroom from the basement below. They were led up a steep flight of steps that came out in the middle of the courtroom behind the lawyers' tables and in front of the public gallery. The steps led directly to a long wooden prisoners' dock built specially for this trial, where they sat facing the judge's bench with their backs to the audience. Two warders accompanied each prisoner and took seats behind the dock, acting as a human *cordon sanitaire* between the defendants and the audience.

Although Hilda knew the ordeal that the detainees had gone through, she was nonetheless shocked when she saw how they looked. Nelson Mandela had lost at least twenty-five pounds. His face, once well rounded and a deep, glistening brown, had turned sunken and hollow; there were thick bags under his eyes and his flesh was a sickly yellow. He was dressed in the humiliating prison garb that was regulation for Africans: khaki shirt and shorts and open-toed sandals on his bare feet.

Rusty appeared to be ill and much older; he looked down and never glanced at Hilda or the audience on his way to the dock. Govan Mbeki's hair had turned completely gray. Jimmy Kantor, normally ebullient, looked pale, haggard and subdued. Only Ahmed Kathrada seemed jaunty and unperturbed.

Taking his place at the prosecution table alongside two assistants was a small, dapper, balding man with a deformed left hand and a supercilious smile. Hilda knew from reading the newspapers that he was Percy Yutar, Deputy Attorney General for Transvaal province, and she had read of his reputation as an aggressive, flamboyant prosecutor with a flair for cross-examination and a passion for publicity. He had worked hard to prepare for this case, and he seemed eager for the proceedings to begin.

There were five lawyers at the main defense table. Bram Fischer was senior counsel for the team, which had been put together by Joel Joffe, Jimmy's former law partner. Vernon Berrange, perhaps the country's most aggressive and accomplished cross-examiner, had agreed to help. Hilda knew him well—he had been a communist in the days before the party was banned, and he had served on the defense team during the four-year Treason Trial. His presence reassured her—at least the police would know they could not lie with impunity on the stand because Berrange was waiting to pounce on their every claim. The other two lawyers, George Bizos and Arthur Chaskalson, both of them young and extremely talented barristers who were serving as junior counsel, were less familiar to her. At a nearby table sat the legal team for Jimmy, who was expected to conduct a separate defense, led by his friend George Lowen.

Presiding was Justice Quartus de Wet, the sixty-five-year-old senior Judge President of the Transvaal. Son of a prominent judge and politician, de Wet was known as an experienced, independent and no-nonsense jurist. Unfortunately, he was also known for his obstinacy, short attention span and lack of patience. Once he had made up his mind about a case—and he usually seemed to do so long before all the evidence was in—he tended to lose interest. Hilda took some hope from the fact that he had been appointed to the bench before the Nationalists came to power in 1948; he would not feel obliged to deal out death sentences just because the Justice Minister demanded them. At the same time, he was a white judge presiding over a white man's court weighing the fate of black men whose experience and feelings he knew nothing about and could not even begin to fathom. He might be able to deliver his own personal notion of fairness, but for these defendants he could never dispense justice.

The usher called for silence and de Wet entered, dressed in the scarlet robes reserved for criminal trials. He gave a perfunctory nod to counsel at the prosecution and defense tables immediately before him and took his seat on the elaborate raised dais of carved mahogany and teak that reminded Hilda of a four-poster canopied bed. Beige curtains hung from the walls on either side of the dais. A single ceiling fan at the end of a long rod spun lazily above his honor's head, stirring the stale air.

Yutar rose. In a conspicuous display of pomp and circumstance, he adjusted his robes decorously, then introduced himself and the two lawyers assisting him. "My lord," he declared in sonorous tones, "I call the case of *The State versus the National High Command and Others*." He handed in the indictment and annex. For the first time the defendants received a copy of the charges against them. The State alleged that the defendants, "acting in concert and conspiring and making common purpose" with seventy named co-conspirators, the ANC and the Communist Party, had "incited, instigated, commanded, aided, advised, encouraged or procured other persons to commit the wrongful and willful acts of sabotage, preparatory to and in facilitation of guerrilla warfare in the Republic of South Africa, coupled with an armed invasion and violent revolution."

The newspapers had been given the indictment hours earlier. Even as Yutar spoke, a special edition of the *Rand Daily Mail* was hitting the streets with the banner headline "REVOLT, INVASION, CHARGES" and a front-page photograph of the smiling prosecutor.

Bram stood next. The defendants had been held under extreme conditions of solitary confinement, he told the court, and would need weeks to properly prepare their defense. "The accused in this case are people who carry the deep respect of a very large proportion of the population," said Bram. "There should be no urgency to bring them to trial. We want justice to be seen to be done." He asked for six weeks to review the case. "By then we will be able to give the court an indication of when we hope to be ready."

But the State was not interested in delay. It had the climate and the momentum and no desire to let either cool down or falter. Yutar argued that the case must begin quickly for the sake of his witnesses. "I fear for their safety!" he proclaimed.

Bram had wanted six weeks. The judge granted three. The proceeding would resume on October 29, he ruled. Less than a half hour after it started, the first session of the most important trial in South Africa's history was over.

The court scheduled a hearing that afternoon to review Jimmy's request for bail. His lawyers were confident; there appeared to be no substantive evidence linking Jimmy with Rivonia. He had been indicted with the others either because of a terrible miscarriage of justice or because the police had chosen to take him hostage for Harold Wolpe, his brother-in-law. Surely even Yutar would see this and would see as well that Jimmy, a fellow lawyer, was no threat to flee a trial in which he had every hope of vindication. And Yutar must have known that Jimmy had suffered a nervous breakdown in prison. The other defendants were taken back to their cells at Pretoria Local, but Jimmy was allowed to remain below until the bail hearing. The court staff permitted Barbara to come downstairs to see him. They embraced for the first time in months. The staff found an easy chair for Barbara, who was pregnant with her first child by Jimmy. She was even allowed to use a phone and order a steak for Jimmy from a nearby restaurant. Things were looking up.

But Jimmy's lawyers had underestimated how badly the police wanted him to remain behind bars. Willie van Wyk was convinced that Jimmy was the moneyman behind Umkhonto. Others were just happy to have a member of Harold Wolpe's family in the dock to send a message to the comrades that they could not embarrass the South African police without someone paying the price. After Harold Nicholas, one of Jimmy's defense team, addressed the court, Yutar rose to assure the judge there was no doubt whatsoever that Jimmy was a full-fledged conspirator.

Bail was denied.

After the hearing, Nicholas stormed over to the prosecutor's table and demanded that Yutar substantiate the allegation. Gathering his papers, Yutar hurried for the door. But on the way out he told Nicholas that he had an affidavit from "a responsible policeman" alleging that James Kantor had recruited Africans for military training abroad. Nicholas was stunned. Jimmy laughed at the outlandishness of the charge. But he understood what it meant: that the police would stop at nothing to keep him locked up until he either agreed to testify against his fellow defendants or was himself convicted of a crime he did not commit. Jimmy, who as a lawyer had once thought the police were the good guys, was now reaching the opposite conclusion.

It should have come as no surprise that Percy Yutar would show Jimmy no mercy. The two men had clashed during the Oppenheimer Jewel Case several years earlier, when Jimmy had defended two of the men charged with stealing nearly 500,000 rand in jewels from the wealthy family's home. Yutar had led the prosecution team. His star witness was a third alleged conspirator who had turned state's evidence. The judge did not believe his testimony. Jimmy's clients went free and he had not shied away from claiming credit. Now he was convinced that Yutar wanted revenge. Besides, Yutar trusted the security police. If they told him Jimmy Kantor was guilty, that was good enough for him.

In truth, Yutar knew only one style of prosecution: bulldog fast, furious and derisive. For years, he had used it with great success in criminal cases. He would not—perhaps could not—change, now that he was dealing with a political one. He did not see that Rivonia was indeed a different kind of case with very different defendants, not common criminals who would deny their guilt and be easily unmasked as liars, but men of dignity and integrity who would admit who they were and what they had done, and who planned to put the State itself on trial. In such a situation, all of the tricks, shortcuts and oratorical embellishments that had served Yutar so well during the hard years of climbing the prosecutorial ladder might end up betraying him.

Fifty-two years old at the time of the Rivonia Trial, Percy Yutar was one of South Africa's most prominent and experienced prosecutors. He had a tough, logical mind, a flair for the dramatic and an unquenchable thirst for headlines. The press, which was not inclined to delve too deeply into the personalities of those behind the levers of the state's legal machine, was fawning. One article entitled "The Yutar Legend" called him "far and away the most qualified legal brain this country has ever possessed." It added in a subheadline, "Ruthless avenger is also gentle."

He was many things, but perhaps the most fundamental fact about Percy Yutar's identity was that he was Jewish. He was born in Cape Town of parents who had come to South Africa, like so many of the radicals he pursued, from the ghettos of Lithuania. Percy was one of eight children and money was scarce. As a young man he was expected to work in his father's butcher shop. Even though the Yutars were a religious family, his father would violate Jewish law and open the shop on Saturday morning to service the weekend trade. One Saturday, Percy was jamming slick cuts of raw beef through the electric mincing machine when his left hand slipped and his fingers plunged into the blades. The fingers were mangled beyond repair, leaving Percy with raw stumps at the end of his hand and a constant reminder of the price he had inflicted upon himself for violating the Sabbath.

Yutar attended the University of Cape Town on a scholarship and eventually became the first student in South Africa in a century to be awarded a doctorate in law. Still, even with the highest of degrees, Jews were not welcome in the cozy, inbred offices of the South African civil service. He was given a lowly position as an "Outdoor Officer" for the office of the Telephone Manager in Johannesburg, tracking down illegal phone hookups and delinquent subscribers through the dusty summer heat and the winter chill. After five years of such work he finally received an appointment as a junior law clerk in the accounts department of the Ministry of Justice. He worked in Room 66 at the Palace of Justice, one floor above the courtroom where he now performed as prosecutor. The anti-Semitism among his co-workers was intense; there were nights when a frustrated Yutar would return home to his lodgings in Pretoria, close the door, and cry himself to sleep. But he hung on. He finally was promoted to junior prosecutor and assigned to Johannesburg in 1940.

This was what Yutar had been waiting for. As a prosecutor, he finally felt in control of his own fate. He could write the script for a trial, direct the drama and play the principal role. Neither his father nor the Jew-hating bastards in Pretoria could tell him what to do. He quickly completed his apprenticeship and became an expert in criminal fraud. Soon he was prosecuting a much wider range of crimes—murders, jewel thefts, public corruption. He was respected by his colleagues in the prosecutor's office and feared or despised by the criminal bar. No one worked harder, or seemed to enjoy his power more. Eventually he became Deputy Attorney General for the Transvaal. But his ambition to rise even higher remained profoundly transparent. "The office of the Attorney General is a laurel I would much like to pluck," he told the *South African Jewish Times* in 1958. No one doubted it.

The law was not just a job for Yutar, it was a way of life and a gentleman's code. He lined his shelves at home with law books and books about famous legal cases—the Lindbergh kidnap case and the Eichmann trial became two of his fascinations—and fancied himself an authority. His walls were covered with pen-and-ink caricatures of British legal figures in wigs and robes, and especially of his hero, Lord Birkenhead, the nineteenth-century doyen of the British legal establishment.

Along the way Yutar made compromises. He had no political views and was indifferent to apartheid. Still, he became one of Special Branch's favorite prosecutors. Policemen like Swanepoel would sit behind the prosecution table to smirk and enjoy the show while Yutar demolished defense witnesses. Often he would turn and smile at the police before resuming the rhetorical decapitation at hand. He was their agent and willing tool. They brought him big cases, helped promote his career. When the ninety-day detention law came to pass, some prosecutors might have had qualms about what it meant to build a case on tainted testimony from witnesses so thoroughly at the mercy of the worst kind of policemen. Percy Yutar was not so fastidious. He would take the new weapons the apartheid police state was providing and he would use them to their utmost. It was, as he often solemnly said, his duty.

Beyond this, Yutar had an obsessive need for love and attention. He pandered to the police, to judges, to other lawyers and to the press in part because he craved their recognition and respect. When he was winning in court, he could be imperious and disdainful. When he lost, his voice would lose its timbre, ascend to a sad falsetto that mimicked a child's lament, powered by a lifetime of grievance and self-pity. He could be a bad winner and a sore loser. Among his faults, this was perhaps his most unattractive.

One thing he never compromised was his religion. Even as a junior clerk in the Jew-hating Afrikaner bureaucracy, he proudly wore a signet ring in the shape of the Star of David. Every Saturday morning he would attend *shul*. For more than a decade he served as president of the United Hebrew Congregation, Johannesburg's largest Orthodox synagogue. His religion in a sense was his justification. He could do nothing immoral, for his faith would not allow it.

The Rivonia Trial was itself a test of faith. Yutar had hungered for it because of his ambitions. What better stepping-stone to the state's top prosecutorial post than to successfully dispatch the state's most dangerous enemies to the gallows or a life sentence on Robben Island? But the Jewish question was also important. All six of the whites arrested at Rivonia came from Jewish backgrounds, as did Harold Wolpe, Ruth

First, Joe Slovo, Michael Harmel and many other prominent leftists. The four white defendants at the trial—Bernstein, Goldberg, Hepple and Kantor—were all considered Jews, even those who were resolutely atheistic or of mixed origin.

The security police, of course, were well aware of the Jewish backgrounds of the white defendants, and tried to use it for leverage with the black defendants. "You must understand that you are in a sinking ship," one of his interrogators told Govan Mbeki. "Let me tell you that the Jewboys are crumbling and you will be left alone in this shit. Whom can you blame for this state but yourself? You won't work, you eat from the cupped hand of the Jewboy, you sleep in the Jewboy's blankets." (Mbeki was not swayed; he told the police nothing.)

The Jewish weekly press steadfastly ignored the Rivonia raid and its implications. When, two weeks after the raid, the chairman of the Cape Council of the South African Jewish Board of Deputies issued a "Call for Tolerance," he was referring to the conflict between Orthodox and Reform Jews, not between blacks and whites. But the implications did not go unnoticed by the progovernment Afrikaans press. *Dagbreek en Sondagnuus*, the Sunday newspaper, reported that it had received a number of letters from readers commenting upon the "high percentage" of Jews among ninety-day detainees. It asked the Board of Deputies, the country's foremost Jewish institution, why this was so and whether it was an indication that Jews were not happy in South Africa.

The board ducked the first question in its official reply. "The facts show abundantly that the Jewish community of South Africa is an established, loyal and patriotic part of the population," it stated. "The conduct of individuals of any section is their own responsibility and no part of the community can or should be asked to accept responsibility." As for those individual acts: "The Jewish community condemns illegality in whatever part of the population it might manifest itself."

Perhaps so. But where some Jews saw the radicals' Jewish origins as an embarrassment that they needed to conceal or distance themselves from, Percy Yutar saw an opportunity. Who better to prosecute Jewish traitors than a loyal Jew? Who better to put things right and prove that not all Jews were radicals hell-bent upon overthrowing the government?

In many ways the Rivonia defendants and Yutar represented two traditional Jewish responses to tyranny. The radicals had chosen to oppose the state. Even though they themselves as whites were among the beneficiaries of apartheid, they sided with its victims. Those among them who identified themselves as Jews cited the moral imperative to oppose evil as well as the pragmatic argument that, in the long run, Jewish interests would best be served by siding with the oppressed majority that would inevitably come to power someday.

Yutar's response came from a different tradition. Often during the Middle Ages, when Jews were faced with a tyrannical ruler, an interceder would emerge to defend Jewish interests in the court of the tyrant. This person became known in Yiddish as the *shtadlan* or Court Jew. By paying tribute or doing other favors for the tyrant, the Court Jew sought the ruler's protection for himself and his fellow Jews. When the relationship succeeded, the *shtadlan* often gained prominence and riches. For anyone in the Jewish community who had a serious problem with the tyrant's thugs, he became the man to see. Yutar in effect became the symbolic *shtadlan* for South African Jewry. By prosecuting his fellow Jews, he was providing protection for the larger community.

Many Jews were not pleased about Yutar's self-appointed role; they felt moral qualms about apartheid and preferred that the community keep the lowest of profiles. When Julius Lewin, a prominent law professor and liberal, used a memorial meeting for the Warsaw Ghetto as a forum to criticize Jewish apathy on racial issues, the Board of Deputies sought to quickly smother the debate. Lewin had said it was "a betrayal of religion" for Jews to submit to "political blackmail" and remain silent about apartheid. "South Africa is a sick society and the Jews cannot hope to enjoy permanent security while other nonconforming groups feel threatened in the atmosphere created by the ruling race," he warned. But the board responded with censure and alarm: "Appeals to Jews as Jews to support any political program are without justification and do the Jewish community and also the country as a whole a disservice. It is particularly to be deplored when such appeals emanate from individuals or groups within the Jewish community itself."

Still, some members of the Jewish establishment sympathized quietly with the defendants. When AnnMarie Wolpe was released from detention following Harold's escape, a two-man delegation from the King David School paid a visit to the house. They expressed deep disapproval of Harold and Arthur's deeds; at the same time, however, they offered to waive nursery-school fees for Peta and Tessa until AnnMarie felt able to pay again. Such was the ambivalence of most Jews. For them, Percy

Yutar's enthusiastic championing of the state was as unseemly as Harold Wolpe and Rusty Bernstein's indefatigable talent for treason.

One of the first decisions Yutar faced was what charges to lodge against the accused. Both treason and sabotage carried the death penalty. But treason was an older, more traditional charge, one that had been on the statute books since the days of British colonial rule, and it bore the distinct rigor and odor of English jurisprudence. It required a lengthy and arduous preliminary hearing at which the State would be compelled to divulge much of its evidence, and it required two witnesses to corroborate each charge. And treason had fallen into something of disrepute following the 1956 Treason Trial, which had dragged on for five years and ended in fiasco for the State. Some of the same people charged then—Mandela, Sisulu, Bernstein—were in the dock again. To try them for treason once more, Yutar argued, would be like taking two bites of the same cherry.

Yutar opted instead for sabotage, which had been legislated as a capital offense the previous year. As a "new" offense, it had certain police-state conveniences courtesy of Justice Minister Vorster and the Nationalist-controlled Parliament. No preliminary hearing was required, and only one witness need testify to each alleged act. Better still, from the prosecution's point of view, once a destructive criminal act had been shown to have occurred, the burden shifted to the defendant to prove that the particular deed was *not* meant as an act of sabotage.

There was only one problem. Treason was a classic charge, one that the public itself held in far more awe than sabotage and, in the minds of the officials weighing the charges, treason was what the Rivonia men ultimately had committed. To charge them with anything less suggested the State did not have total confidence in its case. Yutar's boss, Transvaal Attorney General Rudolf Rein, implied as much when he learned that his deputy was proposing sabotage rather than treason. "Percy," he asked, "are you afraid to prosecute this case? If so, we'll be prepared to replace you."

But Percy Yutar had no intention of surrendering the reins of the biggest case of his career. "Rudy, I'm not afraid to do my duty," he replied. The Attorney General demurred. Sabotage it was.

The men of the defense team were a very different breed of lawyer than Percy Yutar. A half dozen attorneys had turned down Hilda already—too busy or too wary to take on such a controversial case—when one day she paid a visit to the office of a little-known but highly respected solicitor. Joel Joffe was thirty years old and a liberal of traditional stripe. He was helping Jimmy Kantor wind down his legal practice as a last act before leaving the country. He could see what was happening to South Africa's legal system—safeguards for the accused were slowly being ground to dust—and he wanted no part of it. He also did not want to raise his two children in an atmosphere of paranoia and repression. He and his wife Vanetta had obtained entry permits for Australia and fully intended to use them. They had sold their house and packed their belongings. Their furniture was sitting boxed and crated at the port of Durban awaiting the next freighter for Sydney. Within a few months, they planned to follow.

Joffe was a close friend of Arthur Chaskalson's, who was close to Bram. He had never met Hilda or Rusty or any of the other detainees. He did not know how long the case would last or even what the charges would be. But he knew enough from reading the newspapers to judge that a trial would be a mere formality. The State apparently had a mountain of evidence. The police were conducting an unprecedented media campaign, leaking documents and allegations. A defense would be a waste of time.

Nonetheless, Joffe grew angry as Hilda described her futile efforts to find a lawyer. There had been a time, he believed, when the legal profession in South Africa was known for its proud and principled men. Where had they all gone? He, of course, was about to leave as well. But he did not feel he could turn his back on people who were being chewed up in the machinery of state repression.

He told Hilda he would take the case.*

In the next few weeks, a number of other concerned relatives stopped by Joffe's office: Albertina Sisulu; Annie Goldberg, Denis's el-

---

*It was a most significant decision, not only for the defendants, who benefited from Joffe's humane blend of thoughtfulness and thoroughness, but also for history. Once the trial ended and Joffe moved to London, he spent his spare time while job hunting writing down his memories of the case. Burdened by his lawyerly style, Joffe's account was pinpoint but dry and he sent the draft to Rusty Bernstein. At that point, memories and sensibilities diverge. Joffe claims that what he got back was so polished and better written that Rusty must have thoroughly revised the entire work. Rusty says he cannot recall doing anything so elaborate. In any case, the finished work was not published for thirty years, but Joffe showed it to anyone who asked. The manuscript became the foundation for the trial sections of Hilda's, Jimmy's and Nelson Mandela's memoirs—and for this book as well.

derly mother, who was staying at the Bernstein house; and Winnie Mandela. Press reports indicated that Nelson Mandela, who was already imprisoned when the raid on Lilliesleaf took place, would be charged along with the Rivonia men. If so it would confirm that the men were going to be accused of criminal acts that predated the Rivonia meeting.

Joffe went to the Grays to see if he could learn more. Percy Yutar had set up an office on the seventh floor, a few doors down from Colonel Klindt. The two men refused to divulge anything about the charges they were considering. They did volunteer that Joffe himself need not worry about being investigated or harassed for representing the defendants. Given that he had not asked for such an undertaking, and knowing how they were treating Jimmy Kantor, Joel found this assurance more of a warning than a comfort.

After they left Klindt's office, Yutar escorted Joffe to his own temporary quarters and offered a curious encomium to the security police. "I have been at the Grays' for three weeks now," he told Joffe, "and in all that time I have not heard a single word of anti-Semitism from any of these people."

Joffe said he did not believe the absence of anti-Semitism was in itself reason for praise. Yutar replied, "If you were a policeman, Joffe, wouldn't it make you anti-Semitic to have people like Bernstein and Goldberg going around stirring up the Bantu?" Yutar seemed to imply that by working with those he knew to be anti-Semites, he could heal their hatred and restore the good name of the Jewish people that Rusty and his ilk had so wantonly besmirched.

As a solicitor under the British-style legal system, Joffe served as the general manager of the defense. It was his job to organize the team, hire other lawyers and brief the barristers who would actually be arguing the case in court. From the beginning, however, Joffe had help from behind the scenes from the man who really orchestrated the Rivonia defense. Bram Fischer was working tirelessly for his comrades. It was he who had sent Hilda to see Joffe, sensing in advance that his young colleague would not turn her down. Bram felt an enormous sense of responsibility for the accused. As lead counsel, he would make the main argument in the defense case. But the men he was defending were not just clients. They were comrades, and many, like Nelson Mandela, Walter Sisulu and Rusty Bernstein, were also dear friends. He felt it was up to him to save their lives.

At the same time, Bram knew that the case posed severe personal danger to him. It was, after all, only a matter of luck and timing that he himself had not been caught at Rivonia. Several of the documents there were in his handwriting or carried his fingerprints, and several of the servants in police custody had seen him at the farm time and time again. Surely the police were building a case against him. To work openly as lead counsel might leave him vulnerable to arrest. On the other hand, it might buy him a certain immunity, at least for the duration of the case. Even the police might be reluctant to arrest a defense lawyer in the midst of a highly publicized trial. In the end, Bram felt he had no choice. Whatever the danger, he could not refuse to appear for the accused. Although he was spending countless hours working with Hilda to rebuild the clandestine network that the Rivonia raid had destroyed, Bram agreed to take on the trial as well.

He relied upon Molly as always to help him. Molly came to court virtually every day, took notes and provided services, legal and otherwise. She also served as social worker for the families of the defendants, making sure everyone had enough money to get by for the duration of the trial. Each evening, the lawyers would gather at the Fischer house on Beaumont Street to confer about the next day's session. Often they would meet in the garden with a radio blaring classical music to confound listening devices. Molly would bring out trays of sandwiches and tea and a generous supply of moral support as they worked past midnight.

All the time the police were watching and waiting. Bram and Molly held a party one night for foreign diplomats and journalists to drum up international interest in the trial. Pat Davidson, a new house guest, looked out one of the downstairs windows and was startled to see someone staring in. She went directly to Bram, who told her not to worry. It's just Special Branch, he said, you'll have to get used to it because they're around all the time.

The local Defense and Aid Fund, set up years earlier to help people charged with political crimes, refused to foot the bill for cases where acts of violence were involved. Instead, Joffe and Bram turned to the British Defense and Aid Fund. Its founder and director, Canon John Collins of St. Paul's Cathedral, set about raising nearly twenty thousand pounds, the minimum needed in a trial where the defense advocates had agreed to charge less than one-fifth their normal fee.

The day before the opening hearing, Joffe, Bizos and Chaskalson were allowed to meet with the accused for the first time. Joffe describes the meeting in his account of the trial. He had to joust with the prison authorities for permission to see all of the defendants, blacks and whites, together in the same room and he was not even certain how many there were until the police delivered them. It turned out there were eleven: the seven Rivonia men—Sisulu, Mbeki, Mhlaba, Kathrada, Hepple, Goldberg and Bernstein—plus alleged Umkhonto members Elias Motsoaledi and Andrew Mlangeni, who had been arrested several weeks before the raid, Nelson Mandela and Jimmy Kantor. In his memoir, Joffe describes how each man appeared to him that day: the haggard Mandela, the prematurely aged Mbeki, the nervous, wisecracking Goldberg, the round-faced, pink-cheeked Hepple, who was the youngest of the group. But he saves his saddest description for Rusty, who looked depressed, listless and nervous. "He struck me as the one most obviously affected by his detention," Joffe recalls.

Hepple, the only one who had made a statement to police, volunteered at the outset that he had been "asked" to become a witness for the prosecution and was weighing whether to do so. Because of this he left the room. Jimmy explained that he would conduct a separate defense. Everyone agreed that this was wise, and he then left as well. The other nine made clear that they would stand together.

George Bizos was somber. He told the defendants they were facing a very serious trial and that the death penalty was a real possibility. But the men were too giddy and disoriented after their release from isolation for a serious discussion that day. This was, after all, the first time any of them had seen outsiders in months. None of them could focus on legal matters. Instead, they wanted to hear about their families. Joel passed on what little he knew, promising they would talk again after the hearing.

When the lawyers and accused met again a few days later, Joel and Bram explained that they were heading into uncharted legal waters. For one thing, until the Ninety-Day Act, police could not compel a suspect to answer their questions. Now no one could refuse to answer. Because the police could detain anyone at any time for any cause with no possibility of judicial review, any witness whose testimony the police found wanting could find himself back in detention that same day. Under such circumstances, the police would have little trouble convincing a witness to say exactly what they wanted him to say. The dice were well and truly loaded.

Also, in the past the law had banned both police and politicians from making statements or divulging material to the press that might prejudice a case. But because the Rivonia men had not been charged during their eighty-eight days in detention, the law had not applied. The newspapers had been filled with statements of self-praise from the police and the Justice Minister, and innuendo against the defendants, all of which abated only slightly after the indictment.

The defendants nodded soberly as they took in the information, but none of it seemed to faze them. Mandela and Sisulu took the lead in explaining to the lawyers what they planned to do. They had decided that they would plead not guilty, but they would not deny what they had done. They wanted the facts made clear—even though those facts would convict most of them of the charges. Many of them had participated in sabotage operations, but they had not endorsed guerrilla warfare or foreign invasion. For three of the defendants—Bernstein, Kathrada and Mhlaba—there was little evidence linking them with sabotage.

All of the nine agreed to allow their lawyers free rein to challenge the State's case on legal grounds. But none of them would deny membership in the illegal organizations to which they had belonged. They all saw the trial as a political event and saw themselves not as defendants in a criminal proceeding but as representatives and spokesmen for their cause. The lawyers had outlined two objectives: first, to get not-guilty verdicts for as many of the defendants as possible; second, to avoid the death penalty for those convicted. To this, Mandela demanded they add a third: to turn the proceedings into a trial of the government rather than of the accused. The defendants were willing to go along with the first two aims, he said, only to the extent that these did not interfere with or compromise the third.

Rusty was part of this consensus, yet at the same time he stood somewhat apart from the others. He insisted that his lawyers apply for bail, even though everyone knew it was a hopeless exercise. The request subtly differentiated him from the other defendants in the eyes of the judge. Later, perhaps, when it came time for a verdict, the judge himself would make the differentiation.

The defense effort was not confined to the courtroom. Oliver Tambo and the international antiapartheid movement were also active. Two days after the opening hearing, the United Nations General Assembly passed a near-unanimous resolution—South Africa was the only nay vote—calling for the release of all South African political prisoners and especially the Rivonia Trial defendants. Bram, who had been under enormous strain worrying about how to save Mandela and his comrades from execution, showed up at George Bizos's garden at five-thirty the next morning waving the *Rand Daily Mail.* Pointing to the front-page headline about the UN vote, he told Bizos to take it with him to Pretoria to show the defendants that day. "They dare not hang them now!" Bram proclaimed. It was more a wish than a prediction.

Bizos was more skeptical about the effect the resolution would have on an Afrikaner judge. But the article had a soothing effect on the accused. They showed no exuberance, but there was a sense of relief, even joy. The prospect of death was a constant companion, and anything that helped put distance between it and them, no matter how remote, was welcome.

The defense team began meeting daily with the accused in a ground-floor room at Pretoria Local. It took several days to persuade the reluctant prison authorities to violate one of apartheid's most basic precepts by providing a room where whites and blacks could mingle. Because the defendants were certain the room was bugged, much of their conversation was conducted in code. Key words of sentences were omitted, key people referred to only as "A" or "B" or "C," and key concepts were conveyed only in written notes, which they then carefully burned in ashtrays. Warders constantly watched through the doors of the conference room, occasionally joined by Special Branch officers, who grew increasingly frustrated by their inability to comprehend what was happening inside.

One day while Swanepoel was standing at the door, Govan Mbeki began to write a note in an ostentatiously secretive manner. He handed it to Mandela, who read it, nodded somberly and passed it on to Kathrada, who placed it in an ashtray and took out a box of matches. Before he could light it, Swanepoel swooped in, grabbed the ashtray with the paper and fled out the door muttering something about having left his ashtray in the room. He did not come back, nor did they see him again for several days.

The note read: "Isn't Swanepoel a fine-looking chap!"

The shift in category from detainee to awaiting-trial prisoner meant that Rusty could receive two half-hour visits each week. Children under sixteen were not allowed. But Hilda persuaded Patrick, fifteen but big for his age, to accompany her one day. Together they drove silently up the Pretoria Road and sat on a hard wooden bench in the waiting area.

The benches and the tiled walls reminded Patrick of the changing room of the gym at high school, only there were bars on the windows here and men in uniform with large rings of keys dangling from their belts. He and his mother were beckoned to another room, where they were told to sit before a window of glass and wire with an opening at the bottom, not unlike a teller's window at a bank. A warder stood nearby, close enough to hear everything that was said. Then Rusty's face appeared on the other side of the glass. Patrick felt overwhelmed. He had not seen his father for months. He wanted to cry, but he remembered what Ivan Schermbrucker had told him the day before—"You've got to be strong, you can't break down." He sat frozen, choking back tears and words. Rusty said, "Hello, Patrick," and gently asked a few questions about home and school. Patrick heard nothing, said nothing.

Hilda did not bring him again.

Rusty appeared for a bail hearing in October. His lawyers argued that because of his past record of never having fled the country despite facing serious charges, Rusty could be trusted to remain and face trial again. But Yutar cited recent incidents where accused communists such as Walter Sisulu, Duma Nokwe and Michael Harmel had skipped house arrest. The judge was not disposed to take any chances. As Hilda had expected, bail was denied.

What she had not anticipated was what happened during the lunch break. Under the courtroom were two or three small cells and a large hallway. Hilda came downstairs hoping for a brief chat with Rusty, who was talking in the hallway with his lawyers. To her surprise, after the lawyers left the courthouse, warders allowed Hilda and Rusty to walk into a cell together, sit on a bench and talk. There they were alone for nearly an hour with the door almost closed. She held him, kissed him, ran her fingers through his hair. It had been more than three months since they had touched. She thought, if I could only do this for an hour each day, hold your hand and talk, life would be bearable.

It was their only contact visit.

The indictment that Percy Yutar had handed in on October 9 was as sweeping as it was vague. There were four counts: that the defendants had recruited persons for the purpose of committing revolution, guerrilla warfare and sabotage; that they had conspired to commit these acts themselves and to aid a foreign military invasion; that they were acting to further the objectives of communism; and that they had raised money for these purposes from foreign governments. It did not state which defendants had committed which particular acts, nor did it state how, when and where the alleged conspiracy had been entered into. When Joel Joffe and the defense team requested more particulars, they received a mystifying reply to many of their questions: "These facts are peculiarly within the knowledge of the accused." It was, Joffe thought, as if the State were saying: you know you are guilty and you know what you did, therefore we do not have to spell it out for you.

The unprofessional nature of the indictment gave the defense team its first line of attack. Bram decided to appeal to the judge's sense of proper legal procedure and ask him to throw out the entire bill of particulars. Such a move would mean a postponement of the trial, perhaps for several months, during which time some of the frenzy and hysteria surrounding the case might subside, along with public pressure to send the accused to the gallows. It was worth a try.

When court resumed on October 29, Nelson Mandela was brought in first. Hilda could see that three weeks of decent food and human contact had made an amazing difference. Mandela looked fit and healthy again. He was wearing a suit rather than prisoner's garb. And his regally defiant spirit was back on full display. As he reached the top of the stairs, he turned to face the audience and raised his clenched right fist, calling out "*Amandla!*" ("Power!"), to which Hilda and the Africans in the audience responded "*Ngawethu!*" ("It shall be ours!")

Each defendant, except for Hepple, also gave the power salute as he came in and received a response from the crowd. Jimmy Kantor, whose only hope was to separate himself from the other defendants, came in quietly. The police were furious, standing up and scanning the public gallery to note the faces of those responding. Yet there was nothing they could do. All the king's horses and men could not prevent the accused from connecting with the audience that considered them its leaders.

Things settled down when the judge entered and took his seat on the dais. Bram rose to launch the assault on the indictment. His analysis was meticulous, thorough and dispassionate. There were no rhetorical flourishes, no dramatic gestures, just dogged, solid, implacable logic. Bram dissected every paragraph in the four-page indictment, sentence by sentence and clause by clause. The indictment did not disclose who had carried out each of the alleged acts of sabotage, or their connection to the defendants, he noted. How could the accused defend themselves if they did not know with whom they had allegedly conspired? And if the State did not know, how could it allege that the defendants had been involved? Some of the alleged acts had occurred before the Sabotage Act had been enacted. And Nelson Mandela was charged with conspiring to commit 156 acts of sabotage that had taken place while he was in jail. The State needed to explain all of this. Otherwise, Bram concluded, it seemed to be operating under the assumption that the accused were guilty and that mounting a defense was a waste of time.

Next rose Jimmy's advocate. Whereas Bram was low-key, George Lowen was fiery, passionate and scornful. Kantor was being charged not for his own alleged acts, argued Lowen, but for those undertaken by Harold Wolpe, his brother-in-law. Yet the indictment offered no specifics about Wolpe's conduct or activities. Lowen read out with sarcastic flourishes the State's responses to questions he had submitted: "These facts are not known," or "These facts are peculiarly within the knowledge of your client." And in one instance, said Lowen, "the answer given by the State is dash, dash, dash, exclamation mark!"

Justice de Wet looked up and smiled weakly. "In my copy there are four dashes, Mr. Lowen," he deadpanned.

The judge then asked Bob Hepple if he also had objections to the indictment. But before he could reply, Yutar sprang to his feet and announced triumphantly that the State was withdrawing its charges against Hepple, who had agreed to appear as a witness for the prosecution. The audience gasped. Hepple stood up, mumbled "good luck" to his comrades and walked down the stairs to freedom.

Like a captain on a sinking ship, Yutar tried to salvage his leaky indictment. Rather than argue the law or rebut the specifics of Bram's argument, he accused the defense of attempting "to harass and embarrass the State." This was an attack on the motives and sincerity of the defense argument, not its logic, a tactic Yutar would resort to time and time again as the trial progressed. Then he made a curious offer, one that he said would be a test of the defendants' good faith. If they wanted to know the specifics of the allegations, he would be prepared to hand over to them a copy of his opening address in lieu of further particulars.

The defense team was stunned. Every lawyer in the room—Fischer, Joffe, Mandela and Kantor included—knew that an opening address was a speech, not a charge. An indictment must set out precisely what the accused had allegedly done to break the law.

Bram rose to protest, but the judge beat him to it. "I can see no reason why I should allow you to hand that in, Mr. Yutar," he stated. "Have you any authority that I can do that?"

Yutar hemmed and hawed. He was only attempting to accommodate the defense, he said. Its refusal to accept the speech, "I make bold to say, my lord, obviously illustrates quite clearly that the defense do not want further particulars."

De Wet was having none of it. "This is a legal argument as to what particulars the defense may be entitled to, and the motive is irrelevant," he told the prosecutor.

Yutar went on to attack the ANC and Communist Party. Because they were banned and illegal organizations, the State could not spell out exactly how or when they had entered into an illegal conspiracy with the accused—"they do not keep minutes of their proceedings," said Yutar. Nonetheless, witnesses would testify, and the documentation captured at Rivonia would corroborate, that such a conspiracy did exist. The judge again intervened with withering effect. Yutar's criticism of the liberation movement was irrelevant, said de Wet. "This is not a political meeting, this is a legal argument and this is a court of law, Mr. Yutar."

Yutar was bereft. His voice rose an octave and he seemed close to tears. He begged and implored de Wet not to throw out the indictment. In the official transcript he uses the word "quash," but Joffe, a keen observer, says Yutar mistakenly said "*squash* the indictment," a malapropism that had the defense team struggling not to laugh.

Yutar began to give details of the evidence the State planned to produce in court. None of this was germane to the argument, but Bram and the defense team let him rattle on, hoping to learn more about the State's case. But the judge, whose patience was far more finite, soon cut off Yutar again.

"The whole basis of your argument as I understand it, Mr. Yutar, is that you are satisfied that the accused are guilty, and you are arguing the case on the assumption that the accused are guilty and that they know of all these documents," said the judge, echoing Bram's own words. "You can't beg the question. . . . A preliminary matter like this must be approached from the assumption that the accused are not guilty."

The judge had heard enough. He announced he was dismissing the charges, rose and left the court. Yutar slumped in his chair like a defeated rag doll. The defense team was ecstatic.

But any defendant who thought he could now walk out of the courtroom a free man was greatly mistaken. Even before the judge's door swung shut, Swanepoel was up and vaulting over the small railing of the dock. He thumped each defendant on the shoulder. "I am arresting you on a charge of sabotage," he said to each as he moved down the row. And with that, the police herded the prisoners back downstairs to their holding cells.

Hilda and Toni stood silently as Rusty was led away once again. The day had begun so promisingly, yet despite the legal triumph, Rusty and his fellow accused were right back where they started. A young policeman came over to Toni. In keeping with puritanical notions of female propriety, women were required to wear head coverings in court, and Toni's makeshift scarf kept slipping off. As he approached her for a third time that morning, Toni blurted out, "Oh, Mummy, tell him to leave me alone!" and burst into tears. Everyone turned toward her—policemen, ANC supporters, reporters and officers of the court. The room fell silent except for the sobs of Rusty Bernstein's daughter.

Jimmy had come to court that morning fortified by a new sense of confidence. His lawyers told him they were certain he would be granted bail. Barbara had sent in his favorite brown suit of lightweight silk, along with a matching tie, silk shirt, gold cuff links and polished English-made shoes. He felt more like himself—the suave, successful professional man—than he had in months.

The lawyer making the case for Jimmy's bail was Harry Schwarz, a prominent liberal who had little use for the other Rivonia defendants but believed Jimmy had been caught in a terrible miscarriage of justice. "His biggest crime, if it is a crime, is that he was a partner of Harold Wolpe, and that Harold Wolpe was his brother-in-law," Schwarz told the court at the hearing that afternoon.

The judge seemed inclined to agree. "I don't think you need go on," he told Schwarz. "Assuming I am disposed to grant bail, what conditions do you suggest?"

But Yutar and the police were not prepared to let Jimmy slip from their grasp. Yutar told the judge that Jimmy was a threat to flee, in part because he had sold his house and liquidated his law practice. "There are no assets to keep him here," said Yutar, who reminded the judge yet again that other communists—Sisulu, Nokwe, Harmel—had fled after promising to honor bail. "What these solemn statements under oath mean to communists, my lord, is quite different to what other people mean thereby," said Yutar.

Schwarz rose deeply angry. "It is very difficult to endeavor to reply in a restrained fashion," he told the judge. He accused Yutar of using "the tactics of McCarthyism" because, unlike the others Yutar had mentioned, Jimmy was not a communist but was being smeared as one. The suggestion that Jimmy had liquidated his law practice in order to facilitate his flight left Schwarz shaking with rage. The practice "has been ruined, my lord, because the accused was arrested, was kept in custody for a long period of time, and his practice has dissipated, broken up, because of it. So if anyone has liquidated Kantor's practice, my lord, it is not Kantor. *It is not Kantor!*"

When Schwarz sat down, it was clear he had won. The judge indicated he would render judgment on bail the next day, after he had heard the conclusion of other procedural matters. Jimmy was frustrated to have to spend yet another night in a cell. Still, he was confident he would be released the next day.

The police had other ideas. Special Branch still hoped to turn Jimmy into a witness for the prosecution and wanted to keep him in custody until he submitted. Yutar came back the next day with more ammunition, courtesy of the security police. First he introduced an affidavit taken from former constable Greeff, who was awaiting sentence for his role in the Wolpe-Goldreich escape. Greeff claimed that while he and

Jimmy were both in custody in Marshall Square, Jimmy had called out to him and told him not to worry about the money he was supposed to receive for helping in the escape—he should just come to Jimmy's office after his release and Jimmy would arrange everything. The affidavit sounded phony. Why would Jimmy run such a risk? Even the judge looked skeptical.

But the police came up with more. A uniformed major entered the courtroom and handed Yutar a sheet of paper. Yutar began whispering excitedly to his colleagues. Then there was a quick conference at the prosecution table. When Jimmy's lawyer sat down after demolishing the Greeff affidavit, Yutar popped up yet again. He waved the sheet of paper—"this confidential secret document," as he called it.

"I cannot, dare not, read the whole of it," Yutar declared. "It is to this effect, my lord: that there is a movement afoot to get Kantor, and whatever other accused will get bail, out to Lobatse" in Bechuanaland.

Jimmy's legal team argued that no evidence had been presented to court, only a mysterious slip of paper. They demanded to cross-examine the police officer who had produced the document. The judge refused. No responsible police officer would present such information before the court without good cause, he said.

Bail was refused again.

Jimmy could see that the legal system no longer offered any protection even to an innocent man. He believed that the police no longer were pursuing him only because of his connection to Harold Wolpe but also to serve as a warning to other lawyers to refrain from taking on political cases. He had never been inclined to overly concern himself about ethical issues, but he had always believed that no one who was truly innocent could be found guilty. Now he realized how naive he had been to put his faith in such a tainted system. He was certain he would be convicted.

His newfound skepticism was confirmed a few days later when one of his lawyers told him that the authorities had indicated the State might be willing to drop the charges against him if he agreed to inform against the other accused. That afternoon he discussed the matter with Rusty and Denis Goldberg. Their response was supportive. They told Jimmy that he should buy his freedom if he could. They were even willing to supply him with information about harmless matters the police were already aware of, but that might lend credibility to Jimmy's pose as an informer. He could claim he had overheard them discussing these points during exercise breaks.

Back in his cell that evening, Jimmy wrestled with the idea. It was a source of bitter irony to him that the legal system he had believed in now wanted him to falsify information in order to purchase his release. Meanwhile, Rusty and Denis, the supposed criminals and ruthless communists, had such a sense of fairness and human sympathy that they would risk further jeopardizing themselves for his benefit. How could he become an accomplice and informer against men such as these? He desperately wanted to be free, to be back home with Barbara and the boys, but he would not pay the price.

He rejected the offer.

After Rusty's request for bail was denied, Hilda decided to approach Percy Yutar herself. Yutar remembers nothing of the meeting, but Hilda describes it in her memoir with such understated and calm detail that the scene rings true. During a break in the proceedings, she climbed the stairs to his second-floor office in the Palace of Justice. A large contingent of security policemen was camped out in the room. She ignored them and spoke directly to Yutar, asking him why he had opposed bail for her husband.

"Well, you know it is not in my power to grant bail," he replied. "Only the judge can do that."

"But you know very well that if you do not oppose it, he will get bail."

They argued back and forth for a long time. Hilda noted that Yutar never refused her request outright. Eventually he suggested that she return to see him in two weeks. She did so—and later went yet again. Each time it was the same—certainly never a yes, but never quite a definite no either. By the third session, Hilda had concluded that Yutar never said no because he keenly wanted to be loved and respected by everyone, even a hated communist like herself.

This time when Hilda was ushered into the office only Yutar and a senior Special Branch officer were present. "Colonel," Yutar told him, "Mrs. Bernstein wants us to let her husband have bail."

The colonel was looking out a window with his back to the room. He swiveled his head, eyed Hilda briefly and said, "No." Then he returned to scrutinizing the view.

"You see how it is," Yutar said. "I would very much like to help you, I would indeed. It's not in my power, really. I'm sorry, it can't be done."

Two weeks after the original indictment was quashed, the defendants were taken back to the Palace of Justice and presented with new charge sheets. The new indictment was nine pages long, and had a nineteen-page list of further particulars and a twenty-one-page annex detailing 193 acts of sabotage. It named 122 persons who were alleged to have committed those acts as agents of the accused—but it failed again to specify which "agents" had committed which specific acts.

The defense moved to quash the new indictment, but this time Mr. Justice de Wet was not interested. In a hearing in late November, he sat back in his chair, gazed at the ceiling and occasionally stifled a yawn. He played ostentatiously with his pencil but took no notes. He appeared irrevocably bored by Bram's arguments.

Harold Hanson, appearing for Jimmy, stood up next. He noted that the first allegation in the new indictment was that Jimmy and his firm had handled many cases for members of the ANC and Communist Party. This was, said Hanson, one of the most sinister charges ever to be made in an indictment in South Africa. "Am I to refuse to appear on behalf of any of these people because some of them may have committed sabotage, and in appearing for them may I involve myself and thus create evidence against myself?" he asked.

Hanson went on to argue that the indictment did not disclose any specific crime committed by Jimmy. The judge was unimpressed. "You will have great difficulty in convincing me that this indictment does not implicate Kantor," he said.

Hanson exploded at the judge. "Is your lordship inviting me to sit down? My application is made seriously, I am not here to play the fool."

De Wet sought to calm him, saying the crime had been implied. But Hanson kept on. "I have yet to hear that an indictment is made good by implication."

None of it mattered. The judge was unmoved. After two days of futile arguments by defense lawyers he upheld the new indictment.

Bram then asked for another postponement. After all, he said, the defense had to track down 122 alleged agents with no addresses and take statements on nearly 200 acts of sabotage. This could take months.

Yutar was opposed. He explained in a falsetto both mournful and indignant why he could not allow any more delays. Bob Hepple had fled to Dar es Salaam after his life had been threatened, Yutar announced. "The State is no longer prepared to expose its witnesses to threats of this kind, or to run the risk of them being spirited away," he declared.

The judge denied Bram's request and ordered the trial to commence the following day.

The next morning Yutar looked pained. On the front page of the *Rand Daily Mail* was an interview with Hepple in Tanganyika in which he said he had fled not because of threats from his comrades in the movement but because of the police. "I believed I was not safe, even if I gave evidence for the State, and I might have been rearrested and placed under ninety-day detention," he told the newspaper. "I left because of broken promises made to me by the police." Hepple also said he never had any intention of testifying against his fellow defendants, whom he said he admired and respected. What he did not say was that his escape had been arranged by Bram Fischer and Ivan Schermbrucker, who at great personal risk had come to see him three times after his release.

Soon thereafter Denis Goldberg said goodbye to his wife Esme and their two children, who left for London permanently on an exit permit. Denis had feared she would be arrested again if she stayed in South Africa. He had pleaded with her to leave.

On December 3 the case resumed with the accused asked to plead. Nelson Mandela was the first to reply. "My lord, it is not I but the government that should be in the dock today," he declared. "I plead not guilty."

The judge looked annoyed, Joffe thought, while Yutar appeared horrified. Walter Sisulu was next. "The government is responsible for what has happened in this country," he said. "I plead not guilty."

The judge sternly intervened. "I am not interested in hearing political speeches in answer to the charges. You will plead not guilty or guilty, that is all."

But Denis Goldberg followed the same path as the others: "I associate myself with the statements of Mr. Mandela and Mr. Sisulu. I plead not guilty."

All of the other accused gave similar responses, except for Jimmy. He declared simply: "I am not guilty, my lord."

Next Yutar stood. He held before him a leather-bound copy of the opening address. Yutar had spent weeks preparing for this moment and he expected that his words would be heard far beyond the confines of the courtroom. On the table before him was a small black microphone from the government-controlled South African Broadcasting Corporation to be used for live broadcast of the prosecution's address. But Bram objected. Such a broadcast would be unprecedented and certain to foment prejudice against the accused, he argued. The judge sheepishly revealed that he had approved an earlier request for broadcast "in order to inform the public," but added quickly that the approval had now lapsed. He asked Yutar for his opinion. "My lord, I have no share in this matter at all," the prosecutor replied. The judge ordered the microphone removed. Joffe thought he saw a cloud of disappointment pass over the prosecutor's face.

Now Yutar began. It was, perhaps, his finest moment, Joffe thought. In calm, controlled language, the prosecutor outlined the main points of the State's case. The evidence would show that after being driven underground in 1960, the African National Congress had embarked upon a campaign of violence designed to lead in carefully planned stages from sabotage to guerrilla warfare to armed invasion, all for the purpose of overthrowing the state. To carry out the scheme, the movement had formed a clandestine military wing called Umkhonto We Sizwe and had purchased a secluded farm property at Rivonia, which served as secret headquarters for the military campaign. Much of the violence was planned at the farm and a transmitter was set up there for the broadcast of Radio Liberation. Arthur Goldreich and his family had gone to live there as cover for the secret operations. Several of the accused, including Mandela, Sisulu and Mbeki, had resided on the property from time to time, and others like Bernstein and Goldberg had visited there frequently, along with co-conspirators like Joe Slovo and Harold Wolpe. The law firm of James Kantor & Partners had been instrumental in providing the legal paperwork for the purchase of the property by a fictitious company and in laundering at least fifty thousand rand used for the sale and for other subversive purposes. Young African men had been recruited, taken from their homes without the knowledge of their parents and sent across the border for military training. Plans had been made to build and deploy various types of bombs and explosives, and Goldberg had been assigned to lease a second property at Travellyn, which was to be used to manufacture grenades, bombs and other explosives.

Yutar went on to discuss briefly some of the 193 acts of sabotage he said the accused were responsible for. He mentioned the collection of funds both at home and abroad. He said the accused planned to deploy thousands of armed guerrillas throughout the country, followed by an invasion of armies from African-ruled countries. He even offered a timetable: "The documents and the witnesses will reveal to the court that the accused, together with the other persons and associations named in the indictment, had so planned their campaign that the present year—1963—was to be the year of their liberation from the so-called yoke of the white man's domination." Behind the entire operation, Yutar concluded grandly, had stood the "vast communistic machine and organization with all its manifold avenues of cooperation and assistance."

Hearing Yutar's detailed account reaffirmed to Joffe that most of his clients would be found guilty. Some of the State's case was fantasy, especially the absurd claim that 1963 was the target year. Pan Africanist Congress leaders had talked in such grandiose terms; ANC leaders never. The defendants were also adamant that they had never adopted Operation Mayibuye. Nonetheless, the amount of detail and documentation that the State had at its command was impressive and would be hard to refute.

The trial began with a police photographer describing various pictures he had taken at Lilliesleaf after the raid. Then came the domestic servants from the farm, who were asked to identify some of the various accused as having been there. It was routine testimony. But cross-examination revealed that all of the servants—none of whom were alleged to have been connected with politics or committed any crime—were still being held in custody under the Ninety-Day Act. "They said that if they were satisfied with the answers that I gave they would release me," testified Edith Ngopani, the first of the servants to testify. Bram immediately challenged the legality of her detention. Yutar leaped up to insist she was not being held in detention but rather in "protective custody." This was another of the prosecutor's ad-libbed legal fantasies—there was no such procedure as protective custody in South African law. Nonetheless, the judge let the testimony stand.

Thomas Mashifane, a foreman at Lilliesleaf, identified the various accused, except for Jimmy, as people he had seen visiting the farm. Yutar asked if Mashifane could identify anyone else who had gone there. Mashifane looked directly at Bram, whom he had seen at the farm at least a dozen times—and said no.

Mashifane concluded his testimony by requesting permission to ask the judge a question. He said police had not been happy with his original statement, and had made him undress. Then they took turns kicking and punching him. "My ear is still sore and my top front tooth is loose," he said. "I just want to know, must I be assaulted like this when I was not committing any offense?"

The judge ordered Yutar to look into the matter. But after the lunch break, Yutar announced that a senior police officer had investigated and that Mashifane did not wish to make a statement. "He asked, nay begged me, my lord, not to take the matter any further," said Yutar. Neither the judge nor the prosecutor thought to inquire as to why the witness had changed his mind.

Jimmy, newly wise in the ways of the police, believed he knew exactly why.

The servants were the first of a long and tedious parade of witnesses to testify on the most trivial aspects of the case. It began to dawn on Joffe that Yutar had misapprehended both the character of the accused and the nature of the defense they were planning. Because the defendants had pleaded not guilty, Yutar assumed they would dispute the allegations against them in an attempt to win acquittal. Therefore he felt the need to nail down every trivial point. But tedium does not attract front-page headlines. To spice things up, Yutar fell back on two ploys. The first was to attempt to inject drama through a surprise witness or document every few days. The second was to keep everyone, especially the defense team, constantly guessing what was coming next.

Bram stayed away from court on days when many of the farmhands testified because of fear they would identify him. Joffe had no idea how deeply implicated Bram was until one day when Yutar produced a handwriting expert who linked documents found at Rivonia to various defendants or co-accused. The expert identified one document as being the handwriting of Harold Wolpe. Bram, before opening his cross-examination, asked to see the evidence. He studied it thoughtfully for a moment, then passed it on to Joffe without comment. To his horror Joffe immediately recognized the handwriting—it was not Wolpe's but Bram's. "No questions, my lord," said Bram calmly and sat down.

Joffe also did not know that even during the trial, Bram was working with the remaining cadres of Umkhonto to put together a new sabotage campaign. He smuggled out court documents such as maps and other papers found at Lilliesleaf and delivered them to David Kitson and Wilton Mkwayi. Bram ordered all operations suspended until after the trial in order to avoid inflaming the judge or public opinion. But he was determined to help Umkhonto start up again once the case ended.

Jimmy, sitting at the defense table, often found his mind wandering. Most of the testimony was boring, the acoustics in the courtroom were so bad he could barely hear what was said and almost none of it was about him anyway. He took to smuggling in crossword puzzles, which he would surreptitiously work on. When he got stuck, he would pass it down the line to his fellow accused. Inevitably it would get to Rusty, who would finish it in a matter of minutes and send it back to Jimmy with a small smile.

Throughout the long, tedious days, Jimmy found himself drawing closer to Nelson Mandela. The tall, regal son of a Transkei chieftain and the short, jocular Jewish lawyer seemingly had little in common, but they shared a sense of humor and appreciation for the absurdity of their situation. With Jimmy, Mandela could relax. There were no pretenses and no political points to be scored, just genuine respect and affection.

Their spouses became striking symbols of wifely beauty and devotion. Jimmy's wife Barbara, accompanied by his and AnnMarie's mother, attended most days looking cool and fashionable in the stifling courtroom. Barbara was six months pregnant when the trial began, and the news photographers kept daily track of the growth of her womb as well as her changing outfits. Winnie Mandela was also a regular visitor. She dressed elegantly in tribal outfits. But the public galleries thinned out noticeably after the first few days, especially in the nonwhite section. It did not help that Special Branch officers had started taking down the name and address of every spectator and a police photographer took their picture as they left the courtroom.

During the proceedings the empty jury box was converted into a public gallery for VIPs—members of the diplomatic corps or, on one particular day, a visiting cricket team from one of the provinces. One day the box was occupied by two visiting American political scientists, Gwendolyn Carter of Indiana University and Thomas Karis of City College of the City University of New York. After spending the morning at the headquarters of Special Branch, they watched Berrange verbally dismantle a shaky prosecution witness in the afternoon. Carter, who along with Karis had embarked upon the monumental task of compiling the primary documents of the liberation struggle, had met Nelson and some of the other defendants during a previous visit to South Africa. From the VIP box, she greeted them warmly and smiled. Yutar was furious. The next day, the box was closed permanently.

Sometimes the police engaged in other forms of retribution. Walter and Albertina's fifteen-year-old son Max was arrested by Dirker one day for not carrying his pass—an arrest that ignored the fact that because Max was still in high school he did not need one. Joffe had to intervene, threatening to sue the commanding officer of the prison for false arrest to gain Max's release.

Elias Motsoaledi's wife Caroline, mother of seven children, the youngest of whom was five months old, was arrested that same afternoon. "What about my babies? They'll be all alone!" she cried out as she was taken away. When Bram rose to object in court, Justice de Wet refused to intervene. "I cannot see how it affects the proceedings of this court," he said. "It was not done while this court was in session. The police presumably had good reasons for doing what they did."

Caroline Motsoaledi was held for 156 days without charge before she was released.

After three weeks of tedious introductory detail, Yutar called the first and most crucial of the State's witnesses. Striking his most melodramatic note, Yutar asked that members of the public be excluded from the courtroom. "His evidence will cover a wide field, and he is definitely in mortal danger," said Yutar. Nonetheless, the prosecutor wanted the witness to receive the fullest publicity, so he asked that the press be allowed to remain, provided they agreed not to disclose the witness's name. Yutar called him "Mr. X." This added an air of mystery and danger to the testimony, although little in the way of protection. After all, every defendant in the dock but Jimmy had met this man before. They all knew his name, where he lived and the damage he could do to them on the witness stand.

Bruno Mtolo was tall, powerfully built and self-confident, with a seemingly photographic memory. He was a petty thief from Durban with a criminal record who had risen to a high post in the Natal Regional Command of Umkhonto because he was smart, streetwise, articulate and seemingly fearless. He had been on the active police list of Umkhonto suspects for several months before he had been arrested in early August. Like any smart criminal, Mtolo had a nose for opportunity and a healthy fear of prison. He was also angry with Umkhonto's leadership for a variety of transgressions, real and imagined. It took less than twenty-four hours after his arrest for him to conclude it was time to change sides.

Mtolo was in many ways an ideal witness. He remembered names, dates and faces. Yutar planned to make him the human centerpiece of the State's case, an eyewitness who had functioned at a senior level deep inside the command structure of Umkhonto. The prosecutor got straight to the point with his first question. "Bruno," he asked, "are you a saboteur?"

"Yes, I was!" Mtolo readily agreed.

The witness spent the next three days describing his career as an activist and saboteur, the twenty-three separate acts of sabotage he admitted to personally having participated in and the inner workings of Umkhonto We Sizwe. Mtolo said he had been an ANC member since the mid-1950s when he had come in contact with the movement while serving a four-year jail term for railroad theft. Later, he joined the Communist Party as well, and when Umkhonto started up in 1961, he was one of the region's first recruits. He attempted to incriminate Rusty by saying he had been told by someone that a man named Bunstead or Bernstein had come to Durban to help set up a regional branch of the organization there. The first bomb Mtolo planted, outside the door of the Bantu Administration building in Durban, had failed to go off, but others had destroyed electric substations, government offices, power lines, beer halls and even the local headquarters of the National Party.

Mtolo discussed how he had traveled to Johannesburg and met Jack Hodgson, Umkhonto's chief munitions expert, who had showed him how to make various kinds of bombs from dynamite and chemicals. He testified about meeting Nelson Mandela in Durban in August 1962, the day before Mandela's arrest. Mandela had reported on his recent mission abroad and, according to Mtolo, had warned the Umkhonto cadres not to reveal their Marxist leanings when they were sent out of the country for training. Mandela purportedly said the African states were prepared to help Umkhonto but were so backward economically and politically that they did not understand communism.

After Mandela's arrest, Mtolo said, Umkhonto had committed twenty-three acts of sabotage in retaliation. At the same time, however, he confirmed that saboteurs had been instructed not to harm people. Even when they placed pipe bombs in the houses of three alleged "collaborators," he testified, the bombs were placed in a way to cause property damage only. "We just wanted to frighten them," he said.

Mtolo described his own rising misgivings about the sabotage campaign, spurred by conflicts between Umkhonto cadres and members of the ANC who were opposed to violence. He said that at the beginning of 1963 communist leaders issued directives ordering party members to infiltrate the ANC and steer it in a procommunist direction. He said he had never lost faith in the principles of the ANC, but contended he had grown disenchanted as he came to realize that the organization and Umkhonto were mere tools of whites in the Communist Party. Added to this, he said, was his growing realization that the young Africans recruited for training abroad were being exploited and neglected by the leadership. His disaffection had become stronger after he made a trip to Johannesburg in May 1963 and was taken to Lilliesleaf to see Walter Sisulu and other underground leaders. He said he had observed the posh conditions in which the Umkhonto leaders were living. At Sisulu's house in Soweto, for example, "the house and the furniture inside, everything was like that of Europeans." And both Sisulu and Andrew Mlangeni owned motorcars! When any danger arose, he added, Umkhonto's leaders were quick to abandon the cause and flee into exile, where they could report to comfortable offices and attend tea parties. Meanwhile, he claimed, he, his family and his comrades were starving.

Mtolo's account offered a ready-made justification for his betrayal of the movement. It also fit seamlessly into the government's contention that communists had captured the movement for their own nefarious purposes and bought off its compliant black leadership. But while his descriptions of Umkhonto's activities and structure were accurate, his complaints about the life styles of the leadership were largely fantasy and seemed designed not merely to convict the accused but to discredit them in the eyes of their followers. Walter Sisulu, for example, did not even know how to drive, let alone owned a motorcar. His cramped three-room house was as modest as any in Soweto. Mlangeni's car belonged to Umkhonto and was used to haul supplies and saboteurs. The last thing either of them had gained from the movement was affluence.

Truth and lies were so entwined in Mtolo's testimony that it was virtually impossible for the defense team to devise an approach for attack during cross-examination that would not involve a tacit admission that much of what he said was indeed accurate. But the accused insisted that their lawyers rebut the lies he had told about the leadership and the movement. Nelson Mandela did not deny attending the meeting Mtolo had described, but denied saying many of the things Mtolo had ascribed to him. He insisted that the Red-baiting smears had to be refuted. Joffe warned him: if you admit, even tacitly, that you were leader of Umkhonto and had solicited aid from foreign nations you are effectively signing your own death certificate. But Mandela said he did not care. A leader who holds a responsible position must accept the consequences. His responsibility, he told Joffe, was to clarify to the country and the world what Umkhonto We Sizwe was, what it stood for and why. If this jeopardized his own fate, so be it.

Berrange, intellectually agile and ruthless, slashed away at Mtolo during cross-examination. He got on record Mtolo's three previous convictions for theft and the witness's selective memory in testifying in an earlier bombing case. And he riddled Mtolo's claim to have been inside Walter Sisulu's house during his trip to Johannesburg. But the witness's basic testimony stood unscathed. By the time Mtolo left the stand, he had implicated Mandela, Sisulu, Mbeki and Mlangeni.

The defendants were especially disheartened by the fact that Mtolo had been one of them. They could understand if he had been broken by torture. But he was never touched by the police, yet he had willingly implicated not only the accused but many other former comrades. Having made their own choices based on deeply held beliefs, the defendants could not seem to grasp that Mtolo's betrayal was not the result of a change of conviction, but simply of his impulse to survive. They had not known of his criminal record when he was recruited and had not realized that his motives were so different from their own. He was willing to sell them out without a minute's hesitation when it became expedient to do so.

Mtolo's testimony opened a window on the psychology of betrayal that was beginning to infect the entire movement. Some comrades had been battered by police and changed sides for self-preservation. Others were weak and easily frightened. Still others, like Mtolo, were shrewd. The cause meant far less to them than their own personal welfare. At first the comrades entertained the hope that once informers appeared as witnesses in open court, they would grow ashamed of their betrayal and recant under cross-examination. But it did not happen that way. Having changed sides, those who betrayed the movement could never go back again. They stayed loyal to their new masters. Attacks by defense counsel simply drove them further into the State's camp. They became wholly dependent on the police. Hilda, who watched Mtolo's testimony unfold, saw him and other turncoats as drowning men, pulling down their friends and comrades in order to save themselves. And to justify it to themselves, they had to denigrate the movement, to turn reality on its head and claim it was the movement and their comrades that had betrayed *them*, not the other way around.

The worst betrayal came in the Cape Town trial of leaders of the African Resistance Movement, the small, predominantly white sabotage group consisting largely of disgruntled younger radicals from Alan Paton's Liberal Party. ARM's leader was Adrian Leftwich, a bright, twenty-four-year-old antiapartheid activist and former head of the National Union of South African Students. Although the ARM suspects were mostly white, the police had not shied from using physical abuse against them. When sleep deprivation did not work, Special Branch detectives assaulted several of their prisoners. But like Mtolo, Leftwich had broken quickly during interrogation without resort to physical means. And as with Mtolo, once he changed sides he went all the way. He implicated his girlfriend and persuaded her to divulge where the group stored its dynamite, then he gave police names of co-conspirators throughout the country. Later he agreed to pressure other detainees to become State witnesses, and finally he agreed to become one himself. "On the wall of one of his cells he had written that he had learnt for the first time how weak he was, but how great was the power of love," wrote lawyer Albie Sachs, who defended two of Leftwich's fellow accused. "We were more inclined to think that he had discovered for the first time how weak he was and how great was the power of the police."

Unlike Mtolo, however, Leftwich did not remain cool and collected once he got on the witness stand. After dispensing testimony that ensured the conviction of his former comrades and friends, he broke down and sobbed loudly under cross-examination. He begged for forgiveness, saying he had testified only because of his fear of receiving a long prison sentence. "It is not easy to give evidence against people you love, your friends, but, sir . . . " Here he sobbed loudly before going on. "If I stood to get only five or ten years, I would not give it, under any circumstances." Then he stopped again for a moment. "I loathe, oh God, I loathe apartheid and all it means. This tragedy here I place at the door of the system."

Leftwich's former friends went to prison with his self-pitying denunciation of apartheid ringing hollowly in their ears.

Bruno Mtolo's testimony gave Joel Joffe a clearer sense of what the defense was up against. Twenty-nine of the State's witnesses had been held by Special Branch in solitary confinement for unlimited periods before the trial. All of them knew their only chance of freedom was to say on the stand exactly what the police wanted them to say. As with Mtolo, they were prepared not just to lie but to tailor their testimony to fit the exact requirements of the State's case.

Mtolo was followed by several such witnesses. One was "Mr. Y"— Cyril Davids, who described attending a training camp that Denis Goldberg had organized and staged outside Cape Town in December 1962. Davids said Goldberg had invited him to lecture camp participants about the basic uses of electricity for circuits, telephones and other devices. Davids had first told police the camp was strictly for health and social purposes. But after three months of detention he had changed his statement. The purpose of the lectures, Davids now testified, was "for use in guerrilla warfare."

Davids, who was still in detention when he appeared on the stand, denied he had agreed to testify because he had been ill treated in prison. He insisted he had actually enjoyed his time in solitary. It gave him a chance for peace and quiet away from his family, he said. But under Berrange's painstaking cross-examination, Davids admitted that he did not much care for solitary confinement and had finally given police the statement they had sought in order to be released.

"You realize perfectly well that if now you were . . . to tell this court what you had originally told the police—namely, that this was an innocent camp—you would again be detained. You realize that?" Berrange asked.

"Yes, I do," Davids replied.

"Mr. Z" was Patrick Mthembu, a member of Umkhonto's Johannesburg Regional Command who had trained in China before infiltrating his way back to Johannesburg. His testimony conclusively fingered Elias Motsoaledi as a saboteur. Under cross-examination, Mthembu said he had been kept in solitary confinement, where he had lost thirty pounds before agreeing to testify for the prosecution. The food in detention, he hastened to add, had been "excellent."

Many of the police witnesses were also difficult. Willie van Wyk's testimony was straightforward and uneventful. But a Sergeant Card from Port Elizabeth appeared determined to show off his apparently photographic memory. He raced through a list of nearly sixty activists, giving full names for each along with their supposed rank within the movement. He had obtained all of this information by questioning detainees and informers, he testified. How exactly did he persuade detainees to divulge such information? Berrange asked. "We tell them what we want to know, and wait until he confirms it," the honest sergeant replied.

Then there was Dirker, van Wyk's deputy, who lied at least twice on the witness stand by Joffe's calculation. He said he had found a copy of Operation Mayibuye on the table in the center of the thatched cottage living room, when in fact it had been found in the heating stove where Bob Hepple had shoved it during the raid. This was an important discrepancy for defendants like Rusty and Ahmed Kathrada, who were denying that they were members of the Umkhonto High Command. If they had been sitting around discussing Operation Mayibuye with Umkhonto's acknowledged leaders that day, the implication was clear that they themselves were ringleaders as well.

Dirker also sought to bolster the case against Rusty by testifying that he had checked Rusty's car after the raid by opening the hood and putting his hand on the engine. It was cold. This suggested that Rusty had been at Lilliesleaf for several hours, not for the ten minutes he had claimed. But Dirker had not reckoned with the fact that Rusty had checked in at Marshall Square earlier that afternoon and that his signature had been witnessed and co-signed by the desk sergeant there. Nor could Dirker explain why his purported examination had not set off the car alarm that sounded anytime someone opened the hood.

The 200 documents seized at Lilliesleaf proved more reliable for the State's case. Ten of them were in Mandela's handwriting, including a diary that gave a day-by-day account of his six-month trip abroad in 1962 and provided full details of his efforts to raise money and obtain military support—irrefutable proof, in other words, of his guilt. Papers written by Govan Mbeki demonstrated his knowledge of Umkhonto's sabotage operations and his role in keeping track of funds received from abroad. And a series of notebooks and sketches written by Denis Goldberg documented his role in designing and manufacturing explosive devices.

The Cape Town engineer proved easy to nail. A small parade of manufacturers and merchants testified that Goldberg, using various aliases, had paid visits to their factories bearing specifications and seeking price estimates for components used in making weapons. Desmond Todd, a timber merchant, said Goldberg had asked him for a quotation to make wooden boxes that fit land mines. F. C. Millburn, a foundry manager, said the defendant wanted a price for buying several thousand iron castings that could be used to produce hand grenades. F. J. Marovec, an engineer, said Goldberg had wanted estimates for building a small furnace for smelting cast iron. And Leon Ruff, technical manager of a fan manufacturer, said Goldberg had inquired about buying a high-pressure blower to be used in a smelting furnace.

The case against Jimmy Kantor, fabricated as much of it was, was more difficult to substantiate. The prosecution called Ismail Essop Makda, a law clerk who had worked for Jimmy for seven years. Loyal and precise, Makda described meetings Harold Wolpe had held at the firm with banned and listed persons. Harold would often borrow Makda's office on the assumption that it was not bugged, shut the door and lower the blinds. Makda also told of carrying a bag of cash at Harold's request to another law firm in connection with the sale of the Rivonia property. He described the firm's system of issuing checks—how each check required two signatures, one from Harold and one from Jimmy or his father. Some of the files relating to matters handled by Harold had no notes attached or written on the outside cover, which was highly unusual, said Makda.

In the end, Makda's testimony was devastating for Harold. But nothing he said suggested Jimmy was involved. Indeed, under cross-examination Makda made quite clear in answer after answer that so far as he knew, Jimmy had no knowledge or involvement in any of Harold's clandestine activities at the firm. He testified that Jimmy never examined any of the checks he countersigned for Harold and never questioned them. Often, said Makda, Jimmy was so busy he signed blank checks for other members of the firm. Of the more than 10,000 checks issued during the time period covered, only thirty-four were related to political matters and only seven were unexplained. Jimmy may have been guilty of naiveté, but he was on trial for sabotage and the State was producing no proof.

Yutar was furious with Makda for exonerating Jimmy during cross-examination. During his reexamination he sought to discredit Makda's testimony. "You agreed with a lot of things," the defense attorney had put to him, Yutar told Makda. "You said 'yes, that is so, that is so, that is so' so often, I thought I was listening to a gramophone record at one stage."

But the judge swooped. "I cannot allow you to cross-examine your own witness, Mr. Yutar." The prosecutor sat down.

Much of the time it was not so clear that Justice de Wet was paying attention. Hilda noticed a gradual change in his behavior. At the beginning, the judge was brisk and impatient with all of the lawyers. But as the trial unwound, he seemed to save most of his rudeness for Bram and the defense team, while giving Yutar free rein. When the defense team objected to prosecution witnesses whose testimony it contended was irrelevant, de Wet refused to hear the motion. This was not a trial before a jury, he said testily, and he was quite capable of deciding for himself what was relevant and what was not.

Later, however, the same rule did not apply to defense witnesses. When Berrange attempted to call two professors of psychology to describe the physical and psychological damage suffered by ninety-day detainees, the judge asked, "How can that possibly be relevant?"

Yutar jumped in. "This is nothing less than to make political capital out of the ninety-day detention law," he declared.

De Wet declared that, as judge, it was his function to assess the evidence of all witnesses—including those held as detainees—and decide to what extent their testimony could be relied upon. The fact that other courts had allowed testimony about the effects of detention did not bind him to do so.

The professors were not allowed to testify.

Despite Yutar's claim to have "overwhelming evidence" of Jimmy's guilt, all the prosecutor had produced by mid-December was Ismail Makda's exculpatory testimony. Jimmy knew the judge was planning a long Christmas recess until mid-January and he dreaded the prospect of spending the Christmas holidays in prison waiting for the trial to resume. He also feared he would miss the birth of his first child. He was so desperate he sought a personal meeting with Yutar to ask for bail. But the prosecutor was not alone in his office. Willie van Wyk, Dirker and a police colonel named van Niekerk were present. Jimmy pleaded; he even groveled. The men were unmoved. It looked like Christmas in prison.

That afternoon before the trial resumed, Jimmy told his fellow accused what had happened as they waited at the bottom of the stairs to climb up to the dock. Nelson Mandela came over and solemnly put his arm around Jimmy's shoulder.

"Tell Barbara I apologize," he said.

"What for?" asked Jimmy.

"Because you are here."

But on the last day before the recess, Justice de Wet himself raised the question of Jimmy's bail and ordered a hearing for that afternoon. Yutar, to Jimmy's surprise, agreed to bail of 10,000 rand. By evening Jimmy was safely home with Barbara and the boys.

He was so tired he could not sleep that night. When morning came he rose and took a long hot bath. Then he went for a walk. It was a warm Saturday morning and traffic was light. He thought of his fellow accused. He suddenly realized that they had probably already finished their morning exercise and were locked away for the day in their cells. Despite the warm sun, Jimmy shivered.

Hilda desperately wanted to get away from Johannesburg for Christmas. Ruth wanted to leave as well, but her banning order restricted her to the city. She loaned Hilda her Citroën and Hilda took Gillian and Robyn along with Frances and Keith to the Indian Ocean resort town of

Port Alfred 500 miles to the south for a week. They stayed at the Grand Hotel, a sprawling Victorian relic on a hilltop overlooking the sea.

The idea was to get a break from the claustrophobia suffocating all of them, but white South Africa was a small, self-contained world and it was not long before the other guests knew who Hilda and the children were and what their connection was to those on trial. For the most part, they were left alone. It rained almost every day and the children soon ran out of diversions. Hilda was clearly depressed and distracted, and this upset Frances and Keith as well. Then there were occasional incidents involving the other guests. One man questioned Frances until she revealed that her father's name was Lionel Bernstein.

"Lionel? Lionel Bernstein?" Slowly it dawned on him. "Do you mean Rusty Bernstein?"

Frances feared she had divulged too much and fled to her mother, with Gillian running behind. Hilda gave Frances a hug, then took the children for a long walk in the rain. They said little for a while until Keith spoke up.

"It's like eating peanuts," he said.

"What is?"

"Thinking about Daddy—once you start, you can't stop."

The trial resumed on January 13, 1964. The first witness was Essop Suliman, a taxi operator, who testified that Sisulu, Kathrada, Mlangeni and Matsoaledi had all employed him at various times to transport young Africans to the border, where they crossed over illegally to Bechuanaland. Berrange got Suliman to admit he had been kept in custody for 120 days and had given evidence in three previous trials that had differed in names and dates from what he was saying now. Still, his testimony established the basic outlines of the smuggling route for Umkhonto recruits. He was followed to the stand by several young Africans who had been recruited for military training and been captured by the Rhodesian authorities and returned to South Africa for trial.

Sitting in the dock one morning listening to the drone of testimony, Nelson Mandela received a note from Jimmy at the other end.

Barbara and I have discussed godfathers at length. We have come to the conclusion that, whether the baby is a girl or boy, we would consider it an honor if you would agree to accept this office as an adjunct to the more disreputable positions you have held in the past.

Mandela's reply took a while to arrive.

I would be more than delighted, and the honor is mine, not the baby's.

When the court recessed for morning tea, Mandela hung back as the others filed out. When Jimmy passed, Nelson beamed. "Now they dare not hang me," he said.

The prosecution's case wound on for more than a month as Yutar paraded witness after witness to the stand to nail down the charges against each of the defendants. Bruno Mtolo made a return appearance and underwent another bruising bout of cross-examination from Vernon Berrange, who was armed this time with detailed information about Mtolo's extensive criminal career.

Jimmy was excused from most of the sessions after Yutar advised his lawyer that none of the witnesses would be testifying about his alleged role. He was home for the birth of his daughter in late January. The police, convinced he was a threat to run to Bechuanaland, kept a constant vigil over the house. During one bizarre weekend after van Wyk received a dubious tip-off supposedly confirming Jimmy's escape plans, the Special Branch officer and his subordinates did shifts inside the house so that Jimmy could remain at home rather than have his bail canceled. It was a humanitarian gesture on van Wyk's part; perhaps he was beginning to realize that Jimmy was innocent. Jimmy fed the various officers; he and Barbara even double-dated with one detective and his young girlfriend, taking in a movie together. But it was nerve-wracking and depressing to know that with one quick trip to a magistrate's office for an arrest warrant these men could send him back to a cell in Pretoria Local.

It was mid-February when Yutar finally called a witness against Jimmy. He was a Johannesburg accountant named Geoffrey Cox, whom the State had retained to examine the books of James Kantor & Partners. Cox testified that the accounts were in order except for the presence in some cases of original receipts—these should have gone to the client making payment—and a lack of notes on the covers of some of Harold Wolpe's political cases. Once again, these were facts that might incriminate Harold, but not Jimmy. After hearing Cox's testimony, Jimmy and his lawyers were more certain than ever that the State had no case.

Nonetheless, the following weekend van Wyk phoned again to warn Jimmy that Swanepoel was on his way over with another arrest order. Police purportedly had new evidence of Jimmy's plans to flee. Swanepoel triumphantly arrived and marched Jimmy, dressed in an old shirt, shorts and sandals, back to the Supreme Court building for a bail hearing. By evening, Jimmy was back at Marshall Square occupying Cell 16 on the ground floor.

He concluded that the police had been baiting him in the hope that he would flee. Then either he would get away or they would catch him and try him for unlawful flight. Either way, the case against him for sabotage would fade away, along with the embarrassing fact that the State had failed to prove the charge.

By Monday he was back in the basement at the Palace of Justice alongside his fellow accused. Restrictions had been eased and blacks and whites were now held together in a large holding cell during trial recesses. Shortly after he arrived, someone delivered the morning tea tray. Nelson insisted that Jimmy join them. Later, Jimmy learned that Nelson had given Jimmy his own cup and had gone without tea that morning.

The prosecution concluded its case on February 29, 1964, after a final parade of police witnesses. They recounted Jimmy's allegedly suspicious behavior at Lilliesleaf the day after the raid when he had fed the dogs and chickens. This purportedly demonstrated his familiarity with the grounds. One police sergeant also recounted that Jimmy while in detention had said "thank God" when informed that Harold and Arthur were safely in Bechuanaland after their escape. This was supposed to infer his support for the escapees. The judge scowled. He was, he interjected, "totally unconcerned with idle chitchat between a prisoner and a member of the Security Branch."

Still, under cross-examination the sergeant conceded that Jimmy's full statement was "Thank God, that means I will be released."

That morning before proceedings started, Nelson Mandela and Jimmy discussed the new application for discharge that Jimmy's lawyers were about to file. Mandela said he was confident it would succeed. Suddenly he turned to Jimmy and said, "Let's exchange ties for luck."

Jimmy was wearing one of his expensive narrow Italian-silk models, while Mandela had on an old-fashioned wide-bodied red-and-white check. When Jimmy entered the dock later, Barbara, sitting in the public gallery, gave him a puzzled look. "Nelson," he mouthed.

Jimmy's luck was indeed improving. That afternoon the prosecution's case came to an end and Justice de Wet announced he was reinstating Jimmy's bail. The defense made a motion to dismiss all charges against the accused, which the judge agreed to hear the next morning.

Joffe and the other lawyers knew the motion would not succeed. But de Wet had one pleasant surprise for the defense team. The following morning he announced he had found Jimmy not guilty and discharged him from the trial. "I have come to the conclusion that there is in fact no case for Accused Number Eight to meet," de Wet declared, saying he would give his reasons in his final judgment at the end of the trial.

The other defendants swarmed over Jimmy, pumping his hand and slapping him on the back. Mandela was the last to greet him. He gripped Jimmy's arm tightly and said, "I knew that tie would bring you luck."

The judge recessed the trial until April 7. On that day the accused would begin their defense.

While Shawn spent the holidays with friends, and Gillian and Robyn went off with Hilda, Ruth First spent Christmas and New Year's at home alone. Her banning order prohibited her from seeing most of her friends and, in any case, most of them were gone now. Some, like her, were banned. Others were in prison, or in hiding, or in exile trying to scratch out a new existence in London or Dar es Salaam, or one of a hundred other cities. The house that had once vibrated with the sound of laughter, music and glasses tinkling on holidays was now silent. The party was well and truly over.

At night she heard strange noises and feared intruders. Perhaps it was the police, or perhaps self-appointed white vigilantes out to scare a communist or two. Or perhaps it was only rabbits or birds or one of the small nocturnal creatures that still prowled the northern suburbs. Like most former detainees, Ruth felt disoriented and had trouble concentrating. Even letters were a chore. She needed help in making decisions, but Joe was nearly 6,000 miles away in London. She knew he could never return—his would be the next Rivonia Trial if he did—and that she and the girls would have to join him abroad. But she felt a terrible sense of guilt about leaving at a time when the movement was in crisis. She could do little or nothing for the cause while sitting in isolation on Mendelssohn Road. But the act of leaving felt to her like an act of abandonment and surrender.

She wrote frequent letters to Joe—"My J," she began each of them. She addressed the envelopes to Mr. H. Watson on Heath Drive in London.

"It is over," she wrote on December 7. "At least so they say. They say no rearrest. After all that. At last the nightmare begins to recede."

She could not sleep, she told Joe. She wanted to take a short holiday, but as a listed person she needed permission to leave Johannesburg. The authorities might have been willing to grant her that, but the one place she knew she would have been welcome was at Jack and Ray Simons's sea cottage outside Cape Town and because Jack and Ray were also banned, she would have needed a further permission to communicate with them, which she knew the police would refuse. She wrote about the children and her mother's car accident that sent Robyn's head into the windshield. It shattered but did not splinter, and so Robyn avoided anything worse than a slight bump. She did not tell Joe what had happened to her in detention. "We have so much to discuss," she wrote. "Love you. You me?"

Two weeks later, after a letter from Joe urging her to drop everything and leave as soon as possible, she told him, "I'm in a state of indecision, difficulty, dither. There are so many difficulties, Joe."

She was still considering whether to take her library exams. "I need time to think about what you write. The problems are not solved as fast as you seem to wish. . . . So many people who would earlier have been able to help me are inaccessible.

"You might think I am being bogged down in a trivial matter like exams. But I can't suspend myself here in limbo while you and I work out plans for a new life. I have to face the fact that my earning capacity is nil at present. In spite of what you say about so-called talents, I admit that survival in a place like London terrifies me. You don't seem to share my apprehensions. But I've got them all the same.

"I need to talk to you. There are things I must tell you because you are you & I can tell no one else. . . . Look, I'm not given to expansive declarations of ecstasy. I know you hold that against me. Not now, perhaps, but at times. And I was always more inhibited than you. But don't worry about me and you. It's the best. Always. And will be the best ever, in time."

Ruth applied for a passport, which would have allowed her to return to South Africa. But political people like her were almost never granted such documents. For weeks, she heard nothing. She repeatedly phoned the passport office in Pretoria, but no one could seem to help her. Vorster had told Helen Suzman that Ruth could have a one-way exit permit, not a passport. He would be happy for her to leave, but she could never return.

On December 26 she wrote of how gloomy things were with the children gone. She told Joe that Ruth Fischer, Bram's older daughter, was getting married in a few days—"we can't go to the wedding, of course."

"This is a helluva life. More uncertainty than anything else. It's one of the occasions you could handle so well. But you're not around to solve all my troubles!

"Miss you so, my J. Need you. More than ever. No good living in the past, but we've had wonderful years here. Is it infantile to be fearful of years ahead somewhere else?"

December 30: "I want to come very much. I can't see this half-life for you and for me going on much longer . . . I'm anxious about the future and don't see how I can last, even ticking over at one-eighth of my former capacity for living and working for this coming year. But I don't want to be indecently hasty for reasons you will understand. Rushing ahead oblivious to some local considerations will be sad—and misunderstood. I feel so split and divided against myself. . . . I think I must have an overdeveloped and oversized conscience."

She wrote of going alone to the cinema to see *The Servant, Electra* and *Billy Liar*. Still, she wrote that Christmas was hell. "Empty, deserted house . . . no parties. You've forgotten what these bans can be like! Never mind, I'll survive. . . ."

By the end of February she finally gave up on her passport application and applied instead for an exit permit. Still, the authorities were infuriatingly slow in responding. "Your telephone calls succeed in making me miserable, if nothing else," she wrote to Joe in early March. "You seem to think I'm responsible for the delays in my getting traveling papers. . . . I don't have influence in those circles!

"And now to hear that when I do succeed in coming you'll be leaving for heaven knows how long . . . it's all too bloody. At this rate what will we have left? . . . I'm not angry, just wretched.

"Now you write and tell me how to persuade Special Branch to give

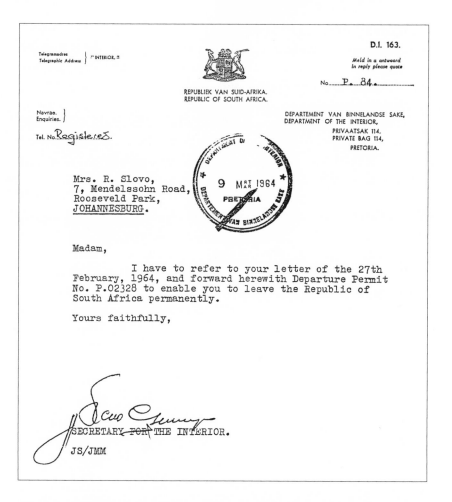

D.I. 163.

Telegramadres
Telegraphic Address } :" INTERIOR. ::

Meld in u antwoord
In reply please quote

No......P...84..

REPUBLIEK VAN SUID-AFRIKA.
REPUBLIC OF SOUTH AFRICA.

Navrae. }
Enquiries. }

DEPARTEMENT VAN BINNELANDSE SAKE,
DEPARTMENT OF THE INTERIOR,

Tel. No. Registered.

PRIVAATSAK 114,
PRIVATE BAG 114,
PRETORIA.

9 MRT 1964
PRETORIA

Mrs. R. Slovo,
7, Mendelssohn Road,
Rooseveld Park,
JOHANNESBURG.

Madam,

     I have to refer to your letter of the 27th
February, 1964, and forward herewith Departure Permit
No. P.02328 to enable you to leave the Republic of
South Africa permanently.

Yours faithfully,

SECRETARY FOR THE INTERIOR.

JS/JMM

me an exit permit in my time, not theirs. Perhaps a letter from you to Col. van den Bergh will tip the scales. Ha ha ha."

She went to see Bram at his home one night and they sat in the bathroom with the bathtub taps running to cover the conversation as they spoke about her leaving. Bram was gentle and supportive. He was adamantly opposed on principle to anyone's going, but he knew what Ruth had been through and he told her he understood why she had to leave.

The exit permit finally came through in early March. Ruth was ready. The house had been sold; her books and papers—those that Special Branch had not seized already—had been packed and shipped. She packed up Gillian and Robyn's things and booked a flight for March 13, two days before Gillian's twelfth birthday. Shawn had already boarded a boat to England with friends. Tilly was set to fly out at the end of the month. Cousins drove Ruth, Gillian and Robyn to the airport, while a car of security police trailed behind.

Hilda understood why Ruth had to leave. Nonetheless, she felt abandoned. Ruth and Joe had been such key members of the movement. Their optimism, their intelligence, their dedication, even their sense of fun had helped sustain her. They seemed to characterize the best of what the movement was about.

Hilda drove to the airport on the afternoon of the thirteenth to see Ruth off. Legally the two women were not allowed to meet or converse. They sat at separate tables in the lounge while a Special Branch man hovered behind a pillar nearby. Finally they each retreated to the ladies' toilet, where they hugged each other briefly and whispered a hurried goodbye. It was the only place where the detectives did not follow.

SEVEN

WITNESS FOR THE DEFENSE

This Court . . . is a pointless institution from any point of view.
A single executioner could do all that is needed.
Franz Kafka
The Trial

E ven while the Rivonia Trial dragged on, normal life—or what passed for it in that year of terror and grief—went on for the Bernstein family. Toni, who had been living away from home, became involved with Ivan Strasburg, a young activist from Durban whom she had met at college. She wanted to visit Rusty to tell him of their plans to marry, but it was not a simple proposition.

A few weeks earlier, Justice Minister Vorster had sent out notices to former members and active supporters of the banned Congress of Democrats adding them to a new roster of people listed under the Suppression of Communism Act. Toni was among those receiving the letter. As a banned person, Rusty was prohibited from communicating with any listed person other than Hilda. This meant he was no longer legally allowed to speak to Toni.

Hilda hoped the prison authorities would ignore the new restriction—after all, it was up to Rusty himself to decide whether to break the regulation and invite prosecution, and she doubted that even Vorster would risk the public embarrassment of prosecuting a father for speaking to his own daughter. She took Toni along on her next prison visit. But the head warder, knowing that Toni was now a listed person, insisted that she leave the prison immediately. "She is not allowed to see her father," he stated flatly.

Hilda pleaded, cajoled and argued, all to no avail. Surely the Minister of Justice did not intend to deny a father and daughter the right to speak to each other, she said. But the warder held firm. No one would be allowed to break any rules on his watch, he told her.

Weeks passed with no official reply to Rusty's request for permission to speak to Toni. Hilda phoned the Chief Magistrate, who offered her the same kind of rationale that Colonel Klindt specialized in. "I am not concerned with the intention of the law, only with what it says," he told her. "It is my duty to see that it is carried out."

In desperation Hilda turned to Helen Suzman. On her next visit to Vorster, Helen obtained permission for Rusty to speak to Toni.

Toni and Ivan were married in April. They had a civil ceremony on a Friday, then, at the behest of Ivan's parents, a Jewish wedding on Sunday in the garden at 154 Regent Street. Ivan's relatives were disturbed to find Special Branch men lurking among the trees in the driveway and on the street outside taking down license plate numbers. Dogs barked, Patrick got drunk. On Sunday morning before the ceremony, the couple drove to Pretoria, where they were allowed a special visit with Rusty.

Toni told Hilda that she and Ivan would live with her for as long as Rusty remained in jail. Hilda did not want to hold her to that pledge— Rusty, after all, might receive a life sentence—but she needed Toni to look after the other children during the weeks and months of the trial, when Hilda spent virtually every weekday trekking to Pretoria and back, and she needed the company as well. The house was now a lonely citadel. The Bernsteins, isolated from the rest of the neighborhood—indeed, from the rest of white society—could rely only upon themselves and the handful of comrades who remained at large. Toni and Ivan fixed up the basement and moved in, expecting to live there for the duration of the trial.

While they were moving in, Patrick was moving out. Athlone Boys High School had become too much for him. He had skipped school so many days that he was afraid to return. He would walk out of the house each morning supposedly to catch the local bus. Instead, he would sneak off to the empty Scout Hall off Frances Street behind the house, where he would smoke cigarettes, climb trees, devour the lunch he carried and generally goof around. He was in his own world there, far from grown-ups and policemen and fathers in prison. No one at home seemed to take much notice. The trial monopolized their time and attention. But the school authorities would ask for sick notes. He kept putting them off. Soon it got to the point where he could not go back at all.

Patrick came up with an alternative he was certain his parents would accept. He said he wanted to go to Waterford, a progressive and racially mixed boys' school in Swaziland, about four hours' drive from Johannesburg. They would look after him there, make sure he got his work done.

Patrick was right about Hilda's reaction. She was relieved at the idea of sending him off. Having a sullen teenaged boy lurking around the house was one burden she did not need in this time of crisis. She cared about Patrick, but she did not know exactly what was wrong with him or how to reach him. Money was scarce, but tuition at Waterford was low and some of Rusty's relatives agreed to chip in. Angry, wounded and more desperate than even he could know, Patrick headed off to Swaziland.

Rusty knew few of the details of Patrick's unhappy life, but he knew the broad outlines and he felt that his imprisonment was partly to blame. The trial had added to Patrick's anxiety, and at the same time had removed Rusty from the possibility of being home to help put things right. For a man who already felt deeply that he had let his family down, abandoned them in the name of a cause he still believed in but saw as increasingly hopeless, it was another burden—and another reason to try to find a way out.

Throughout the tedious days and weeks of the prosecution's case Rusty had watched the judge closely. De Wet was the kind of establishment authority figure Rusty had always despised—pompous, self-satisfied and overly fond of his own dubious intellect. But Rusty had been dealing with such men since his days at boarding school. He was naturally polite with such people, talking to them as if they were intelligent and blunting their wrath and disapproval. It was not a premeditated strategy on his part, but more of a reflex. And the fact that Rusty was white certainly would not hurt his cause.

All of this was a bitter pill. Rusty had spent his adult life as a collectivist in a movement dedicated to racial equality. To take advantage, even unconsciously, of his intellect and his skin color was repugnant to him. It could put an invisible barrier between him and his fellow accused, and between him and the movement he cherished. Looking back more than thirty years later, Rusty denies he made any attempt to separate himself from his comrades in the dock. He certainly did nothing to betray them or the movement. But somewhere in the course of the trial, his case became distinct from those of the other defendants, at least in the eyes of the judge.

One day during the long break in the trial, an Afrikaner prison warder who had become friendly with Nelson Mandela asked him the big question: "Mandela, what do you think is going to happen to you in this case?"

"Ag, they'll hang us," Mandela replied. He had always thought so, and now that the prosecution's case was finished he was even more convinced. Still, he secretly hoped that he was wrong, and he longed for the warder to offer him a few words of encouragement, and perhaps even a plausible theory for optimism. To Mandela's chagrin, the warder fully agreed with his own appraisal. "I think you're right," he told Mandela. "They're going to hang you."

From the moment they had been charged with sabotage, Nelson Mandela, Walter Sisulu, Rusty Bernstein and their co-defendants were all convinced that one or more of them would hang. They seldom talked about it, but the possibility haunted them and their families day after day. Everything they said, every decision they made, was said and made under the shadow of the hangman. The temptation to adopt a legal strategy that might enhance their chances of escaping the gallows even while damaging their cause was always there. It was their lawyers' duty to suggest such a strategy, and they did so repeatedly. But the defendants never succumbed. Looking directly at the hangman, they did not blink.

The defendants had five weeks to prepare their case. Everyone agreed that Mandela should be the first to appear. The original idea was for him to take the stand in his own defense. But during the practice question-and-answer sessions in which Mandela rehearsed his testimony, the case he wished to make emerged only in thin, piecemeal fashion. Mandela also feared that his appearance as a witness might seem to contradict the stand he had taken in his earlier trial in which he had refused to enter the witness box as a protest against being tried by an all-white court. There was an alternative. Rather than appear as a witness he could choose instead to give a statement from the dock. Under South African rules of legal procedure, a defendant could make such a statement without being cross-examined. The statement did not carry the same weight as regular testimony, but it did offer a defendant the opportunity to explain himself, his cause and his motives. Mandela had nothing to lose; his guilt was a foregone conclusion. From the dock he could speak to his demoralized followers, to all South Africans and to the world. Mandela had done the same thing very effectively at his 1962 trial. All of the accused, and the lawyers as well, agreed he should do so again.

But what of the other defendants? The State had not done a good job in presenting evidence against Kathrada, Mhlaba and Bernstein. All three, it was agreed, would have to take the witness stand to deny their guilt. As for the other five, they were clearly as guilty as Mandela, and would probably only make the cases against them worse by testifying. Also, all of them had pledged not to answer any questions that might implicate other comrades or their organizations. The lawyers worried that if the defendants took that position on the witness stand, they would antagonize the judge and further diminish their chances of escaping the death penalty. Was there any point in their testifying? And would they not be better off avoiding Yutar's scathing cross-examination?

All of the lawyers agreed the defendants should not testify, except for one. George Bizos was at the beginning of a distinguished career as one of South Africa's most prominent criminal lawyers and he was a shrewd judge of character. He had been watching Percy Yutar perform in court for the past four months and he believed that Yutar was after more than mere convictions in this show trial. The prosecutor also wanted to defeat the defendants politically, to show that their cause and their characters were defective. He would not resist the opportunity to cross-examine them on political issues.

This was an opening that the defendants could take advantage of, Bizos argued. Most of them were experienced politicians. They could handle themselves in a public forum. If Yutar tried to take them on, they would acquit themselves well—and perhaps gain enough sympathy from the judge to cheat the hangman.

Then there was the human factor. Once the defendants testified, Bizos contended, the judge would know them as human beings.

Whether he approved of their politics or not—and most certainly he would not—it would be harder for him to send them to the gallows. "Look," said Bizos, "if you really get the judge to understand these people, to see them in front of him behaving impeccably, it's very difficult to hang them."

The other lawyers believed Bizos was dreaming. Yutar was too shrewd to wander from the basic facts of the case, which were so overwhelmingly in his favor, into a political thicket. "Yutar will cross-examine them on the facts, and in a few swift moments confirm their role in Umkhonto," Joel Joffe argued. But Bizos was so confident he was willing to take bets.

During the five weeks of preparation for the defense, Joffe came to know his clients far better and began to see how much each of them looked to Mandela as their natural leader. Nelson had all the necessary qualities—intelligence, stature, calm, tact and conviction. Even the warders seemed to show him a certain respect, as if they realized grudgingly that they were in the presence of greatness. Nonetheless, Joffe loved Walter Sisulu best. His warmth, his calm even when facing the death penalty and his gentle sense of humor—all impressed Joffe enormously. Joffe had never had black friends growing up. Despite his attempt to treat Africans as equals, he had always harbored the sense that they were somehow inferior. It was something bred into him since childhood. To be among blacks who were truly great men—wise, considerate, caring—was a great revelation. Yet in some ways it increased his burden. These men were more than clients, more even than friends, Joffe felt. They were a national treasure he had been entrusted to protect and defend. He needed to find a way to save their lives without damaging the cause they were devoted to. There were many nights when he could not sleep.

Just as Yutar had flouted legal tradition by springing surprise witness after surprise witness upon them, so the defense gave no advance warning to him that Nelson Mandela would not take the stand. In fact, the defense team did its best to mislead the prosecutor by ordering up the entire 100-volume transcript of the Treason Trial, hoping he would feel obliged to do the same and waste valuable preparation time poring over it. In a regular criminal case Mandela would certainly have taken the stand to deny his role in the conspiracy—after all, he had been in prison when most of the bombings had occurred. Yutar went about preparing to cross-examine Mandela as if he were an ordinary defendant who would lie, distort and otherwise seek to escape conviction. The next time Joffe went to visit Yutar's office, he noticed with grim satisfaction that volumes of the Treason Trial record were stacked on the desk.

Mandela worked on the draft statement for weeks. But he had much professional help in the polishing. Nadine Gordimer, one of South Africa's best-known novelists, had been asked by her friend George Bizos to write brief profiles of each of the accused for publicity purposes based on notes made by the defendants themselves. Bizos brought Mandela's draft to Gordimer to check the grammar and make suggestions. Visiting British journalist Anthony Sampson, who had once been editor of *Drum* magazine, a popular black weekly, was staying at Gordimer's house. He looked at the draft with a newsman's eye, suggesting that they move to the top sections on Nelson's attitudes toward violence and communism, two vital issues for Western audiences. Sampson also advised them to punch up the prose by inserting highly quotable sentences here and there that reporters could cite in their news reports.

Bizos took these ideas back to Mandela, who eagerly welcomed them. But there was one part of the draft he refused to change. At the conclusion of the address Mandela planned to assert his willingness to die for his beliefs. Both Bram Fischer and Joel Joffe argued that such a statement could only antagonize the judge, who might be overly tempted to grant Mandela his wish. When they typed up his handwritten draft, they deleted the sentence. But Mandela would not budge. In the end, at his insistence, the lawyers had to put it back in.

After the long delay, the courtroom was packed on Monday, April 20, 1964. Bram led off with a summary of four major legal points that the defense would make in presenting its case. First, the defense would stipulate that most of the accused had participated in Umkhonto We Sizwe but would strongly deny that Mhlaba, Goldberg, Kathrada and Bernstein were members of the High Command or, indeed, in the case of Kathrada and Bernstein that they were members of Umkhonto at all. Second, the defense would dispute the claim that Umkhonto was a wing of the ANC; the two organizations had much in common, Bram argued, but had maintained as much separation as possible under the difficult circumstances they faced. Third, the defense would dispute the claim that the ANC was a tool of the Communist Party with the same aims and objectives. And finally, the defense would deny that Umkhonto had adopted Operation Mayibuye. Guerrilla warfare had been contemplated and some preparatory steps had been taken, conceded Bram, but no decision had been made to go ahead. Indeed, said Bram, the Umkhonto leaders would not have launched guerrilla warfare so long as they felt there was any chance, no matter how slim, that the sabotage campaign would succeed in bringing the white government to the bargaining table.

Bram then introduced Mandela, who he said would commence the defense case with a statement from the dock. As Joffe recalls in his account, Yutar looked stunned. The prosecutor leaped to his feet as Mandela rose and slowly adjusted his reading glasses. "My lord!" Yutar called out in the wounded falsetto that had become his trademark. "My lord, I think you should warn the accused that what he says from the dock has far less weight than if he submitted himself to cross-examination!"

The judge eyed him sternly. "I think, Mr. Yutar, that counsel for the defense have sufficient experience to be able to advise their clients without your assistance."

Bram, who also rose, was less cutting. He appreciated his learned friend's advice, he said drily, but "neither we, nor our clients, are unaware of the provisions of the Criminal Code."

Mandela, who had stood patiently during this exchange, now began to read his statement. "I admit immediately that I was one of the persons who helped to form Umkhonto, and that I played a prominent role in its affairs until my arrest in August 1962."

Mandela read slowly and deliberately in a flat voice that grew in power and effectiveness as he went on. The drama was all in the content and the circumstances, not the delivery. Within minutes, the entire room was silent. Judge, prosecutors, defense lawyers, defendants, public audience, even the warders and the officers of Special Branch all seemed spellbound.

As Sampson had suggested. Mandela wasted no time in seeking to dismiss one misconception. "At the outset, I want to say that the suggestion made by the State in its opening that the struggle in South Africa is under the influence of foreigners or communists is wholly incorrect. I have done whatever I did, both as an individual and as a leader of my people, because of my experience in South Africa, and my own proudly felt African background, and not because of what any outsider might have said."

Mandela spoke of his own life: his childhood in the Transkei, his decision to join the African National Congress and its struggle for political freedom and equality, his rise to a position of leadership and his founding of Umkhonto. "I do not deny that I planned sabotage. This was not done in a spirit of recklessness or for any love of violence. I planned it as a result of a calm and sober assessment of the political situation that had arisen after many years of tyranny, exploitation and oppression of my people by whites."

He put Umkhonto into the context of the ANC's long history of nonviolence. "When we took this decision, and subsequently formulated our plans, the ANC heritage of nonviolence and racial harmony was very much with us. We felt that the country was drifting towards a civil war in which blacks and whites would fight each other. We viewed the situation with alarm. Civil war would mean the destruction of what the ANC stood for."

Next, Mandela reviewed South Africa's postwar history and the persistent refusal of whites to share political power. "The hard facts were that more than fifty years of nonviolence had brought the African people nothing but more and more repressive legislation, and fewer and fewer rights."

Then he discussed his relationship with the communists. The idea that the ANC was communist-dominated was false, he declared. "The ANC has never in its history advocated a revolutionary change in the economic structure of the country, nor has it, to the best of my recollection, ever condemned capitalist society. . . . The Communist Party sought to emphasize class distinctions whilst the ANC seeks to harmonize them.

"It is true that there has often been close cooperation between the ANC and the Communist Party. But cooperation is merely proof of a common goal—in this case the removal of white supremacy—and is not proof of a complete community of interests."

Nonetheless, Mandela added, "for many decades communists were the only political group in South Africa who were prepared to treat Africans as human beings and their equals, who were prepared to eat with us, talk with us, live with us and work with us. . . . Because of this, there are many Africans who today tend to equate freedom with communism. They are supported in this belief by a legislature which brands all exponents of democratic government and African freedom as communists." He himself was not a communist and had always regarded himself as an African patriot. He was attracted by the idea of a classless society and had been influenced by Marxist thought. Still, he added, "I have gained the impression that communists regarded the parliamentary system of the West as undemocratic and reactionary. But, on the contrary, I am an admirer of such a system."

The defendant gave a ringing restatement of the ANC's commitment to multiracial democracy. "Political division based on color is entirely artificial and, when it disappears, so will the domination of one color group by another. The ANC has spent half a century fighting against racialism. When it triumphs, it will not change that policy."

Then he concluded. "During my lifetime I have fought against white domination, and I have fought against black domination. I have cherished the ideal of a democratic and free society in which all persons live together in harmony and with equal opportunities."

Mandela paused for one long moment, and raised his head to look squarely at the judge. "It is an ideal which I hope to live for and to achieve," he said. Then came the line that Joffe and Fischer had begged him to delete. "But if needs be, it is an ideal for which I am prepared to die."

Nelson Mandela sat down. He had spoken for more than four hours. The room remained silent. No one moved or said a word. A handful of women in the public gallery were crying softly, and their muffled sobs began wafting eerily through the chamber. Finally the judge looked at Bram and said—almost gently, Joffe recalls—"You may call your next witness."

Jimmy Kantor missed Mandela's speech by a few days. By the time the defense case started he was safely in exile in London. The fact that his law degree was not recognized in Britain was of no consequence; he had no intention of ever practicing law again.

The final straw for Jimmy came soon after his release when he read an article in a local newspaper quoting the speech of a Nationalist senator. The speech, a long-winded denunciation of communist subversion, made two direct references to Jimmy. The senator said that even though Jimmy had been found not guilty, that did not necessarily mean he was innocent. And the senator could not help but note that many members of Jimmy's "race"—meaning Jews—were notoriously active in subversion. Jimmy took the message very seriously. He could see no point in sitting around and waiting for the security police to fabricate another charge against him. He still had a passport and he decided to use it before it was revoked. He waited until late Saturday morning, a time when most of Special Branch would be home for the weekend, then phoned South African Airways and bought a ticket to London for that same evening. Barbara and the children could join him later.

Jimmy was tense as he waited for takeoff. The plane sat on the runway for forty minutes fully loaded with passengers while the junior authorities on duty contacted their superiors and weighed whether to let it go. Eventually they did. As the plane finally left the ground, a mightily relieved Jimmy, irrepressible as ever, could not help turning to the older couple sitting next to him. "I hope you weren't too worried about the delay because I think that I was responsible for it," he told them. He explained who he was, adding rather lamely, "I suppose you have heard of the trial?"

Indeed they had. The woman explained that her husband was Justice Milne, who had just finished presiding over a similar sabotage trial in Natal province, where he had sentenced members of the regional branch of Umkhonto to twenty-year prison terms. The case had been a great strain for him and they were going abroad to get away.

Off they flew together, the jurist and the former accused, both seeking to escape, at least temporarily, their troubled homeland.

Walter Sisulu was to be the key to the defense case. Nelson Mandela's speech had been addressed to the world, but Sisulu's testimony had to convince the judge. No one on the defense team doubted his courage and convictions, but several of the lawyers feared he would falter under Yutar's cross-examination. They were pitting a defendant with eight years of education against an experienced prosecutor who held one of the country's few doctorates in law. On the surface it seemed like a most uneven match.

Bram handled the direct examination, gently leading Sisulu through the story of his childhood, his gradual interest in politics, his membership in the ANC and his rise to leadership. He also had Sisulu recount how he had suffered personally for his beliefs.

"I have been banned under the Suppression of Communism Act," Sisulu recalled. "I have been confined. I have been ordered to resign from political organizations to which I have belonged. I have been house-arrested. I have been detained. I have been separated from my family."

The witness discussed the ANC's decision to continue working underground after it was banned in 1960 and the decision to form Umkhonto. He himself had never been a member of Umkhonto's High Command, he said, but after Mandela's arrest in 1962 he had attended its meetings as a representative from the ANC. He said he had been present when Operation Mayibuye was first proposed, and that the High Command was deeply divided over its adoption.

"Looking back on it, Mr. Sisulu," Bram asked in conclusion, "do you consider that you could or should have acted otherwise than you did?"

Sisulu's reply offered no apologies or regrets. "I can't see how I could have done otherwise, other than what I have done. Because even if I myself did not play the role I did, others would have done what I have done instead."

Yutar rose and went straight to work. "Did the African National Congress or Umkhonto ever take precautions to see that, as a result of the commission of various acts of sabotage, nobody was injured, that nobody was killed?" he asked.

The witness replied that the Umkhonto manifesto had made clear that property, not people, was its target. "The intention was not to injure anybody at all."

Here the judge intervened. He recalled an incident during World War II when Nazi sympathizers had placed a bomb outside a local post office. Someone who came by to mail a letter at the wrong time had been killed by the blast. "If you are going to start bombing buildings, is it possible to avoid that type of accident?" the judge asked. "Can you ever be sure that you have avoided killing or injuring people?"

"My lord, an accident is an accident," Sisulu replied. "But the precaution in fact is in the intention and the method used—for instance at night, when people are not there."

The judge was not persuaded. "Your argument is that as long as you have not got the intention to kill people, it does not matter if you kill people. Is that your argument?"

Sisulu did not back down. "I'm not saying that it can't happen. But I am saying that precautions are taken that it should not happen."

Joffe and the defense team were made uneasy by the judge's interven-
tion. The indictment had not accused the defendants of committing
murder. In fact, the only person who had been killed in any of
Umkhonto's bombings was one of the saboteurs. If the judge did not accept that the defendants had done what they could to prevent injury,
would that make it easier for him to send them to the gallows?

Yutar sought to take full advantage of the opening the judge had
given him. He peppered Sisulu with allegations about killings and injuries, none of which were charged in the indictment. Then he moved
on to a series of questions that, while irrelevant to the case, seemed designed to give the security police more information about people they
were seeking. For example, Yutar asked where one ANC document had
been discussed. "In Johannesburg," Sisulu replied.

"Where in Johannesburg?" asked Yutar.

"In the townships."

"Whereabouts in the townships?"

"Are you trying to get the house?"

"I am not trying to get the house! I am trying to get the truth!"

The two men went around again.

"I want to know where in the townships," Yutar repeated.

"That means what house it was."

"Really!"

"I am not prepared to answer that. . . . I am not going to implicate
people here. What difference does it make in whose house?"

"Don't ask me questions, please."

Yutar was getting nowhere. "Well, unless his lordship stops me," he
said, "I'm going to insist on a name. I want to know who, on behalf of
Umkhonto, drafted this pamphlet."

"It doesn't help you to insist on the name," Sisulu replied. "I have explained that insofar as people who are in the country are concerned, I
will certainly not answer."

This was breaking new ground in a South African court. Once a defendant agreed to take the stand, he had no right to refuse to answer a
question unless it was self-incriminating. Yet Walter Sisulu was blatantly
refusing to answer. But the judge, as mercurial a jurist as Joffe had ever
seen, did not seem to mind.

"You are not prepared to answer?" he asked Sisulu.

"I am not prepared to answer."

"Yes, very well," said the judge.

Yutar had other purposes besides fishing for information. Albert Luthuli had not been named as a co-conspirator, but Yutar appeared determined to discredit the ANC's most prominent leader—"the Nobel Prize winner for peace," as Yutar sneeringly referred to him. He pressed the witness for information on Luthuli's role in the founding of Umkhonto. Here again Walter Sisulu would not help. "You won't get anything from me about Chief Luthuli," he informed the prosecutor.

They clashed again over the police. In explaining why Denis Goldberg had left Cape Town, Sisulu said he had been afraid of being arrested there.

"What for?" asked Yutar. "The police don't arrest people indiscriminately unless . . ."

Sisulu cut him off. "They arrest many people indiscriminately. For no offense people have been arrested."

"Would you like to make a political speech?" Yutar asked mockingly.

"I'm not making a political speech. I am answering your question."

"How do you know they arrest people innocently?"

"I know. They arrested my wife; they arrested my son."

"Yes, without any evidence whatsoever?"

"What evidence?"

"I don't know, I'm asking . . ."

It was here, Joffe recounts, that Walter Sisulu momentarily lost his composure. "I have been persecuted by the police, Special Branch," he said angrily. "In 1962 I was arrested six times. *I know the position in this country.*"

"You do?" asked Yutar.

"I wish you were in the position of an African!" Sisulu shouted. "I wish you were an African to know the position in this country!"

For five days Walter Sisulu withstood Percy Yutar's verbal assaults and the occasional interventions of the judge. While he was testifying he spent each night in solitary confinement, kept in isolation from his fellow accused and the defense team. Yet except for that one moment, he acquitted himself calmly and with dignity.

Operation Mayibuye was the crucial issue. If Yutar could prove that the plan for guerrilla warfare had already been launched, the judge would have little choice but to sentence the defendants to hang. But Sisulu insisted that the plan was only a draft for discussion and that it had never been approved. What's more, he testified that he and others of the accused believed it was premature. "My view," he told Yutar, "was that conditions did not exist at that time for Operation Mayibuye." As for the idea of an invasion by foreign armies, Sisulu insisted it, too, had never even been contemplated, let alone approved. "There was certainly no such arrangement," he said.

Arthur Goldreich, Sisulu maintained, had gone too far in commissioning Denis Goldberg to gather estimates on equipment needed to manufacture and store explosives on a large scale. "This was a fantastically big proposition," said Sisulu. "There was no place to store arms. The plan was not capable of being fulfilled."

Yutar then went off on a sidetrack in an attempt to discredit the ANC. He elicited from Sisulu that the ANC's membership at the time it was banned in 1960 was 120,000 people.

"So," concluded Yutar triumphantly, "despite your fifty years of trying to persuade the Bantu in this country that they were being oppressed, you only had in 1960 a total enrollment of about 120,000 out of twelve million?"

"Yes," agreed Sisulu. But he added, "The reason is obvious. There is no country which conducts greater intimidation against political movements than South Africa. And yet that does not mean that because we have 120,000 we do not represent the aspirations of the African people."

When Sisulu asserted that black people wanted the right to vote, the judge intervened again. "How do you know that the ordinary Bantu around town wants the vote?" he asked.

Walter Sisulu could only marvel at the judge's incredulity. "Well," he replied, "I have not come across meetings where I have heard people saying, 'No, we don't want the vote!' People always support the idea of the vote."

Yutar kept tearing at Sisulu's denials about Operation Mayibuye. But Joffe noticed that Yutar was neglecting to raise a basic question: What exactly were the defendants doing at Lilliesleaf on July 11?

Came the weekend and Sisulu remained in solitary. Joffe was certain that Yutar would start in on the July 11 meeting the following Monday. But when court resumed, Yutar announced that he planned to curtail his cross-examination. He was finished by the morning tea break. Walter Sisulu's testimony was complete.

Joffe was relieved. Sisulu had held up well. Beyond the legal points his testimony had established, he had shown himself to be thoughtful, careful and straightforward. George Bizos was right. Surely it would be hard, Joffe reasoned, for a judge to sentence such an impressive man to hang.

Ahmed Kathrada was next. There was little hard evidence implicating him beyond the fact that he had been arrested at Rivonia, had spent several weeks there previously and was wearing a disguise when captured. But Kathrada could not restrain himself on the witness stand. When Yutar baited him, he leaped to respond.

"You have called them [the government's cabinet], amongst other things, criminal?" asked Yutar.

"That's what they are," Kathrada snapped back.

Yutar's attack was blatantly political. He pointed out that India, Kathrada's ancestral homeland, had a three-year-detention-without-trial law, and he elicited the fact that Kathrada had never protested against it.

"I suffer from the laws in South Africa," Kathrada replied. "My objection is to what goes on to me and my people."

And what about seeking support from Ghana, which has a five-year detention statute? Yutar demanded.

"I'd get assistance from the devil, provided it was for my people in this country," Kathrada replied.

Soon it was over. Once again, Yutar had neglected to link Kathrada to the July 11 meeting. But he had elicited the admission that Kathrada was a member of the underground Communist Party and a staunch supporter of Umkhonto. Both admissions, Joffe feared, would be damning in the eyes of the judge.

Raymond Mhlaba, who took the stand next, was even less convincing in denying he had played any role in Umkhonto. It was clear from the judge's lack of interest that he did not believe anything Mhlaba said—a discouraging prelude to Rusty Bernstein's appearance on the stand.

"My lord, my views have been communist for twenty-five years. . . . I don't think anybody who knows me is in any doubt about them," Rusty began. "I was a foundation member of the Congress of Democrats, and I helped to edit the publication *Fighting Talk*. I have done a great deal of leftist writing."

From the beginning, Rusty's approach on the witness stand was direct and unapologetic. His strategy was to tell the truth about what was obvious and undeniable, hoping to build enough credibility so that the judge would accept his testimony on the crucial matters that would determine his guilt or innocence.

Less evidence had emerged against Rusty than against any other defendant. Witnesses had testified that he had been a regular visitor to Lilliesleaf, that he had designed the alterations to the outbuildings and that he had been attending a meeting there on the afternoon of the raid. One witness had also claimed that Rusty had helped erect the radio mast on the roof of the thatched cottage. Bruno Mtolo had given hearsay evidence, easily discredited, that Rusty had helped set up a branch of Umkhonto in Durban. Finally, there was Dirker's claim, which had been immediately refuted by the defense, that Rusty had been at Lilliesleaf for hours, not minutes, on the day of the raid. But in the high-risk contest taking place inside the courtroom, perceptions were at least as important as facts. Certainly the evidence against Kathrada was no stronger than that against Rusty, but Yutar had managed to make him appear argumentative and sarcastic on the witness stand. Rusty was the first white defendant to testify. He had the opportunity to present the judge with a very different impression.

Berrange carefully walked Rusty through his political history, starting with his first joining the Communist Party in 1939, his role in helping found the Congress of Democrats and his writing for various left-wing publications. Rusty gave brief descriptions of each organization, its activities and its position within the overall Congress Alliance. The judge seemed interested. He had heard much testimony about these groups without any real explanation of what each one was. Now Rusty clarified these matters. The judge intervened at times for further elucidation; the dialogue between him and Rusty was polite and informative.

One crucial part of Rusty's testimony concerned his frequent visits to Rivonia. Rusty said he had originally been invited to the property in 1961 by Michael Harmel to inspect it and design alterations to one of the outbuildings. Rusty did not conceal the fact that he understood the farm was to be used for political purposes. But he said he had refrained from asking Harmel about those purposes so that he would neither implicate himself nor learn damaging information that the police might later force him to reveal. "I had a very shrewd suspicion," he recalled. "It was not necessary to ask, and I deliberately did not want to ask."

Rusty recalled finding Nelson Mandela living at Lilliesleaf and visiting him on occasion, bringing him books to read. After Mandela left the premises, Rusty said he continued to visit from time to time, attending various political meetings. He had also brought to Rivonia pamphlets and newspapers discussing two of the major issues in the Communist world of that era: the Sino-Soviet rift and the 1962 border war between China and India. He said he had come to the July 11 meeting at the invitation of Bob Hepple to discuss the launching of a protest campaign to demand the release of those held under the Ninety-Day Act.

Berrange asked Rusty to help explain the decision to initiate armed struggle. Rusty replied that the ANC had not endorsed violence so much as it had stopped preaching passive resistance to its followers. Given the climate in 1961 after the government crackdown had closed all doors to peaceful dissent, he said, "the congresses at that stage had to face the alternative of finding new methods, or . . . allowing the leadership to slip into irresponsible, reckless, adventurous hands." He called the Umkhonto manifesto "a highly responsible, sober and well-considered document."

Rusty also tried to give the judge a sense of what it was like to be under constant harassment by the state. He had been under continuous restrictions since 1954. He had attempted to start his own architectural practice in 1956 but had been arrested soon after for treason. The practice had withered and Rusty had been forced to close down his office and work from home. Just when he was beginning to make some headway in 1962 he was subjected to house arrest. His clients "could not come and see me . . . and I had extreme difficulty in getting to see them at all." Police raided his house frequently, seizing his papers. "They must have a better library than I have at this stage," he said.

He denied helping to erect the radio aerial at Lilliesleaf. "There is not a word of truth in it," he replied. His statement was true. Foreman Thomas Mashifane's teenaged son Joseph had seen a white man helping put up the antenna one Saturday and had mistakenly identified the man as Rusty.

But on three other matters, Rusty was not truthful. He flatly denied knowing that Rivonia was being used for work in connection with Umkhonto. "No, sir, I never knew until I heard the evidence in this case."

Nor, he said, did he participate at any stage in the sabotage campaign. "My lord, I never had anything to do, either directly or indirectly, with acts of sabotage."

Finally, he told the court he had never heard of Operation Mayibuye before his arrest. "I did not know of the existence of such a document," he said. Which was, of course, a lie.

Joel Joffe expected Yutar to attack the holes in Rusty's story. To his surprise, the prosecutor did no such thing. Instead Yutar began by tearing away at the Communist Party and at Rusty's political views. "Mr. Bernstein, you have been in the Communist Party an awful long time?" he began.

"I was in the Communist Party from 1939 until it was dissolved in 1950."

And the banning of the party did not deter you? Yutar asked. "It did not deter me from being a communist."

"And an ardent communist?"

"I think that is fair enough, yes."

"A very loyal disciple of Karl Marx?"

"Yes, sir, I think that is fair."

And after the party was reconstituted underground, Yutar asked, "Did you rejoin?"

The question was a trap. If Rusty told the truth he would incriminate himself by admitting he was a member of a banned organization. If he lied he could be charged with perjury. And if he declined to answer he would leave little doubt in the mind of the judge that he had something to hide. Yutar asked again. Rusty felt he had no choice.

"My lord, I am afraid I must decline to answer," he replied.

The prosecutor asked the judge to instruct the witness to reply. De Wet did so, and warned Rusty that if he failed to answer he could be held in contempt of court. But then the judge smiled slightly. "If you refuse to answer, all I can do is detain you for eight days, which is not going to do much harm to you under present circumstances," he said, well aware that Rusty had already been held for nine months. Police-state penalties were undermining judicial ones.

"Of course, Mr. Bernstein," Yutar continued, pointing out the obvious. "If you had not rejoined it, the answer would have been a simple no."

"That is deduction, sir, which I leave to the court to draw."

Yutar tried another tack. "Who is the leader of the Communist Party in South Africa?"

"I am afraid that is another question I must decline to answer."

"On what ground?"

"I am afraid my conscience will not permit me to disclose the names of people who participated in unlawful organizations."

"You know who they are?"

"I know some of them."

The exchange summed up Rusty's attitude as a witness in his own defense. He was sticking to his principles, yet even when he refused to cooperate with the court he did so in a conciliatory, almost apologetic fashion.

Hilda could tell that Rusty was nervous when he first took the stand. But he visibly relaxed as the testimony went on. After the friendly exchange over the contempt-of-court question, he realized that the judge was warming to him. He became an excellent witness—soft-spoken, concise and extremely polite. His years of experience as a speaker and lecturer stood him in good stead. When Yutar popped a double-barreled question—a two-parter in which the answer to the second part implied acceptance of what Yutar had asked in the first—Rusty patiently separated out the parts and answered each in turn. He formulated a line and he stuck to it. And he kept his cool.

Yutar took Rusty through a series of party documents, asking him to comment on each. The prosecutor made no attempt to show that Rusty had written them or even that he knew of their existence before they had been entered before the court. Rusty agreed with some, disagreed with others, always maintaining an air of calm authority and thoughtfulness. Yutar, after all, was questioning him about his one true area of expertise: politics and ideology. Rusty felt in control.

Yutar helped him inadvertently. Throughout the trial the prosecutor had addressed black and Asian witnesses by their last names only. Rusty, on the other hand, he called "Mr." It was one of many ways that the judge might differentiate between Rusty and his fellow accused.

Was it not true, Yutar asked next, that the Communist Party had used the ANC to propagate its aims and objectives? Not so, replied Rusty. "I don't think the leaders of the African National Congress are people of a caliber who allow themselves to be used by just anybody who wants to make use of them. They are capable of deciding their own direction, and they do so, sir, not because they are being used by others but because they have decided for themselves what is correct."

Still, Rusty would not back down from defending his own beliefs.

"Being a communist, you are a revolutionary?" Yutar asked.

"Yes, in the sense of wanting a radical change in society," Rusty replied.

"And let us face it, the aim of the Communist Party is the overthrow of the South African government?"

"That is so."

"If need be, by force and violence?"

"My lord, in certain circumstances, yes."

"A policy to which you subscribed?"

"Yes."

Yutar then cited a book entitled *Kill or Get Killed* that police had seized at the Travellyn hideout. It was a police manual about riot control and it discussed so-called communist tactics. Yutar quoted its claim that communists regularly sought to discredit the regular police and military forces. Noting that activists had made accusations of torture and abuse of detainees against the South African police, Yutar asked, "Has an attempt not been made in this case to discredit the police?"

"I think the police succeed in discrediting themselves very satisfactorily without assistance," Rusty replied.

Under further questioning, Rusty calmly explained that the Communist Party had never incited nonwhites to overthrow the government but only to struggle for their freedom. Africans had turned to violence, he said, not because their demands had not been met but because the government had closed off all avenues of peaceful protest. He said he believed that the existence of militant forces in South Africa might actually increase the prospects of a peaceful transition to majority rule.

"Do you call it peaceful," Yutar interjected, "if you have a firearm, and you say 'Give me your money' to someone and he hands it over?"

Yutar was pushing Rusty onto dangerous ground. He was inviting the witness to preach revolution. This was no academic seminar but a courtroom, with charges that could send him to the scaffold. Rusty did not flinch.

"My lord, that is not the analogy," he replied. "If the gun is being pointed at a man who is unarmed, it is being pointed by the government at the unarmed nonwhite people. . . . If one man should have a gun, the other man should have a gun to defend himself. Then there might be prospect of talk."

"In other words, you agree that the only way to force the government to talk peacefully around a table is to embark on sabotage and guerrilla warfare?" Yutar demanded.

"It is not the only way, sir," Rusty replied. "I think that this is a help."

One of Joel Joffe's lawyer colleagues who was in attendance that day told him during tea break that he believed Rusty was cooking his own goose by freely discussing such issues. But Joffe disagreed. Yutar had laid no foundation for the evidence; the documents he was asking Rusty about had not been found in the defendant's possession and there was no proof that Rusty was even aware of their existence, let alone had written any of them.

Yutar returned to the name game. Who was the secretary general of the Communist Party? he demanded several times. Rusty refused to co-operate, although both he and the prosecutor knew that Yutar was referring to Bram Fischer, who was sitting just a few feet away at the defense table. Bram tensed visibly and his face turned bright red. Yutar kept hammering away. He referred to a 1953 edition of *Fighting Talk*, the leftist magazine Rusty had edited and written for before his banning order prohibited him from working there. In it was a laudatory profile of Bram, written after the Justice Ministry had banned Bram from all political organizations. "I am not going to mention his name, I will just call him Mr. A," said Yutar coyly of the subject of the article.

The author, identified as "LB," wrote that whenever he despaired for the future of South Africa, he recalled Bram and felt restored in the be-lief that not all white South Africans were racists and reactionaries. Yutar first got Rusty to confirm he had written the piece. Then he asked again, "Who was the secretary general of the Communist Party?"

Rusty declined to answer, Bram's face tightened. He threw a sharp glance over at Yutar and whispered loudly, "Percy, *los*"—Afrikaans for *"leave it alone."* The prosecutor smiled thinly and kept scraping away. He was clearly attempting to discredit and embarrass Bram. Dirker and Swanepoel, sitting behind the prosecution table, snickered. The judge said nothing.

Hilda and Joffe were both astonished. The article had said nothing about sabotage or violence and had no relevance to the case at hand. What possible purpose could entering it as an exhibit have except to smear Bram as a communist in the eyes of the judge? Bram himself must have realized that the line of questioning was designed to send a message to him as well—that the police knew exactly who he was and would not hesitate to harass him under any circumstances.

"Mr. Bernstein, you are a listed communist?"

"That is correct, sir."

"So is your wife?"

"Yes, that is correct."

"You made it perfectly clear that you were not prepared to have your name taken off the list of listed communists?"

"Not on the basis on which the offer was made."

"What was the basis of the offer?"

"I objected to the fact that no hearing was given to those people who were being subjected to this form of punishment, that no attempt was being made to provide us with the evidence on which the government was acting, and I refused to participate in such a travesty of judicial procedure."

Yutar went back to quoting from communist pamphlets and literature. He had Rusty read aloud a passage that characterized South Africa's judicial system as unfair and politically corrupted, a place where legal procedure and the rule of law were "thrown to the winds." "Is that not a shocking misrepresentation of the true position in this country?" demanded Yutar.

"No, sir, I don't think so."

"Points of law and court procedure are thrown to the winds?"

"That is correct, sir."

"What courts have you in mind, then?"

"My lord, I had procedure in mind. Such things as, for instance, holding a person under duress in order to force him to make a statement. Such matters as not releasing a prisoner on the expiration of his sentence."

"Have you not personally misrepresented the events in this very case itself?"

"I don't understand what you mean."

"Have you ever accused the State of coaching its witnesses?"

"I possibly have said that, sir."

"That is a reflection on the state prosecutors?" demanded Yutar.

"I am afraid so, sir," replied Rusty.

Yutar went on. "Did you ever say 'Apart from police evidence and documents . . . all the substantial witnesses have been detainees who made statements under pressure and while subject certainly to threats of either indefinite detention or prosecution or both?' "

"Yes, I did, sir."

"Is it true or false?"

"I think it is probably true, sir."

Rusty realized that the statements came from a letter he had written from prison to his sister Vera and her husband in Britain. The prison authorities had confiscated the letter and forwarded a copy to Special Branch, which had handed it to Yutar. It was a shameless ploy for Yutar to use this violation of Rusty's privacy in court. Yutar's purpose, it seemed, was to demonstrate to the judge that Rusty held the court and its proceedings in contempt—thus draining the goodwill Rusty seemed to have established with de Wet.

"You wrote this letter, didn't you?"

"I did."

"Then you go on to pay me this compliment: 'Here too Vernon [Berrange] did a great job of exposing this very patent, blatant is a better word, coaching of witnesses.' How dare you say that if you have got nothing to support it?"

"My lord, I have explained the case on which I think it is an adequate statement."

"And one final extract: 'And yet the whole thing disgusts me, the unprincipled timidity of people and even more the unprincipled willingness, eagerness, of the authorities to use them.'"

"I adhere to that."

Yutar felt compelled to run down the entire list of twenty-nine witnesses who had been detainees. He insisted in each case that the testimony had been freely given and had not been contested by the defense. Rusty refused to agree.

Speaking of Cyril Davids, for example, Rusty said, "His statement was taken from him under conditions which I regard as conditions of torture."

"Of torture?"

"Yes, having suffered it."

"That does not happen in Soviet Russia?"

"If you want my description of Soviet Russia, I will deal with it. I consider these conditions as torture."

Yutar seemed to get angrier and angrier, straying further and further from the evidence at hand. Had Rusty any proof that witnesses had been coached?

"I say that every detainee who gives his statement under duress and conditions which I regard as torture is being forced to make a statement, and his statement is subject to suspicion."

Joffe and the defense team kept waiting for Yutar to pursue the highly incriminating issue of why Rusty had been at Lilliesleaf on the day of the raid and to challenge Rusty's claim that he knew nothing of Operation Mayibuye. But Yutar never got back to those matters. After exhausting himself with the issue of Rusty's letter to his sister, the prosecutor sat down.

Bram rose for a brief re-direct. He had Rusty explain that his advocacy of revolution did not mean he necessarily endorsed violent overthrow of the state. Revolutions could be accomplished peacefully as well, according to the witness. Bram asked Rusty once again why he had refused to name those he had met with at Rivonia. "Did you realize in declining to answer you might prejudice yourself?"

"Yes, my lord, I'm aware of that fact. I fear that anybody whose name I mention in this respect will be subject to persecution, and I'm not prepared to open anybody with whom I've ever associated up to persecution at all."

He asked Rusty to describe how he was treated by police in detention. "Were you offered any rewards? Were any threats made?"

"I was told repeatedly in interrogation sessions that if I did not give the information they required satisfactorily I would be detained indefinitely for ninety days and ninety days and another ninety days. One of the interrogating officers in fact told me he had got twenty-three years to go in the service, so he can afford to wait longer than I can. Toward the end of my detention, continued reference was made to . . . the death sentence." Finally, "suggestions were made that perhaps I could name my price for giving information. I was told about people who got considerable sums of money for giving information."

Bram asked Rusty why he considered solitary confinement a form of torture.

"One has to go through it, to spend ninety days without talking to a solitary human being at all, to be locked in a tiny room, gray walls, only able to see a piece of light through a very high window, and spend twenty-three hours a day contemplating those walls, because you are not allowed to read or write, and you have got no work to do and nothing to occupy yourself at all."

Rusty talked about the nervous tremor that had developed in his hands, his inability to concentrate for more than a few minutes at a time and the extreme anxiety he still suffered from. He was so desperate, he said, that when his interrogators came, "it was a great relief to have somebody to talk to."

The judge interrupted. "What is the relevance of this, Mr. Fischer?" he asked. "You are now trying to get evidence at the back door which I excluded from the front door?"

But Rusty had said enough to make the point. With Bram's gentle guidance he concluded his testimony with a warning to white South Africans. "If they choose to shoot it out, in the long run they are going to fail. By that time there will be such bitterness in this country that white South Africans, even if they then choose to want to live here, very likely will find life as intolerable as many whites in Algeria."

"Would it be fair to say that you spent many years of your life trying to prevent South Africa coming to [such] a stage?"

"I think almost all my political life has been spent in that direction."

Rusty walked back to the prisoner dock, exhausted but relieved.

How had he done? By any objective standard he had acquitted himself well. He had stuck to his principles, giving a ringing and even courageous defense of his beliefs even while dodging the facts about his actual role in and knowledge of Umkhonto's activities. In Yutar's zealousness to tackle Rusty on political grounds, Joel Joffe believed, the prosecutor had neglected to make the fundamental legal points he needed for conviction. But would the judge agree?

Watching from the gallery, Hilda also sensed that Yutar had gotten carried away. Her heart pounded wildly as Rusty returned to the defendants' bench. Could it be that he might be acquitted? She knew, of course, that the police would never allow him to go free. In all likelihood he would be rearrested immediately. But at least the threat of hanging would be lifted. For the first time in months, Hilda began to harbor a small kernel of hope.

One evening following Rusty's testimony, Hilda paid a visit to Gertrude, an old friend who had been giving her money each month to help pay the bills while Rusty was in custody. Gertrude was a German Jew who had fled her homeland after the rise of the Nazis. She knew what repression was, and she was shocked to see it recur in her adopted new home.

"Rusty has a chance of getting off," Hilda told her.

Gertrude looked at Hilda with an expression of great sadness, even pity. "How can you say that?" she asked.

"There is no evidence against him."

"But you know it is not a normal situation, it is not a question of evidence." Gertrude took Hilda's hand, held it firmly and looked in her face. Gertrude's eyes were filled with tears. She spoke from bitter experience. "Don't allow yourself to believe it. You will only suffer the most awful disappointment."

Hilda understood her friend's warning. But she had to cling to something, no matter how slender. "Gertrude," she said finally, "I cannot live without hope."

The other four defendants came and went from the stand in quick succession. Govan Mbeki gave a sweeping review of the inequities of South African political oppression. He did not budge one inch from the truth, damaging as it was to his own case. When Yutar put to him all four of the charges in the indictment in the form of a question, Mbeki readily admitted he was guilty of each.

Yutar was perplexed. "Why have you pleaded not guilty to the four counts?"

"I did not plead guilty for the simple reason, firstly, that I should come and explain from here under oath some of the reasons that led me to join Umkhonto We Sizwe. And secondly, for the simple reason that to plead guilty would to my mind indicate a sense of moral guilt to it. I do not accept that there is any moral guilt attached to my actions."

Denis Goldberg was equally unrepentant but managed to fend off Yutar's cross-examination without undue sarcasm. Elias Motsoaledi and Andrew Mlangeni, both of them rank-and-file members of Umkhonto, made brief but moving statements to the court but did not testify. Mlangeni described being tortured with electric shock at the Central Police Barracks in Pretoria.

With that, the defense rested. The State had presented 173 witnesses, the defense only eleven.

EIGHT

THE VERDICT

What is important in the end is that a man should choose to live,
rather than choose to die.
C. J. Driver
Elegy for a Revolutionary

Percy Yutar had worked on his closing address for weeks, often late at night at his suburban Johannesburg home, which was heavily guarded by police following anonymous threats against Yutar and his family. Now on the morning of May 20, he and his colleagues wheeled in a stack of thick blue-bound volumes, with four volumes to a set. Joel Joffe recalls that Yutar gave several bound sets to members of the press gallery but allocated only one unbound copy without covers to the defense team. As Joffe thumbed through it, he could see it was simply a summary of the evidence, rather than an organized, cogent argument or analysis of the case. He could not help blurting out so that Yutar could hear, "This is not a closing address. It's just a garbled summary."

Nonetheless, the prosecutor read aloud three of the volumes from cover to cover. "Although the State has charged the accused with Sabotage, this is nevertheless a case of High Treason par excellence," Yutar began. "It is a classic case of the intended overthrow of the government by force and violence with military and other assistance of foreign countries."

From there he launched into a personal attack on the defendants.

"The deceit of the accused is amazing," he declared. "Although they represented scarcely more than one percent of the Bantu population, they took it upon themselves to tell the world that the Africans in South Africa are suppressed, oppressed and depressed. It is tragic to think that the accused, who between themselves did not have the courage to commit a single act of sabotage, should nevertheless have incited their followers to acts of sabotage and guerrilla warfare, armed insurrection and open rebellion and ultimately civil war.

"Having done that, they would then, from the safety and comforts of their hideouts at Rivonia, Travellyn and Mountain View, have surveyed the savage scene of slaughter on both sides."

Yutar singled out for special scorn Denis Goldberg, who "having created the Frankenstein monster and put it into action, would have gone abroad to join the band of brothers; this included that great and glorious guerrilla, Goldreich, the heroic Harmel and Hodgson, Slovo the soldier and the wise Wolpe. From a safe distance of 6,000 miles or more they would behold the tragic works of their handiwork."

Referring to some of the propaganda pamphlets seized at Rivonia, Yutar added: "It is a great pity the rank and file of the Bantu in this country, who are peaceful, law-abiding, faithful and loyal, should have been duped by false promises of free bread, free transport, free medical services and free holidays. They forgot to mention free air."

Judge de Wet listened to Yutar's oratorical flights without comment. But then Yutar soared a bit too high. "The day of the mass uprising in connection with the launching of guerrilla warfare was to have been the 26th of May 1963," he declared. This was a mystifying six weeks before the Rivonia raid. Joel was astonished. What kind of warfare could Yutar be talking about when the only firearm at Lilliesleaf was an air rifle Nelson Mandela had once used for target practice?

The judge intervened. "Dr. Yutar," he said, "you do concede that you failed to prove guerrilla warfare was ever decided upon, do you not?"

Yutar looked stricken. He paused to gather himself, then replied that he believed the State had proven that preparations had been made.

"Yes, I know that," the judge wearily replied. "The defense concedes that. What they say is that preparations were made in case one day they found it necessary to resort to guerrilla warfare. But they say that prior to their arrest they never considered it necessary, and took no decision to engage in guerrilla warfare. I take it that you have no evidence contradicting that, and that you accept it?"

Yutar's face collapsed like a deflated balloon. "As your lordship pleases," he murmured.

Next Yutar sought to pin the blame for the Sharpeville Massacre on the ANC and the Communist Party, saying they had incited the crowd to violence. No matter that the rival PAC had organized the mass campaign that led to Sharpeville and that it was the police, not the crowd, who had opened fire that afternoon.

Then Yutar began summarizing the evidence against each defendant. The judge again intervened. Mandela had already admitted his guilt on all charges, so what was the point? he asked. He intervened again when Yutar turned to the case of Walter Sisulu.

As for Denis Goldberg, Yutar said the evidence was so overwhelming he did not know where to begin. "Well, why try?" loudly interjected Vernon Berrange.

But Yutar saved his most elaborate rhetorical excursion for last. "My lord, for the edification of your lordship, I have decided to nominate a shadow cabinet for the provisional revolutionary government."

Because of Goldberg's role at the Mamre training camp near Cape Town, Yutar said he would nominate him as Minister of Health. "But he will have to learn the truth first, which he will find difficult to do if one takes into consideration the lies he told this court." Dirker and the other security police sitting behind Yutar's table chuckled appreciatively.

Yutar proceeded to nominate Kathrada as Minister of Indian Affairs and Mbeki as Minister of European Affairs. Rusty became Minister of Information and Bob Hepple became Minister of Informers. Walter Sisulu was to be Minister of the Interior and Nelson Mandela Minister of Defense. Yutar said he would leave blank the office of Prime Minister since it rightfully belonged to the head of the Communist Party, a man whose name had not been revealed. Then he turned and looked meaningfully at Bram.

At no point did Yutar ask for the death penalty. But his argument left little doubt that the State believed this was the appropriate penalty. "Because of the people who have lost their lives and suffered injury as a result of the activities of the accused, it is apparent that this case is now one of murder and attempted murder as well," he declared.

Yutar concluded on a note of praise for the policemen sitting behind him. "On the evidence it is clear that without the action of the police, South Africa might have found itself in a bloody civil war," he said. "The public owes a great debt of gratitude to the police."

With a final flourish, finger pointing to the ceiling, the prosecutor concluded: "I make bold to say that every particular allegation in the indictment has been proved."

Thus having judged his own performance and found it pleasing, Percy Yutar sat down.

The histrionics disappeared and the volume dropped considerably when the defense team took over. First came Arthur Chaskalson. He attacked large portions of the State's case on legal grounds, carefully explaining why vast amounts of its evidence were either inadmissible or irrelevant. Many of the 193 acts of sabotage that the State alleged had been committed by Umkhonto had actually been carried out by other groups, Chaskalson argued, including all of the attacks in which anyone had been injured. The judge did not disagree. "I accept that there were other organizations in South Africa committing acts of sabotage at the time in question," he said.

The point was a critical one because Yutar was alleging that Umkhonto had engaged in acts of murder and attempted murder. Chaskalson's argument exonerated Umkhonto of most of the actual sabotage attacks charged by the State and showed that the organization had lived up to its pledge to solely attack property, not people. It would not make the difference between innocence and guilt, but it could be the difference between life imprisonment and the hangman.

Then Bram took over. His purpose was to reiterate that neither Umkhonto nor the ANC had ever decided upon a plan to launch guerrilla warfare, and that in any case the two organizations, although closely cooperating, were separate and independent institutions. But the judge intervened almost immediately to say he accepted both arguments. "I do not, however, accept that the plan would never have been implemented," he added.

Bram sparred briefly with the judge over this question. But there was no point in Bram's fighting a battle he had already won. Despite weeks of meticulous preparation, he quickly sat down.

Next came Berrange. He was to focus on the cases of Bernstein, Kathrada and Mhlaba, the three defendants who had a chance of acquittal. But first he delivered a stinging rebuke of Yutar's conduct, especially of the prosecutor's sarcastic naming of the Umkhonto fantasy cabinet. "With the dignity that has characterized the accused throughout this trial, they have instructed us to ignore these remarks," Berrange said sternly. But he could not help adding, "It is, however, unusual and not in the best traditions in which prosecutions are conducted in this country." Berrange was not only attacking Yutar, he was implicitly criticizing Judge de Wet for tolerating such a farce. De Wet did not respond.

Then Berrange focused on Rusty's case, quickly disposing of the evidence against him. "The cross-examination of Bernstein covers 153 pages of transcript," he said. "What is remarkable is that, in that 153 pages, there is not one word of cross-examination as to the facts deposed by Bernstein. The only direct evidence against him related to the erection of the radio masts and this evidence had been given by a servant at Rivonia who was in police custody under ninety-day detention when he gave it."

Berrange was referring to Joseph Mashifane, the teenaged son of the foreman at Lilliesleaf, whose mistaken testimony had been contradicted by Rusty and another witness. Berrange argued that Mashifane, one of the twenty-nine prosecution witnesses who had been held under the Ninety-Day Act, could easily have confused Rusty with other whites on the premises. "This was the only piece of evidence against Bernstein," Berrange concluded. "And on this basis, he is entitled to his discharge."

Berrange then analyzed the case against Kathrada and Mhlaba, poking holes wherever he could and attempting to persuade the judge that on purely legal grounds, the State had failed to prove its case against either man.

After Berrange sat down, Yutar made one more feeble attempt to review the evidence against Rusty, but the judge cut him short. "You know, Dr. Yutar, you are only entitled to reply on questions of law."

And so it ended. The judge announced that court was adjourned for three weeks while he considered his verdict. The lawyers went home. The Rivonia defendants went back to their cells. The waiting began.

The Rivonia Trial took place in the age before communications satellites prowled the skies. Foreign correspondents still sent their dispatches by telex, and television footage, such as there was, had to be sent by overnight flight to Europe and America. South Africa itself did not have television until 1977. The ruling Afrikaner fathers deemed the medium too dangerous for their brave new society; they feared it would only spread Western-style depravity and social unrest.

Still, even if from a distance, the whole world was watching as the case unwound inside the Palace of Justice. The press gallery was full most days. A BBC radio correspondent broadcast daily reports to London and the world, and BBC television carried the news regularly. *The New York Times* and other American newspapers gave periodic updates, as did American television networks. The international wire services filed short reports virtually every day. Various Western embassies, including those of the United States and Britain, sent regular observers.

In June, two days before de Wet issued his verdict, the United Nations Security Council (with four abstentions: the United States, Britain, France and Brazil) urged South Africa to end the trial and grant amnesty to the defendants. Dockworkers' unions throughout the world threatened to boycott South African goods. Soviet President Leonid Brezhnev wrote to South African Prime Minister Verwoerd demanding freedom for the defendants. Fifty Members of Parliament staged a march in London and an all-night vigil was held at St. Paul's Cathedral. Adlai Stevenson, U.S. representative to the United Nations, wrote a letter saying Washington would do everything it could to prevent the death sentence from being carried out.

It was almost winter again when the day of judgment arrived—June 11, 1964, eleven months to the day since the Rivonia raid. Hilda made the familiar trek to Pretoria early that morning, accompanied by Denis Goldberg's mother, Annie. Harold and Jean Bernstein, Rusty's brother and sister-in-law, also made the drive. They braved the gauntlet of roadblocks and checkpoints and made it to their seats just as the judge entered. It was precisely 10 a.m. He sat down and ordered the accused to rise. Then he read his verdict quickly and quietly. The lawyers and the defendants could barely hear him. Hilda strained to catch his words. Most of the audience, still settling in their seats, heard nothing.

Nelson Mandela, Walter Sisulu, Denis Goldberg, Govan Mbeki, Raymond Mhlaba, Andrew Mlangeni and Elias Motsoaledi were guilty on all four counts. Ahmed Kathrada was guilty on count two only.

As for Rusty: "Lionel Bernstein is found not guilty. He will be discharged."

The judge set the following morning for sentencing, then adjourned the court and swiftly exited. The crowd was puzzled. Hilda felt numb and disbelieving, and she turned behind her to glance at Harold and Jean, who gestured to her to signify that they had heard it too. Then she caught a glimpse of Rusty's face. He looked as pale and solemn as if the verdict had gone the other way.

She rushed forward to try to reach him. He tried to push toward her, but police and warders stood in his way. They demanded that he return to the cells with the other defendants. He resisted. He was determined that if they were going to rearrest him they should have to do it in open court before the press and public. "Are you arresting me again?" he demanded as he struggled toward Hilda. Arms outstretched, their fingertips were nearly touching when Swanepoel clasped Rusty on the shoulder, formally declared him under arrest and marched him back toward the stairway. Rusty had been acquitted by the court, not the police, and in the new South African police state he was not free.

Afterward, Vernon Berrange confronted Dirker in the corridor. "After that disgraceful exhibition in court, I will expect you people not to oppose bail when we apply for it on Bernstein's behalf," he told the detective. Dirker muttered something unintelligible and walked off.

Berrange decided to take it for a yes.

The defense lawyers stopped at Pretoria Local to consult with their clients before driving back to Johannesburg. The accused made clear once again that while they were willing for the lawyers to ask the court not to impose the death penalty, they were not prepared to apologize for their acts or in any way renounce their comrades or their movement. There was a long discussion of what would happen if the death penalty was handed down. The judge would begin by asking Nelson Mandela, the first accused, "Have you any reason to advance why the death sentence should not be passed?"

Mandela said he would reiterate in his response that he was prepared to die for his beliefs and was confident that his death would inspire others to follow in the struggle. He said he would add that the judge was wrong if he believed that by hanging the defendants he could stop the cause of black liberation.

Joel Joffe gently suggested that such a response would be of dubious assistance in appealing the death sentence to a higher court. But Mandela stunned the defense team by saying that he, Walter Sisulu and Govan Mbeki had discussed the matter at length and had decided that any appeal would be seen as an act of weakness. Their legacy to their supporters and their movement would be to stand fast and die like martyrs. Death sentence or no, there would be no appeal.

The decision was no act of false bravado. The defendants had heard that Justice Minister Vorster had told friends that former Prime Minister Smuts had blundered in not hanging him for treason during World War II. The Nationalist government would not make the same mistake. Mandela and Sisulu both believed the death penalty was inevitable.

The next morning the Palace of Justice again appeared under siege. Despite roadblocks and checkpoints on the main highways and at the train and bus stations, hundreds of Africans found their way to Church Square. A large group of white youths gathered as well. They were students from the University of Pretoria, come to cheer for death sentences for the enemies of Afrikaner nationalism. It was a tense standoff.

Inside, the courtroom was packed with relatives, policemen and reporters. The defense lawyers had a few quick minutes with the accused in the holding cell below the courtroom, but everyone was too tense to say much. Then they slowly climbed the steps to the dock for the last time.

Bram and Joel Joffe had searched for weeks for prominent white South Africans to appear before the court to speak in mitigation of sentence. Few were willing to consider speaking out for men convicted of violent acts. Some were sympathetic, but feared that stepping forward would turn themselves into targets for Special Branch and its vigilante allies. But one man who showed no reluctance was Alan Paton.

South Africa's best-known novelist was the spiritual leader of the Liberal Party, a devout Christian, a vocal anticommunist and an opponent of violence. He disagreed intensely with the sabotage campaign. Nonetheless he believed that the defendants had acted from pure motives, and he was prepared to speak on their behalf. He was also an ardent opponent of capital punishment.

Bram went to see him several weeks before the verdict at his home outside Durban to ask for his help.

"Are their lives in danger?" Paton asked.

When Bram replied yes, Paton did not hesitate. "In that case there is no question at all," he said. "I will give evidence if I am called."

Harold Hanson, who had been one of Jimmy Kantor's advocates, agreed to lead testimony for the defense for the penalty phase of the trial. He called Paton to the stand.

Paton gave three reasons for sparing the lives of the Rivonia men. He cited the attitude that South African Prime Ministers had taken in pardoning Afrikaner rebels who opposed the government's decision to fight alongside Britain in World Wars I and II. He said liberals understood that African leaders had been condemned by the National Party to a lifetime of knocking on a door that would never open, which made their turn to violent resistance understandable. And he said he feared Afrikanerdom would never recover from the stain it would suffer throughout the world if it executed men such as Nelson Mandela. Paton spoke of those among the accused whom he had met personally. Mandela, Sisulu and Mbeki were honorable and sincere men who were deeply devoted to the cause of their people, he told the court. He spoke on their behalf out of his love for his country. He concluded, "It seems to me, my lord, with respect, that the exercise of clemency in this case is a thing which is very important for our future."

Yutar stood next. The night before, Special Branch officers had handed him a thick dossier on Paton and the Liberal Party. The government and the police were convinced that the Liberals were at best communist dupes and at worst enemies of the state themselves. Having an acknowledged leader of the party on the witness stand was too good an opportunity to pass up. And Percy Yutar, eager to please as always, was prepared to do their bidding once again.

Yutar had accused the defendants of murder and attempted murder—crimes that, if proven, cried out for hanging. Now he sought to smear and ridicule the one witness they had called to plead for mercy.

He explained to the judge that he did not as a rule cross-examine witnesses speaking in mitigation of sentence but felt compelled "to unmask this gentleman and make perfectly clear that his only reason for going into the witness box, in my submission, is to make political propaganda."

Yutar started out by asking Paton if he was a communist or a fellow traveler. When Paton answered no, Yutar asked if it was true that Paton "moved a lot with communists in this country," and he specifically mentioned Rowley Arenstein, a radical lawyer who lived in Paton's hometown of Durban. "Met him largely through Defense and Aid," Paton replied, naming the organization that had raised money to fund the defense in the Treason Trial.

"That is another organization with a high-sounding name which assists the saboteurs in this country, isn't that so?" sneered Yutar.

No, replied Paton. "It assisted in defending people who were brought before the courts so that they might get a fair and just trial."

On it went. Yutar discussed Paton's support for an international economic boycott against South Africa and strafed him rhetorically for speaking out "against your country."

"Against my country?" answered an enraged Paton. "No, no! Against certain politics that are followed in this country, yes. But against my country, no."

Joel Joffe found the cross-examination a degrading spectacle, but both the judge and the security police seemed to enjoy it. Paton was dismissed.

Hanson rose to make a last plea. Just as Afrikaners had armed themselves in the struggle against British imperialism, so had black patriots taken up arms against the Afrikaner state. Indeed, there would be no Afrikaner-led government today had such acts of rebellion not occurred. Hanson warned that whatever sentence the judge imposed would echo down the halls of South African history for many years to come.

The judge, who looked pale and uncomfortable, seemed not to be listening. As soon as Hanson finished, he told the accused to rise. Once again he spoke so softly that almost no one but the defendants themselves could hear him.

He said he had heard often during the course of the case about the grievances of nonwhites and the defense's claim that the accused were motivated entirely by a wish to ameliorate those grievances. "I am by no means convinced that the motives of the accused were as altruistic as they wish the court to believe," he declared. "People who organize a revolution usually take over the government, and personal ambition can't be excluded as a motive.

"The crime of which the accused have been convicted, that is the main crime, the crime of conspiracy, is in essence one of High Treason," the judge went on. "The State has decided not to charge the crime in this form.

"Bearing this in mind and giving the matter very serious consideration, I have decided not to impose the supreme penalty which in a case like this would usually be the proper penalty for the crime. But consistent with my duty that is the only leniency I can show. The sentence in the case of all the accused will be one of life imprisonment."

It was over. The judge stood up swiftly and marched out. The accused, who seemed stunned at first, slowly turned toward the public galleries with smiles slowly appearing. Annie Goldberg called out to her son, "Denis! What is it?"

He called back joyously, "Life! Life! To live!"

Walter Sisulu, too, felt relieved. Life imprisonment seemed almost like an acquittal. All of the accused now were grinning broadly. Somehow, they felt, they had won.

As the defendants were led away, Joel Joffe looked at Bram. They had saved the lives of their clients, which was the most they could have hoped for. But neither of them felt any sense of achievement or satisfaction, not even a sense of relief. These special men, clients, friends and comrades, were going to prison for life. They felt numb.

Outside, Winnie Mandela announced "Life!" to the crowd from the bottom of the courthouse steps with her arm raised in a militant salute. African women broke into song. Banners were unfurled reading "Our future is bright," and "Sentence or no sentence, we stand by our leaders." Police with dogs sought to push people back. Members of the crowd and the police followed Winnie to her car. Before she got in, Toni Bernstein put her arms around her and gently kissed her.

Joffe, emerging from the Palace of Justice, watched the crowd moving slowly toward the back of the building, straining for one more glimpse of their leaders being driven back to prison. These were people who should have been broken, leaderless and without hope, thought Joffe. Yet here they were, singing, marching and displaying the forbidden green, gold and black of the ANC. It seemed to him that they, not the court, were having the last word. They and their leaders were innocent; it was the state that was guilty.

Bram, as always, tried to see the bright side. In a letter he wrote later that day to John Collins, the Anglican priest in London who had pro vided most of the funds for the Rivonia defense, Bram contended that uniform life sentences were best because they would make a better focus for an international campaign to have the men released. He also believed that "in many ways, important and unimportant, this trial has changed attitudes." He cited instances where white warders had treated Nelson and the other accused with dignity and even affection. He quoted one anonymous Afrikaner warder as saying, "We have all learned a great deal during this case."

International reaction to the verdict was condemnatory. The world press and many governments, East and West, accused the government of staging a show trial in a society devoid of justice. In the United States, the story generally received limited play. *The New York Times* played it at the left-hand bottom of the front page, just below "Laos Neutralists Lose a Vital Post." *Time* magazine opined that "the outcome could have been worse." But an editorial in the *Times* the following day warned, "If disaster is to be averted in South Africa, those who now hold the reins of power there must re-examine the policies that are sowing the seeds of holocaust." South Africa had always identified itself with the West, and its Afrikaner leaders took pride in comparing the history of their pioneering society and their racial policies to that of the United States. But the day before the Rivonia verdict, the U.S. Senate had voted by 71 to 29 to end the filibuster against the watershed 1964 Civil Rights Act. By the end of the year the bill was law, followed the next year by the Voting Rights Act. While America's leaders were attempting to enshrine racial equality in its laws and practices, South Africa's were determined to eradicate it in theirs.

The South African government was defensive but unrepentant. Prime Minister Verwoerd declared that those who had been found guilty at the Rivonia Trial were "communist criminals in the same way as any communist spy found in the United States and sentenced to death." Justice Minister Vorster told Parliament he would press for an extension of the Ninety-Day Act, which he called "one of the most important means of keeping South Africa peaceful." South Africa's newspapers rallied to defend the court and the verdict. But the *Rand Daily Mail*, while lauding the sentences as "wise and just," agreed more was at stake than just one trial.

"The case has captured the imagination because it seems to tell a classic, ancient story of the struggle of men for freedom and dignity, with overtones of Grecian tragedy in their failure.

"Rivonia," it concluded, "is a name to remember."

Rusty was not in court the morning of the sentencing. He had been transferred back to Marshall Square in Johannesburg to await charges of violating his banning orders and belonging to an illegal political organization—namely, the Communist Party. When Hilda brought him food that evening, the young warder in charge asked if she would like to see him and told her she could bring the children as well. Keith and Frances came for two long visits, and the warders even allowed Rusty to hold and kiss them.

On Saturday morning Hilda, Toni and Ivan went to the Magistrate's Court, where Rusty was to be formally charged. The prosecutor said police had instructed him to oppose bail. But Berrange thundered indignantly that he had been assured by Warrant Officer Dirker that Special Branch would not contest bail. Berrange was a gambler and something of a con man. He knew Dirker had said no such thing. But he and his client had nothing to lose. When the prosecutor balked, Berrange demanded that Dirker be called to the stand to explain why the police had changed their minds. It was the day of a championship rugby match between Transvaal and Western Province at Johannesburg's Ellis Park, and Berrange calculated correctly that Special Branch officers would be hard to find. After much fulmination and browbeating, the prosecutor agreed to bail of 2,000 rand.

After eleven months in prison and a trial in which his life was at stake, Rusty at last was free go home.

Early that afternoon the lawyers came by Regent Street to greet him. Hilda hugged each of them in gratitude, but she saved her strongest hug for Bram. He had worked so hard for so long and he looked exhausted. The trial had been a great strain. He and Molly, who had served as a combination secretary, coach and informal legal advisor, had worked full-time for months on the case. There had been little time for family matters. Their younger daughter Ilse's twenty-first birthday was coming up in a few days. Ilse was attending the University of Cape Town, and everyone had encouraged Bram and Molly to go down south to see her.

There would be time to tie up the loose ends of the trial when they returned. They were leaving that afternoon for the first leg of the 800-mile trip and they stayed only a few minutes at the Bernsteins' house to share in the bittersweet joy of Rusty's return. Then they headed off for the long drive to Cape Town.

NINE

SUNSET

For the Afrikaner people, Lionel Burger was a tragedy rather than an outcast; that way, he still was theirs . . . that way, they were themselves absolved from his destruction.
Nadine Gordimer
Burger's Daughter

B ram and Molly Fischer left for Cape Town in their gray Mercedes sedan that afternoon with Elizabeth Lewin, a young friend who ran the Johannesburg office of the Defense and Aid Fund. The Fischers planned to spend the night at the home of Bram's brother Paul in Bloemfontein. Bram was still exhausted from the climax of the Rivonia Trial, which had only ended two days before, and Molly drove the first leg. But at six-thirty that evening Bram took over.

It was dark as he approached the Sand River Bridge in the Orange Free State going about seventy miles per hour. He saw a cow moving slowly across the road, then a motorcycle coming in the opposite direction. The cow stepped back into the path of the Mercedes. Bram swerved sharply to avoid the animal and the car plunged off the road into the riverbed. Neither he nor Liz could open their doors, so they rolled down the windows and scrambled out. To their surprise they found themselves in several feet of water. Molly made no move to get out—she must have been knocked unconscious from the crash. But as Bram and Liz tried to yank open a door and pull her out, the car suddenly slipped under the surface and disappeared. Dazed, cold and wet, Bram dove in over and over, even climbing up on the bridge to try to get more momentum for his dives, while Liz scrambled to the road to get help. But the sinkhole was thirty feet deep and Bram could not reach the car. Eventually, onlookers had to drag him from the site.

They took him and Liz to a local hospital, and Bram phoned his brother Paul, who drove up immediately. Paul wanted them to come to his house for the night, but Bram insisted on going straight back to Johannesburg so that he could be the one to tell his son that Molly was dead. On the way he agonized constantly. It was all his fault, he kept saying over and over, for going so fast and for not rescuing Molly from the murky depths. "My poor wife," he moaned. "*My poor, poor wife.*"

Hilda and Rusty learned of Molly's death early the next morning when their neighbor and comrade Ivan Schermbrucker showed up at the house, sat down on the bed and burst into tears. By the time they arrived at Beaumont Street the house was already filled with visitors, some sitting silently or sobbing gently. Bram wept when he saw Hilda, and again at the arrival of Arthur Chaskalson's wife Lorraine, a close friend of Molly's. But he pulled himself together, offering food and drink to his guests, moving from room to room and occasionally taking refuge in the garden that Molly had planted and nurtured and that they both had cherished for twenty-five years. Sometimes he would retreat to their bedroom, where Pat Davidson found him at one point weeping quietly.

Even in his grief Bram knew to be vigilant. When his brother Paul went back to claim the body, Bram asked him to retrieve a tissue box from the car. Paul found a small map pasted to the bottom with a pattern of dots. Paul thought the dots might have been sabotage targets, but he returned it to Bram without asking.

Both Hilda and Rusty needed written permission from the Chief Magistrate of Johannesburg to attend Molly's cremation service at the Braamfontein Crematorium the following Saturday. It was granted the day of the ceremony, too late for them to attend. Bram had asked Hilda to speak, but later he came to the house with George Bizos to plead with her not to because to do so would violate her banning order. Hilda said she did not care, but Bram gently insisted that she not put herself at risk. In the end she prepared the words and Vernon Berrange read them aloud at the chapel without saying who wrote them.

Three hundred people, including leading members of the Johannesburg bar, came to the ceremony, among them many of the banned—the

```
81/172690,
(Z. 14 8)
/MS                          Republiek              Republic
Verw. Nr./Ref. No.  17/33/4/41         VAN SUID-AFRIKA       OF SOUTH AFRICA

                                                    KANTOOR VAN DIE—OFFICE OF THE
NAVRAE/ENQUIRIES:                                       MAGISTRATE,
        Tel. No.  835-8396                             JOHANNESBURG.

                                                       17th June, 1964.



              Mrs. H. L. BERNSTEIN,
              154, Regent Street,
              Observatory,
              JOHANNESBURG.


              Madam,

                    PERMISSION is hereby granted for you to

              attend the Cremation Service of the late Mrs.

              A. Fischer at the Braamfontein Crematorium,

              Johannesburg, to-day (17.6.1964.) at 4.45 p.m.


                                    Yours faithfully,




                                    CHIEF MAGISTRATE OF JOHANNESBURG
```

comrades that the government had effectively declared nonpeople. Whites, Africans and Indians, many of them weeping, stood silently as Berrange read messages of tribute. Molly was "a true daughter of South Africa," he declared. "She belongs to all of us."

A week later Bram flew down to Cape Town with Joel Joffe to visit Nelson Mandela and the other Rivonia prisoners at their new home on Robben Island. Bram felt strongly that they should lodge an appeal of the verdict and sentence, but Mandela and the others were adamant. Not even Ahmed Kathrada, whom Bram was certain had good grounds for reversal of his conviction, would budge. Once again. Bram was thinking like a lawyer while they were thinking like politicians. Mandela, who had no idea that the accident had occurred, asked after Molly. Bram said nothing but excused himself from the room. He came back a few minutes later and resumed the discussion of legal matters, but he never answered Nelson's question. On the way back to the cells afterward, a prison officer who had sat in on the interview took Nelson aside and told him of Molly's death.

Mandela wrote Bram a letter of condolence—but the authorities never sent it. Nelson Mandela never saw Bram Fischer again.

Molly's death did not deter the police from closing in. Hendrik van den Bergh, head of the security police, had waited patiently for the end of the Rivonia Trial, and now he was preparing another strike at the heart of what remained of the South African Communist Party. Long Hendrik had several dozen suspects in mind, but his primary target was Bram himself. Now that the trial was over, so was the temporary immunity that Bram had enjoyed as chief defense counsel. But Long Hendrik wanted to achieve more than merely arrest Bram. He also wanted to destroy Bram's credibility with his comrades. He decided to begin the process by harassing his quarry. He assigned a surveillance team to Bram, ordering his men to be conspicuous enough so that Bram and everyone he met with would know he was being watched. This, Long Hendrick figured, would heighten Bram's paranoia and the anxieties of everyone around him. Long Hendrik hated all communists, but he seemed to hate Bram most of all. As a fellow Afrikaner, he looked upon Bram as the ultimate traitor, a man who deserved not just punishment but humiliation. And Long Hendrik was a gamesman; he liked turning this particular investigation into a contest, one in which he held all the cards.

After he visited with the Rivonia men. Bram gathered his children for a brief holiday. Borrowing Ivan Schermbrucker's big American sedan, the Fischers drove east along the Garden Route through some of the Cape Province's most beautiful countryside, staying for a few days at the beach house of a friend. Everywhere they went the police were close behind, always making their presence felt. Bram grew anxious. There were incriminating documents in the car that he did not want to fall into the hands of Special Branch, but there was no safe place to dump them. Finally the police pulled them over in a seaside town named George. Bram insisted on following the patrol car to the station, and en route he slipped various papers to Ilse and Ruth. The girls stuffed everything into their bras. Bram stood around with the police as they searched the vehicle, while the girls excused themselves and ducked into a local coffee shop. There they flushed the evidence down the ladies' toilet.

They arrived back in Johannesburg on July 8. At 5 a.m. the following day the police came for Bram. They held him for three days, interrogated him perfunctorily and let him go. They then spread word that he had given them a statement. It was an attempt to discredit him and persuade others to talk. Few of his comrades believed such a rumor, but Bram came home under a cloud of suspicion.

He faced the prospect of a protracted legal battle against the police and a house filled with painful memories. In a letter to Tilly and Julius First replying to their condolence note upon Molly's death, Bram wrote: "During the past twenty years, we have had to make many important decisions which might have had grave consequences for ourselves and our family. I know that there was no single occasion when Molly ever let herself be influenced in any way by possible personal consequences. She had the rare quality, supposed to belong to judges, of being able to exclude entirely from her mind what the consequences might be to her and—what was perhaps even more remarkable—what such consequences might be to our family."

In fact, the opposite was more often true. Molly had deeply loved and protected her family and she was inevitably influenced by personal considerations. She had cut back her own political activities considerably to care for their son Paul. Rather than exclude the personal consequences of her deeds, she had been acutely aware of them and worked hard to shelter her children from them.

Molly had been Bram's anchor tethering him to reality. Now, as the letter suggested, his mind was beginning to drift. There were times when his imagination seemed to take flight beyond the bounds of reality. Perhaps he was only expressing a sense of what he ideally would have liked. Or perhaps, without Molly to keep him grounded, he was beginning to slip into a world of his own. Pat Davidson, who moved back to the house after Molly's death, accompanied him to a jeweler's shop where he insisted on ordering an alarm clock for Ilse's birthday that was an exact replica of the one that had been lost with Molly in the back seat of the Mercedes. He even insisted on the same engraved message. When he saw it he broke down and wept.

Hilda, too, believed Bram was losing control. He was taking crazy risks. She went to his law office one day to discuss party matters. They knew they could not talk there because it was bugged, so Bram took a key from his drawer and opened a colleague's office next door. Hilda was uneasy—the colleague was not a political man and had no idea Bram might use his office for illegal purposes. Halfway through the meeting, the man walked in. He could have easily decided to go to the police, but he did not.

Bram seemed more driven than before. He felt responsible for everyone and everything. As people left the country or were arrested, he took on more and more of the burden, and more and more risks. "Whatever we left unfinished was on his shoulders," said Hilda.

The joy that swept the Bernstein family upon Rusty's release was short-lived. Molly's death punctured it, then the police set to work rolling up the remaining activists who were among Rusty and Hilda's closest friends. Mac Maharaj, one of the most important leaders of the new Umkhonto, was arrested near the end of June. Others were picked up soon after that. Hilda knew it was only a matter of time before she herself would be taken. Each night after dinner the family would huddle by the fireplace in the living room and do word games and other activities. But any sense of normality was gone. They were cut off not only from comrades and friends but even from each other. They could say nothing of importance for fear of listening devices in the phone or the walls. Rusty appeared in court on June 26, and his case was remanded until September. No evidence was presented, but little would be needed. His candid testimony at the Rivonia Trial about his communist views would be enough for a conviction. They all understood in advance what the verdict would be. They had two and a half months to consider and agonize over the possibilities.

The northern suburbs were like an echo chamber that July. Rumors reverberated powerfully, picking up volume and momentum as they careened from house to house and whispers became cries. Informers were everywhere. When word spread swiftly that a new raid was in the works, Hilda packed an overnight case and spent the weekend with nonpolitical friends to avoid arrest. The following week the police raided hundreds of homes and detained dozens more people. Still they did not come to Regent Street. Hilda took Keith and traveled to Durban to stay for a week with Ivan's parents, her new in-laws. Soon she was back home and the waiting began anew.

Bombs were going off again. Led by Wilton Mkwayi and David Kitson, Umkhonto mounted a series of small actions in July. But the worst attack had nothing to do with Umkhonto. On a Saturday afternoon in late July, a man phoned the Johannesburg Railway Police to warn that a bomb had been placed in a suitcase at the new train station. It was set to go off in fifteen minutes, and the caller told police to evacuate the area immediately. They took no action—no one has ever determined why—and the bomb went off on the concourse between Platforms 5 and 6 just as the caller had warned, injuring twenty-three people. One of them, a seventy-seven-year-old grandmother named Ethel Rhys, died of her wounds. Her twelve-year-old granddaughter Glynnis was badly burned. Police swept furiously through the ranks of activists and political prisoners that evening, assaulting anyone they believed might have information that would lead them to the bomber. Within seven hours they had located and arrested John Frederick Harris, an Oxford University graduate, schoolteacher and member of the Liberal Party, who had been a fringe member of Adrian Leftwich's African Resistance Movement. Lieutenant J. J. Viktor led the interrogation. He kicked Harris twice in the jaw and once in the stomach, according to journalist and police informer Gordon Winter's account, and extracted a swift admission of guilt.

The bombing further inflamed white public opinion against the left. The police saw it as a rationale for further toughening their war against the opposition. A few days later Justice Minister Vorster declared confidently that police were closing in on those known to be the brains behind the wave of subversion. "The masterminds were white South African communists who shield behind and posed as liberals," Vorster told reporters. "They found among the liberals willing musket-bearers to direct a long-term communist plan, dating back to the 1930s, to take control of South Africa." Soon they would be crushed, he promised.

———

Hilda and Rusty took Toni and her husband Ivan for a picnic in the Wilds that weekend to tell them they were planning to flee the country. They asked if Toni and Ivan were prepared to care for the other children for an indefinite period. The police might even decide to detain Toni or Ivan or both of them. None of this fazed their daughter or son-in-law. Toni and Ivan said they had long wished for Hilda and Rusty to leave, fearful that more arrests and another round of trials lay just around the corner.

The following Monday, Rusty took the bus into the city to meet someone he was banned from seeing. In the afternoon a police van parked outside the front gate and Hilda began to worry. Rusty was late. The afternoon seemed like a chilling replay of that nightmarish July day a year earlier when the police had raided Rivonia. The clock ticked down. Toni said nothing; Hilda avoided her anxious gaze. This time I will die, Hilda thought. At 6:15 p.m. she could bear it no longer. She jumped into the car and drove to the corner. The van followed. Then she saw Rusty. He was hurrying toward home past the trees down the dusk-filled street. She threw open the passenger-side door for him and he climbed in. She began to cry and he hugged her tightly. They headed home, safe for now, and the van peeled off.

The following morning she woke at dawn to find him peering out at the street from behind the bedroom curtain. A Volkswagen pulled up to the front gate and two men got out. He turned to Hilda. "Quick, go!" he said. "They're here."

She ran to the basement, following the drill they had worked out long ago. Police might come to both the front and back doors, but there was a side basement window that opened to the garden at a spot concealed from both doors. Rusty had cut through the bolts holding the security bars so that someone could push his way out, and he had placed a table under the window. She climbed up, pushed out the window and the bars and pulled herself through, then headed through the thick wet grass toward the next-door yard. As she ran off she could hear the doorbell ringing behind her.

No doubt the Schermbruckers' house would be raided too. She headed instead to a more distant and apolitical neighbor a few blocks away, persuading him to drive her to friends in another part of town. Rusty phoned later to say the police had seized two typewriters and left. Although her friends warned her not to go back, she returned home that evening.

A few nights later Hilda met with Ivan Schermbrucker in the back garden. Ivan was like Bram—totally opposed to anyone leaving the country. Yet he knew Hilda was thinking of fleeing and she urged him to consider it as well. "You know you are going to be arrested soon," she recalls telling him. "You know it's only a matter of days."

"Hilda, I can't go," he replied. "I can't bloody well go. I can't run away and leave L. and M. and N. stuck in under ninety days. I can't go and leave Helen shut for five years alone in her house. *I can't go.*"

But what Hilda remembers most painfully from that discussion was her sense of a growing divide between her and Ivan, one of her dearest friends. She was leaving and he was not. As far as he was concerned, she was giving up.

The next day Ivan was arrested.

With the constant threat of arrest gnawing at her, Hilda left home again and moved in with friends. She quietly visited a few of the people she had been close to over the years, silently saying goodbye without divulging her plans. She was afraid to go back to Regent Street, although she risked it to spend time with Keith on the last day of his winter holidays, and again the next morning to see him off to school. Each time she walked to the house, taking a circuitous route to avoid being followed. One morning as she drew near her neighborhood, she was too afraid to go to the door. Instead she stood on a nearby hill and watched the house as if it were forbidden territory across a foreign border. Her heart and her home were there, as was everything she loved and cared for. Yet it was denied to her. She saw smoke rising from the chimney and the dog racing through the yard. She felt like a ghost, looking back on a world she could no longer inhabit yet not quite bring herself to leave.

Hilda packed her bag that Friday afternoon and told her friends she was returning home. Rusty was irritated with her and anxious for her at the same time. He feared she was taking too great a risk. The children were uncertain why she had come back and how long she would stay. She had no answers. She could no longer live with the tension of not knowing when Special Branch would strike again and she wanted to bring things to a head, force them to make their move. Yet when a stranger phoned the following day and tried to fix a meeting, she immediately fled, figuring the man was a security policeman setting her up for arrest. She went to the house of a friend, who drove her to another friend's house. Neither place was safe for her, so she was taken to a third house, owned by a sympathetic stranger. She was welcomed there. Even Rusty did not know where she was.

The police came twice to Regent Street that weekend looking for her. Rusty sent her a note. "I am trying to find a way," it read. Full of dread, she wrote back: "If they come again and don't find me, they may take you—if we go, it must be soon."

The new Umkhonto High Command did not last long. Within a few weeks of the July bomb blasts the police net fell. Wilton Mkwayi, David Kitson, John Edward Matthews and Laloo Chiba were all arrested within a few days of each other.

Soon the police came again for Bram. This time they formally charged him with participating in an illegal organization—the banned Communist Party. Thirteen others were charged as well, including Ivan Schermbrucker and Eli Weinberg, a professional photographer responsible for some of the most memorable photographs of the era. Another prominent communist, fellow Afrikaner Piet Beyleveld, was detained but not charged. This led some in the movement to fear that Piet was talking to the police.

Bram was in the midst of preparing for a major legal case over patent rights that pitted the German pharmaceutical giant Bayer against his client, Bayer's former South African subsidiary. Bram had won the initial case, and was due to travel to London to argue against the German firm's appeal before the British Privy Council. He asked the South African court for bail in order to make the trip. Coming at a time when accused communists such as Michael Harmel and Duma Nokwe had skipped bail and fled the country, such a request seemed unlikely to be granted. But Bram was no ordinary defendant. Peter Rissik, a prominent Johannesburg lawyer who was co-counsel in the Bayer case, appeared on his behalf, telling the court, "I have absolute faith in his integrity and shall accept his word without hesitation."

"I fully believe I can establish my innocence," Bram told the judge. "I am an Afrikaner. My home is South Africa. I will not leave South Africa because my political beliefs conflict with those of the government ruling the country." Over the vehement objections of the security police, the judge set bail at 10,000 rand.

Before he left, Bram sought to put the party's Central Committee back together. He persuaded Lesley Schermbrucker and Violet Wein-berg to take the places of their imprisoned husbands, and Ilse tem-porarily took Bram's place. The fourth spot was assigned to Bartholomew Hlapane, a black activist and Umkhonto member who had fallen under suspicion because he had been detained during the time of the Rivonia raid. People feared Hlapane had turned informer. But things were so desperate Bram felt he had no choice.

The group met a few days before Bram left for London. He made them one promise: no matter what happened, he would return.

With Hilda away, Rusty had to find a means of escape for both of them, yet without raising the suspicions of the police. He was still under house arrest, required to report to Marshall Square daily and remain home for twelve hours each night. There was no one to consult with or seek approval from. It was too dangerous even to try to communicate with Bram. Most of the escape networks had been smashed. The people who had manned them had disappeared or used them for their own flight. One comrade offered to smuggle them to Bechuanaland in a steel oil tank; Rusty was afraid they would die of heat and dehydration on the way. But Lesley Schermbrucker knew someone who knew someone else.

The someone else was Arthur "McClipper" Magadlela, proud owner of a 1949 Chevrolet Impala with 200,000 miles on the odometer. The car was McClipper's most valuable possession—he called it "the Myste-rious Impala" because how it kept running was a mystery to him— and he needed money to keep it alive. He had made two successful runs across the border with ANC people. For 150 rand and gas money he was willing to try it again.

After some negotiating, the move was finally set for the first Wednes-day in August. But Hilda could not go without seeing the children one more time. That afternoon she left her refuge and went to Bezuiden-hout Park, not far from the house. Rusty and the children met her there, all except Patrick, who was away at the Waterford school; with him there would be no goodbyes. Frances thought her parents looked strange. Her mother was disguised in heavy makeup, a strange hat, borrowed clothes and high heels; her father had blacked his red hair. Hilda told them she and their father were leaving but it would be all right. Toni and Ivan would stay with them and they would follow in a few days or weeks. What she did not tell them was that if she and their father were caught, it could be years before she might see them again. The children may not have known all the dire possibilities, but they could sense the danger and uncertainty. Frances began crying and Toni held Keith tightly as Hilda walked away.

As dusk fell that evening, Rusty made his way through the back garden to Lesley's house. He had a water bottle, a small canvas bag and a wad of 600 rand in his pocket, a gift from an old friend. Lesley had him lie down in the back of her station wagon, covered him with a rug and drove him to the tall gum trees opposite the Planetarium behind the University of Witwatersrand. Hilda made her way there separately. They climbed in the back seat of the Impala and McClipper headed northwest. He took a circuitous route to the border, at one point passing a roadblock of two police cars whose officers did not stop talking to each other long enough to check out what a black man was doing with two white passengers near the border in the middle of the night.

During the four-hour car ride, Hilda recalls in her book, she was more afraid than she had ever been in her life. There had been many moments of fear and anxiety over the years, but they had been tempered by the fact that she was serving a cause she believed in and fighting against something she knew was evil. But there was no way to ease the fear she felt now. She was serving no cause but her own, she felt, running away from the only world she cared about, admitting defeat and surrendering to the principle of self-preservation. For an idealist like Hilda, it was humiliating to sit huddled in the rattletrap sedan and flee like a frightened bird.

McClipper got within five miles of the border and pulled over. He led Hilda and Rusty across acres of elephant grass and drought-hardened ground. After an hour he pointed them in what he said was the general direction of the border and said goodbye. It would be another hour to the fence, he told them. But without a guide on a moonless night Hilda and Rusty stumbled along for several hours through the rugged, stony terrain, thornbushes, ant holes and deep darkness. They had a flashlight and a compass but feared that any light, even a cigarette, would attract a border patrol. Bruised and exhausted, they finally decided to stop and rest until dawn, but it was cold and one of Hilda's legs was so stiff she feared if she did not keep going she would not be able to walk on it. As dawn rose, they found themselves near a dirt track and began walking along it until Rusty realized it must be used by border patrol vehicles. They veered off quickly in search of cover. At last they came upon a kraal, a traditional African village. They sat down outside and waited. Eventually a man emerged from a hut. Rusty approached him warily and asked for directions. The man said little but beckoned them to follow. After walking just ten minutes they reached the fence—a double line of barbed wire with a thin strip of no-man's-land in between. They must have spent hours walking in circles in the darkness. After paying their guide, they pulled themselves over the two wires and entered Bechuanaland.

Hilda had to lie down. Rusty left her under a tree and walked on, eventually coming to another hut. The woman there, who had worked as a domestic in Johannesburg and spoke some English, helped fetch Hilda, then made them tea and massaged Hilda's legs and feet with warm salty water. She then cajoled a man from a neighboring kraal into taking them in a horse-drawn cart to a nearby settlement, where she knew they might find a visiting agricultural agent with a car. They found the agent, and he gave them a lift to Lobatse. He dropped them at the post office, where they sent a telegram to Toni telling her they had arrived safely, so that when the police came by looking for Rusty she would have something to show them. Then they found their ANC comrades and started making the complex arrangements for safely leaving the country.

Lobatse was a dusty crossroads outpost only three miles from the border. Except for a handful of British colonial officials, virtually all of the whites living in the area were South Africans whose loyalties were to the apartheid regime. A small contingent of ANC people had set up a way station for refugees. The ANC members feared that Rusty and Hilda's notoriety might attract unwelcome attention and endanger the safe house, so Rusty and Hilda stayed instead at a local hotel. They could not sleep securely, however, knowing that South African police squads roaming freely through the area had kidnaped other refugees.

After three days, South African newspapers broke the story of their flight and the phone at the hotel rang constantly. Soon a yellow Ford Galaxy with South African license plates appeared, following them around town, then a red Volkswagen. The local British agent, polite but guarded at all times, kept inquiring as to when they were leaving.

After a week of desperate phone calls and telegrams, their ANC contact in Lusaka, Northern Rhodesia, arranged for a charter plane to fly to the airstrip at Palapye, about 200 miles to the north—the same place where Harold Wolpe and Arthur Goldreich had caught their flight to freedom a year earlier. The plane would pick them up early on a Monday morning and fly them to safety. Because none of their contacts in Lobatse had a car to get to Palapye, they decided to board a train late on Saturday night. It was a South African Railways train that came up from Mafeking, crossed the border and went on to Francistown, stopping along the way at small towns like Lobatse and Palapye. Rusty and Hilda did not buy their tickets in advance to avoid tipping off anyone to their plan, but they had to inform the local British agent.

A trusted ANC contact named Maulvi Cachalia arrived after dark and walked them to the one-room station. A single lightbulb barely illuminated the rickety wooden platform. Cachalia left them to go buy the tickets inside. Moments later a Land Rover and another car pulled up in the yard. Six men in civilian clothes got out. They climbed the stairs and stood on the platform a few yards away from where Hilda and Rusty were sitting. Then one of the men left the group and walked slowly down the platform, silently passing Hilda and Rusty, who sat motionless on a bench. Rusty recognized him as a colonel in the security police. At the end of the platform, the man turned around and walked back at the same deliberate pace.

Cachalia came hurrying back from the ticket office. "It's Special Branch," he told them. "You mustn't get on the train."

Hilda argued. "If we don't get on the train, what are we to do? How can we get away from them? We must get on the train."

But Cachalia insisted that they stay put. A few weeks earlier men like these had stopped the train outside of town, taken off a South African passenger and beaten him. Someone had taken Cachalia aside at the ticket office and warned him that the South Africans were planning to kidnap Hilda and Rusty and haul them back to Pretoria. All of the men who operated the train were South Africans. Once the Bernsteins boarded, they would have no one to turn to for help. A kidnaping that might be an embarrassment if it took place in Lobatse would not be seen or heard out in the bush along the desolate track.

Cachalia had a plan. As the train pulled into the platform, he, Hilda and Rusty jumped from the platform onto the sandy yard, ran past the cars, crossed a street, pushed open a gate and huddled in the back yard of a house. They waited until they heard the train pull out, then cautiously made their way to the house of a friend of Cachalia's. They were safe, for now, but stranded.

That morning Hilda approached another ANC contact and pleaded with him to take them to Palapye in his truck. The man had not volunteered the vehicle before, but now he readily agreed. The four of them left after dark and drove much of the night. The plane was late and they spent several anxious hours in Palapye, dirty, exhausted and drained of both hope and fear.

In a letter she wrote later to Toni and Ivan, Hilda says she did not believe in the existence of the plane. She never thought it would come. Now that it had, she understood why she had tried to deny its existence. The little red-and-white three-seater was her final defeat, an admission of failure and the vehicle of her despair. It would take her far away from everything she cared about.

As it bumped along the dirt airstrip, their friends on the ground raised their clenched fists and called out, "*Amandla! Amandla!*"

From inside the small plane, Rusty and Hilda raised their fists in return and called back, "*Ngawethu Afrika—Mayibuye!*" But the sounds of their voices were drowned out by the steady hammering of the single engine and the bleak, solitary moan of the desert wind.

Bram arrived in London in early October. He stayed with his daughter Ruth and her husband, Anthony Eastwood, in their basement flat in Primrose Hill. The legal case went well; the judgment for Bram's client was sustained on appeal. But his efforts to reach agreement with his comrades-in-exile were less successful. He met at Ruth and Tony's flat with Joe Slovo, Yusuf Dadoo, Michael Harmel, Brian Bunting and the newly arrived Rusty— he had made it to London with Hilda and two of the children a few weeks earlier. The men argued for several hours over the wisdom of Bram's plan to return to South Africa.

These were Bram's comrades and some of his closest friends, men he had worked with for twenty years and more. They pleaded with him not to go back. There was no point in his returning to stand trial before a court that was certain to convict him. "You're putting your life at risk," Rusty told him. "What's the point? What are you going to achieve?"

But Bram insisted that he had to return to South Africa as a matter of both personal honor and political necessity. Someone had to rebuild the underground party and convince blacks who felt they had been abandoned to the ravages of apartheid that the communists were still on their side and prepared to make personal sacrifices on their behalf. If the trial looked hopeless, Bram pledged, he would flee and go underground. From there he could continue working for the party and inspire the liberation movement in the same way Nelson Mandela had done during his months as the Black Pimpernel. In any event, said Bram, he had made a promise to return not only to the court but to his remaining comrades on the Central Committee. They needed his leadership and they expected him to come back. He would not let them down. "I've given my word," he said over and over.

The comrades could have invoked party discipline and ordered him not to return, but they chose not to. The decision, they said, was his to make. Perhaps they were responding in part to the unspoken rebuke of Bram's position. While he did not say so, he felt they were wrong to remain in exile. South Africa needed all of them, even if it would destroy them. They told him they would support with money and other means any effort he made. They would also try to arrange to send people back to help restore the party, although by necessity these would have to be fresh, unknown cadres rather than those whose names and faces were prominently featured in police dossiers. None of them believed Bram was doing the right thing, and few thought he could survive for long underground. They would do what they could to help, but there was no enthusiasm for such a self-destructive act.

Hilda and Rusty both felt that Bram was over the edge. Without Molly to keep him stable and organized, he seemed lost and confused. He was obsessed with returning home, even if it cost him his life. Hilda had seen this before—Bram's feeling that he and he alone could overcome the problems. He had always believed his country was just at the dawn of a new era, if he and his comrades could hold on just a little longer. Where others saw darkness, Bram anticipated sunrise.

A few days before his return, Bram and Hilda went for a walk on Hampstead Heath. More than thirty years later, Hilda remembers little of what they said to each other, but she remembers the affection and anxiety she felt. They had known each other for so long, two people who had worked together and who loved each other. But there was so much they could not say. Hilda made no effort to talk him out of going back, but she pressed him to make one promise. "If you can possibly stay out of jail, do so," she told him. "Do whatever you have to do, but don't let them get you."

"Don't worry about me," he replied softly.

It was the last time she ever saw him.

Bram stopped off briefly for a visit at his alma mater, New College in Oxford. Then he took an overnight flight back to Johannesburg. When the trial resumed on November 16, Bram was sitting in the dock with his thirteen comrades.

From the moment he arrived, the Waterford School in Swaziland was a disaster for Patrick Bernstein. He got there in the middle of the school year. Everyone else was settled and had made their friends. Patrick was unsettled and made none. He hated the classes, the teachers, the homework. Most of all, he hated the feeling that there was no way out. In Johannesburg at least, he could miss the bus in the morning and spend the day hiding out, alone with his own thoughts. There was space, even if it was space to be unhappy. But at Waterford, Patrick felt totally isolated and yet without privacy or time to himself. It was the worst possible combination. No one told him that his parents were thinking of fleeing South Africa. It would have been too great a risk. So when he found out, it was a complete surprise and it sealed his sense of total isolation. Now all he wanted was out. Legally, he could not leave. When he had arrived, the school's headmaster had taken his passport and locked it away in the office. But that did not stop Patrick. As his parents had done in Johannesburg, he carefully planned his escape.

One night he stayed awake long after lights-out, wearing his street clothes under the blanket. After midnight, he got up and slipped out the door of his dormitory room, out of the building and past the unmanned front gate. Even in the thick of darkness Patrick knew the route. He headed down the hill, then turned onto the main road a few miles from the border. It was a misty night, but he could see the lights of the occasional cars from far off. Each time one came, he ran off to the side of the road and lay flat in the dewy grass until it disappeared. He was scared and he was tired but he kept moving. It was perhaps 5 a.m. when he reached the border post and veered off across the veld.

He reached the border fence at a point far enough from the checkpoint so that no one could see him. The fence was about six feet high and topped with barbed wire. He had heard stories about its being electrified, but he had to get over it. He screwed up his courage and whacked the fence with his hand with a quick down-and-up motion. He felt nothing. He did it again. Nothing. And again. Finally he reached out and grabbed the fence with both hands. He pulled himself up over the wire. He fell to the ground, picked himself up and walked for a mile or so across the veld, then headed back to the road and started to hitchhike. When a man stopped, Patrick said he had been working as an electrician in Swaziland. On the way to Johannesburg, they stopped at a bar and Patrick had the first beer of his life. It tasted terrible, but he drained his glass so as not to raise the suspicions of his host. He was back in Johannesburg before sunset, and on a plane to join his parents abroad a few weeks later. Patrick's South African school career was over. But his anger and his emotional isolation would linger for a very long time.

Over the months Long Hendrik's men had refined ninety-day detention into a brutally effective tool. The old rules that had protected white detainees from physical abuse had long been scrapped. Now some were assaulted, while others were subjected to acute sleep deprivation, made to stand up without food or water for as long as it took until they collapsed physically and mentally and signed statements. Interrogators worked in tag teams, tough ones alternating with soft. Judges never interfered.

Ivan Schermbrucker was questioned continuously for twenty-eight hours, punched and kicked. Afterward, he managed to smuggle a letter to his wife Lesley, telling her what had happened. When she visited him, he looked pale, depressed and exhausted. Lesley brought an application in court for the police to release Ivan or at the least to produce him to testify about how he had been treated. Colonel George Klindt of Special Branch refused to allow Ivan to see a lawyer, and testified before a judge that he had questioned the officers involved and was satisfied that no mistreatment had occurred. The judge saved his outrage not for the police abuse but for the fact that Lesley had received a written message "apparently surreptitiously, and in the circumstances unlawfully." He said that while the Ninety-Day Act did not allow torture or other third-degree methods, it did call for the isolation of detainees to induce their cooperation. "An interruption by the court of a detention would frustrate the general policy of Section 17," he declared. Only the Minister of Justice or a senior police officer could intervene. Ivan stayed in detention, under the authority of the very people who had beaten him.

The two main prosecution witnesses in what became known in the press as the Little Rivonia Trial were not subjected to such abuse. Piet Beyleveld made a statement to police after only a few days of detention with no coercion at all except for the threat of a long jail sentence if he was convicted.

At first Bram could not believe his old friend and comrade would testify against him. Beyleveld had been chairman of the Congress of Democrats and had chaired the historic Kliptown meeting where the Freedom Charter was formally adopted in 1955. Like Bram he was an Afrikaner. "For years Piet and I were comrades," Bram told his friend Mary Benson. "I do not believe that when he comes into court, when he looks me in the eyes, he will be able to give evidence against us."

But Bram was wrong. Beyleveld, who avoided eye contact with Bram throughout his testimony, proved a persuasive and knowledgeable witness for the prosecution. He testified that he, Bram, Ivan Schermbrucker, Eli Weinberg and Hilda had been members of the Central Committee since August 1963. He described the party's structure and methods and offered incriminating evidence against virtually every one of the thirteen defendants. By the time he finished, the defense case was in serious trouble.

Asked by defense attorney Harold Hanson why he had agreed to testify, Beyleveld described it as an act of self-preservation. "I wanted to be released from the ninety-day detention. My liberty became very important to me. I can think of nothing but my liberty and I am prepared to forsake my lifelong principles for it."

"Were you not also motivated by a desire to save your own skin?" asked Hanson.

"If you want to put it that way," Beyleveld replied.

He said he still revered Bram as a champion of the oppressed. "He is a man who carries something of an aura of a saintlike quality, does he not?" Hanson asked.

"I agree," Beyleveld replied.

The second key witness was Gerard Ludi, or Agent Q018 as he was known by his superiors in Special Branch. Ludi testified that he had been recruited by the police in December 1960 to infiltrate the left and try to join the Communist Party. He claimed he had been handpicked for the task, although the comrades believed he had been turned more recently after being caught by police in a compromising position with a black woman. A graduate of the University of Witwatersrand and a reporter with the *Star* and the *Rand Daily Mail*, Ludi first joined the Congress of Democrats, then was recruited to the party in May 1963. He dated Toni Bernstein for a while and testified about a 1962 trip to Moscow they had taken together under the auspices of the World Youth Congress, a Soviet front group. He titillated the press with lurid accounts of illicit parties at the Fischer and Slovo houses. "Some parties were nothing but sex orgies where married white women made overtures to nonwhite men," Ludi testified. "People swam and walked about naked."

Under cross-examination from the relentless Vernon Berrange, Ludi admitted to his own illicit liaisons across the color line. "In order to gain the confidence of these people I had to pretend I was one of them," he explained. "I tried to do it as little as possible."

He described a party at Bram's where guests had plunged into the swimming pool.

"Naked, of course?" asked Berrange, his voice dripping with sarcasm.

"Of course," replied Ludi to loud laughter from the audience.

"You must have been filled with revulsion?" asked Berrange.

"At times I was."

"With yourself?"

"No, not with myself."

Ludi testified that he was placed in the same party cell as Bram, who was known to other members as "Jan." When the cell's post office box became compromised, Ludi arranged for a new one. From then on every piece of mail was read by Special Branch before it was received by cell members. Police also rented a flat next to that of Jean Middleton, another cell member, photographed those who came and went and recorded all conversations. Among their take were recordings of an alleged adulterous affair between Piet Beyleveld and a young female comrade.

Ludi's credibility was less than profound, but the fundamental claims of his testimony varied little from Beyleveld's. Together, they made a powerful case for the prosecution. Bram was lawyer enough to know that his conviction was all but guaranteed. He had no intention of meekly submitting. In December, at a meeting with Violet, Lesley, and a comrade named Issy Heymann, Bram told them he believed it was time to go underground. With their help he started making plans.

As she had predicted, Ruth First and her family had trouble adjusting to life in London. They rented a flat in Swiss Cottage in north London, then bought a small house on Lyme Street in Camden Town—Julius and Tilly lived in the ground-floor flat. Joe was away much of the time overseeing from exile the frantic efforts to keep the underground alive in South Africa and to build political and military structures abroad. Ruth had no job and few prospects in British journalism, where she was quickly pigeonholed as a Marxist who could not be entirely trusted to be "objective." But her most difficult task those first few months was the book she was attempting to write.

Her old friend Ronald Segal, the former editor and publisher of *Africa South*, who fled into exile in 1960, had become editor of the Penguin African Library. While Ruth was still in South Africa he wrote to her clandestinely to plead that she undertake the writing of a narrative of her time in detention. She started on it before she left South Africa, but she found it hard to focus. Once in London, distractions were multifold. In early June she confessed in a letter to Segal that she had written only a few paragraphs, but she signed a contract with Penguin for the book to be delivered by the end of the year. It was the most personal writing she had ever attempted. Segal persuaded her that the book would be meaningless unless she revealed much of herself, but she did so reluctantly and with only the greatest of effort. At one point she wrote to him to say she did not know if she could continue because she found the reliving of her experience so painful. He wrote back pleading with her to carry on, insisting that such an account would help rally public opinion abroad against the apartheid regime. In the end she pierced her own facade of confidence and command with a brutally honest account of her vulnerability and confusion in prison. When Segal received the final chapter, he was stunned to learn of her attempted suicide. She had said nothing about it. She wrote about it with restrained, spare, but powerful prose.

Ruth never quite came to terms with how much she had revealed. In a letter to a friend, South African poet Lionel Abrahams, dated January 1965, she wrote: "I didn't want to wallow in self-discovery and write too explicitly but a description of what happened makes it all, alas, too clear, and there is space to read between lines. . . . Old habits die hard. In future I shall stick to facts, like land ownership and mission schools and annual general meetings."

In some ways the book was Ruth's declaration of independence. Having given everything to the movement, having even been willing to forfeit her own life, she seemed liberated from ideological convention. The Ruth who worked in South Africa for nearly twenty years was a gifted but largely orthodox leftist intellectual. The one who emerged in London seemed far more willing to challenge the party line and leaders of the movement, including her own husband. She never quit the Communist Party, but she found herself increasingly isolated and critical. She favored China over the Soviet Union during the Sino-Soviet split; and the Soviet invasion of Czechoslovakia deeply angered her. Her views alienated her from mainstream members of the party, who seemed to bask in their allegiance to Moscow. This bothered her very little—she clung to her stubborn independence; she had, after all, paid the price of admission in the hardest of currencies.

On a Friday night in late January, the Fischer Volkswagen pulled out of the driveway on Beaumont Street. Ilse was behind the wheel, Pat Davidson in the passenger seat, and wedged on the floor behind their seats was Bram. Ilse drove around aimlessly for a while to lose anyone tailing them, then made her way to the nearby suburb of Killarney, where Violet Weinberg had arranged for a young man to meet the car. Bram popped out and the young man took him off to a secret location. Ilse and Pat drove home, where Ilse dressed in Bram's pajamas, drew the curtains and pretended to be her father for the rest of the weekend. She even set out meals for him and she and Pat spoke as if he were in the next room so that anyone listening in would not realize he was gone. They had a close call on Saturday afternoon when an American journalist came to the door asking to see Bram. Pat insisted that Bram could not be disturbed and that the journalist should contact him again on Monday.

That morning in court the surprise was sprung. Harold Hanson read a letter in which Bram announced his decision to go underground. His primary motivation, he said, was his fear that unwavering white attitudes would lead inevitably to widespread bloodshed. "If by my fight I can encourage even some people to think about, to understand and to abandon the policies they now so blindly follow, I shall not regret any punishment I may incur," he wrote. "I can no longer serve justice in the way I have attempted to do during the past thirty years."

Rather than flee abroad, he added, "I believe that it is the duty of every true opponent of this government to remain in this country and to oppose its monstrous policy of apartheid with every means in my power. That is what I shall do for as long as I can."

He left two letters for Ilse. One of them was for police consumption and was written to make it appear that she knew nothing of his flight. The other was more personal. In it he spoke of the house and garden on Beaumont Street, all they had meant to him and how it broke his heart to have to leave them behind. "They have been a sort of epitome of all that Molly was and what she stood for: friendliness and warmth, strength and love," he wrote. "God, what a terrible thing I did when I had that accident. At times I could nearly go mad with remorse & despair."

The state was outraged by Bram's flight. J. H. Liebenberg, the prosecutor, called it "the desperate act of a desperate man, and the action of a coward . . . a disgraceful act." But there was no concealing the fact that Special Branch had been caught completely by surprise. Offering what he called "a substantial reward," General Keevy, Commissioner of Police, said Bram was "somewhere between the South Pole and North Pole." After months of victories, the police had suffered a stunning defeat.

In fact, Bram was considerably closer than Keevy could possibly imagine. His first hideout was on a remote farm in Rustenberg, eighty miles northwest of Johannesburg, where he rented a small guesthouse from seventy-one-year-old Felicia Midlindton, a secret sympathizer. She knew who he was, but the cover story she gave was that he had told her he was Charles Thompson, a recent widower in need of refuge following his wife's death. While there Bram lost weight, which eased his high blood pressure and reduced the florid glow of his face. He changed his appearance in other, more artificial ways with the help of Cecil Williams, a theatrical producer and longtime activist. He shaved the hair at the front of his head, grew a goatee and dyed it and the rest of his hair auburn. Some of his comrades thought he looked like Lenin, but the children of one of his helpers called him "Professor Calculus" after the character in the Tintin comic books. He took to smoking a pipe, and kept it in his mouth when he talked to change the timbre of his voice. He also learned a new walk and used a cane to conceal the limp he had walked with ever since he had hurt his knee playing rugby at Oxford. He replaced his trademark black horn-rimmed glasses with a pair of rimless spectacles and traded his lawyer's suits and Afrikaner khakis for an English-style tweed jacket and cap. After six weeks at the farm, a forged identity card and driver's license arrived from London, along with several thousand British pounds. The name on the new papers was Douglas Black.

A young woman who said her name was Ann Getcliffe opened a bank account in Black's name. She also rented him a house at 57 Knox Street in the northern suburb of Waverley and bought him a light gray Volkswagen. She told friends that Douglas Black was her uncle, a retired insurance broker who had moved to Johannesburg from London for health reasons. In March, Bram moved in.

At first he relied upon a circle of only a half dozen party members including Violet Weinberg, Lesley Schermbrucker, Issy Heymann and Minnie and Ralph Sepel, secret activists who had helped Harold Wolpe arrange the Lilliesleaf sale and helped hide Harold and Arthur Goldreich at Mountain View after their escape from Marshall Square. Ilse and Pat Davidson were excluded at first; it was feared the police would tail them. But as time went on, Bram became lonelier and more isolated. He longed for human contact. Despite the dangers, Ilse and Pat each took to phoning him nightly and visiting him at least once a week. His friend Mary Benson, author of a book on the ANC and a close friend of Ruth First, also started coming around to see him.

Ilse first saw him at a deserted warehouse where she had been taken by a friend. An odd little man walked in and at first Ilse thought she'd been followed by the police. But then she saw his eyes—bright blue, same as her own—and she laughed with surprise and delight.

The disguise was so good that Bram decided to test it out by riding the elevator in the Innes Chambers, where he had kept his law offices. A judge he knew got on and stood beside him but did not recognize the peculiar little man with the walking stick.

Pat Davidson would meet him at a parking garage or at her club, where he would pick her up in the evening after she finished playing squash. He would drive her to his hideout and cook dinner. She could see how Bram was slowly deteriorating. He was used to being constantly busy and having his day mapped out so that every moment was full. Even on weekends he had always been active. Now he had endless time on his hands, hours and hours with nothing to do.

The Sepels were crucial members of Bram's inner circle. Ralph had been detained for thirty-four days after Harold and Arthur's escape, but had been released without charge. He and Minnie had a heightened sense of discipline and the need for security. They constantly tried to persuade Bram to cut off contact with Violet, Ilse and Pat for fear Special Branch would tail anyone they suspected might be in contact with him. "Don't see Violet, for God's sake," Ralph told him, "they've got to be watching her all the time." You've got to build up a new set of apolitical friends, said the Sepels. Join a camera club, go to a bridge club. Bram said he agreed, but he did none of this. In the opinion of the Sepels, he remained so traumatized by Molly's death and by the strains of living underground that he was incapable of taking positive steps for self-protection. Instead, knowing that they would disapprove strongly, he simply did not tell them about his constant contacts with Violet, Pat and Ilse.

Bram tried to remain politically active. He posted letters to newspaper editors from mailboxes in different parts of the country. He knew the letters would taunt the police, but his real purpose was to try to spark some sort of dialogue within the white community about race and politics.

Bram also wrote a long letter to Beyers Naude, director of the Christian Institute and a fellow Afrikaner, after reading that Naude had been prevented from giving a speech condemning apartheid. After praising Naude's attempt, Bram added: "I hesitated in writing to you because I doubted whether you would consider the support of a Marxist to be genuine, but this is the case. The conception of the brotherhood of man, and the idea that you must do unto your neighbor as you would have done unto yourself, are the fundamental contributions of Christ's philosophy and trust; these are the objects we are striving for, although by other means than yourself.

"Is it not now a suitable time to write a play showing what Christ would see if He should return now and visit South Africa? And how He would be crucified?"

Christ was unavailable. But in his absence, Bram seemed to be preparing himself for the role.

Many fellow Afrikaners looked at Bram as a traitor to his people. White liberals tended to see him as a tragic figure. "With his background, his family connections and his own brilliance, his future success was looked upon as a formality. Would it be Prime Minister or Chief Justice? That was the only question," wrote Joel Mervis, editor of the *Sunday Times,* a few days after Bram's disappearance. "However much one may disagree with Bram Fischer, however much one may condemn him, what we are witnessing here is the picture of a man who has deliberately sacrificed the richest rewards that life can offer for his beliefs and his ideals."

Mervis had known Bram for forty years, ever since college days. He noted that Bram had joined the Communist Party when it was legal, and that in doing so "he was deliberately throwing away the great material and professional rewards that would otherwise have been his for the taking.

"That decision, made in good faith, with the best intentions and with his eyes wide open, has now led to his downfall—and his humiliation and disgrace. Those who remember the brilliance of this remarkable man, his rich promise, his warm, likeable personality, will mourn for the tragedy that has overtaken him."

Even many of Bram's white comrades saw his decision to go underground as the delusion of a man pushed over the edge by the collapse of the movement and the death of his wife. But many blacks saw it differently. They welcomed and appreciated the sacrifice he was making. Nelson Mandela, Walter Sisulu and other prisoners on Robben Island heard of his exploits and cheered him on. They accepted the meaning that he himself gave to his flight—that it was designed, above all, to reassure blacks. "The madness of the brave is the wisdom of life," Maxim Gorky once wrote. Bram, it seemed, had not crossed the line between courage and madness; he had erased it altogether.

Bram tried to reorganize the underground party. He wrote a paper analyzing the political situation in South Africa and appealing to fellow communists to remain in the country despite recent defeats. It called for members to participate in rebuilding the party and allied organizations like the ANC, "expose and isolate" informers and campaign for better treatment and early release of political prisoners. But he was preaching to a shrunken and demoralized choir. Only a handful of party members remained free inside the country. They were scattered, isolated and powerless, unable or unwilling to emerge even long enough to try to communicate with each other, let alone engage in collective action. The party as an organization operating inside the country was finished.

One of the final blows was the verdict in the Little Rivonia Trial in April. Twelve of the thirteen remaining defendants were found guilty. As Central Committee members, Ivan Schermbrucker and Eli Weinberg received the longest sentences of six years each. The others each got four to five. Citing the fact that Ivan had lied on the stand about being a communist, Judge S. C. Allen said he concluded that Ivan's claim he had been tortured in prison was "just blatant propaganda." Judges in the new police state had gone far beyond giving police the benefit of the doubt; they were now actively helping the security forces dismantle the rule of law.

Bram observed the verdict from a safe distance, disappointed but not surprised. He stayed at the house on Knox Street until the middle of July, then moved to 215 Corlett Drive in the suburb of Bramley, renting a semi-detached house known as Mon Repos. He felt even more alienated and isolated there. Seeing his spirit deteriorate, Violet and Lesley arranged more visits from family and friends. Still, he told Mary Benson, he was desperately lonely.

He read the newspapers avidly searching for signs of life of the revolution he still fervently believed in. When the *Rand Daily Mail* and the *Sunday Times* published a series of articles on prison conditions, he asked Mary, "Do you think it's the flaring up of a new flame, or old ashes dying?" Before she could reply, he answered his own question with his old Bram-like enthusiasm: "I believe it is a new flame!"

The new Bram was a mass of contradictions. He told Mary he was studying the underground methods of the Portuguese Communist Party, learning how it was necessary to be ruthless even with one's own family and friends and to renounce all personal ties in order to be an effective revolutionary. Yet here he was taking ever greater risks to meet with her, Ilse, Pat and Violet each week. He also told Mary he was reading the Bible.

Part of his depression stemmed from his long, fruitless wait for help from his comrades abroad. He wrote letters in code and invisible ink to Joe Slovo in London twice a week addressed to "Kim" and signed

"Paulus," pleading for more money and reinforcements. He also asked for a fake passport so that he could travel abroad to ease the burden of loneliness and consult with those in exile. But the comrades, who had their own problems adjusting to life in a foreign country, were slow to respond. When an angry Ruth Eastwood confronted her father's friends in London that August demanding help for him, she was told that everyone was out of town. Some of them, she knew, were in Italy on vacation.

But what troubled Bram most were not the actions of his comrades but of his lawyer colleagues. Just two days after he went underground, the Bar Council of Johannesburg decided to file an action in the Supreme Court seeking to expunge his name from the Roll of Advocates on the grounds that he had broken his word to the court and dishonored the law. Bram was furious and deeply saddened. For years he had been a distinguished member and leader of the Bar Council. Everyone there knew how much he valued his personal integrity. To accuse him of dishonor was a rank insult and a sign of contempt. It was a sign also of how desperate his colleagues were to curry favor with the government. His colleagues had no legal reason to launch such an action—once he was convicted of being a communist the government could itself strike him from the roll. For his own legal brethren to do so in such haste was a betrayal he could only swallow bitterly.

He wrote to the press to defend his honor. "When an advocate does what I have done, his conduct is not determined by any disrespect for the law," he wrote. "On the contrary, it requires an act of will to overcome his deeply rooted respect of legality, and he takes the step only when he feels that, whatever the consequences to himself, his political conscience no longer permits him to do otherwise. He does it not because of a desire to be immoral, but because to act otherwise would, for him, be immoral."

In explaining why he had gone underground, Bram argued that the judicial system had been fundamentally compromised by the government's police-state laws. No proceeding that relied upon evidence extracted from ninety-day detainees could be regarded as fair, he wrote. And a new act allowing the Justice Minister to extend indefinitely the sentences of convicted political prisoners meant that the judiciary was no longer independent.

Prominent defense lawyer Sydney Kentridge and Bram's old protégé Arthur Chaskalson appeared on Bram's behalf at the Supreme Court hearing. The ruling judge was none other than Quartus de Wet, who had presided with such petulance and impatience over the Rivonia Trial. On November 2, 1965, de Wet ruled that Bram was guilty of "dishonest and dishonorable conduct" and struck his name. Thirty years of service as a lawyer was brought to an abrupt end. "Why couldn't they let the government do its own dirty work?" he plaintively asked Mary.

It was around this time that the fake passport under a new alias, Peter West, finally arrived from London. It was said to be the work of the KGB's forgery unit and it looked impressively genuine. Bram hoped to travel to London soon; he needed a break from the pressure and isolation. But he decided he must first switch houses again. The Sepels helped him find a place in the suburb of Dunkeld. It would be more secure; this time only they would know where he was living. The others would have to arrange to meet him at separate secure locations. But he needed cash to close the deal and London was infuriatingly slow in responding. In a coded letter written in early November, Bram pleaded with "Kim." "This item is now very urgent," he wrote. "I'm afraid I cannot understand your attitude . . . I sit here unable to do anything until I know what the trouble is."

Then he made a more general complaint. "I assume that you have been unable to do anything more than you have during the past few months. If you have and you have failed to do so, this would be absolutely unforgivable."

Bram was waiting for a reply when, on Tuesday night, November 9, Ilse phoned. Violet had been picked up at her workplace that afternoon, she told him. Bram agreed that he would have to move soon. But first he needed to close the deal with the owner of the Dunkeld house. A meeting was set for Friday morning. Surely that would be soon enough. The Sepels met with him at the Craighall Park Hotel and told him it was too long to wait. You should move at once into the hotel, they told him, you must not go back to the house. But Bram hesitated. He just had to pick up a few things, he replied. Perhaps he was too weary to move or too self-confident, too dismissive of Long Hendrik's Special Branch men.

By the time of Violet's arrest, Minister of Justice Vorster had scrapped the Ninety-Day Law for a new act that allowed for 180-day detention. Violet knew the police could hold her indefinitely and no judge could order her release. She was taken to security police headquarters in Pretoria that evening. The police found a spare house key in her purse and demanded to know where it was from. She refused to respond. They then went to work. They ordered Violet, who was forty-nine, to stand up, and they kept her standing for three days and nights without food or sleep, while a team of officers working in relays interrogated her. Her legs ached, her ankles swelled and her eyes were reduced to slits. Sometimes she leaned against the radiator, but the only time she was allowed to sit was when she went to the toilet, accompanied by a female guard. If she fell asleep her interrogators would bang the table to wake her up or threaten to douse her with water. They also threatened to arrest her son Mark, who was deaf, and her daughter Sheila. "You are like a group of sadistic schoolboys pulling the legs and wings off a fly," she told them. None of them felt any shame. "We will crack you," one of them replied.

Violet managed to hold out until Thursday afternoon. Finally, exhausted and broken after seventy hours of sleep deprivation. she collapsed and told them the address of the house where the key would fit.

An undercover team took up positions around 215 Corlett Drive. Long Hendrik ordered them to be patient. It would be easier to capture Bram Fischer alive once he emerged from his lair. He did so early that evening, loading some of his things into his Volkswagen for the impending move to Dunkeld, then heading off in the car. Unmarked patrol cars followed him from the house and pulled him over at the corner of Beaumont and Stella streets, just a few blocks from his old home. At first he insisted they had the wrong man. But when an old and familiar adversary, Captain J. C. Broodryk, arrived on the scene, Bram admitted who he was and accompanied the police back to Corlett Drive.

Pat had borrowed Ilse's white Volkswagen to meet Bram after squash that evening, but he never showed. She and Ilse feared the worst. Pat drove down Corlett Drive to the house, where she could see a collection of hard-looking men in the yard and driveway. She wanted to flee at once, but all of the activity had caused a major traffic jam and Pat found herself stuck directly in front of the house. She had a scarf on her head and stared straight ahead, hoping they would not spot her. But one of the detectives recognized the car and suddenly a group of men were running toward the road. Just then the traffic eased and Pat pressed the gas pedal to the floor. A police car gave chase. Pat weaved in and out of traffic—at one point she took a turn so rapidly that the car almost flipped over. After that the cops backed off. Later they accused Ilse, whom they had assumed was the driver, of knowing where her father had been hiding.

Broodryk opened the door of the house with Violet's key. Inside, he and his men found face creams, "tan-in-a-minute" lotion, mascara, glasses, two false beards, a wig, a mustache and tweezers. They also discovered spare cash, false license plates and identity papers, coded letters, Communist Party propaganda and a complete outfit of women's clothing—white blouse, green skirt, blue hat, white panties and two pairs of shoes. The clothing sparked a legend that the strange-looking elderly woman who had sat in the back row at the climax of Little Rivonia Trial was none other than Bram. The fact that she did not have a goatee was somehow overlooked.

Bram had held out underground for 294 days.

The police had captured Bram's body. His spirit was another matter. When George Bizos came to visit him at the new jail cell, the lawyer embraced Bram and asked him if it had all been worthwhile. Bram flared with anger. Had George ever asked the same of Nelson Mandela or Walter Sisulu or Govan Mbeki? he demanded to know. Didn't they have families and jobs as well? Bizos admitted he had never thought to ask them such a question. Well, then, don't ask it of me, Bram told him.

Back in court to face a preliminary hearing in January, Bram looked thin and pale. His semi-comic goatee was gone, the hair above his forehead was slowly growing back and he was wearing his old horn-rimmed glasses. The prosecutor made clear that this time the State would press charges far more serious than the crime of membership in an illegal organization. Now there were fifteen charges instead of the original four, and one of them alleged that Bram had approved sabotage missions and helped organize the recruiting and training of Umkhonto members: It was the same charge that Nelson, Rusty and the Rivonia men had faced. The maximum penalty was death by hanging. Ruth and Ilse were there to comfort their father. But Paul had been so ill over Christmas and looked so frail that they decided not to bring him to the courtroom so as not to alarm their father.

The prosecutor called Lesley Schermbrucker to the stand. The police had arrested Lesley one week after they captured Bram and had held her in detention ever since. Lesley had every reason to cooperate with the police. She was the mother of two teenaged children and her husband Ivan had already begun his six-year prison term. Bram was in captivity and there was no way he would go free. The pragmatic thing for her to do was to tell the truth and testify for the prosecution in return for an agreement to drop charges or suspend her sentence. But Lesley refused. "I don't wish to be disrespectful and I don't want to go to jail, but it is a question of principle," she told the magistrate in explaining her decision. Astonished and dismayed, he sentenced her to three hundred days' imprisonment, telling her she could gain her release at any time by satisfactorily answering questions.

As she stood up to leave the courtroom, Lesley looked back at the public gallery, smiled at her daughter Jill, who was eighteen, and whispered, "Don't worry." Then her eyes briefly met Bram's. He smiled warmly at her as she was taken away.

Violet, despite the statement she had already made to police, also refused to testify. But Bartholomew Hlapane, their former comrade, took the other route. He not only testified against Bram but became the star witness in a number of Umkhonto trials. Like Bruno Mtolo, Hlapane told a sordid tale of white communist domination of the liberation movement, all of it tailored to fit the State's harrowing conception. The money all came from Moscow, and whites were the masterminds, according to Hlapane, who said he had turned state's evidence because black members of Umkhonto had been left behind to die while whites had fled to London, where they were enjoying afternoon tea at luxury hotels. But his most damaging testimony concerned Bram's personal role. He revealed that Bram was chairman of the Central Committee, had visited Rivonia frequently and was aware of and had approved plans for sabotage.

The formal trial began March 23, 1966. It was held in the Palace of Justice in the same courtroom where Bram had defended Nelson Mandela, Walter Sisulu, Rusty Bernstein and their fellow accused. The same wooden prisoner's dock built for twelve men now held only one. Paul was now sufficiently recovered to join his sisters in the public gallery.

The prosecution's case took just two days. Beyleveld, Ludi and Hlapane all testified for the State. Thomas Mashifane, the hapless foreman at Lilliesleaf who had complained of being beaten by police, took the stand again. During the Rivonia Trial he had failed to identify Bram as someone whom he had seen at Lilliesleaf. This time was different. "I saw Fischer on the farm on several occasions," he told the court.

The prosecution sought to portray Bram's clandestine sojourn as orchestrated by Moscow. The KGB had ordered Bram to go underground, according to prosecutor Liebenberg, arranged for plastic surgery and financed the elaborate network that kept him going for nearly ten months. Only a masterful police effort had uncovered the fugitive. The truth was far simpler and closer to home. The decision to flee had been Bram's alone, against all advice from his comrades. There had been no plastic surgery, very little money and only a small and tattered band of accomplices. The KGB had provided some forged documents, nothing more. Like the cause he served, Bram was almost entirely on his own.

Nadine Gordimer, who attended the trial and later based the character Lionel Burger on Bram in her novel *Burger's Daughter*, wrote that Bram listened and took notes with the same calm demeanor he had shown during the Rivonia Trial. He remained tranquil even when Beyleveld took the stand. It all seemed normal—the courtroom setting was like an everyday scene from Bram's working life as a lawyer, noted Gordimer, except that this time it was he who was on trial. "Spectators in the gallery stared into the well of the court as into Fischer's private nightmare, where all appeared normal except for this one glaring displacement."

Sydney Kentridge for the defense announced he had no witnesses to call, but the accused would make a statement from the dock.

Bram stood where Nelson Mandela had stood before him, and spoke for four hours in his characteristic low-key and meticulous manner. He could have been a lawyer dispassionately dissecting the case against a client. Only this time he was speaking on his own behalf and the principles he was defending were those he had lived by for fifty-eight years.

He started out by declaring that all of the activities of which he had been accused arose from his membership in the Communist Party. "I engaged upon those activities because I believed that, in the dangerous circumstances which have been created in South Africa, it is my duty to do so," he told the court.

"When a man is on trial for his political beliefs and actions, two courses are open to him. He can either confess to his transgressions and plead for mercy or he can justify his beliefs and explain why he acted as he did. Were I to ask for forgiveness today I would betray my cause. That course is not open to me. I believe that what I did was right."

He went on to talk about his childhood in Bloemfontein and his growing awareness of racial prejudice and its consequences. He described his attraction to Marxism as an antidote to injustice and he discussed how Marxism offered what to him were logical explanations for the rise and fall of societies, the relationship between economics and politics and the evolution of history. "Marxism is not something evil or violent or subversive," he declared, and its adherents in South Africa were moral people. "We have never aimed at a despotic system of government, nor were any efforts ever directed towards establishing a dictatorship of the proletariat."

He reiterated that he and his comrades had created Umkhonto We Sizwe to stave off a civil war, not foment one. Its sabotage campaign was very different from terrorism. "This was to be a demonstration. It might achieve its object of making the white voter in South Africa reconsider his whole attitude.

"The sole question for the future, for the future of everyone, is not whether change will come, but whether it can be brought about peacefully and without bloodshed."

Bram spoke, he said, as an Afrikaner. Apartheid, he warned, was breeding "a deep-rooted hatred for Afrikaners, for our language, our political and racial outlook amongst all nonwhites. . . . It is rapidly destroying amongst nonwhites all belief in future cooperation with Afrikaners."

That was why ultimately he had decided to break bail and go underground. "In such circumstances there was an additional duty cast on me, that at least one Afrikaner should make this protest actively and positively even though as a result I now face fifteen charges instead of four. It was to keep faith with all those dispossessed by apartheid that I broke my undertaking to the court, that I separated myself from my family, pretended that I was someone else and accepted the life of a fugitive. I owed it to the political prisoners, to the banished, to the silenced and to those under house arrest not to remain a spectator, but to act. I knew what they expected of me, and I did it."

Ruth, Ilse and Paul sat in the public gallery, listening intently to their father's political testament. The night before his address, he had ordered them to go to the statue of Paul Kruger in the center of Church Square and write down the inscription at its base—words spoken by Kruger in 1881. Now, in conclusion, the defendant read them to the court:

"With faith we lay our whole case bare to the world. Whether we win or die, freedom shall rise over Africa like the sun from the morning clouds."

For most whites, Bram was the symbol of a lost cause that they feared and despised. They looked forward to his imprisonment. Although his speech from the dock was published in many newspapers, few thought about the significance of his accusations. Africans saw him very differently. Bram was a hero, a man of conscience who had kept faith with them. A few days before sentence was passed, an African couple begged Ilse to loan them one of Bram's suits so that a witch doctor might use it to concoct a spell on the judge.

Even as he awaited the verdict, Bram kept faith with his comrades and his cause. He wrote a letter to Ruth First late in April thanking her for her own letter to him. His reply was full of the warmth and tenderness that had made Bram such an extraordinary friend. "Despite the desperate distance of which you speak and which we all feel, you were actually here with me, encouraging me," he wrote. "I wonder if you can understand. Perhaps it is our common experience, though heaven knows I have not been through one-tenth of what you went through. Whatever it is, it is very real, and though I cannot keep your letter with me, it will remain with me in spirit until the day I'm released."

Bram was sober about what had happened. "I'm afraid what really sticks out, if one gets down to the tacks, is that I made a failure of what I set out to do. Well, I suppose one must risk that sort of thing sometimes even if one is an amateur. What you must never talk about, however, or even allow to enter your mind, is a sense of guilt on your part. You above all have nothing to feel guilty about."

He pleaded with Ruth and Joe not to grow too comfortable in London. "You will be needed far too desperately here some day." And he concluded: "Keep yourselves well and fit as I am doing. I shall be with you in spirit whatever happens. And thank you again for bringing your spirit here to me. My love to both of you, Bram."

On May 4, 1966, presiding justice W. G. Boshoff returned his verdict:

guilty on all counts. Five days later he sentenced the accused to life imprisonment. Bram turned and smiled at Paul and Ilse, then raised his clenched right fist.

In a letter to his children that he wrote the night before he was sentenced, he refused to surrender the optimism that had always been at his core. "Goodness, we seem to have been through several lifetimes in the past two years, don't we? [But] just as there is a 'last night' as an awaiting trial prisoner, so there will be a 'last night' for me as a prisoner. Just think what a night that will be."

Like Nelson Mandela, Walter Sisulu and the others, Bram refused to appeal the verdict. The authorities transferred him that same afternoon to Pretoria Central to begin the rest of his life as A. Fischer, Prisoner 3331/66.

Bram Fischer's conviction marked the last gasp of the movement he had helped lead. All of its major figures had been removed from the South African scene. Nelson Mandela, Walter Sisulu, Govan Mbeki and Bram were in prison serving life sentences, while Oliver Tambo, Moses Kotane, Ruth First, Joe Slovo, Rusty Bernstein, Michael Harmel, Yusuf Dadoo and many others were in exile. But Bram's story did not end here.

At Pretoria Central the head warder, du Preez, the same man who had tormented Jimmy Kantor, set out to break Prisoner 3331/66. The warder slowly ground Bram down, giving him a ridiculously large jacket and trousers to wear that he could barely keep on, hacking off most of his silver hair. De Preez kept Bram isolated from his fellow prisoners and made him clean toilets down on his knees with a brush and rag. Bram, as always, remained polite and courteous. He would not give du Preez the gift of his rage.

The years passed slowly and the humiliations were many. Only personal matters could be discussed during family visits. No news was allowed. Ilse was not even allowed to tell Bram when the Americans landed a man on the moon.

One day in January 1971, Bram was called out just before dinner and taken to the visiting room, where his brother Gustav met him through a glass-and-wood partition. As two warders listened in, Gustav announced that Bram's son Paul had died that morning. He had gone to

Groote Schuur Hospital in Cape Town for an ordinary checkup, but sometime during the morning his lungs had suddenly collapsed. He could not be revived.

The warders would not let Bram have a contact visit with his brother that evening. He came back from the visiting room just as his fellow prisoners were being locked in for the night. He was locked in as well, left alone in his cell for fourteen hours to contemplate the news that his only son, who had fought so long and hard for life, was no more. Bram was refused permission to attend the funeral. And when Ilse and Ruth came to see him, they too were not allowed any physical contact with their father. Rules were rules.

Soon after Paul's death, Ilse married Tim Wilson. The couple asked for permission to hold the wedding at the prison. Bram was allowed to have two visitors at a time, but since the ceremony would have required a minister's presence as well, the request was refused.

Later that year, the Beaumont Street house was sold. Bram never saw it again.

Nineteen seventy-one was also the year that Bram was reclassified as an "A" category prisoner, which meant he could now receive one letter per month. He added the Slovos to his list of correspondents under the pseudonyms of Jean and Jonathan Robbin. Ruth was amazed to hear from him after all this time, and her first letter showed the depth of her feelings. "Dear dear Bram," she began. "I'm not sure that you can ever properly know how profoundly all who have ever known you love and admire your special self. This year because of Paul and the year of Molly's death especially, we were shaken at how painfully unjust it was that a man who has so selflessly devoted himself to others as well as to his great vision of the new, should have to endure such agony in his personal life."

Helen Suzman worked hard over the years to ease the many restrictions the prisoners were subjected to, even arranging for them to receive a phonograph and record albums. Bram wrote to Ruth later in the year mentioning how the politicals now had some three hundred records, including Beethoven, Brahms, Bellini and the American folk-rock duo Simon and Garfunkel ("May their souls never rest," he added). Suzman visited Bram regularly in prison, where he served as spokesman for his fellow political prisoners. He would present her with a concise list of grievances. One day when she arrived, he gave her a bunch of flowers that he had grown in the small patch of prison yard the authorities had turned over to him. Suzman cherished them.

In May 1974 Bram fell ill. He was hospitalized with internal hemorrhaging from a bleeding ulcer, but the doctor suspected he was suffering from prostate cancer as well, and in July his prostate was removed. It showed no signs of cancer, and no further treatment was ordered. But there was cancer, and it was spreading. Bram was also suffering from arthritis of the left hip. In September the pain became acute, but the authorities denied him use of a crutch until his fellow inmates fashioned him one from a broomstick. On November 6 he slipped and fell in the prison shower, breaking his leg. For thirteen days while he struggled with intense pain he was ignored by the warders and the medical staff. Finally, he was admitted to the hospital. By this time he had become delusional. There were times when he could not recognize his fellow inmates and did not know where he was. Yet in early December he was discharged back to his cell, where his fellow prisoners came upon him that afternoon, confused and unable to speak. Denis Goldberg and Dave Kitson tended to him, carrying him up and down the stairs and making sure he ate. Goldberg began to keep a secret written account of the authorities' negligent treatment of Bram, which was later smuggled out of prison.

One week later Bram was returned to the hospital in critical condition. The cancer was spreading to his brain and he slipped into unconsciousness. But he responded well to treatment, pulled out of his coma and appeared to improve. At this point Ilse and Ruth petitioned Minister of Justice Jimmy Kruger for their father's release on medical grounds. Kruger rejected their plea, saying he was not certain Bram had cancer.

When Helen Suzman visited Bram at the Verwoerd State Hospital prison ward, she did not recognize her old friend. He had shrunk to a tiny mummy. He was fast asleep when she came in, but a warder urged her to wake him. "He'll want to see you."

When he woke, Bram seemed dazed and agitated at first. But he soon calmed down and asked the warder to fetch his notebook. "These are the things that I want done," Bram told Suzman, rattling off a list of requests on behalf of his fellow prisoners.

In Cape Town a few days later. Suzman went to see Kruger. "The man is dying and it would be a very fine gesture of compassion if you would let him die at home and not in hospital or in prison," she told him.

Compassion was not one of Kruger's strengths. He was the cabinet minister who later said "it leaves me cold" when informed that black leader Steve Biko had died from injuries received from a beating during police interrogation. Kruger told Suzman, "I can't do that."

"Yes, you can," she replied. "You phone his doctor and you'll learn that he only has a couple of months to live." Eventually Kruger made the call. On March 10 he agreed to place Bram in the custody of his brother Paul, a physician. Paul's house in Bloemfontein was formally declared a state prison, so that technically Bram was not being released. Kruger arranged for Bram to be flown to Bloemfontein by military helicopter. Before allowing him on the helicopter the authorities made Bram sign a statement pledging he would see no visitors beyond his immediate family.

Bram arrived at the house on a stretcher. By then he was paralyzed in both legs and unable to walk. He spent a month in captivity with his brother and his daughters by his side. Soon after his sixty-seventh birthday on April 23 he slipped into unconsciousness. He died on May 8.

The funeral was held four days later in Bloemfontein. Many of those who had been closest to Bram were not able to be there. The Bernsteins, Slovos and hundreds of other activists in exile whose lives had been touched by Bram's were only able to read newspaper accounts. Bram's fellow inmates at Pretoria Local held a memorial service for him. So did the prisoners at Robben Island. Nelson Mandela presided over the ceremony for his mentor and friend; Walter Sisulu was among those who spoke.

Helen Suzman was in London at the time of Bram's death. She told reporters she was pleased that at least he had been able to spend his last few weeks with his family. As for the meaning of his life and death, Suzman gave the conventional judgment. "Bram Fischer was a man of great promise and, alas, his life turned out to be a tragic waste."

But Afrikaner novelist André Brink, who gave one of the eulogies at the funeral, offered a far different assessment. It was a facile distortion to call Bram's life "a tragic waste," said Brink. Bram's life was tragic only in the sense that tragedy requires a sacrifice before sanity and progress can be restored to a corrupt and destructive society. His life was not wasted. Not only had he "enlarged and deepened the concept of Afrikanerdom," said Brink, but Bram had achieved nothing less than to set the stage for the liberation of South Africa.

After the funeral it emerged that the security police had come to Paul's home the day after Bram's death with a letter stipulating that the family could hold the ceremony only if it agreed to return Bram's remains to the Department of Prisons after the service. When the press found out, an embarrassed Jimmy Kruger told reporters he would gladly reconsider the matter if the family would apply to him. But Ilse and Ruth refused to cooperate. They were not prepared to negotiate with the state over their father's corpse. It was one last symbolic act of defiance. The authorities could never hold Bram's spirit, even if they held his remains. The ashes were shipped to Pretoria. There they remain, lost or scattered, to this day.

EPILOGUE

The noises of the town were still beating like waves at the front of the long line of
terraces, but tonight they told not of revolution but of deliverance.
Albert Camus
The Plague

By the time of Bram Fischer's death, South Africa was firmly in the grip of police-state rule. The radical movement had been crushed after Rivonia, mainstream black leaders imprisoned, banned or exiled and new protest movements buried by legal restrictions and security police harassment even before they could surface. After scrapping the ninety- and 180-day detention laws, Parliament in 1967 enacted the Terrorism Act, which legalized indefinite detention without judicial review. Even the sham of weekly magistrate's visits was dispensed with. One result of this unrestrained police power: between Looksmart Ngudle's death in 1963 and 1990, seventy-three people died in detention, many in suspicious circumstances.

Having dispatched its most visible enemies, the security police apparatus next turned its attention to "fellow travelers"—liberals, student activists and other critics of the apartheid regime. Lawyers, journalists and leading members of Alan Paton's small but energetic Liberal Party were subject to house arrest, raids, surveillance, wiretapping and other malignant forms of police attention. Paton himself was tailed constantly during trips to political meetings, and police smashed his car windshield and back window in the driveway of a country hotel where he was staying. Finally, in 1968, Parliament passed the Prevention of Political Interference Act, which made it a criminal offense to belong to any racially mixed organization that propagated or even studied political views. Unwilling to divide itself along racial lines, the demoralized Liberal Party shut itself down. The cruel fact was that once their radical counterparts had been crushed, liberals had been too few, too weak and too divided over tactics and philosophy to pose any challenge to the state. They went almost gently into the night, leaving Helen Suzman in Parliament and a handful of hearty editorial-page writers as the sole remaining public voices of liberal dissent.

Then in June 1976, one year and one month after Bram's death, Soweto exploded in an uprising that shook South Africa. The spark that set off the revolt was an edict requiring that students be taught half their classes in Afrikaans, a language many Africans did not know. A new generation of young urban blacks, frustrated and humiliated by their relentlessly third-rate schools, lack of economic opportunities and the seeming docility of their own parents, were not prepared to swallow this new form of humiliation. They challenged the power of the state with strikes, protest marches and rioting. Other townships throughout South Africa followed suit. It took more than a year for police to restore control. Over six hundred people were killed, and thousands more were jailed or forced to flee into exile. The Soweto uprising became the first of a sporadic series of grassroots rebellions against white rule that gradually gained momentum while eroding white control.

Few in the Soweto generation had heard of Bram Fischer or his comrades. Fewer still knew of the comrades' role in launching Umkhonto We Sizwe, or of their ties to Nelson Mandela, or of Rusty Bernstein's role in composing the Freedom Charter, or of the Marshall Square jailbreak. But the radicals of Rivonia had laid the foundation for much of what followed. When members of the new generation of activists arrived in exile, the ANC was there to absorb and train them; the exiles in turn helped replenish and revitalize the movement. Umkhonto became the armed wing of the African National Congress, and eventually grew into a full-fledged guerrilla force that harassed the apartheid state with a series of high-profile attacks. Joe Slovo, who for many years was chief of staff of Umkhonto, became a popular figure in township song and mythology. But even more important was the comrades' contribution to the ANC. The work they had done in the 1940s and 1950s in strengthening the organization and broadening the outlook of its leaders helped the ANC maintain its primacy as the enduring voice of South Africa's black majority during the long years in exile. And thanks in large part to their influence, the ANC never forgot its commitment to a multiracial society. In 1969, it opened its doors to members of all races. Critics warned that the move would allow white and Indian communists to dominate the congress from within, and there is no question that the movement became increasingly close to Moscow as time went on. But the critics failed to see how vital it was for South Africa's future that the movement working for its liberation include within its ranks representatives from all ethnic groups.

Government security forces responded to the new challenge with the same police-state tactics they had first employed in the early 1960s. John Vorster, who had risen to the post of Prime Minister after Hendrik F. Verwoerd was assassinated by a crazed, knife-wielding parliamentary employee in 1966, personally oversaw the crackdown. His right-hand man, Major General Hendrik van den Bergh, continued to lead Special Branch, which was renamed the Bureau of State Security (BOSS). The Soweto uprising created some unease in the white community about Vorster and van den Bergh's leadership; they clearly had not anticipated this challenge. But it took an internal scandal involving government abuse of a secret slush fund to finally bring them down. Vorster was forced to resign. The new Prime Minister, P. W. Botha, a former Defense Minister, swiftly set about diminishing Vorster's old power base and securing his own. He dismantled BOSS, squeezed out van den Bergh and transferred primacy from the security police to the military establishment. Long Hendrik retired to his farm near Delmas, east of Johannesburg.

Under Botha's military-oriented leadership, South Africa's security forces launched a dirty war against the ANC and its allies that made the abuses of the 1960s look mild. Officially sanctioned death squads stalked antiapartheid activists. At least forty-nine dissidents were assassinated in a decade-long campaign, while hundreds more disappeared or were gunned down in suspicious circumstances that could not be traced directly to the security forces. Meanwhile, Umkhonto We Sizwe was actively infiltrating fighters into South Africa who carried out a handful of armed attacks on police stations and other targets identified with the regime. While none of these raids did serious physical or financial damage, their psychological impact was considerable; they effectively declared the ANC's return to the battlefield. Perhaps the most spectacular was a coordinated assault in June 1980 by a special operations unit under Joe's command that blew up a state-of-the-art coal-to-oil conversion plant and a nearby refinery outside Johannesburg and a power plant in another part of Transvaal province. Fuel tanks were still burning the following morning and the smoke could be seen drifting within sight of Soweto, nearly forty miles away.

Joe planned these attacks from the Mozambican capital, Maputo, the former Lourenço Marques, after Mozambique gained independence from Portugal in 1975 following a long guerrilla war. The old colony's black leadership was eager at first to have the ANC use its territory as a launching pad against the apartheid regime. But Botha's men were quick to strike back. In 1981, South African commandos staged a retaliatory raid on the special operations barracks in Matola, south of Maputo, killing twelve fighters and an unarmed Portuguese electrician who had happened upon the scene. The raiders clearly had mistaken him for Joe.

Joe carried a pistol in an ankle holster and tried to vary his routine. ANC military leaders in general became more security-conscious and better protected. As a result, South Africa's security establishment turned its attention to softer targets. Joe Gqabi, who had worked as a reporter and photographer with Ruth First on *New Age* and who was the ANC's representative in Zimbabwe, was gunned down in front of his house in Salisbury in July 1981. The ANC's London headquarters was firebombed. The ANC's chief representative in Swaziland, Petros Nyawose, and his wife, Jabulile, were killed in front of their three children in a car bomb explosion in June 1982. Meanwhile, the South African security police set up shop at Jan Smuts Airport in Johannesburg, monitoring international mail against a long list of ANC activists in search of prey.

Ruth First had returned to Africa in 1976 with Joe. Their marriage was shaky at times, but still intact. Their three daughters were grown. Despite long stretches apart and occasional affairs, they shared an apartment in Maputo and a bed. Ruth became director of research for the Center for African Studies at Eduardo Mondlane University. They left the girls behind in London. "In most families it's the children who leave," said Gillian Slovo. "In ours it was the parents."

Despite the hardships of living in an economically deprived Third World capital, Ruth thrived in Maputo. The center, under her direction, became known as a place of serious and innovative research into rural conditions. Her success seemed to make her less competitive with Joe, and they seemed to enjoy each other's company more. When Ruth's old friend Hillary Kuny paid a visit early in 1982, she found Ruth warm and relaxed, in both manner and appearance. With no hair salon in sight, Ruth had abandoned her old heavily made-up style, washed her hair herself and let it dry as it fell, in a semi-Afro. She wore simple cotton dresses and talked with self-deprecating humor about her past obsession with fashion. Part of the change was the result of the rugged circumstances of life in Maputo, but part was no doubt the result of maturity. You learn things when you get older, Ruth told Hillary, like the fact that you don't need more than four dresses.

There were times when she worried about Joe's safety, but never about her own. Occasionally there would be a warning telephone call from ANC security to members. "There are unwelcome visitors in town," was the signal to go sleep elsewhere for a few nights. Even then, Ruth never stopped going to work. Although still a member of the ANC, she was not involved in armed struggle, and her days as an active member of the South African Communist Party were also at an end. Except to the extent that her writing and her academic work forced people to think critically about the costs and consequences of apartheid, she was a threat to no one. But she was Joe Slovo's wife.

In August 1982 police at Jan Smuts intercepted a large manila envelope addressed to Ruth from a United Nations agency. Under directions from its commander, a special unit unsealed the envelope and inserted a small explosive device, closed it and sent it on. A few days later, Ruth opened it in her second-floor office at the university. The force of the blast, Gillian later wrote, was enough to blow out the window and send half of the industrial air-conditioning unit crashing to the ground. To compound the atrocity, Ruth's killers leaked to the South African press the claim that Joe himself had ordered the murder because Ruth had left the Communist Party and become an ideological rebel.

Ruth was buried in the national cemetery south of Maputo alongside the fallen Matola fighters. Joe, Shawn, Gillian, Robyn and Ruth's mother

Tilly were all there, standing in a stolid, silent line at the front. Harold Wolpe, who had been visiting Maputo at the time of the bombing, was also present. At the end of *117 Days*, Ruth had written that even though she had been released from detention, she had the feeling that the police were not through with her, that they would come again someday. And now they had.

Joe was deeply shaken by Ruth's death. He blamed himself to some extent, knowing the South Africans had destroyed her as a way of getting back at him. He drank heavily for a time. Two years after the murder, he and the rest of the ANC's military operatives were expelled from Maputo following a mutual security pact between the hard-pressed Mozambican government and South Africa. At the signing ceremony, General Johann Coetzee, South Africa's new Police Commissioner and a former Special Branch detective who had known Ruth in the old days in Johannesburg, told one of Ruth's friends that the bomb had been "a terrible mistake." He did not bother to explain.

When I met Joe the following year at ANC headquarters in Lusaka, Zambia, he still seemed depressed. He wept openly when he discussed Ruth's murder and spoke with deep admiration and affection of the role she had played in challenging Marxist orthodoxy—both the party's and his own. He insisted that his own thinking had changed; he had closed his eyes for too long to the crimes of Stalin and other communist leaders, and while he was still grateful for Soviet support for the liberation movement, he said he no longer slavishly followed Moscow's line. The ANC, when it took power, would be a moderate, pragmatic government, he insisted. There would be no radical rush to seize the commanding heights of the economy and impose a revolutionary regime. Or so he told me. I could not tell for certain whether he was saying what he truly believed or what he knew readers of *The Washington Post* wanted to hear.

Joe remained the eternal optimist—and a man given to making jokes at his own expense. "We will win in the end—there's absolutely no question. I have no doubt we will see South Africa liberated in my lifetime," he told me. "But I must warn you," he added with a smile. "You're talking to a man who's been predicting ever since 1948 that the Nats would be out of power in five years. I tell my friends that I still see no reason to change my mind."

This time, however, Joe's prophecy was not so far off. The grassroots rebellions in black townships were taking their toll. P. W. Botha's government embarked upon a campaign of limited reform that divided white Afrikaners while stimulating even more unrest among blacks. A revolution of rising expectations was taking hold. Botha needed to co-opt an emerging urban black middle class to maintain power, yet he was unwilling to share political power as they demanded. A campaign of tougher international sanctions helped tighten the noose. In February 1990, almost five years to the day after my interview with Joe, Nelson Mandela was released from prison by Botha's more pragmatic successor, F. W. de Klerk. The ANC, PAC and South African Communist Party were unbanned.

Within weeks Joe himself was back in South Africa as part of the ANC team negotiating the end of white rule. He proved to be a realistic and flexible negotiator. He pressed Mandela to declare a unilateral halt to the armed struggle when the talks flagged early on. And he was an architect of the crucial "sunset clause" that required the ANC to share power with the National Party and other political groups for an interim period in order to allay white fears that an ANC takeover would be sudden and unfettered. In other words, Joe came through. He had claimed in Lusaka that he had evolved from the hard-liner of the Rivonia era, the utopian architect of Operation Mayibuye, to someone more moderate and practical, and he had. And because of his impeccable radical credentials, his advocacy of compromise carried great weight within the ANC. No one could legitimately accuse Joe Slovo of selling out (although some tried). In a sense, he became Rivonia's representative at the bargaining table, a man whose ideological certainty had been tempered by years of struggle and personal sacrifice.

Along the way, Joe had married Helena Dolny, a British ANC supporter who had worked with Ruth at the Center for African Studies in Maputo. It was, by all accounts, a warm and happy marriage. Helena, who was more than twenty years younger than Joe, gave him the unreserved devotion he felt he never totally got from Ruth.

Joe wore red socks to the ceremony at which Nelson Mandela was sworn in as President in 1994 following South Africa's first free election, and he became Housing Minister in Mandela's cabinet. He launched an ambitious program of low-income housing in an effort to make good the ANC's promise to raise living standards for the long-neglected black majority. But Joe was fighting a losing battle with bone-marrow cancer.

He died in January 1995 and was buried outside Soweto. Shawn, Gillian and Robyn gathered once again to mourn.

Nelson Mandela came by the house the morning after Joe's death to pay his respects. He told Joe's daughters how one day he had tried to hug his own grown-up daughter and she had rejected him. "You are the father to all our people," she told him, "but you have never had the time to be a father to me." This was, he said, his greatest regret in life, that his children and the children of his comrades had paid such a high price for their parents' commitment to the cause.

Mandela had been sworn in on a brilliant day in May. The ceremony was held outside the brown sandstone Union Buildings—the fortress of white rule where Verwoerd, Vorster and apartheid's henchmen had drawn up the Ninety-Day Act and the Sabotage Act and the other tools of police-state rule. U.S. Vice President Al Gore, First Lady Hillary Clinton, Prince Philip, Yasser Arafat and Fidel Castro were among the 6,036 foreign dignitaries in attendance. Also on the platform that day were two elderly guests from Britain whom few in the crowd recognized.

Rusty and Hilda Bernstein, both now in their seventies, had traveled a long road to arrive back in Pretoria. For several months after they landed in London in 1964, Rusty and Hilda had hoped to return to Africa. Rusty had received promises of a post in the Ministry of Public Works of the newly independent republic of Zambia, the former Northern Rhodesia. But the position never materialized and Rusty eventually took a job with an architectural firm in London. He and Hilda spent the next seventeen years in London, living during most of them in a terraced house in Primrose Hill.

For a long time after they moved to England, Hilda was depressed and listless. Removed from the intense excitement and anxiety of South Africa, she felt she did not know who she really was or what she was doing. Bram's eventual capture and life sentence only added to her sense of powerlessness and despair. What kept her going was the necessity of caring for three children who themselves were going through the difficult adjustment to life in exile. After months of ennui, she began to read the new wave of feminist books coming out of the United States by Betty Friedan and others. In their depictions of how women had been subjugated in male-dominated societies, Hilda recognized something of her own situation. She began to see how she herself had long suppressed her personality and her interests to the male-controlled movement she had served with devotion. And she began to regain her formidable self-confidence.

Over the ensuing years Hilda wrote several books about South Africa, including *The World That Was Ours* and a prize-winning novel entitled *Death Is Part of the Process*. She stayed active in the London-based Anti-Apartheid Movement but felt increasingly estranged from the Communist Party. After the Soviet invasion of Czechoslovakia in 1968, she finally left the party altogether. She was tired of toeing the Moscow line, and fed up with the excuses her comrades—Rusty included—offered for the inexcusable. When Rusty attempted to defend the invasion, they argued intensely. For a time, she even refused to share her bed with him.

Joe Slovo took Hilda to lunch one day and she vented her anger at the party and told him she was planning to quit. Whatever doubts Joe himself was beginning to have, he concealed them from Hilda that day. "You realize that you're opting out of our struggle?" he told her. She interpreted this as a warning more than a question. By leaving the Communist Party she would be cutting herself off from many of the people she had been associated with for so many years. But she could no longer stay in. The price had become too high.

Hilda never doubted that the struggle against apartheid was a moral crusade worthy of the sacrifices it had demanded of her and her friends. But as the years went on, she questioned her decision to devote her life to politics. She was a person of many talents—a gifted artist and singer as well as a writer—but she had put much of these aside to serve the cause. Now she began to produce etchings, many with African motifs. Some of them sold quite well, and she was proud of her work and wondered where it might have led her had she started earlier and pursued it with the same passion she had spent on the movement.

Rusty never dropped out of the Communist Party but he slowly loosened his connection to it. He felt he had dedicated himself completely to the cause during his adult years in South Africa. While in detention awaiting the Rivonia Trial, he had promised himself that if he ever regained his freedom he would put his family first. Once in London he kept that promise. He continued to enjoy a reputation among the political cognoscenti who knew that this was the man who had written the

Freedom Charter and who was one of the intellectual giants of the movement. Both he and Hilda were invited occasionally to speak at gatherings. Once the children were grown, they lived and worked for a year at the ANC school in Mazimbu, Tanzania. But life there was too chaotic and disorganized, and both of them decided they were wasting their time.

Eventually they settled in a small, semi-attached property outside Oxford in an anonymous housing estate known as Garden City ("Neither garden nor city," Rusty would complain). They traveled to South Africa after receiving indemnification from prosecution following Mandela's release, and again in 1994 at the time of the first free elections. At Frances's urging, Hilda and Rusty both cast their ballots, and Rusty participated in a reunion of the Rivonia Trial defendants at Lilliesleaf. It was a day of nostalgia and absurdity. Rivonia had changed into a dense, residential suburb and the group got lost searching for the farm and arrived more than an hour late.

The Bernsteins enjoyed their visits to South Africa, but they never moved back. Although Rusty could have gotten a position with the unbanned Communist Party, he decided not to try. Their four children and most of their seven grandchildren lived in Britain, and they did not want to leave them. Hilda compiled *The Rift*, an oral history of South African exiles published in London. But while the exiles were welcomed back to the new South Africa, many of them felt they were denied the public recognition they had earned through years of sacrifice. Rusty saw this as sad but inevitable; as an unreconstructed Marxist, he knew better than anyone that society moves on and personal histories fade quickly. Still, at times he felt the pangs of his own obscurity. He began writing his memoirs, in hopes of setting the historical record straight and modestly explaining his own role. Eventually he received a small pension from the South African government for his work in the liberation movement. Both he and Hilda were awarded honorary doctorates from the University of Natal in Durban, and they basked in the attention and respect they received from faculty and students there.

But perhaps the sweetest moment came on the day of the President's swearing-in. Nelson Mandela's voice echoed above a vast sea of thousands of supporters—a "rainbow nation," he called them, of blacks, whites and Asians—on the sloping hillside of Government Lawn. Mandela spoke of "the depth of pain we all carried in our hearts as we saw our country tear itself apart in terrible conflict." He dedicated this day "to all the heroes and heroines in this country and the rest of the world who sacrificed in many ways and surrendered their lives so that we could be free." And he pledged: "Never, never and never again shall it be that this beautiful land will again experience the oppression of one by another and suffer the indignity of being the skunk of the world."

Hilda was swept away by her feelings. She knew South Africa still had a long way to go, that the destruction of the apartheid regime and its legal edifice would not necessarily mean the end of social, economic and racial inequality, and that democracy was a means to social justice and not the final goal in itself. Still, she felt enormously proud of Nelson Mandela and of all her comrades. They had not merely survived or even endured; they had, finally, won.

Mandela's swearing-in launched a process of reconsideration and reflection in the society at large, including South Africa's Jewish community. The rift between the Pretoria government and the state of Israel that had culminated in Verwoerd's ban on the transfer of funds to Israel had continued until the Six-Day War in June 1967, when sympathy for Israel swept across white South Africa. A deputation of South African Jewish leaders pleaded with Prime Minister Vorster to waive the funds ban, and he readily agreed "on purely humanitarian grounds." That marked a turning point in relations.

As Israel's links to black Africa gradually deteriorated, its ties to South Africa strengthened. By 1975 the two countries had raised their diplomatic representation to ambassadorial level. One year later Vorster visited Israel and signed a series of trade and technical cooperation agreements. Israeli Prime Minister Yitzhak Rabin also paid a secret visit to Pretoria. Rabin, a former general, professed to hate apartheid but pressed for closer military cooperation, arguing that Israel needed all the friends it could get. At some point the two sides began sharing nuclear technology and Israel was widely reported to have helped South Africa detonate a nuclear device in the Indian Ocean in 1979. Afrikaners began to shed the anti-Semitism that had been part of their mystical nationalism and identified with Israelis as another Chosen People in an alien land, beset by dark-skinned native peoples. Israeli technicians, engineers and retired military officers increasingly took up places as consultants and planners of the new tribal homelands, the nominally independent puppet states that the Pretoria government created out of rural wastelands. As ties between the two nations improved, South Africa's Jews became increasingly identified with the government and less with its opposition in the liberation movement.

All of this began to unravel with Mandela's release, and ended upon his taking office. In denying their own culpability, many Jews pointed to the fact that their brethren were prominently involved in the antiapartheid movement; indeed, some used this to suggest that the Jewish community as a whole had been committed to the liberation cause. The fact that three of the whites who stood in the dock with Nelson Mandela at the Rivonia Trial were Jews became a point of pride, even for some who had considered this same fact an embarrassment during the days of white rule. But Todd Pitock, writing in a special issue of *Jewish Affairs*, the quarterly publication of the South African Jewish Board of Deputies, rejected both the self-congratulatory view that Jews did more than other whites to fight apartheid and the self-flagellating view that Jews had shirked their special moral responsibility. Both viewpoints contained some truth yet both were misleading. "Jews were not, of course, mere witnesses to apartheid, and apartheid bears testimony to the fact that Jews are morally the same as other people," Pitock wrote. "Perhaps that is a humbling realization to some."

One establishment Jewish leader who never backed down from her opposition to apartheid was Helen Suzman. She continued to give as good as she got in Parliament and in the newspapers. When Vorster accused her of being an "agent" for Christian Defense and Aid, the London-based organization that helped fund legal defenses for South Africa's political prisoners, she introduced a resolution to halve his salary. Her reputation for political courage became international. Typical was a two-page spread in *Life* magazine in May 1970 that hailed her as "South Africa's lonely liberal"—and also noted that her critics dubbed her "Mother Superior" for her caustic and condescending manner. She remained the sole Progressive in Parliament until 1974, when her party unexpectedly won six additional seats. She held office until 1989, when she retired after thirty-six years of service. But the last few years were not easy ones. Suzman never hesitated to take a political position that offended supporters as well as detractors, and in the 1980s she spoke out firmly and frequently against the international campaign for economic sanctions on South Africa. As a classic liberal, she feared sanctions would wreck the country's economy and harm black workers. She was making—and at times overstating—an important point, but she was denounced by left-wing critics at home for taking the same stand on this issue as the white-ruled government she had always opposed. Abroad, where sanctions became a matter of faith for liberals as well as radicals, the vehemence of her argument both surprised and disappointed many who had always admired her. None of which bothered Helen Suzman in the least. She liked to be right and she liked a good fight. In her view, the sanctions debate allowed her to be both.

Suzman had pressed for Nelson Mandela's release for many years and was one of the first to visit him after his triumphant return to Soweto, where they shared a hug in his garden. But she felt increasingly removed and isolated politically. White liberals who stood apart from the ANC had a shrinking role in the new South Africa, in part because they had not directly participated in the liberation struggle and in part perhaps because they could not fully embrace the reality of black majority rule. Still, Suzman maintained a place of honor in the antiapartheid pantheon because of her lonely stand in the 1960s and because she had been the patron saint for two generations of political prisoners, many of whom now ran the country. Mandela appointed her to his Human Rights Commission and insisted that she continue serving even after she felt she was playing no useful role (she finally stepped down in 1999 at around the same time he was ending his term as President). But she feared for the future of liberal values in South Africa, even while she took great satisfaction in the downfall of apartheid.

Toni, Keith and Frances Bernstein all returned to South Africa for the 1994 elections, Toni as a United Nations observer, Keith as a news photographer and Frances as a companion to her parents. For each the return was a moment fraught with memories and complex emotions.

After Hilda and Rusty had fled South Africa, Toni's husband, Ivan, had been arrested by police and held for thirty days. When he was released they left the country and settled in London. Ivan became a freelance cameraman working on documentaries and feature films. Toni worked as a documentary film writer and producer as well. They had two sons. Keith Bernstein always considered Toni his second mother. He grew up to become an award-winning photojournalist. Together he and Toni traveled to southern Africa in 1988, two years before Mandela's release, and collaborated on a photo-essay book about the struggles of the black-ruled states bordering South Africa.

Frances had cried for months after leaving South Africa. She missed the garden at Regent Street and the comfortable life, the weather, her friends. Her first year at the formidable Camden Girls' School in London was a disaster. The other girls were full-fledged swinging London teenagers with bras and boyfriends, obsessed with the Beatles. Frances wept each morning in her room before heading off to school. She became shy and withdrawn, her self-confidence drained away. She fell behind academically, emotionally and physically. She eventually got a degree in economics from Manchester University, then drifted into factory work and radical Maoist politics—a distinct act of rebellion given her parents' affinity for the Soviet Union. She married a fellow Maoist and had two sons. Gradually they drifted out of the movement and settled in Leeds. There she got a job, first in the city office for women's issues and later in the Department of Education, where she became a senior manager. Her self-esteem slowly returned. She had inherited her mother's mellifluous voice and sang in a people's choir that specialized in folk and political songs. Still, at times when she was upset or needed to calm down, she dreamed of the garden on Regent Street. In her mind she played among the trees and flowers, or sat in the warm South African sun by the old swimming pool.

Frances finally decided to revisit the land of her dreams by joining her parents, who had already made the trip in order to visit friends and watch the first free election campaign unfold. When Hilda met her at the airport, Frances asked to go straight to 154 Regent Street. So much had changed—the row of tall jacaranda trees that once graced the front yard was gone, chopped down a decade earlier. The wildness of the back yard had been severely cut back. And the house seemed so much smaller. But Frances recalled the touch of the shiny polished wooden floorboards and the string gate that Rusty had made to separate two sections of the basement, where it still stood guard. "A warm, funny glow came over me seeing it," she recalled later. "I didn't expect that feeling. I felt that something that had been severed was reconnected. It was a lovely feeling."

One thing struck Frances as dramatically different. The ANC had opened a local campaign office in a corner storefront near the house, where ANC workers gave out flags, posters and leaflets. All the activity was wide open and very public. Frances could not help but notice the remarkable contrast with 1963, when everything was underground, cloaked and dangerous. She returned home to Britain encouraged by what she had seen and happy for her parents.

Some of the Marxist-Leninist tracts from the old bookshelf in Regent Street still sit in the main hallway of Frances's house in Leeds. When I visited her not long ago we took down a few. One of them had Ruth First's name penciled at the top of the opening page. Perhaps Ruth had loaned it to Rusty or Hilda at some point. Leafing through it, Frances thought about her parents and South Africa and everything that had happened there. She now saw it from the perspective of a woman in her forties—the same age her parents were when the Rivonia Trial took place.

"They didn't so much choose to take those risks and do those dangerous things as much as they took a step that led down a path that ended up doing things that were riskier and riskier," she told me. "If you had a conscience, you really didn't have a lot of choices. If you wanted to do anything about it you were forced to do illegal and dangerous things." Like her brother Patrick, she was proud of her parents, and pleased that the changes they had struggled for had finally come to South Africa. But like him, she was wounded somehow. In her heart.

After reading Hilda's novel, Frances told me, she had called her mother and then wrote her a rambling and intense four-page letter about herself, South Africa and the Rivonia years. She showed it to me. The writing was passionate, proud and sad—similar in that way to what Ruth, Hilda and AnnMarie had themselves written about their lives and their painful moment of truth a generation earlier—and it seemed to me that Frances in her letter had declared herself, and her siblings, as Rivonia's final children, the last of a haunted, troubled yet honorable line.

The book upset me very deeply (Frances wrote). *Is it a good book? I find it hard to say, as for me it is too intensely personal. It stirred great emotions in me, these caused as much by what is in me as what is in the book. The same emotions were stirred by Ruth's death, which I couldn't share very well with anyone. Guilt. Frustration. Dissatisfaction with my life and what I am. Frustration because I am trapped in what I am, not by anything or anyone, but because the turn of events has placed me here, events that I am powerless to change.*

Now in this moment of clarity, I can trace many facets of my life, trivial ones perhaps, to this fount, to South Africa. I don't mind injections, try not to let physical pain bother me. It is so little to bear in comparison. I don't fret about money, what to spend it on. What can it buy really? Nothing that matters. I don't fuss Sean, don't want him to be fussy. What has he got to fuss about? It seems silly, but all these trivial aspects of my character come from the awareness & yes, guilt about the suffering in South Africa, the things that people endure. . . .

Although the whole experience was so long ago, so far away, it never fades away completely. Sometimes I look at people through its eyes, even now. People at work, embroiled in their pointless little world, spouting meaningless words. They've never seen real suffering, real struggle.

In her life and those of her siblings, Frances wrote, there was:

. . . a hole where South Africa was, nothing is big enough to fill it. No purpose worthy enough. We work at this, at that, for this and that, it scratches but never cures the itch. Maybe it's better that it doesn't. . . .

Well, Mom, all these things lie in me still, like dead fallen leaves. Your book, Ruth's death . . . are like a fierce hot wind that blows them all up so they are swirling round in my head and my heart.

The one Bernstein child who made no attempt to return to South Africa was the one who was probably most troubled by what had happened there. Like his sister Frances, Patrick Bernstein had settled uneasily in London, still in the throes of a surly and rebellious adolescence. He left school at age eighteen for an unsuccessful apprenticeship with an electronics company, then sold books door to door and eventually, with his parents' financial help, took a six-month computer maintenance course. He married Yvonne, a woman who came from a working-class London family. Hilda and Rusty were not comfortable with the emotional distance that Patrick maintained with them. He and Yvonne had two sons and he began to achieve some financial success, eventually launching his own software business with Yvonne's help. Slowly the walls that Patrick had built around himself began to come down. But the wounds he still felt from the Rivonia Trial year were still very close to the surface.

Patrick refused to read *The World That Was Ours* for fear that it would devastate him. But in the late 1980s he and his parents attended a play by a visiting South African drama troupe. In the last scene one of the characters was shot by the police, and Patrick was left badly shaken. Afterward, he drove his parents home and he and Rusty went for a walk in the garden. He asked about Rusty's time in detention, what it was like, whether his father had feared being hanged, how he had managed to keep sane. It was the first time Patrick had raised these questions, and the first time Rusty had attempted to talk to his son about these most painful of times. Afterward, when he returned home, Patrick wrote his parents a letter. He told them he had been deeply upset by the conversation, but wanted them to know how proud he was of who they were and what they had done, and that whatever price he himself had been forced to pay had been worthwhile.

Patrick was finally opening up, coming closer to his parents and to Yvonne as well. But some of the emotions never changed. Ten years later when I met with him at his home in Suffolk, Patrick still could not speak of the Rivonia years without crying. On a rational level, he could understand and even accept what had happened, but his heart still felt the pain. He was certain that it always would.

One of the first acts of the new government was to establish a Truth and Reconciliation Commission to deal with the crimes of the apartheid regime and its victims. The panel was the official response to a section of the interim constitution that acknowledged "gross violations of human rights" and "a legacy of hatred, fear, guilt and revenge" and called for understanding, reparation and *ubuntu*—the spirit of community. The language was conciliatory and generous, but in fact the commission was the result of hard and rancorous bargaining. Representatives of the regime had insisted upon a total amnesty for police and security officials when the ruling National Party sat down with the ANC to negotiate the historic transition to democratic rule. The ANC had its own reasons for supporting an amnesty. Some of its leaders had been implicated in atrocities that the movement acknowledged had taken place in ANC camps outside South Africa during the long, hard years of struggle.

After fourteen months of talks, the two sides agreed to a compromise: amnesty would be granted to those who provided a complete, truthful and public accounting of their activities. No one was particularly happy with the arrangement—government officials faced the humiliation of a public confession of crimes they had indignantly denied in the past, while families of the victims forfeited the right to seek justice and punishment from the judicial system. But without the compromise, as one of the ANC negotiators later told me, the country could have been plunged into civil war and further racial conflict.

The commission, chaired by Anglican bishop Desmond Tutu, set out to investigate and expose the abuses of the apartheid years in order to bring some sense of closure. It held a series of public hearings at which victims of apartheid or their surviving relatives testified. Among them were Ruth and Ilse Fischer, who in July 1997 gave a presentation about their father and the treatment he suffered in prison. In quiet, dignified voices they described how the warder du Preez had sought to humiliate Bram, how Bram had been denied access to visitors when their brother Paul died and how Bram's cancer went untreated for weeks. Asked by the commission what form of remembrance the family wanted, Ilse gently choked back her tears and replied, "I suppose we just never want it to happen again."

Around the same time, another witness from the distant past was summoned by the commission. Retired policeman Johan Jacobus Viktor, who had been Ruth First's interrogator in detention, was asked to explain his alleged role in the dirty war. Viktor had risen to the rank of major general in the security police, and for a time had run Section C, the ANC/PAC desk, of the security police. According to Dirk Coetzee, a security policeman who turned state's evidence, Viktor was a commander of Vlakplaas, a farm west of Pretoria that police used to train informants and captive Umkhonto members and send them back into the townships to attack and harass antiapartheid activists. Five security policemen named Viktor as the commander who had given orders in 1985 to launch an all-out war against the liberation movements and kill opponents in the townships. Viktor denied he had given such orders—by that time, he testified, he was deputy head of the riot and counterinsurgency unit and did not have the authority to give commands to security police. He had only "suggested" how they should deal with intimidation of civilians in the townships, he said.

Calm, defiant and contemptuous to the end, J. J. Viktor did not apply for amnesty for the 1985 operation. He did apply, however, for his role in a cross-border bombing raid that killed an ANC operative and a seven-year-old child in Swaziland in retaliation for the oil refinery attack.

A year later, the commission's hearing room in Pretoria was filled again, this time with the policemen who had murdered Ruth First. There was Roger Jerry Raven, the explosives expert who had turned a simple manila envelope into a powerful bomb; Craig Williamson, who headed the unit that Raven worked for and had ordered him to make the bomb; and Johann Coetzee, the retired National Police Commissioner who was Williamson's commander. Sitting across from them in the hearing room were Ruth's daughters, Shawn, Gillian and Robyn Slovo, along with Marius Schoon, whose wife Jeannette and daughter Katryn had been murdered by a similar letter bomb. The victims' relatives were represented by George Bizos, one of the lawyers from the Rivonia defense team.

Raven said he had nothing to do with selecting the targets of his bombs. They could have been sent to Bizos or Tutu or Helen Suzman, for all he knew. His duty was to manufacture "improvised explosive devices"; victims were chosen by a separate "target identification" committee, and he never had a need to ask who the target was. In a curious lapse of memory, both he and Williamson said they could not remember whose name was on the envelope they had doctored. It might have been addressed to Joe, or it might have been to Ruth, they could not say. "I have to concede that whether it was the victim or his wife, it made absolutely no difference to me," said Williamson.

After the murder, Williamson recalled, the incident was noted at a security police meeting, but no one made reference to police involvement. Williamson said he glanced over to his immediate superior (the late Piet Goosen), the same security policeman who had overseen the fatal beating of black activist Steve Biko in 1977. "Brigadier Goosen looked directly at me and nodded slightly," Williamson recalled.

Williamson also testified that everyone in the security apparatus, from senior officials on down, knew police were responsible for the letter-bomb attacks. But Coetzee vehemently denied knowing about or approving the decision to kill Ruth. "I never gave an instruction that someone should be assassinated, or killed, inside or outside the country," he told the commission. As for Ruth, he said he had known her from the days when he was a young Special Branch officer and she was a radical journalist. "The case of Mrs. Slovo, I personally would never, ever have acquiesced to, for personal reasons. As far as I was concerned, it should never have happened."

After they completed their testimony, Gillian took the stand. She said that Raven and Williamson clearly had lied about the envelope. It must have been addressed to her mother, she said, for Ruth would never have presumed to open anything addressed to Joe. She implored the commission to deny the amnesty requests. "I thought that coming here would give me and my two sisters some sense of completion, and that the applicants would tell the truth," she told the hearing. "I've been quite shaken up in that belief because we have not been told the truth." The hearing was adjourned for several months while the commission pondered its judgment. If it ruled that the applicants had not told the truth, it could deny their bid for amnesty, leaving them vulnerable to prosecution and civil action.

The Slovos had never expected to be reconciled with their mother's killers, but they had hoped for a sense of resolution and closure. But like so many other relatives of apartheid's victims, they would not find it in the hearing room, or from the hard, pathetic men who had killed their mother. Gillian came away believing she had seen those men for what they were: hateful and devoid of shame. They had killed her mother because they had hated her father. It was not just a ruthless act of state; it was something far more personal. After watching them perform their twisted verbal ballets of self-justification, she feared that she would never feel quite the same about South Africa. "I have looked too deeply into its malevolent heart," she wrote afterward. "I have seen that its evil had a human face."

Joe's old Spanish guitar sits silently in Shawn's living room. Ruth's sturdy Hermès portable typewriter rests on a table in Gillian's flat. Robyn has Joe's Soviet watch commemorating the seventieth anniversary of the October Revolution. Each of the Slovo daughters was left with the memory of parents they had loved and struggled against and never quite known, and whose activism they never fully came to terms with. Shawn wrote *A World Apart*, a fictionalized screenplay about Ruth's detention and their relationship that captured much of the fear and sadness of that terrible year. It was made into an award-winning film starring Barbara Hershey as the mother and Jodhi May as the daughter. After Joe's death Gillian published *Every Secret Thing*, a memoir of family life that revealed much about her parents' courage and commitment, but also about their private lives and secret loves. Some of Joe and Ruth's old comrades were appalled; others praised Gillian's honesty and passion. Unlike her sisters, Robyn did not write about her parents, but she supported Shawn's and Gillian's work, and the three daughters maintained a sense of sisterhood and solidarity. The struggle between parents and children continued, it seemed, even after death.

Unlike what they did to Ruth First, the security police did not kill Jimmy Kantor with a bomb. But they were nonetheless responsible for his death. When Jimmy arrived in London in 1964, he was still deeply angry at his sister, AnnMarie Wolpe, and her husband, Harold. While still in prison, he had written to a friend: "I think that the less said about the Wolpes the better. How Harold could allow me to be put in a position where I could be charged beats me. I'm livid about the whole damn thing and would like to chop both their heads off. They are fine in London and little me sits in jail for Harold Bloody Wolpe." For many months Jimmy refused to talk to AnnMarie and Harold, but eventually the rift began to heal. As his marriage to Barbara dissolved in acrimony and accusation, he drew closer again to AnnMarie. Still, they never fully discussed what had happened in South Africa, and AnnMarie never read Jimmy's book; each time she started it, she had nightmares and had to stop. She realized she could not cope with the pain and the guilt of knowing what Jimmy had suffered on her and Harold's behalf.

At first Jimmy had trouble finding work, but he soon became involved in several successful business schemes. Eventually he bought a comfortable house in Teddington on the river Thames and a yacht, and he sought to duplicate the same lavish lifestyle he had enjoyed in Johannesburg. By 1972 he and Barbara had separated. His health had never recovered from the rigors and anxieties of prison and the sabotage trial. He died of a massive heart attack in 1974 at age forty-seven. AnnMarie always felt that she and Harold were partly to blame. But she put the main responsibility on the heads of the police and of a judicial system that had betrayed a lawyer who had deeply believed in it.

Life was not easy for Harold and AnnMarie in London. There was little money and Harold was often away on Communist Party and Umkhonto business. Eventually he got a fellowship to attend the London School of Economics and became a lecturer in sociology. The same pattern of family life continued as in Johannesburg; Harold became fully absorbed in his work, political and academic, while AnnMarie—

dutiful and resentful simultaneously—held the family together in his semi-absence. But then AnnMarie went back to school as well. She and Harold both got teaching posts at Bradford University and then back in London. AnnMarie first became a researcher and later a sociology lecturer at Middlesex University, where she developed a women's studies program. She published academic works on feminism and education, and became a founding member of *Feminist Review*.

After Mandela's release from prison, Harold desperately wanted to return to South Africa. AnnMarie hesitated. Besides health issues—she was recovering from a recent hip operation—she feared leaving her children and the country she had come to call home and returning to a land she had left behind twenty-seven years earlier. She also feared that as a white feminist she would not fit in the new South Africa. Harold would not be denied. Once again he offered AnnMarie the same kind of stark choice he had given her during the dark days of 1963. I am going back, he told her. It's your decision. You can come with me or remain here.

AnnMarie chose, once again, to follow his lead. But at the same time she embarked upon *The Long Way Home*, her memoir of the Rivonia years and the 1963 prison escape. It was during the process of putting together the book that Harold began to open up about his feelings during that time. He said he had always been upset and concerned for the family and keenly aware that his political choices had made their lives harder and fraught with danger. AnnMarie still felt some residual anger, but she also knew that she had chosen to accept Harold's politics and his shortcomings. She could have opted out, but she never did. In the end, it was her choice as well as his.

Upon their return to South Africa, Harold and AnnMarie both accepted research positions at the University of the Western Cape. He helped turn the school's education department into one of the most effective research units in the country and produced a blueprint for reforming institutions of higher learning. While he never got the public recognition he deserved, he felt he was making an important contribution to the country he loved. AnnMarie worked for equal treatment of women in South Africa's education system. They lived in a comfortable house on one of the picturesque hillsides that make Cape Town one of the world's most glorious cities. Two of their children moved to South Africa as well. Then without warning Harold was struck by a massive fatal heart attack in January 1996 at age seventy. AnnMarie felt cheated and angry—at Harold for working so hard and at circumstances that were beyond his or her or anyone's control. Somewhat disillusioned, she remained deeply committed to the new South Africa. After all, it was what she and Harold had sacrificed for and built so much of their lives around.

Even in a time of reconciliation, the South African Bar Council was not inclined to review the past. After Nelson Mandela took office, Arthur Chaskalson, Joel Joffe and some of Bram Fischer's other close colleagues in the legal profession applied to the council to reverse its decision purging him from its ranks. But the council ruled that there was no proper procedure for reinstating a dead man. Faced with this rejection, Bram's friends organized a memorial lecture in his name to honor his memory and advance the cause of human rights in South Africa. The first lecture was given by Nelson Mandela.

Mandela recalled the last time he had seen Bram in June 1964, a few days after Molly's death, and how Bram had refused to let his grief interfere with the business at hand of discussing whether Mandela and his comrades should appeal their life sentences. He shared memories of Bram's kindness and determination. And Mandela invoked Bram in explaining why, despite all of the suffering they had caused him, he maintained an open-hand policy toward South Africa's whites.

"Afrikaners have given us a lot of pain, a lot of suffering; they have been insensitive beyond words," Mandela said. "It is difficult to imagine that human beings can do what Afrikaners have done to blacks in this country. . . . But when an Afrikaner changes he changes completely. He becomes a real friend. And Bram exemplified that type of Afrikaner."

Unlike some of the others who invoked Bram's memory, Mandela did not shy away from acknowledging Bram's dedication to communism. "With the exception of small numbers of religious leaders, communists were the only ones prepared to treat blacks as true equals," he said. "Bram's commitment helped change many of us in the ANC," himself included.

Finally, Mandela recalled the day during the Rivonia Trial when Bram had brought him the revised draft of Mandela's statement from the dock, having deleted the last sentence in which Mandela had invited for himself the death penalty. Mandela had read the draft and demanded that Bram restore the missing passage. Bram pleaded with him, but Mandela said he had insisted upon this, "not out of bravery, but it was duty." Bram, he added, had later made the same kind of gesture by insisting upon staying in South Africa, going underground and subjecting himself to life in prison when he could have easily fled abroad. Nelson Mandela and Bram Fischer were, in the end, comrades in the truest sense of the word.

As for the other principals from the Rivonia era:

Joel Joffe forfeited his travel permit to Australia because of his role in defending the Rivonia accused, and he and his family ended up in London instead. Fortune smiled: he became head of the Abbey Life Insurance Company, acquiring wealth that allowed him to buy a fine English mansion outside the city of Swindon. One of his top deputies was Ralph Sepel, who had fled South Africa with his wife, Minnie, after Bram Fischer's arrest and settled in London. Joffe later became chairman of Oxfam, U.K., the international charitable group, and of course served as unpaid financial and legal advisor to a generation of South African political exiles and their families.

Walter Sisulu, Ahmed Kathrada and Govan Mbeki survived more than two decades on Robben Island and Pollsmoor Prison. Upon their release, Sisulu became a senior advisor to the ANC, holding court daily in the movement's Johannesburg headquarters. Kathrada served as political advisor to President Mandela, while Mbeki retired to Port Elizabeth. His son Thabo, who had demonstrated on his behalf in London in 1964, went on to become a senior leader of the ANC and was slated to succeed Mandela as President of South Africa.

Willie Van Wyk was promoted to police captain and eventually to brigadier. He retired peacefully to a farm in Cape Province after a distinguished career. He remembered his former foes fondly, even telling a South African newspaper while Nelson Mandela was still imprisoned that he had the greatest respect for the ANC leader. After the release of the Rivonia prisoners, Ahmed Kathrada sought to locate van Wyk to compare notes and assure him that they shared his sense of goodwill and bore him no animus.

The career of Percy Yutar continued to ascend after the Rivonia Trial.

Four years after it ended, he was appointed Attorney General of the Orange Free State, fulfilling his long-stated ambition to become South Africa's first Jewish Attorney General. In 1975 he returned to the Palace of Justice as Attorney General for the Transvaal. When he retired a few years later, Justice Minister Jimmy Kruger praised him as "the official with the highest sense of loyalty I have ever found in a public servant." Yutar seldom spoke publicly about his role in the Rivonia Trial, but over the years he came to the conclusion that he had saved the lives of Nelson Mandela and the other accused by charging them with sabotage rather than treason. In 1983, the twentieth anniversary of the trial, Yutar wrote to Prime Minister P. W. Botha and three cabinet members asking that Nelson and the others be released. The request was ignored. But Mandela did not forget his diminutive prosecutor. In November 1995, at the behest of a film documentary crew, President Mandela invited Yutar to lunch at the official residence in Pretoria. Yutar looked relieved and grateful as Mandela, painfully uncomfortable, said he did not hold the prosecutor responsible for his imprisonment. Mandela agreed with Yutar's characterization that he had only played "a minor role" and had only done what duty required.

Others were less forgiving. Ahmed Kathrada was so upset by Yutar's appearance that he made up an excuse to avoid having lunch with him. Walter Sisulu, in the subsequent documentary, said Yutar had "wanted to show the Nationalist government [that] he as a Jew was even more vicious than anyone else." Harry Schwarz, who had been one of Jimmy Kantor's lawyers and who later became South Africa's ambassador to the United States, accused Yutar of prosecuting Kantor without "one little bit of real evidence."

Despite Mandela's public blessing, Yutar repeatedly found himself the subject of public opprobrium. In 1997, it was revealed that he had sold his copy of the complete Rivonia Trial transcript for an undisclosed sum to the Brenthurst Library, a private collection owned by gold and diamond magnate Harry Oppenheimer. For unstated reasons, Oppenheimer stipulated that the transcript not be made public until after Mandela's death. The transcript was a rare document—there were several incomplete versions in the state archives and in various libraries, but Yutar's apparently was the only full one—and the fact that Yutar had profited from its sale deeply upset many former members of the liberation movement. A small band of concerned archivists contacted Mandela's office, where Kathrada spearheaded a drive to have the transcript made public. Finally, in late 1997, Brenthurst allowed the copy to be microfilmed for public use.

Throughout the controversy Percy Yutar railed in private at the personal attacks made against him. Still searching for vindication, he began work on his own account of the Rivonia Trial. When I last spoke to him by phone, he declared himself shocked by what he had discovered in going through the evidence. "It's frightening, some of the things I've quoted," he told me. "They planned a revolutionary and a military invasion on a massive scale." Yutar said he'd decided on a title for the book: *The Rivonia Trial: The Facts Based on Authentic Documentary Exhibits.*

Still, for all of Percy Yutar's righteous indignation, it pained him to know that his role as prosecutor was a source of embarrassment and discomfort not only for himself but for Cecilia, his wife of more than fifty years, and David, their only child. During the days of white rule, the Rivonia Trial had been the jewel in the crown of Percy Yutar's illustrious career. In the post-apartheid era it had turned into a curse.

Toward the end of my writing of *Rivonia's Children*, I paid a trip to Britain to spend more time with Rusty and Hilda Bernstein and their family. While I was there, a woman named Ray Harmel died. She was the ex-wife of the late Michael Harmel, the radical ideologist of the South African Communist Party and one of the prime movers behind the sabotage campaign. Ray had fled Lithuania as a young woman after police cracked down on her union-organizing activities, and in Johannesburg she had served the movement as a sort of all-purpose clerical worker—everything from licking envelopes to answering the phones to participating in countless rallies and protests. A memorial service was held for her at the Golders Green Crematorium in northwest London, and many of the old comrades attended—those who were still alive and had not had the wherewithal or desire to return to South Africa after its liberation. There was Denis Goldberg and Mannie Brown and Hazel Goldreich and the Sepels, Ralph and Minnie. A young black woman came as representative of the South African High Commission. Barbara

Harmel, Ray and Michael's daughter and a childhood friend of Toni Bernstein's, said a few words between tears. Then Rusty Bernstein, who had come to the ceremony with Hilda, rose to speak.

I knew Rusty was an intelligent man and highly articulate in private sessions. But I had never heard him in a public setting. He spoke without notes, slowly and carefully, yet he was spellbinding in a quiet and thoughtful way. He made no mention of class struggle or any other part of Marxist dogma that might once have been standard rhetorical fare at the parting of a comrade. He also made no attempt to glorify Ray or the role she had played. Her life had been a hard one, he said: her marriage to Michael had been difficult, her work for the movement simultaneously tedious and dangerous. In midlife, she had had to pick up and flee yet again, this time to the unfriendly environs of London. Nothing had ever come easy.

And yet, Rusty added, Ray had been involved in something bigger than herself, had contributed in her own small way to a great movement that had turned the tide of history. This was, he said, no small thing. It was, in fact, what all of them there had been part of. They could be proud of her and of themselves.

Rusty sat down. Hilda smiled shyly at me, as if to note how well her husband had spoken for them both. I looked around the old stone chapel. Everyone there had been bit players in the same struggle. They were elderly now and, like Ray, would soon be gone. Their lives had been reduced to the concerns of old age—the size of their pensions, the cost of living, the fortunes of children and grandchildren, the weather. Yet they had been part of a remarkable and historic moment. They had resisted one of the century's great tyrannies. They had taken a risk that others of their background and social status would not take, had eschewed comfort and thrown away security when others chose to go along and reap the benefits of silence and moral compliance. They had lost their battle, but the war had been won. They would die in relative anonymity—history claims a thousand like them by lunchtime each day—but they had made their stand.

"The meaning of life is not a fact to be discovered, but a choice that you make about the way you live," Hilda had told me when we first met. Hilda, Rusty and their comrades had made their choice.

NOTE ON SOURCES

T his book is based upon interviews, primary documents and the
written accounts of many of its principals. I have used the standard journalistic technique of interviewing and reinterviewing
the main subjects and others, and I have also relied heavily upon five
books that inspired me to explore this subject and that provided the
basis of many of its scenes and dialogue. They are Hilda Bernstein's *The
World That Was Ours* (1967), Ruth First's *117 Days* (1965), Joel Joffe's
The Rivonia Story (1995), James Kantor's *A Healthy Grave* (1967) and
AnnMarie Wolpe's *The Long Way Home* (1994). Full listings for them
are in the Bibliography. The Bernstein, First and Kantor books were
written soon after the events they describe. While the Joffe and Wolpe
books are of more recent vintage, they are based upon contemporane-
ous materials. Joel Joffe wrote his manuscript soon after he moved to
London in 1964, but it went unpublished for thirty years. AnnMarie
Wolpe and her husband, Harold, tape-recorded their remembrances
sometime in the late 1960s after they moved to London, and AnnMarie
used those in her account. I have sought to check, verify and scrutinize
everything I have used from these sources, and at times my account dif-
fers from theirs.

Any researcher into this recent era of South African history runs into one troubling problem: the activists who fought apartheid, although silenced within their own country, have enjoyed a near-monopoly on writing and interpreting events. They were more articulate spokesmen and better writers than their foes, and they gained access to sympathetic book publishers and journalists abroad. This was as it should have been, but it puts an extra burden on researchers to seek out other viewpoints and people—especially those who worked for the state's security apparatus. Many of them are understandably reluctant to speak, both because they fear possible prosecution for past deeds and because they do not trust those who are writing on this subject. Those who felt they once controlled South Africa's history do not always welcome independent historians. In some cases I was able to overcome this reluctance—Percy Yutar, the Rivonia Trial prosecutor, spoke to me in detail, as did retired police captain W. P. J. van Wyk, a key figure in the campaign against the activists. Others were resolutely silent. After several faxes and phone call attempts, I received the following fax from retired major general J. J. Viktor, the chief police interrogator of Ruth First:

I have received your fax seeking a meeting to discuss your book on the Rivonia era. It would be kindly appreciated if any further attempt to contact me on the above-mentioned issue could be avoided as I have no interest whatsoever in rendering any comments.

Faced with such adamancy, I have sought other sources of information. I've relied upon the public record: what government officials said in Parliament and in the press; what they told American writer Allen Drury, when the conservative author of *Advise and Consent* traveled throughout the country in 1966 and wrote "*A Very Strange Society,*" an ambitious, 523-page account that was part travelogue, part analysis and part apologia. But perhaps the most useful of all was a collection of works produced at the time by South African journalists allied with the government. These writers enjoyed privileged access to police files and government officials and published a group of Red Scare books—including Lauritz Strydom's *Rivonia Unmasked!* and various works by Chris Vermaak and Gerard Ludi—that in effect had a government stamp of approval. Their depictions of the brilliance of police officials and the nefariousness of the activists are largely fantasy. Still, they go a long way toward providing a definitive view of the security establishment's work and attitudes in the early to middle 1960s.

A brief note about dialogue: Because *Rivonia's Children* is a narrative, it reproduces scenes and dialogue as described by firsthand participants. I have followed some well-established ground rules about the use of such material. All quotes come from someone who was present at the time the statement was made. Where I have taken dialogue from previously published books, I have sought to check its accuracy with the participants. The chapter notes that follow attempt to give the source of every scene and quotation in this book.

Nonetheless, people's memories are fallible, as is their ability to recall precisely what was said or done in a given moment years, months or even hours after the fact. Except when tape recordings are available, the reproduction of what people said, when they said it and how they said it is never an exact science. I have done my best to provide an accurate account. But there are things I cannot know for certain. The dialogue that Ruth First uses in her book *117 Days* rings true, and she repeated some of it in interviews after writing the book. The fact that the book was written just months after her imprisonment lends additional credibility. But with Viktor and other police participants either dead or unwilling to be interviewed, there is no independent way to verify a part of Ruth's story. Until others come forward with their own subjective accounts, Ruth's is the best we have.

INTERVIEWS AND CONVERSATIONS

Mary Benson, Johannesburg, August 1995; London, August 1997, March 1998

Monty and Myrtle Berman, Cape Town, July 1997

Frances Bernstein, Leeds, England, March 1998

Hilda and Rusty Bernstein, Kidlington, England, August 1996, August 1997, March 1998; London, March 1998

Keith Bernstein, London, August 1997

Patrick and Yvonne Bernstein, Stowe, England, August 1997

Claudia Braude, Johannesburg, July 1997

Jules and Selma Browde, Johannesburg, August 1995, July 1997

Mannie Brown, London, August 1997

Amina Cachalia, Johannesburg, July 1997

Luli Callinicos, Johannesburg, July 1997

Arthur Chaskalson, Johannesburg, July 1997

Apollon Davidson, Cape Town, July 1997

Helena Dolny, Johannesburg, July 1997

Gail M. Gerhart, Johannesburg, July 1997

Denis Goldberg, London, March 1997

Arthur Goldreich (interviewed by Linda Gradstein), Herzliya, Israel, March 1998

Hazel Goldreich, London, August 1997

Hillary (Kuny) Hamburger, Johannesburg, August 1995, July 1997

Rica Hodgson, Johannesburg, July 1997

Joel and Vanetta Joffe, Swindon, England, August 1997

Ahmed Kathrada, Johannesburg, July 1997

Norman Levy, Cape Town, July 1997

Pat (Davidson) Lewin (interviewed by Andrew Meldrum), Harare, Zimbabwe, February 1998

Beate Lipman, Johannesburg, July 1997

Betty Mansfield, Cape Town, July 1997

Donald Pinnock, Cape Town, July 1997

Benjamin Pogrund, Johannesburg, July 1997

Ruth (Fischer) Rice, Johannesburg, July 1997

Albie Sachs, Maputo, January 1985; Cape Town, July 1995; Johannesburg, July 1997

Marius Schoon, Johannesburg, July 1995, July 1997

Ronald Segal, Walton-on-Thames, England, August 1997, March 1998

Ralph and Minnie Sepel, London, March 1998

Milton Shain, Cape Town, July 1997

Walter Sisulu, Johannesburg, July 1997

Gillian Slovo, London, July 1995, March 1998

Joe Slovo, Lusaka, Zambia, January 1985; Johannesburg, January 1991

Robyn Slovo, London, August 1996

Shawn Slovo, London, August 1995, August 1996

Margaret Smith, London, March 1998

Allister and Sue Sparks, Johannesburg, August 1995, July 1997

Lesley (Schermbrucker) Spiller, Johannesburg, July 1997

Toni (Bernstein) Strasburg, London, August 1997

Helen Suzman, Johannesburg, August 1995, July 1997

W. P. J. van Wyk, by phone from Cape Province, South Africa, December 1997, January 1998

Ilse (Fischer) Wilson, Johannesburg, July 1997

AnnMarie Wolpe, Washington, December 1996, January 1998; Cape Town, July 1997

Harold Wolpe, Johannesburg, July 1995

David Yutar, Cape Town, July 1997

Percy Yutar, Johannesburg, July 1997; by phone December 1997, January 1998, October 1998

I also had access to oral histories recorded and transcribed by Hilda Bernstein, David Everatt, Julie Frederickse and Wolfie Kodesh, copies of which are available at the South African History Archive and the Mayibuye Center (see below). Stephen Clingman and Donald Pinnock made available tapes or transcripts of conversations with interviewees who have since died.

ARCHIVES, COLLECTIONS, NEWSPAPERS AND PERIODICALS

South African History Archive, University of Witwatersrand, Johannesburg

    Records of the Rivonia Treason Trial

    Records of the 1956 Treason Trial

    Records of the South African Institute of Race Relations

    Records of the African National Congress

    Records of the Congress of Democrats

    Records of the South African Communist Party

    Helen Joseph Papers

    David Everatt Interviews

    Benjamin Pogrund Papers

Library of the South African Board of Jewish Deputies, Johannesburg

Mayibuye Center, University of the Western Cape, Bellville

    Wolfie Kodesh Interviews

    Julie Frederickse Interviews

    Oral History of Exile

South Africa Library, Cape Town

Institute of Commonwealth Studies, London
  Ruth First Collection
  South African Materials Project
Cooperative Africana Microform Project, Chicago
Library of Congress

Africa South
Contact
Fighting Talk (Johannesburg)
Guardian (Cape Town)
New Age (Johannesburg)
The New York Times
Pretoria News
Rand Daily Mail
Sechaba
South African Jewish Times
The Star
Sunday Times (Johannesburg)
Weekly Mail & Guardian

BIBLIOGRAPHY

Arendt, Hannah. *Eichmann in Jerusalem.* Harmondsworth: Penguin, 1977.

Barrell, Howard. *MK: The ANC's Armed Struggle.* Penguin Forum Series. Harmondsworth: Penguin, 1990.

Benson, Mary. *A Far Cry.* Randburg: Ravan Press, 1996.

———. *Nelson Mandela.* New York: W. W. Norton, 1994.

———, ed. *The Sun Will Rise.* London: International Defense and Aid Fund for Southern Africa, 1981.

Bernstein, Hilda. *For Their Triumphs and for Their Tears.* London: International Defense and Aid Fund for Southern Africa, 1985.

———. *The Rift.* London: Jonathan Cape, 1994.

———. *The World That Was Ours.* London: Heinemann, 1967; paperback: London: SA Writers, 1989.

Branch, Taylor. *Parting the Waters.* New York: Simon & Schuster, 1988.

Bunting, Brian. *Moses Kotane: South African Revolutionary.* London: Inkululeko Publications, 1975.

————. *The Rise of the South African Reich*. Harmondsworth: Penguin, 1964.

Clingman, Stephen. *Bram Fischer*. Amherst: University of Massachusetts Press, 1998.

Crossman, Richard, ed. *The God That Failed*. New York: Harper & Row, 1949; paperback, 1963.

Dawidowicz, Lucy S. *From That Place and Time*. New York: W. W. Norton, 1989.

de Villiers, H.H.W. *Rivonia: Operation Mayibuye*. Johannesburg: Afrikaanse Pers, 1964.

Driver, C. J. *Elegy for a Revolutionary*. London: Faber & Faber, 1969; paperback: Cape Town: David Philip, 1984.

Drury, Allen. *"A Very Strange Society."* New York: Pocket Books, 1968.

Ellis, Stephen, and Tsepo Sechaba. *Comrades Against Apartheid*. Bloomington: Indiana University Press, 1992.

Everatt, David. *The Politics of Nonracialism: White Opposition to Apartheid*, 1945–1960. Oxford: Lincoln College, Oxford University, 1990 (unpublished dissertation).

Feit, Edward. *Urban Revolt in South Africa 1960–1964*. Evanston: Northwestern University Press, 1971.

First, Ruth. *117 Days*. Harmondsworth: Penguin, 1965; further editions: Penguin, 1982, and London: Bloomsbury, 1988.

Gerhart, Gail M. *Black Power in South Africa*. Berkeley: University of California Press, 1978.

Gordimer, Nadine. *Burger's Daughter*. Harmondsworth: Penguin, 1980.

————. *The Essential Gesture*. Stephen Clingman, ed. New York: Alfred A. Knopf, 1988.

————. *The Late Bourgeois World*. Harmondsworth: Penguin, 1966.

————. *A World of Strangers*. New York: Simon & Schuster, 1958.

Greene, Graham. *The Ministry of Fear*. New York: Viking Press, 1943.

Hooper, Charles. *Brief Authority*. London: Collins, 1960; paperback: Cape Town: David Philip, 1989.

Hutchinson, Alfred. *Road to Ghana*. London: Victor Gollancz, 1960.

Joffe, Joel. *The Rivonia Story*. Bellville: Mayibuye Books-UWC, 1995.

Johannesburg, City of. *Official Guide*. Cape Town: R. Beerman, Second Edition, 1956.

Joseph, Helen. *Side by Side*. Johannesburg: Ad. Donker, 1993.

Kafka, Franz. *The Trial*. New York: Modern Library, 1937, 1956.

Kantor, James. *A Healthy Grave.* London: Hamish Hamilton, 1967.

Karis, Thomas, and Gail M. Gerhart. *Challenge and Violence 1953–1964,* Vol. 111 of *From Protest to Challenge: A Documentary History of African Politics in South Africa 1882–1964,* edited by Thomas Karis and Gwendolyn M. Carter. Stanford: Hoover University Press, 1977.

Kasrils, Ronnie. *Armed and Dangerous.* Oxford: Heinemann, 1993.

Lapping, Brian. *Apartheid: A History.* New York: George Braziller, 1987.

Laurence, Patrick. *Death Squads: Apartheid's Secret Weapon.* Penguin Forum Series. Harmondsworth: Penguin, 1990.

Lazerson, Joshua N. *Against the Tide: Whites in the Struggle Against Apartheid.* Boulder: Westview Press, 1994.

Lewin, Hugh. *Bandiet: Seven Years in a South African Prison.* London: Barrie & Jenkins, 1974.

Lewsen, Phyllis, ed. *Helen Suzman's Solo Years.* Johannesburg: Jonathan Ball and Ad. Donker, 1991.

Lodge, Tom. *Black Politics in South Africa Since 1945.* Randburg: Ravan Press, 1983.

Ludi, Gerard. *Operation Q-018.* Cape Town: Nasionale Boekhandel, 1969.

———, and Blaar Grobbelaar. *The Amazing Mr. Fischer.* Cape Town: Nasionale Boekhandel, 1966.

Luthuli, Albert. *Let My People Go.* New York: McGraw-Hill, 1962.

Macmillan, Harold. *Pointing the Way: 1959–1961.* New York: Harper & Row, 1972.

Mandela, Nelson. *Long Walk to Freedom.* Boston: Little, Brown, 1994.

Mattera, Don. *Sophiatown: Coming of Age in South Africa.* Boston: Beacon Press, 1987.

Meredith, Martin. *Nelson Mandela.* New York: St. Martin's Press, 1998.

———. *In the Name of Apartheid.* New York: Harper & Row, 1988.

Mitchison, Naomi. *A Life for Africa: The Story of Bram Fischer.* London: Merlin Press, 1973.

Mtolo, Bruno. *Umkonto We Sizwe: The Road to the Left.* Durban: Drakensburg Press, 1966.

Ngubane, Jordan K. *An African Explains Apartheid.* New York: Praeger, 1963.

Nkosi, Lewis. *Home and Exile.* London: Longmans, 1965.

Paton, Alan. *Journey Continued.* Cape Town: David Philip, 1988.

Pike, Henry R. *A History of Communism in South Africa.* Germiston: Christian Mission International of South Africa, 1985.

Pinnock, Donald. *Writing Left: Ruth First and Radical South African Journalism in the 1950s.* University of Cape Town, n.d. (unpublished dissertation).

Reeves, Ambrose. *Shooting at Sharpeville.* London: Victor Gollancz, 1960.

Roux, Edward. *Time Longer Than Rope.* Madison: University of Wisconsin Press, 1964.

Sachs, Albie. *The Jail Diary of Albie Sachs.* Cape Town: David Philip, 1990.

———. *Stephanie on Trial.* London: Harvill Press, 1968.

Sampson, Anthony. *The Treason Cage.* London: Heinemann, 1958.

Segal, Ronald. *Into Exile.* New York: McGraw-Hill, 1963.

Shain, Milton. *The Roots of Antisemitism in South Africa.* Charlottesville: University Press of Virginia, 1994.

Shimoni, Gideon. *Jews and Zionism: The South African Experience (1910–1967).* Cape Town: Oxford University Press, 1980.

Slovo, Gillian. *Every Secret Thing.* London: Little, Brown, 1996.

Slovo, Joe. *Slovo: The Unfinished Autobiography.* Randburg: Ravan Press, 1995.

Slovo, Shawn. *A World Apart.* London: Faber & Faber, 1988.

South African Communists Speak. London: Inkululeko Publications, 1981.

Sparks, Allister. *The Mind of South Africa.* New York: Alfred A. Knopf, 1990.

Strydom, Lauritz. *Rivonia Unmasked!* Johannesburg: Voortrekkerpers, 1965.

Suttner, Immanuel, ed. *Cutting Through the Mountain.* London: Viking Press, 1997.

Suzman, Helen. *In No Uncertain Terms.* Johannesburg: Jonathan Ball, 1993.

United States Senate Subcommittee on Security and Terrorism. *The Role of the Soviet Union, Cuba and East Germany in Fomenting Terrorism in Southern Africa. Hearings Before the Senate Subcommittee on Security and Terrorism, Volume 1.* Washington: U.S. Government Printing Office, 1982.

Vermaak, Chris. *Bram Fischer: The Man with Two Faces.* Johannesburg: APB, 1966.

———. *The Red Trap.* Johannesburg: APB, 1966

Weinberg, Eli. *Portrait of a People.* London: International Defense and Aid Fund for Southern Africa, 1981.

White, Monica, and Leonard Thompson, eds. *The Oxford History of South Africa.* New York and Oxford: Oxford University Press, 1971.

Winter, Gordon. *Inside BOSS: South Africa's Secret Police.* Harmondsworth: Penguin, 1981.

Wolpe, AnnMarie. *The Long Way Home.* London: Virago Press, 1994.

CHAPTER NOTES

AUTHOR'S NOTE

3. *"The future was already there"* Nadine Gordimer, *The Late Bourgeois World* (Harmondsworth: Penguin, 1966), p. 40.

6. *"I'd get assistance from the devil"* Joel Joffe, *The Rivonia Story* (Bellville: Mayibuye Books-UWC, 1995), p. 156.

7. *"the sort of people who"* Joseph Lelyveld, *Move Your Shadow* (New York: Times Books), p. 6.

9. *"holes of oblivion"* Hannah Arendt, *Eichmann in Jerusalem* (Harmondsworth: Penguin, 1977), pp. 232–33.

ONE. THE RAID

11. *"Communists are the last optimists"* Nadine Gordimer, *Burger's Daughter* (Harmondsworth: Penguin, 1980), p. 42.

11. *"I'm going in to report"* Hilda Bernstein, *The World That Was Ours* (London: SA Writers, 1989), p. 2. The scene at the Bernstein house on July 11, 1963, is from Hilda's book and from interviews with Hilda, Rusty and Toni Bernstein.

11. *"I'll be busy"* Ibid., p. 2.

13. *"Take care of yourself"* Ibid., p. 3.

16. *"Daddy's late"* Ibid., p. 6.

18. *"a gallant but often fruitless attempt"* During the Rivonia Trial, Jimmy Kantor asked

each of his co-defendants to prepare a short autobiographical note for the book he planned to write. He published them in James Kantor, *A Healthy Grave* (London: Hamish Hamilton, 1967), pp. 144–59. Rusty Bernstein's self-deprecatory remarks are on pp. 150–54.

18. *"sitting hunched in his family drawing room"* Joe Slovo, *The Unfinished Autobiography* (Randburg: Ravan Press, 1995), p. 133.

19. *"The knowledge of being one of those in the lifeboat"* *The God That Failed*, edited by Richard Crossman (New York: Harper & Row, 1963), p. 170.

20. *"Workers of the World, Unite"* Edward Roux, *Time Longer Than Rope* (Madison: University of Wisconsin Press, 1964), p. 148.

22. "There's Nothing Wrong with Rock 'n' Roll," *Childhood*, Vol. XXXIX, No. 6 (June 1957), pp. 9–13.

22. *China's policy toward ethnic minorities* Hilda Bernstein, "How China Is Tackling the National Question," *New Age*, Sept. 14, 1961.

25. *"Sons and daughters of Africa!"* Thomas Karis and Gail M. Gerhart, *Challenge and Violence 1953–1964*, Vol. III of *From Protest to Challenge: A Documentary History of African Politics in South Africa 1882–1964*, edited by Thomas Karis and Gwendolyn M. Carter (Stanford: Hoover University Press, 1977), pp. 759–60.

26. *van Wyk was falling far behind* Lauritz Strydom, *Rivonia Unmasked!* (Johannesburg: Voortrekkerpers, 1965), pp. 23–24.

27. *a new commander had taken over* Gordon Winter, *Inside BOSS* (Harmondsworth: Penguin, 1981), pp. 34–43.

28. *"a master of the unorthodox"* Chris Vermaak, *Bram Fischer: The Man with Two Faces* (Johannesburg: APB, 1966), preface.

28. *"South Africa's own Heinrich Himmler"* Winter, p. 36.

28. *"For me the choice was between revolution"* Martin Meredith, *In the Name of Apartheid* (New York: Harper & Row, 1988), p. 103.

28. *At the same time he traveled to France* Reports that van den Bergh and other security policemen had been trained in France were confirmed in the Truth and Reconciliation Commission's report, Oct. 29, 1998.

29. *van Wyk received a call* This account of how police discovered the Lilliesleaf hideout is taken from Strydom, pp. 15–19, trial testimony and an interview with W.P.J. van Wyk.

30. *"His Bantu visitors are very well dressed"* Strydom, p. 21.

30. *They were just about to pull out* Strydom, p. 23.

31. *"Let's close in"* *Sunday Times*, June 14, 1964, and *Rand Daily Mail*, June 19, 1964. There are many accounts of the raid itself, including Strydom, Kantor, newspaper articles and trial testimony. This chapter has been drawn from all of these, plus interviews with Rusty Bernstein, van Wyk, Sisulu, Goldberg and Kathrada.

32. *the raid yielded stack after stack of pamphlets* The State vs. Nelson Mandela and Others, Vol. 30a, Alphabetical Exhibits, pp. 9–33.

33. *Long Hendrik arrived* Interview with W.P.J. van Wyk.

34. *"You see, Goldreich"* Interview with Arthur Goldreich.

34. *"You know, when a Jew gets scared"* *Pretoria News*, Sept. 30, 1966.

TWO. THE ROAD TO RIVONIA

36. *"This is not yet a police state"* Joe Slovo, p. 104.

36. *"some like volcanoes, some like sand"* Nadine Gordimer, *A World of Strangers* (New York: Simon & Schuster, 1958), p. 130.

37. *"which made it so desperately important"* Lewis Nkosi, *Home and Exile* (London: Longmans, 1965), p. 17.

37. *African stretcher bearers* Roux, p. 307.

37. For a detailed account of the rise of urban black militancy, see Tom Lodge, *Black Politics in South Africa Since* 1945 (Randburg: Ravan Press, 1983).

38. *Sunlight laundry soap* Joe Slovo, p. 35.

38. The official Communist Party account of the mine workers' strike is contained in the pamphlet *A Distant Clap of Thunder: Fortieth Anniversary of the 1946 Mine Strike*, published by the SACP, 1986.

39. The Moroka squatters scene is from interviews with Rusty Bernstein and from Joe Slovo, pp. 38–39.

41. Details of Mandela's childhood and early days in Johannesburg: Nelson Mandela, *Long Walk to Freedom* (Boston: Little, Brown, 1994), and Martin Meredith, *Nelson Mandela* (New York: St. Martin's Press, 1998).

43. *they refused to accompany Sisulu* Interview with Walter Sisulu.

43. *Both of them became more and more Marxist* Sisulu interview and Mandela, pp. 104–5.

44. *Mandela's friendship with Bram Fischer* Meredith, *Mandela*, pp. 90–91.

44. *"Present were Africans"* Nkosi, p. 25.

45. Biographical details of Ruth First: Donald Pinnock, *Writing Left: Ruth First and Radical South African Journalism in the 1950s*, an unpublished doctoral thesis, University of Cape Town, n.d., and Gillian Slovo, *Every Secret Thing* (London: Little, Brown, 1996).

46. *She was bored and sickened* Ruth First, *117 Days* (Harmondsworth: Penguin, 1982), p. 117.

47. *"Is Miss First here?"* Interview with Beate Lipman.

47. *Paton . . . saw a different side* Alan Paton, *Journey Continued* (Cape Town: David Philip, 1988), p. 106.

48. *"You won't always be young"* Interview with Hilda Bernstein.

48. *"My introspection"* Joe Slovo, "Introduction to the New Edition," in Ruth First, *117 Days* (London: Bloomsbury, 1988), p. 5.

49. Biographical details of Joe Slovo are from his unfinished autobiography and Gillian Slovo, pp. 27–28.

51. *"I feel so inadequate"* Ruth First letter to Joe Slovo, April 6, 1960.

51. *"You make me cross"* Joe Slovo letter to Ruth First, May 22, 1960.

51. *"You've got the wrong idea about communism"* Interview with the woman involved, who asked to remain anonymous.

51. *"Are you behaving yourself?"* Joe Slovo letter to Ruth First, n.d.

52. *"While there was a fantastic array"* Nkosi, p. 8.

52. *"As far as the National Party is concerned"* Walter Sisulu in *Africa South,* Jan. 1957.
53. *"The very nature of our activities"* Joe Slovo, p. 111.
53. For the arrival of Lithuanian Jews in South Africa, see Gideon Shimoni, *Jews and Zionism: The South African Experience (1910–1967)* (Cape Town: Oxford University Press, 1980), pp. 5–9.
53. For a description of the Jewish life in Vilna, see Lucy S. Dawidowicz, *From That Place and Time* (New York: W. W. Norton, 1989), pp. 28–51.
54. Shimoni describes in detail Jewish attitudes toward politics and the National Party, pp. 206–34, as does Ronald Segal, *Into Exile* (New York: McGraw-Hill, 1963), pp. 16–19.
56. *"We know that a large percentage"* Cape Times, n.d.
56. *"The Jews will thus now have to choose"* Shimoni, p. 332.
56. *Mandela never forgot the kindness* Mandela, p. 62.
57. *"It was the Jews who tempered"* Nkosi, p. 19.
57. *"When photographs appear"* Transvaler, Sept. 11, 1956.
58. For the breadth and impact of apartheid, see Allister Sparks, *The Mind of South Africa* (New York: Alfred A, Knopf, 1990).
58. *"Give orders one at a time"* City of Johannesburg, *Your Bantu Servant and You* (Johannesburg, 1962), p. 3.
59. For descriptions of Sophiatown, see Sparks, pp. 187–88, and Don Mattera, *Sophiatown: Coming of Age in South Africa* (Boston: Beacon Press, 1987), pp. 49–62.
59. *"We believe, and believe strongly"* Edgar H. Brookes, *Apartheid: A Documentary Study of Modern South Africa* (New York: Barnes and Noble, 1968), pp. 191–92.
60. For details of the Suppression of Communism Act and public reaction, see Roger Omond, *The Apartheid Handbook* (Harmondsworth: Penguin, 1985), pp. 203–4.
61. *"not to become an officer-bearer"* Charles Robberts Swart, NOTICE IN TERMS OF SECTION FIVE OF THE SUPPRESSION OF COMMUNISM ACT, 1950, to Lionel Bernstein, May 24, 1954.
62. *the South African party received limited financial* Interview with Apollon Davidson.
62. *"No one quits the Communist Party"* Interview with Beate Lipman.
63. For a history of the Congress of Democrats, see Joshua N. Lazerson, *Against the Tide* (Boulder: Westview, 1994), pp. 71–75, 115–37.
64. *"WE CALL THE PEOPLE"* Karis and Gerhart, pp. 180–84.
65. *"That South Africa belongs to all"* Ibid., pp. 205–8.
66. *"Soup With Meat"* Mandela, p. 151.
66. *"Mummy's gone to prison"* Gillian Slovo, p. 39.
67. *"communism straight from the shoulder"* Mandela, p. 183.
67. *"Hutch, about that article"* Alfred Hutchinson, *Road to Ghana* (London: Victor Gollancz, 1960), p. 13.
68. *"Don't push me, man"* Ibid., p. 14.
69. *"Decisions were being arrived at"* Gail M. Gerhart, *Black Power in South Africa* (Berkeley: University of California Press, 1978), p. 156.

69. *communists had captured effective control* Jordan K. Ngubane, *An African Explains Apartheid* (New York: Praeger, 1963), pp. 162–73.

70. *a political death wish* Gerhart, p. 230.

70. For the most detailed contemporary description of the Sharpeville Massacre, see Ambrose Reeves, *Shooting at Sharpeville* (London: Victor Gollancz, 1960).

71. *"Some of the children"* *Africa Today*, May 1960.

71. *"It is a matter of concern to me"* *Rand Daily Mail*, March 22, 1960.

72. *Luthuli . . . was slapped hard* Albert Luthuli, *Let My People Go* (New York: McGraw-Hill, 1962), p. 224.

72. *Ruth was not on their list* Gillian Slovo, p. 49.

72. *"They're here!"* Hilda Bernstein's prison diary, April 8, 1960.

73. *"Nobody's going to take me"* Stephen Clingman, *Bram Fischer* (Amherst: University of Massachusetts Press, 1998), p. 273.

73. *"What do you want?"* Interview with Toni Bernstein.

74. *"To see a man about a dog"* Interview with Frances Bernstein.

76. *"The children were simply removed"* *Sunday Times*, May 15, 1960.

77. *"Don't cry, you will upset them"* Bernstein diary, May 26, 1960.

77. *"Please, Pat"* Hilda Bernstein letter from prison, n.d.

77. *One night Hilda dreamed* Bernstein diary, May 21, 1960.

77. *"serious and lasting adverse effects"* Harold Bernstein letter, June 11, 1960.

THREE. SABOTAGE

79. *"What we have aimed to do"* Luthuli, p. 113.

79. *a man who called himself Jacobson* Accounts of the purchase of Lilliesleaf come from Joffe, Kantor, Strydom, and interviews with Ralph Sepel and Arthur Goldreich.

81. *Michael Harmel produced a paper* Meredith, *Mandela*, p. 188.

81. *"Much as I don't like this"* Interview with Ruth Rice.

81. *The ANC took considerably longer* For an account of ANC decision to permit violence, see Mandela, pp. 236–40.

82. *"If the government reaction is to crush"* Ibid., p. 236.

82. *"the attacks of the wild beast"* Ibid.

84. *Joe could see at once* Joe Slovo, p. 153.

84. *the alias David Matsamayi* Mandela, p. 243.

85. *Arthur Goldreich . . . moved into the main house* Interviews with Arthur and Hazel Goldreich.

85. *"How can you go on living like this . . . ?"* Interview with Selma Browde.

86. *"I know that he's a communist"* Interview with Hazel Goldreich.

86. *Hodgson mixed the potash* Interview with Rica Hodgson.

87. *"Can I do anything for you, sir?"* Joe Slovo, p. 154.

88. *"The choice is not ours"* Karis and Gerhart, pp. 716–17.

89. *"As a child and as a student"* Vermaak, *Bram Fischer*, prelude (n.p.)

89. *"I found I had to shake hands"* This and succeeding quotations are from Bram Fis-

cher's speech from the dock, March 28, 1966, reprinted in *The Sun Will Rise*, edited by Mary Benson (London: International Defense and Aid Fund for Southern Africa, 1981), p. 37.

89. For a detailed account of Fischer's life, see Clingman.

91. *"Don't bluff yourself"* Paton, p. 69.

92. *Slovo believed he was too cautious* Joe Slovo interview by Stephen Clingman, Dec. 23, 1991.

93. *"You're misjudging what is going on"* Interview with Monty and Myrtle Berman.

93. *"kaffirboeties"* Clingman, p. 219.

94. For details of Mandela's trip abroad, see *Mandela*, pp. 251–267.

95. *government-planted stories* Meredith, *Mandela*, pp. 220–21.

96. For the abortive Mandela escape attempts, see Mandela, pp. 281–82, and Joe Slovo, pp. 159–65.

96. *"I consider myself neither morally"* Karis and Gerhart, p. 726.

96. *"There comes a time"* Ibid. p. 743.

97. *"I believe the time has arrived"* General Law Amendment Bill, *House of Assembly Debates*, May 21, 1962, Hansard, Vol. IV, Col. 6061.

98. *"We are dealing with people"* Ibid., Cols. 6077–78.

98. *"God, Helen, we can think of ten Progs"* Interview with Helen Suzman.

98. For details of Suzman's life, see Helen Suzman, *In No Uncertain Terms* (Johannesburg: Jonathan Ball, 1993).

99. *"You might try going to Soweto yourself"* Suzman interview.

99. *"Long before the final chapter"* Hansard, Col. 4672.

100. *"Liberalism . . . had never come to terms"* Segal, pp. 117–18.

101. *"you haven't served me"* Interview with Toni Bernstein.

101. *"provided you proceed straight"* Letter to Mr. L. Bernstein from the Office of the Magistrate, Johannesburg, June 7, 1963.

101. *As a listed person* Letter to Mrs. H. Bernstein from the Office of the Magistrate, Johannesburg, April 3, 1963.

102. *What was the point in staying any longer . . . ?* Interviews with Rusty and Hilda Bernstein.

104. *"If they want to go"* Sunday Express, Nov. 11, 1962.

104. *Ruth First's latest set of banning orders* First, p. 11.

104. *"We have to bear in mind"* Hansard 1963, Vol. VI, Col. 4644.

105. *"He is one of the people"* Ibid., Col. 4642.

105. *"It is absolutely essential"* Ibid., Col. 4656.

106. *"on the altar of the holy cow"* Ibid., Col. 4675.

107. *"The white state has thrown overboard"* Complete text of Operation Mayibuye can be found in Karis and Gerhart, pp. 760–68.

109. *An ugly rift began to develop* Interview with Rusty Bernstein.

110. *On the Fourth of July* The Star, July 4, 1963.

FOUR. THE ESCAPE

111. *"As a prisoner, I always contemplated escape"* Mandela, p. 281.
112. *"Mr. Wolpe is out of town"* AnnMarie Wolpe, *The Long Way Home* (London: Virago, 1994), p. 82.
112. *"I will be in touch"* Ibid., p. 83.
114. *He became . . . the movement's main lawyer* Harold Wolpe interview by Wolfie Kodesh, Dec. 16, 1992.
115. *"It's a beautiful night"* Interview with AnnMarie Wolpe.
115. *"It's your decision"* Ibid.
115. *"Harold, this is crazy"* Ibid.
116. *"He is playing an extremely significant role"* Wolpe, p. 96.
116. *The chief attributes for such work* Kantor, p. 4.
117. *When Nelson Mandela became a lawyer* Interview with AnnMarie Wolpe.
118. *"Don't you have any idea . . . ?"* Interview with Betty Mansfield.
119. *"I've got to go into hiding"* Wolpe, pp. 89–90.
119. *"You'll be all right there"* Ibid., p. 90.
119. *"Don't get out of the car"* Kantor, p. 8.
120. *"What about the animals?"* Ibid., p. 9.
120. *Lieutenant Willie van Wyk was standing* Interview with van Wyk.
121. *"We've taken a helluva beating"* Wolpe, pp. 90–91.
121. *"This arrest has been . . . catastrophic"* Ibid., pp. 96–97.
121. *"I've come to give you a new look"* Ibid., p. 99.
122. *"Ag, Herold, it's really you, man"* Ibid., p. 108.
122. *"Say goodbye to your wife"* Ibid., p. 115.
122. *"Well, what do you expect?"* Ibid., p. 119.
125. *three possible means of escape* Ibid., p. 131.
125. *"Have you been to a Jewish funeral before?"* Ibid., p. 144.
126. *"Am curiously calm and collected"* Ruth First letter to Joe Slovo, July 12, 1963.
126. *"I just need to know you're all right"* Ibid., July 27, 1963.
126. *"Will you come with us, please"* Ruth First interview by Jack Gold, BBC tape transcription, n.d., p. 2.
127. *"It's got the children's friends"* Ibid., p. 4.
127. *"If you're interested in your children"* Ibid., p. 5.
128. *"What were you doing at Rivonia?"* First, p. 52.
128. *"There's something special for him"* Wolpe, p. 147.
128. *"Contact D whose cousin A"* Ibid., p. 148.
129. *"Oh, I've got something for you"* Ibid., p. 152.
129. *"You'll have to be quick"* Ibid., p. 153.
130. *Greeff did not understand* Denis Herbstein, "The Smiling Policeman," in *The Independent on Sunday*, July 17, 1994.
131. *"But if we escape, when will I see the children . . . ?"* Interview with Hazel Goldreich.
132. *"I think we may have to borrow your car"* Interviews with AnnMarie Wolpe and Mannie Brown.

132. *"That's where we'll take them"* Interview with Mannie Brown.

132. *"What's doing, AnnMarie?"* Wolpe, pp. 172–73.

133. *"Listen . . . it's going to be tonight"* Ibid., p. 173.

133. *"Marlene, I'm going to tell you something"* Ibid., pp. 174–75.

134. *"If we don't go tonight"* Ibid., p. 179.

135. *"I don't believe it!"* Wolpe, p. 183

135. *Barney Simon was just as amazed* See interview with Barney Simon by Joseph Sherman, March 13 and 27, 1995, in *Cutting Through the Mountain*, edited by Immanuel Suttner (London: Viking Press, 1997), p. 127.

136. *"Apparently this was the weapon"* Strydom, p. 41.

136. *"I was in bad trouble, sir"* Ibid., p. 42.

136. *"Get your clothes on, Mrs. Wolpe"* Wolpe, p. 175.

137. *"You know where they are"* Ibid., p. 185.

137. *"We know exactly what you have done"* Ibid., p. 186.

137. *"I want to deal with her myself"* Ibid., p. 189.

138. *"I'm going to get them"* Ibid., p. 191.

138. *"Why do you have to have people like that . . . ?"* Ibid., p. 192. AnnMarie Wolpe isn't certain who interrogated her after Swanepoel, and van Wyk says he cannot remember questioning her. But in Strydom's book, written at the time with van Wyk's and Special Branch's full assistance, van Wyk questions her that night. See Strydom, p. 45.

138. *"For Christ's sake make sure Jimmy checks"* Wolpe, pp. 192–93.

138. *"She's a bloody good actress"* Ibid., p. 194.

139. *"Those guys are going out"* Ibid., p. 195.

139. *"They're crazy and they'll get caught"* Interview with Hilda Bernstein.

140. *"We have Harold and Arthur"* Bernstein, p. 89; see also Kantor, p. 19.

141. *"Did you recognize me?"* Interview with Hilda Bernstein.

143. *"At no time did the police get anywhere"* *Rand Daily Mail*, Aug. 29, 1963.

144. *Jimmy was furious* Kantor, p. 18.

144. *"We've beaten them for the first time in ages"* Wolpe, p. 201.

144. *"It's a pity he has such vicious parents"* Ibid., p. 223.

144. *"There can be no doubt that two of the big fishes"* *The Star*, Aug. 28, 1963.

FIVE. NOTES FROM UNDERGROUND

145. *"Pain is truth"* J. M. Coetzee, *Waiting for the Barbarians* (Harmondsworth: Penguin, 1982), p. 5.

146. *"Hi, Bob, how are you?"* Kantor, p. 45.

146. *"What's the hurry?"* Ibid., p. 46.

147. *"Is that the right time?"* Ibid., p. 49.

148. *"There was something threatening"* Graham Greene, *The Ministry of Fear* (New York: Viking Press, 1943), p. 8.

149. *"They are the same everywhere"* Ibid., p. 112.

149. *"Oh, Hilda, it can't last"* Interview with Hilda Bernstein.

150. *"We were so anxious"* Bernstein, p. 59.

151. *"Dear Dad"* Ibid., p. 60.

152. *"No! Definitely not!" Klindt proclaimed* Ibid., p. 69.

154. *"Do you really think you can tell me anything?"* First, p. 54.

155. *a narrow, lumpy straw mattress* Ibid., p. 9.

155. *Ruth nicknamed her wardresses* Ibid., pp. 30–38.

157. *"I have been keeping a record"* Undated note from Rusty to Hilda Bernstein.

157. *"I am finding the nights worse"* Ibid.

158. *How was it, Hilda asked him one day* Bernstein, p. 79.

159. *"You can't make war without money"* Interview with W.P.J. van Wyk.

159. *"We don't believe you!"* James Kantor letter to David Suzman, Oct. 15, 1963.

159. *"First [came] the whistle of the cane"* Kantor, p. 103.

160. *"a tough little Jew"* Ibid., p. 104.

160. *"Where are the others?"* Ibid., p. 105.

161. *Maggie Smith . . . came by the house* Interview with Margaret Smith.

162. *"They have reached a decision"* Wolpe, pp. 264–65.

163. *"If you have something to read"* First, p. 83.

163. *"How's Joe?"* Ibid., p. 87.

163. *"If you come again bring a bottle"* Ibid., p. 89.

164. *"So it took only one clout"* Albie Sachs, *Stephanie on Trial* (London: Harvill Press, 1968), p. 61.

164. *"Have a smoke"* Hugh Lewin, *Bandiet* (London: Barrie & Jenkins, 1974), pp. 34–35.

164. *He handed her a small bottle* First, pp. 102–3.

165. *Think it over carefully* Ibid., p. 105.

165. *"The thought of being in prison"* Rusty to Hilda Bernstein, n.d.

165. *"It is not permitted!"* Bernstein, p. 87–88.

166. *"Nothing gives me worse torments"* Rusty to Hilda Bernstein, n.d.

166. *"Where are you going tonight?"* Interview with Frances Bernstein.

166. *"Any complaints?"* Bernstein, pp. 93–94.

167. *sixty leading psychiatrists* Rand Daily Mail, Dec. 17, 1963.

167. *a "mighty weapon"* Rand Daily Mail, n.d.

167. *When Abdullah Jassat . . . was seized* Bernstein, p. 82.

168. *"Dead Man Banned"* First, p. 89.

168. *"The next thing I remember"* Portions of the transcript of the inquest into Looksmart Ngudle's death are reprinted in Joffe, pp. 30–32, and First, pp. 97–102.

169. *"a disgrace to any so-called civilized country"* Hansard, Vol. IX, Cols. 138–47, reprinted in *Helen Suzman's Solo Years*, edited by Phyllis Lewsen (Johannesburg: Jonathan Ball and Ad. Donker, 1991), p. 39.

170. *"This simply indescribable state"* Stefan Zweig, *The Royal Game* (New York: Viking Press, 1944), p. 42.

170. *"The task of all who believe"* Lewsen, p. 36.

170. *"You won't get another one"* Interview with Rusty Bernstein.

170. *"I feel as though here I am"* Rusty to Hilda Bernstein, n.d.

171. *"I now really worry about"* Ibid.

172. *"I think the day he was brought back"* Ibid.
173. *"Colonel Klindt, I want to see my husband"* Bernstein, p. 96.
173. *"just listen to what I have to say"* Ibid., p. 98.
174. *Three brightly scrubbed faces* First, pp. 105–6.
174. *"I've come to tell you to pack"* Ibid., p. 107.
175. *"Just a minute, Mrs. Slovo"* Ibid., p. 109.
176. *wave after wave of self-pity* Ibid., p. 112.
176. *"You see, Mrs. Slovo, we are persistent"* Ibid., p. 114.
176. *"It's a funny thing, isn't it?"* Ibid., p. 121.
177. *"Are you cracking up?"* Ibid., pp. 124–25.
177. *"Do you want a doctor?"* Ibid., p. 131.
178. *"You don't think I'd be so foolish"* Ibid., p. 132.
178. *"I am asking you as one woman to another"* Suzman, p. 76.
178. *"Is that my favorite MP?"* Ibid., p. 77.
179. *"That woman is worth ten United Party MPs"* Ibid., p. 73.
179. *"I hear she's in a very bad way"* Interview with Helen Suzman.
179. *"I've watched when you walk out of here"* First, p. 140.
180. *"I'd rather kiss it"* Ibid., p. 140.
180. *"Don't try that again"* Ibid., 143.
180. *"I'll be there to catch you"* Ibid., p. 144.
181. *"You know, Vic, I've always known"* Kantor, p. 112.
181. *"Good afternoon, gentlemen!"* Ibid., p. 113.

SIX. ON TRIAL

182. *"Everything belongs to the Court"* Franz Kafka, *The Trial* (New York: Modern Library, 1956), p. 288.
183. *When Hilda started over* Bernstein, p. 121.
185. *"My lord, I call the case"* Ibid., p. 108.
185. *"REVOLT, INVASION, CHARGES"* *Rand Daily Mail*, Oct. 9, 1963.
185. *"The accused in this case"* Joffe, p. 28.
186. *Jimmy laughed at the outlandishness* Kantor, p. 120.
187. For Jimmy Kantor's derisory description of Yutar, see ibid., p. 118.
187. "The Yutar Legend," *Sunday Chronicle*, Aug. 29, 1965.
187. For a biographical sketch of Yutar, see *South African Jewish Times*, Feb. 14, 1975.
188. *"The office of the Attorney General"* *South African Jewish Times*, July 23, 1963.
190. *"You must understand that you are in a sinking ship"* Govan Mbeki's account is from p. 46 of the typed manuscript of Ruth First's *117 Days*.
190. "Call for Tolerance," *South African Jewish Times*, July 23, 1963.
190. the "high percentage" of Jews *Dagbreek en Sondagnuus*, Sept. 1, 1963.
190. *"The facts show abundantly"* South African Jewish Board of Deputies Press Digest No. 54, Sept. 5, 1963, p. 343.
191. *"A betrayal of religion"* South African Jewish Times, April 24, 1964.
191. *They expressed deep disapproval* Wolpe, p. 227.

192. *"Percy, are you afraid to prosecute"* Interview with Percy Yutar.
193. *a last act before leaving the country* Interview with Joel Joffe.
194. *"I have been at the Grays' for three weeks"* Joffe, p. 12.
194. *"If you were a policeman"* Ibid., p. 12.
195. *Pat Davidson . . . looked out one of the downstairs windows* Interview with Pat Lewin.
196. *He had to joust with the prison authorities* Joffe, pp. 19–20.
198. *"They dare not hang them now!"* Interview with George Bizos by Thomas Karis and Gail Gerhart, New York, October 1989, p. 38.
199. *"Isn't Swanepoel a fine-looking chap!"* Mandela, p. 313.
199. *"You've got to be strong"* Interview with Patrick Bernstein.
199. *There they were alone for nearly an hour* Bernstein, p. 111.
200. *"These facts are peculiarly"* Joffe, p. 35.
200. *Hilda could see that three weeks* Interview with Hilda Bernstein.
201. *Bram dissected every paragraph* Joffe, pp. 37–38.
201. *"These facts are not known"* Ibid., pp. 39–40.
202. *Yutar tried to salvage* "Application to Quash," Rivonia Trial transcript, Oct. 30, 1963, pp. 1–40.
202. *"I can see no reason why"* Ibid., p. 2.
202. *"This is not a political meeting"* Ibid., p. 5.
203. *"I am arresting you"* Joffe, p. 44.
203. *"Oh, Mummy, tell him to leave me alone!"* Bernstein, pp. 128–29.
203. *He felt more like himself* Kantor, p. 114.
204. *"His biggest crime"* "Application for Bail, Kantor," Rivonia Trial transcript, Oct. 30, 1963, p. 4.
204. *The practice "has been ruined, my lord"* Ibid., p. 15.
205. *"this confidential secret document"* Kantor, p. 142.
206. *Back in his cell that evening* Ibid., p. 128.
206. *"Well, you know it is not in my power"* Bernstein, pp. 134–36.
207. *The defense moved to quash* Joffe, p. 51.
207. *"Am I to refuse to appear . . . ?"* Kantor, pp. 161–62.
208. *"The State is no longer prepared"* Ibid., p. 163.
208. *"I believed I was not safe"* Ibid.
208. *Denis had feared she would be arrested again* Interview with Denis Goldberg.
208. *"My lord, it is not I"* Mandela, p. 310.
209. *a small black microphone* Joffe, p. 60.
209. *It was, perhaps, his finest moment* Ibid., pp. 60–62.
210. *"They said that if they were satisfied"* Ibid., pp. 63–64.
211. *"My ear is still sore"* Kantor, p. 167.
211. *It began to dawn on Joffe* Joffe, p. 65.
212. *Bram was working with the remaining cadres* Clingman, pp. 310–11.
212. *He took to smuggling in crossword puzzles* Kantor, p. 171.
213. *One day the box was occupied* Joffe, pp. 107–8.
213. *"What about my babies?"* Ibid., p. 109.

214. For accounts of Bruno Mtolo's testimony, see Joffe, pp. 70–91; Mandela, pp. 311–12; and Mtolo's memoir: Bruno Mtolo, *Umkonto We Sizwe: The Road to the Left* (Durban: Drakensburg Press, 1966).

214. *"Bruno, are you a saboteur?"* Joffe, p. 71.

215. *"the house and the furniture inside"* Ibid., p. 74.

217. *Mtolo's testimony opened a window* Bernstein, pp. 144–45.

217. For an account of Adrian Leftwich's life and activities, see Paton, pp. 222–36.

217. *"On the wall of one of his cells"* Sachs, *The Jail Diary of Albie* Sachs (Cape Town: David Philip, 1990), p. 73.

218. *"It is not easy to give evidence"* Ibid., pp. 121–22.

218. For an account of Cyril Davids's testimony, see Joffe, pp. 92–99.

219. *The food in detention . . . had been "excellent"* Rand Daily Mail, Jan. 23, 1964.

219. *"We tell them what we want to know"* Joffe, p. 116.

219. For Dirker's testimony, see ibid., pp. 116–18.

220. *The Cape Town engineer proved easy* Interview with Denis Goldberg.

220. *Loyal and precise, Makda described meetings* Rand Daily Mail, Dec. 7, 1963, and Kantor, pp. 168–70.

221. *"You agreed with a lot of things"* Kantor, p. 170.

221. *Hilda noticed a gradual change* Bernstein, pp. 174–75.

221. *"How can that possibly be relevant?"* The Star, May 4, 1964.

222. *He was so desperate he sought a personal meeting* Kantor, pp. 174–75.

222. *"Tell Barbara I apologize"* Ibid., p. 175.

222. *Despite the warm sun, Jimmy shivered* Ibid., pp. 178–79.

222. The Port Alfred trip is recounted in Bernstein, pp. 180–82, and Gillian Slovo, p. 93.

223. For Essop Suliman's testimony, see *Rand Daily Mail*, Jan. 14, 1964.

223. *"Barbara and I have discussed"* Kantor, p. 182, and Mandela, pp. 313–14.

224. *During one bizarre weekend* Kantor, pp. 185–89.

224. For Cox's testimony, see ibid., p. 195.

225. *the following weekend van Wyk phoned* Ibid., pp. 196–98.

225. *Nelson had given Jimmy his own cup* Kantor, p. 202.

225. *Jimmy . . . had said "thank God"* Rand Daily Mail, Feb. 21, 1964.

225. *"Let's exchange ties for luck"* Kantor, p. 213, and Mandela, p. 323.

226. *"I have come to the conclusion"* Kantor, p. 216.

228. *"Your telephone calls succeed"* Ruth First letter to Joe Slovo, March 2, 1964.

230. *Hilda understood why* Interview with Hilda Bernstein.

SEVEN. WITNESS FOR THE DEFENSE

231. *"This Court . . . is a pointless institution"* Kafka, p. 193.

231. *Vorster had sent out notices* Sunday Times, Sept. 8, 1963; Sunday Express, Feb. 9, 1964.

232. *"She is not allowed"* Bernstein, pp. 112–13.

232. *Ivan's relatives were disturbed* Interview with Toni Bernstein.

232. *Patrick was moving out* Interview with Patrick Bernstein.

233. *Rusty knew few of the details* Interviews with Rusty and Hilda Bernstein. Rusty disputes my view that a separation gradually occurred between himself and the other accused. He insists that all decisions taken by the accused were made collectively and that there was no difference between his defense and that of any of his comrades.

234. *"Mandela, what do you think"* Nelson Mandela interview by David Beresford for *Encounters*, a documentary film broadcast by the South African Broadcasting Company, July 1995.

234. For an account of defense preparations, see Joffe, pp. 121–27.

235. *Bizos . . . had been watching Percy Yutar* Karis and Gerhart interview with Bizos, p. 48.

236. *"Look. . . . if you really get the judge"* Interview with Joel Joffe.

236. *Joffe had never had black friends* Ibid.

236. *the defense team did its best to mislead* Joffe, p. 127.

237. For Nadine Gordimer and Anthony Sampson's contributions to Mandela's address, see Bizos interview, pp. 34–36.

237. *Bram led off with a summary* Joffe, p. 129.

238. *"My lord, I think you should warn"* Mandela, p. 317.

238. For Mandela's speech from the dock, see Karis and Gerhart, pp. 771–96.

240. *The room remained silent* Joffe, p. 133.

240. *The final straw for Jimmy* Kantor, p. 217.

241. *"I hope you weren't too worried"* Ibid., p. 218–19.

241. For Walter Sisulu's testimony, see Benson, ed., pp. 24–27, and Joffe, pp. 133–50.

246. *"You have called them . . . amongst other things"* Joffe, p. 153.

246. *"I suffer from the laws"* Ibid., p. 156.

246. *"My lord, my views have been communist"* Extract from Evidence, Accused No. 6, Lionel Bernstein, *The State vs. Nelson Mandela and Others*, May 1, 1964, p. 15.

247. *"I had a very shrewd suspicion"* Ibid., p. 36.

248. *"the congresses at that stage"* Ibid., p. 25.

248. *"a highly responsible, sober"* Ibid., p. 26.

248. *His clients "could not come"* Ibid., p. 34.

248. *"There is not a word of truth"* Ibid., p. 43.

248. Rusty's three lies: *"No, sir, I never knew,"* ibid., p. 45; *"My lord, I never had anything to do,"* p. 45; and *"I did not know of the existence,"* p. 57.

249. *"Mr. Bernstein, you have been in the Communist Party"* Ibid., p. 59.

249. *"Did you rejoin?"* Ibid., p. 61.

249. *"If you refuse to answer"* Ibid., p. 65.

250. *"Who is the leader . . . ?"* Ibid., p. 67.

250. *"I don't think the leaders"* Ibid., p. 74.

251. *"Being a communist, you are"* Ibid., p. 86.

251. *"Has an attempt not been made in this case"* Ibid., p. 124.

251. *"Do you call it peaceful . . . ?"* Ibid., p. 143.

252. *Rusty was cooking his own goose* Joffe, p. 171.

252. *"I am not going to mention"* Extract from Evidence, May 5, 1964, p. 159.
252. *"Percy, los"* Interview with Percy Yutar.
253. *"you are a listed communist?"* Extract, p. 160.
253. *"Is that not a shocking misrepresentation"* The exchange between Rusty and Yutar over Rusty's letter: ibid., pp. 170–74.
254. *"That does not happen in Soviet Russia?"* Ibid., p. 177.
255. *"Did you realize in declining to answer . . . ?"* Ibid., p. 216.
255. *"Were you offered any rewards?"* Ibid., p. 246.
255. *"One has to go through it"* Ibid., p. 247.
257. *"Rusty has a chance"* Bernstein, p. 217.
257. *"Why have you pleaded not guilty . . . ?"* Joffe, p. 177.

EIGHT. THE VERDICT

258. *"What is important in the end"* C. J. Driver, *Elegy for a Revolutionary* (Cape Town: David Philip, 1984), p. 123.
258. *"This is not a closing address"* Joffe, p. 192.
258. *"Although the State has charged"* For summary of Yutar's closing, see Joffe, pp. 192–97, and *Rand Daily Mail*, May 21, 1964.
261. *"I accept that there were other"* Joffe, p. 198.
262. *"With the dignity that has characterized"* *Rand Daily Mail*, May 29, 1964.
262. *"You know, Dr. Yutar"* Joffe, p. 202.
263. *Hilda made the familiar trek* Bernstein, p. 233.
264. *"Lionel Bernstein is found not guilty"* Joffe, p. 203.
264. *"Are you arresting me again?"* Interview with Rusty Bernstein.
264. *"After that disgraceful exhibition"* Bernstein, p. 240.
265. For an account of the convicted defendants' refusal to appeal, see Joffe, pp. 205–6; Mandela, pp. 326–27.
266. *"Are their lives in danger?"* Joffe, p. 191.
266. *Paton gave three reasons* Paton, p. 250–51.
266. *"to unmask this gentleman"* Strydom, p. 145. The most detailed account of Yutar's cross-examination of Paton is Strydom, pp. 145–58.
267. *"I am by no means convinced"* The Star, June 12, 1964; *Rand Daily Mail*, June 13, 1964.
268. *"Denis! What is it?"* Interview with Denis Goldberg.
268. *Joffe . . . watched the crowd* Interview with Joel Joffe.
269. *"in many ways, important and unimportant"* Bram Fischer letter to Canon John Collins, June 12, 1964.
269. *"the outcome could have been worse"* Time, June 19, 1964, p. 25.
269. *"If disaster is to be averted"* The New York Times, June 14, 1964.
269. *"communist criminals"* The Star, June 16, 1964.
269. *"wise and just"* Rand Daily Mail, June 13, 1964.
270. For Rusty's release, see Bernstein, pp. 240–41, and *Sunday Times*, June 14, 1964.

NINE. SUNSET

272. *"For the Afrikaner people"* Gordimer, *Burger's Daughter*, p. 42.

272. For details of Molly Fischer's death, including Elizabeth Lewin's first-person account, see Clingman, pp. 323–26.

273. *"My poor wife"* Ibid., p. 325.

273. *Ivan Schermbrucker showed up at the house* Interviews with Rusty and Hilda Bernstein.

273. *Even in his grief* Clingman, pp. 326–27.

273. *written permission* Letter from Chief Magistrate of Johannesburg to Lionel Bernstein, June 17, 1964.

274. *"a true daughter of South Africa"* *Rand Daily Mail*, June 18, 1964.

274. For Fischer and Joffe's visit to Robben Island, see Mandela, pp. 339–40, and interview with Joel Joffe.

275. *van den Bergh . . . had waited patiently* Vermaak, pp. 137–42.

275. *the Fischers drove east* Interviews with Ruth Rice and Ilse Wilson, and transcript of South African Institute of Race Relations Oral Archive interview with Ruth Eastwood and Ilse Wilson, Oct. 24, 1983.

276. *"During the past twenty years"* Gillian Slovo, pp. 95–96.

276. *Pat Davidson . . . accompanied him* Interview with Pat Lewin.

277. *"Whatever we left unfinished"* Interview with Hilda Bernstein.

278. For accounts of the Johannesburg railway station bombing, see Paton, pp. 336–40, and Winter, pp. 93–100.

278. *"The masterminds were white"* H.H.W. de Villiers, *Rivonia: Operation Mayibuye* (Johannesburg: Afrikaanse Pers, 1964), p. 115.

279. *"Quick, go!"* Bernstein, p. 250.

280. *"You know you are going to be arrested"* Ibid., p. 253.

281. *"I am trying to find a way"* Ibid., p. 263.

281. *"I have absolute faith"* Clingman, p. 339.

282. *He made them one promise* Ibid., p. 340.

282. *"the Mysterious Impala"* Arthur Magadlela, "I Ran Escape Route," in *Drum*, n.d.

282. *Frances thought her parents looked strange* Interview with Frances Bernstein.

283. *Lesley had him lie down* Interview with Lesley (Schermbrucker) Spiller.

283. For Rusty and Hilda's escape to Bechuanaland, see Bernstein, pp. 265–78; letter from Hilda Bernstein to Toni and Ivan Strasburg, Aug. 6, 1964. This account is also based on interviews with Hilda and Rusty Bernstein.

285. *"It's Special Branch"* Bernstein, p. 301.

285. For Rusty and Hilda's flight to freedom, see ibid., pp. 302–9.

286. *"You're putting your life at risk"* Interview with Rusty Bernstein.

286. For Bram Fischer's meeting with his comrades in London, see Clingman, pp. 344–46; Clingman interviews with Joe Slovo, Dec. 23, 1991, and Feb. 17, 1994; and interviews with Rusty and Hilda Bernstein and Ruth Rice.

288. *"If you can possibly stay out of jail"* Interview with Hilda Bernstein.

288. *He hated the classes, the teachers* Interview with Patrick Bernstein.

289. *Ivan Schermbrucker was questioned* *Rand Daily Mail*, Aug. 15, 1964, and interview with Lesley Spiller.

290. *"For years Piet and I were comrades"* Mary Benson, *A Far Cry* (Randburg: Ravan, 1996), p. 162.

290. *"I wanted to be released"* Vermaak recounts passages from Beyleveld's testimony, pp. 162–65.

291. *"Some parties were nothing but sex orgies"* *The Star*, Dec. 8, 1964. See also Ludi's own books: Gerard Ludi and Blaar Grobbelaar, *The Amazing Mr. Fischer* (Cape Town: Nasionale Boekhandel, 1966), and Gerard Ludi, *Operation Q-018* (Cape Town: Nasionale Boekhandel, 1969).

292. *Ruth First and her family* Interviews with Ronald Segal and Gillian, Robyn and Shawn Slovo; Ruth First letters to Ronald Segal, June 3, 1964, and to Lionel Abrams, Jan. 31, 1965.

292. Bram Fischer's move underground: Interviews with Pat Lewin and Ilse Wilson.

294. *"If by my fight"* Clingman reprints the Fischer letter, pp. 355–56.

294. *"They have been a sort of epitome"* Clingman, p. 360.

294. *"the desperate act of a desperate man"* Benson, *A Far Cry*, p. 164.

294. *"somewhere between the South Pole"* Clingman, p. 373.

294. Bram Fischer's time underground: Interviews with Ilse Wilson, Pat Lewin, Ralph and Minnie Sepel, Mary Benson and Lesley Spiller.

296. *"Don't see Violet, for God's sake"* Interview with Ralph Sepel.

296. *"I hesitated in writing to you"* Vermaak, p. 203.

297. *"With his background"* *Sunday Times*, Jan. 31, 1965.

297. *Nelson Mandela, Walter Sisulu . . . heard of his exploits* Interview with Walter Sisulu.

297. *He wrote a paper* Vermaak, pp. 185–90.

298. For details of the Little Rivonia Trial and verdict, see *Rand Daily Mail*, April 3, 1965; *The Star*, April 2, 1965; and Ludi and Grobbelaar, pp. 47–81.

298. *"Do you think it's the flaring up"* Benson, *A Far Cry*, p. 174.

298. *He wrote letters in code* Clingman interview with Joe Slovo.

299. *an angry Ruth Eastwood confronted* Interview with Ruth Rice.

299. *"When an advocate does"* Clingman, pp. 369–70.

300. *"dishonest and dishonorable conduct"* Ibid., p. 390.

300. *"Why couldn't they let the government"* Benson, *A Far Cry*, p. 180.

300. *"This item is now very urgent"* Clingman, p. 396.

301. *"You are like a group of sadistic schoolboys"* *The Star*, May 18, 1966.

301. Details of Bram's capture: Vermaak, pp. 206–13; Clingman, pp. 391–96; *The Star*, Nov. 12, 1965; and interviews with Pat Lewin, Lesley Spiller, Ralph and Minnie Sepel and Ilse Wilson.

302. *Bram flared with anger* Clingman, p. 401.

302. *Paul had been so ill* SAIRR interview with Ruth Eastwood and Ilse Wilson.

303. *"I don't wish to be disrespectful"* Clingman, p. 404.

304. *"I saw Fischer on the farm"* *Sunday Times*, Jan. 30, 1966.

304. *"Spectators in the gallery"* Nadine Gordimer's account of the Fischer trial was first published in *The New York Times Magazine*, Aug. 14, 1966, and reprinted in "Why

Did Bram Fischer Choose Jail?" in Nadine Gordimer, *The Essential Gesture* (New York: Alfred A. Knopf, 1988), pp. 68–78.

304. *"I engaged upon those activities"* Bram Fischer's speech from the dock, reprinted in Benson, ed., pp. 35–50.

306. *The night before his address* Interviews with Ruth Rice and Ilse Wilson.

306. *"Despite the desperate distance"* Bram Fischer letter to Ruth First, April 28, 1966.

307. *"Goodness, we seem to have been"* Clingman, p. 416.

307. There are many accounts of Bram's harsh treatment in prison, including Clingman, pp. 417–41; Lewin, pp. 212–16, 223–25; and a 23-page, handwritten diary from fellow prisoner Issy Heymann, dated Nov. 1, 1982. Ruth Rice and Ilse Wilson also testified before the Truth and Reconciliation Commission on July 21, 1997. See *Business Day* and *The Star*, July 22, 1997.

308. *"Dear dear Bram"* Letter from Ruth First to Bram Fischer, June 17, 1971.

308. *"May their souls never rest"* Letter from Bram Fischer to Ruth First, June 28, 1971.

308. *he gave her a bunch of flowers* Interview with Helen Suzman.

309. *Bram fell ill* Fellow inmate Denis Goldberg kept a secret diary of Bram's illness and treatment, which Marius Schoon smuggled out of prison upon his release. See Clingman, pp. 434–35, and Denis Goldberg interview in Suttner, p. 484.

309. *"He'll want to see you"* Suzman, p. 144.

309. *"The man is dying"* Interview with Helen Suzman.

310. *Bram's fellow inmates* Clingman, p. 444.

310. *"Bram Fischer was a man of great promise"* *Rand Daily Mail*, May 9, 1975.

310. *"enlarged and deepened"* *Rand Daily Mail*, May 13, 1975.

311. *They were not prepared to negotiate* Interviews with Ruth Rice and Ilse Wilson.

EPILOGUE

312. *seventy-three people died in detention* Patrick Laurence, *Death Squads: Apartheid's Secret Weapon* (Harmondsworth: Penguin, 1990), p. 65. A running tally on deaths of political prisoners in detention was kept by the Detainees' Parents Support Committee, an opposition human rights group.

312. For the demise of the Liberal Party, see Paton, pp. 242–45, 276–80.

313. For an account of Umkhonto's military campaign in the early 1980s, see Howard Barrell, *MK: The ANC's Armed Struggle* (Harmondsworth: Penguin, 1990), pp. 30–52.

315. *Joe carried a pistol* Steven Mufson, *Fighting Years* (Boston: Beacon Press, 1990), p. 225.

316. *"In most families"* Interview with Gillian Slovo.

316. *she found Ruth warm and relaxed* Interview with Hillary Hamburger.

316. *"There are unwelcome visitors"* Interview with Helena Dolny.

316. *Under directions from its commander* In hearings before the Truth and Reconciliation Commission in September 1998, security police officials confirmed they were responsible for Ruth's murder. See *The Star Online*, September 10–29, 1998.

317. *"I have no doubt"* Interview with Joe Slovo.

318. *he was an architect of the crucial "sunset clause"* Mandela, p. 528; Gillian Slovo, pp. 149–51.

318. *"You are the father to all our people"* Gillian Slovo, p. 210.

320. *"You realize that you're opting out"* Interview with Hilda Bernstein.

321. *"Neither garden nor city"* Interview with Rusty Bernstein.

321. *"a rainbow nation"* The Washington Post, May 11, 1994.

322. *"on purely humanitarian grounds"* Shimoni, p. 352.

323. *"Jews were not, of course, mere witnesses"* Todd Pitock, "Remembering and Renewing: By Way of an Introduction," *Jewish Affairs*, Vol. III, No. 1 (Autumn 1997), p. 18.

323. *"South Africa's lonely liberal"* *Life*, Vol. LXVIII, No. 18 (May 15, 1970), p. 58c.

325. *Frances had cried for months* Interviews with Frances, Hilda and Rusty Bernstein.

325. *"A warm, funny glow came over me"* Interview with Frances Bernstein.

326. *"They didn't so much choose"* Ibid.

326. *"The book upset me"* Letter from Frances to Hilda Bernstein, n.d.

327. *Patrick Bernstein had settled uneasily* Interviews with Patrick, Yvonne, Rusty and Hilda Bernstein.

328. *"gross violations of human rights"* Graeme Simpson and Paul van Zyl, "South Africa's Truth and Reconciliation Commission," White Paper (Braamfontein: Center for the Study of Violence and Reconciliation, n.d), p. 5.

329. *"I suppose we just never want it"* The Star, July 22, 1997.

329. *He had only "suggested"* Business Day, June 24, 1997.

330. *"improvised explosive devices"* The Star Online, Sept. 1998.

330. *"Brigadier Goosen looked directly at me"* The Star, Sept. 22, 1998.

330. *"I never gave an instruction"* Weekly Mail & Guardian, Sept. 10, 1998.

331. *"I thought that coming here"* The Star, Sept. 29, 1998.

331. *"I have looked too deeply"* Letter from Gillian Slovo.

332. *"I think that the less said"* Letter from James Kantor to David Suzman, Oct. 15, 1963.

332. *AnnMarie never read Jimmy's book* Interview with AnnMarie Wolpe.

333. For the Wolpes' decision to return to South Africa, see Wolpe, pp. 3–59, and interview with AnnMarie Wolpe.

334. *"Afrikaners have given us a lot of pain"* Nelson Mandela, First Bram Fischer Memorial Lecture (videotape), June 9, 1995.

336. *"the official with the highest sense of loyalty"* Weekly Mail & Guardian, March 27, 1997.

336. *"a minor role"* Encounters, July 1995.

336. *"wanted to show the Nationalist government"* Ibid.

336. *"one little bit of real evidence"* Sunday Times, Jan. 28, 1996.

337. *"It's frightening, some of the things"* Interview with Percy Yutar.

ACKNOWLEDGMENTS

R ivonia's Children is the product of more than fifteen years of thinking, reporting and writing, yet the book itself was done with limited time and resources, and I could not have achieved it without the generous support of friends and colleagues.

At the top of my list are four dear South African friends: Allister and Sue Sparks and Hillary and Tony Hamburger. Ever since I first stepped foot in apartheid South Africa in 1983, Allister and Sue have served as hosts, guides and second family, providing me a home away from home, introducing me to many of their fellow South Africans and sharing with me their own deep insights and feelings about the tumultuous events we witnessed. As former editor of the late and lamented *Rand Daily Mail*, special correspondent for *The Washington Post, The Observer* and *The Economist*, author of two essential books on apartheid and its demise and, most recently, editor of the South African Broadcasting Corporation's television news and current affairs, Allister has long been my model of what a committed journalist ought to be. Sue has been a companion, critic, researcher, hostess—and most of all, a moral compass.

Hillary Hamburger introduced me to many of the people portrayed in this book, paving the way and offering her own special knowledge of the Rivonia era. She and her husband, Tony, fed me more meals than I can possibly count and shared their acute observations and wisdom about the people and events in this book.

Next must come some of the subjects of this book. Hilda and Rusty Bernstein first welcomed me into their home outside Oxford, England, in 1996 and spent the next three years talking and corresponding with me. They showed me everything they had written and all of the documents, books and newspaper clippings they had collected. They introduced me to their children and their friends. Most of all, they shared their deepest and most intimate feelings about their activities and their comrades—and even about each other. They did not always agree with my conclusions, but they were always scrupulous in separating disagreements about facts—where they rightly insisted upon rigorous accuracy—from disputes about interpretation, which they knew in the end would have to be mine. We have built a relationship of trust and affection that I cherish.

I feel a similar bond with AnnMarie Wolpe, who was equally generous with her time, her support, her memories, her papers and those of her late brother James Kantor. Shawn, Gillian and Robyn Slovo sat for interviews and allowed me access to their mother's papers, even after they chose, for understandable reasons, to separate themselves from this project. Ruth Rice and Ilse Wilson, the daughters of Bram Fischer, were generous with their time and memories and with access to their father's letters.

In Johannesburg, Rica Hodgson saw me frequently, arranged contacts with key Rivonia figures such as Walter Sisulu and Ahmed Kathrada, and mixed many gin and tonics, which we sipped watching the sun go down from her downtown flat. Helen Suzman, as always, offered much hospitality and good humor along with her unique insights into South Africa's history and its future. Historian Gail M. Gerhart offered expert advice on sources and collections, as well as access to her own files and her personal trove of knowledge. Marius Schoon and Sherry McLean welcomed me frequently and warmly to their table. I must also thank David Beresford, Claudia Braude, Helena Dolny, Benjamin Pogrund, Albie Sachs and Percy and Cecilia Yutar.

In Cape Town, Milton Shain played host and tour guide and offered enthusiastic support. Thanks also to Hermann Giliomee, Betty Mansfield, Donald Pinnock and David Yutar.

In England, Ronald Segal invited me to his lovely, historic Tudor-era home outside London and regaled me with his unique intelligence and insight as author, witness to history and intimate friend of the Slovos. Joel and Vanetta Joffe were gracious hosts at their estate outside Swindon. The Bernstein children welcomed me to their homes as well. My thanks to Toni (Bernstein) Strasburg, Patrick and Yvonne Bernstein, Frances Bernstein and John Clare, and Keith Bernstein. Thanks also to my dear friends and hosts in Chiswick, Michael and Susan Kerr, Lawrence Waterman and Christine Taylor, and Simon and Pat Culshaw. I also thank author Mary Benson, who courageously paved much of this ground.

Thanks, as well, to colleagues Andrew Meldrum of Harare, Zimbabwe, who interviewed Pat (Davidson) Lewin at my request; and Linda Gradstein of Jersualem, who interviewed Arthur Goldreich. Stephen Clingman generously allowed me access to tapes of interviews with the late Joe Slovo.

The Alicia Patterson Foundation granted me half a year's fellowship, which helped pay for an additional reporting trip to London and keep food on the table toward the end of this project. My thanks to Margaret Engel and Cathy Trost.

Among archivists, my primary thanks must go to Michele Pickover and Claire Kruger of the South African History Archive at the Cullen Library of the University of Witwatersrand. For my money, SAHA has the best and most accessible collection of South African materials in the world, and in Michele, it has the most knowledgeable and helpful of librarians. During the apartheid years, the library collected and preserved for history thousands of banned or illegal documents, an act of courage that could have netted its keepers many years in prison. There was extra resonance and meaning in knowing that the room where I worked was the same room where Ruth First was detained by Special Branch while studying library science in 1963.

I must also thank David Ward, archivist of the Institute for Commonwealth Studies in London; Sylvia Tuback, librarian of the South African Board of Jewish Deputies in Johannesburg; and the archivists of the Mayibuye Center at the University of the Western Cape in Bellville, South Africa.

At *The Washington Post*, librarian Kim Klein was a never-ending source of help and good advice in finding obscure books. Olwen Price transcribed interviews with blazing speed and good cheer. Lorraine Adams, Katherine Boo, Jackson Diehl, David Finkel, Fred Hiatt, Steven Mufson and Margaret Shapiro gave moral support and read the manuscript. Rick Atkinson, Steve Coll, T. A. Frail, Robert G. Kaiser, Steve Luxenberg and Tom Wilkinson helped ease my way out of and back into the newspaper.

The manuscript was also read by Allister and Sue Sparks, Hillary Hamburger, Rusty and Hilda Bernstein, AnnMarie Wolpe and Shawn and Gillian Slovo. Ruth Rice and Ilse Wilson read the portions concerning Bram Fischer. Needless to say, no one but me is responsible for errors of fact or interpretation.

Gail Ross, my tenacious literary agent, believed in this book when others did not and rescued it at the crucial moment of its birth. John Glusman at Farrar, Straus and Giroux was a supportive, enthusiastic and perceptive editor who did nothing but improve the manuscript. Rebecca Kurson helped pilot it from manuscript to book.

No one should undertake such a project without firm support from family. I thank my parents, Herbert and Betty Frankel, and my mother-in-law, Betsy Yeager. My children, Abra, Margo and Paul Frankel, tolerated their father's presence behind a frequently closed door. But most of all, I thank my wife, Betsyellen Yeager, who never wavered in urging me to spend whatever it took in time, energy and expense to produce the book she knew I had to write.

Arlington, Virginia
March 1999

INDEX

A

Abrahams, Lionel, 293

African National Congress (ANC), 25,
63, 85, 109, 207, 268, 282, 295, 297,
334, 335; and "African Claims," 38;
banning of, 71, 78; black-only
membership of, 42; Communist Party
and, 21, 23, 26, 42–44, 83, 94–96, 105;
competition between PAC and, 94; in
Congress Movement, 46; and end of
white rule, 318, 324–26, 328, 329; in
exile, 122, 313–17, 321; Freedom
Charter of, 64–69, 290, 313, 321;
military wing of, *see* Umkhonto We
Sizwe; Mtolo's testimony about,
214, 215; National Executive
Committee, 42, 81–83; pass-law
protests of, 70; and Rivonia Trial, 185,
202, 209, 210, 214–15, 237, 239–45,
248, 250, 260, 261; smuggling people
out of South Africa by, 282, 284–86;
trade unions and, 37, 59; during
World War II, 37–38; Youth League
of, 41, 42

African Resistance Movement (ARM),
217, 278

Africanists, 42, 65, 68–69, 83

Afrikaners, 37, 44, 68, 89–93, 154, 198,
265, 275, 281, 290, 296, 297, 305, 310,
334; apartheid and, 58, 60; during
Boer War, 267; Jews and, 55, 57, 322;
in Parliament, 99; as prison warders,
123–25, 128, 130, 269; victory over
Zulus of, 87; during World Wars I and
II, 266

Alexandra bus boycott, 92

Allen, S. C., 298

Anglo American Corporation, 56

Anti-Apartheid Movement (London),
320

anti-Semitism, 53–56, 106, 117, 170, 180,
188, 194, 322

Arafat, Yasser, 319

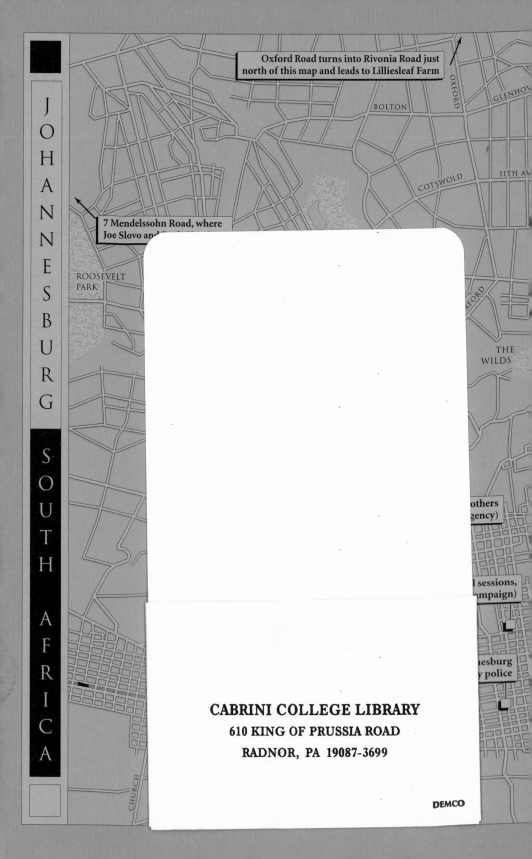

JOHANNESBURG SOUTH AFRICA

Oxford Road turns into Rivonia Road just north of this map and leads to Lilliesleaf Farm

BOLTON

OXFORD

GLENHOV

COTSWOLD

11TH AV

7 Mendelssohn Road, where Joe Slovo and

ROOSEVELT PARK

OXFORD

THE WILDS

others
gency)

sessions,
mpaign)

nesburg
y police